Eamon de Valera
The Man & the Myths

T. Ryle Dwyer

First published 1991 by
Poolbeg Press Ltd.
Knocksedan House,
Swords, Co Dublin, Ireland

© T. Ryle Dwyer 1991

This promotional edition published by Paperview U.K. Ltd. in association
with the Irish Independent (2006)
www.paperviewgroup.com
www.unison.ie

The publishers would like to thank the following sources for their kind permission to reproduce the pictures in this book. Every effort has been made to trace the copyright holders of these images and we apologize in advance for any unintentional omissions.

Pages 1:	Irish Independent
Page 2:	(top) Irish Independent; (bottom) Topfoto
Page 3:	Irish Independent
Page 4:	(top) Irish Independent; (bottom) Topfoto
Pages 5-8:	Irish Independent

CONTENTS

PREFACE

During his lifetime Éamon de Valera inspired intense loyalty and provoked bitter resentment. No matter what one thinks of him, it is not possible to appreciate what happened in Ireland during the twentieth century without understanding his role.

There has been no full-length biography of him since Lord Longford and Thomas P. O'Neill published their quasi-official life in November 1970. Their de Valera was a figure of mythical proportions—an unflawed, charismatic colossus. In the hagiographical account they not only sanctified him with virtual canonisation, but credited him with having had an influence on Ireland that was of divine proportions.

It would be unfair and ungracious not to acknowledge that there are very good aspects to the Longford and O'Neill book. Indeed when dealing with de Valera's successes, it is invaluable, but it provides only part of a whole picture. It explains why he was the most loved man in Ireland, but not why he was also the most hated. In the eyes of many of his contemporaries, he was as infamous as he was famous in the eyes of others.

The object of this biography is not to deify de Valera, nor to denigrate his undoubted accomplishments, but to present an in-depth, objective picture of him, to evaluate what made him tick, and to examine the myths that surrounded him so that his influence on recent Irish history may be better understood. Whether people choose to regard his influence as beneficial or malignant, there can be no doubt, he has been the outstanding Irish leader of the twentieth century.

This book draws heavily on more than twenty years of research for my M.A. and Ph.D theses and for eight different books on twentieth-century Irish historical topics, including a short biography of de Valera and a two-volume study of his quest for national independence, two books on Irish neutrality, and two studies of the career of Michael Collins in which de Valera figured prominently. In the course of this research I had the benefit of discussions and correspondence with a number of people mentioned in these pages: Dean Acheson, the Earl of Avon (Anthony Eden), Tom Barry, Robert Barton, F. H. Boland, Kevin Boland, Ernest Blythe, Dan Bryan, Lord Brookeborough, Liam Cosgrave, James Dillon, James A. Farley, John D. Kearney, Lord Longford, John M. Lynch, John W. McCormack, Frank McDermot, Malcolm MacDonald, Seán MacEntee, Seán MacEoin, Mike McGlynn, E.R. Marlin, the late

Leon O Broin and Maurice Moynihan. I would like to thank them for their courtesy and I would like to thank the others who have helped me in various ways, with special thanks to Michael Costello, Anne Maria O'Sullivan, my brother Seán, his wife Geraldine, and especially to my mother for reading the manuscript and making helpful suggestions.

TRD
Tralee, January 1991

CHAPTER 1

"What About My Vocation?"

Eamon de Valera was an unlikely Irish hero, much less the virtual personification of nationalist Ireland. Born in New York City on 14 October 1882, he was the son of a Spanish father and an Irish immigrant mother. His father, who moved away shortly after the boy was born, died two years later. Under the circumstances Eamon's mother decided to send him to Ireland to be reared by her own family near the village of Bruree, County Limerick, while she remained in the United States.

Young de Valera, who was brought to Ireland by his mother's brother, never forgot his first morning in the Coll family home—a one-roomed thatched cottage, housing himself, his grandmother, two uncles and an aunt.\He woke up to find the house deserted. The family was moving to a new slate-roofed, three-roomed labourer's cottage nearby and nobody had bothered to ensure the child would not be frightened waking up in a strange, deserted house. It must have been a traumatic experience because he never forgot that morning. \

The importance of the first years of a child's life in shaping his future character have long been recognised by psychiatrists. Like all children de Valera would have first looked to his parents for security. Following the early disappearance of his father, he would have become especially dependent on his mother, and his subsequent separation from her would undoubtedly have had a profound effect on him. Not only did she remain on in the United States, but the uncle who brought him to Bruree soon returned to America, to be followed shortly afterwards by the boy's aunt, Hannie, to whom he had become attached. Thus the people to whom de Valera first looked for security during those formative years were in America, with the result that he would inevitably associate the United States subconsciously with security. This helps explain why, in later life, he repeatedly turned to the United States for help in times of trouble or crisis.

His mother visited Bruree briefly in 1887, before returning to the United States, leaving the boy to be reared by her mother and her brother, Pat Coll. She was planning to remarry and de Valera pleaded with her to take him back, but she refused. One can only imagine the scaring consequences of being rejected by his mother, especially when the rejection fuelled speculation about his legitimacy.

Before first emigrating in 1879, Catherine Coll had worked for a time as a domestic servant and there was local speculation that she had become pregnant by the son of the owner and had gone to America to conceal the fact. It would have been understandable enough for an Irish emigrant to send home an illegitimate child to be reared by her family, and even to leave the child in Ireland after she married, but it was something else for a former widow not to reclaim a legitimate child after she had remarried, especially after she had started a second family.

De Valera was born some two years after she had emigrated, so he was certainly not conceived in Ireland. His birth-certificate could have scotched the rumour but it was more than thirty years before anyone bothered to get a copy of it.

Thus the rumour persisted among those ready to believe it. For one thing the boy always seemed older because he was tall for his age. Moreover, when he started at the local national school at the age of five, he was registered under the name of Edward Coll.

This may have been the first sign of a certain sensitivity de Valera would later betray about his foreign background. Maybe his touchiness was the result of conditioning brought on by the attitude of his grandmother or uncle, or just the reaction of a little boy trying to fit into a society in which he quite probably, and indeed justifiably, felt rejected.

He would later recall being irritated that his uncle was known locally as "the Dane Coll," which was one of those family nicknames transferred from father to son. De Valera's late grandfather Coll used to lead prayers in the local church and as a result he was given the nickname, "the Dean," which was pronounced locally as "the Dane," much to the subsequent embarrassment of his grandson, who thought the nickname had something to do with the Norse invaders who had plundered Ireland around the beginning of the millennium.

Charged with supporting his mother and young nephew, Pat Coll was a rather frustrated individual. He could not afford to get married and seemed to take out his frustration on de Valera, with whom he was quite severe. He disapproved of the boy playing games, which he considered were a waste of time. De Valera was expected to perform various duties. "From my earliest days I participated in every operation that takes place on a farm," he later recalled. "Until I was sixteen years of age, there was no farm work, from the spancelling of a goat and milking of a cow, that I had not to deal with. I cleaned out the cowhouses, I followed the tumbler rake. I took my place on top of the rick. I took my place on the cart and filled the float of hay. I took milk to the creamery. I harnessed the donkey, the jennet, and the horse."

The one thing he did not learn was how to plough, because the Colls had only half an acre of land. It was not even enough to support the three or four cows owned by his uncle. As a result they used what de Valera called "the long farm"—the grass margins by the roadside. This was against the law, so he was given the task of keeping watch for the police. If he saw them approaching he would just pretend to be driving the cattle from one field to another.

While on "the long farm," de Valera used to relieve the boredom by reading books about the French revolution, Scottish mythology, and Abbé MacGeoghegan's History of Ireland. He did not take history at school, so he knew little about Irish history. He later credited the local parish priest, Father Eugene Sheehy, with introducing him to nationalist politics, though he could not have been very impressed with the early introduction because it was some years before he showed any interest in the nationalist renaissance taking place at the time.

De Valera's aunt, Hannie, returned from the United States for a while to nurse her ailing mother before the latter's death in 1895. She then returned to the United States, leaving de Valera to undertake much of the housekeeping and the preparation of his uncle's meals. As a result the boy's school attendance suffered. Clearly disillusioned with life in Bruree, he wrote to Hannie in January 1896 pleading with her to intercede with his mother to allow him to return to America, but his efforts were in vain.

He did manage to persuade his uncle, however, to allow him to attend the Christian Brothers' secondary school in Charleville, some seven miles from home. He frequently made the long journey to and from school on foot. After sitting his junior grade examination in 1898, he won a three-year scholarship worth twenty pounds a year. This allowed him to continue his education at boarding school. Although he was rejected by the two boarding schools in Limerick, a local priest managed to get him accepted into Blackrock College in the Dublin suburbs. The twenty pounds did not quite cover his full costs, but the Holy Ghost Fathers waived the remainder. They drew the line, however, when Pat Coll asked the college authorities for five pounds out of the scholarship for himself. The request was indignantly ignored.

Blackrock College had a strict routine. Boys rose at six o'clock in the morning and had a full schedule of prayer, class, study, and recreation outlined for each day. Discipline was strict and they were obliged to remain silent going to class and during meals, as well as during study periods. Among de Valera's classmates were the future Catholic Primate of Ireland, John D'Alton, and the famous Gaelic writer, Pádraic O Conaire. At the outset the Dean of Studies told the students that they were being joined by "a prodigy arriving from Charleville who will set the pace."

It was not easy, of course, for de Valera to fit into a new class midway through secondary school, especially when he had to adjust to a very different environment. For a time he actually considered quitting the college.

It would have been quite normal for a fifteen-year-old boy to have been homesick on going away to school for the first time, but his initial difficulties had nothing to do with homesickness. He was in fact delighted to get away.

On his first night, he later recalled, he lay in bed thanking God for his deliverance from Bruree. He just could not understand the homesickness of the boy in the next bed sobbing in muffled tones. This lack of understanding testified more to the cold, loveless surroundings in which he had been reared than to anything in the other boy's upbringing.

Those boys brought up in the stable atmosphere of warm family surroundings were naturally homesick and sought compensation in forming new friendships, but de Valera had no pressing need for camaraderie and would not become particularly friendly with anyone during his first year. "He had," according to one of his teachers, "a certain dignity of manner, a gentleness of disposition, a capability of adapting himself to circumstances, or perhaps I should rather say, of utilizing those circumstances that served his purpose."

Despite initial misgivings, de Valera fitted into his new surroundings relatively quickly. In the school examinations before Christmas he was placed sixth in a class of eighteen, which was headed by John D'Alton, who later remembered de Valera as "a good, very serious student, good at Mathematics but not outstanding otherwise." The little barb at the end was ironic, because in addition to finishing at the top of his class in arithmetic, de Valera also finished first in religious instruction, leaving the future cardinal in his wake.

Boys would naturally be expected to look forward to going home for the Christmas break, but de Valera asked to be allowed to remain at the school for the holidays. He later said his memories of his first Christmas at Blackrock were his most vivid recollection of his years there. Even at this early stage it was apparent he had begun to look on the college as a kind of home. For a time he would seriously consider entering the priesthood with the Holy Ghost Fathers. In later life he liked to return to the college for the midnight services at Christmas, and he repeatedly made his home in the Blackrock area. He even chose to move into a nursing home in Blackrock when he retired from public life some seventy years later.

Blackrock College was a good school and de Valera was one of its star pupils. In the public examinations at the end of his first year the college won more prizes and scholarships than any other school in the country. Three classmates won gold medals for finishing first in Ireland in specific subjects. Although de Valera was not among the gold medallists, his accumulated marks in the various subjects were the highest in his class, so he had the distinction of being Student of the Year. As such he was appointed reader of prayers in the church, study hall and dormitory, and he was the main reader in the dining-room during retreats. He relished the challenge, and it helped improve his skills as a public speaker.

The one unpleasantness of his new role, he said, was the memories it evoked of that dreaded nickname, "the Dane Coll." His touchiness was probably as much a reflection of his unhappy childhood as his uneasiness about his own foreign background.

Although de Valera made no particularly close friends during his first year at Blackrock, he did become quite close to a new boy, Frank Hughes, the following year. Hughes brought him home to Kiltimagh, County Mayo, for Christmas 1899, and they were to cement a lifelong friendship in which each would act as best man at the other's wedding and stand as godfather to the other's first child.

After finishing secondary school at the turn of the century, de Valera still had one year of his scholarship from Charleville remaining, so he enrolled at University College, Blackrock, an extension of the secondary school. Opportunities for third level education were quite limited for Catholics at the time, seeing that Trinity College, Dublin was almost exclusively Protestant, and the Royal University of Ireland—the alternative prior to the founding of the National University in 1908—was strictly an examining body. The various Catholic colleges scattered throughout the country prepared students for examinations conducted by the Royal University. Blackrock College was handicapped in that none of its teachers were involved either in setting or marking examination papers.

De Valera thought students at other colleges, whose professors helped to set the examination papers, had an unfair advantage, because those professors inevitably made sure the material relating to the examination questions was thoroughly covered in their classes. One day, for instance, a colleague was poring over a textbook outside the examination hall of the Royal University when some friends from another college told him he was wasting his time because their professor—one of those who had set the examination paper—had never opened that particular text in class. They suggested he concentrate on another specific area and, sure enough, there was a question on it in the subsequent examination. Although de Valera felt unfairly handicapped in the competitive examination system, he still received second class honours in his first arts examination. As a result, he got a three year scholarship from the Royal University.

While studying for his degree he was particularly active in the debating society, where he displayed a distinctly conservative outlook. He contended, for instance, that "the old monastic form" of distributing "charity to the poor was preferable to the modern state social services." In view of the excesses of the French Revolution, he also argued that constitutional monarchy was preferable to republicanism, and he even expressed reservations about democracy. "There is," he argued, "no rule so tyrannical as that of them all."

His conservatism was further apparent in his attitude to the Gaelic renaissance sweeping intellectual circles at the time. Although it seemed to herald a new era, de Valera was slow to show any interest in the developments. He shied away from involvement in things Gaelic, despite the presence at Blackrock of enthusiasts like O Conaire and Michael Cusack, one of the driving forces of the Gaelic Athletic Association. Maybe his reticence had something to do with his love of rugby, which was condemned as a foreign game by the rather xenophobic Gaelic enthusiasts. At any rate de Valera was more interested in rugby and educational matters than in political or cultural developments, though his educational interests soon led him into the other two areas. To him knowledge was power, and it was inevitable his views on education would become entangled with politics.

During his second year of university study there was a noticeable softening of his conservatism. In presenting a paper to the debating society on the question of establishing a national university, one of the more hotly debated issues of the period, he candidly admitted having modified some of his views in the course of researching the lengthy paper.

"Is it that the problem is too hard for English statesmen to solve?" he asked on that night in February 1903. "They pretend they can legislate for us better than we could for ourselves. And yet if we had but a free Parliament in College Green for the space of one single hour, this vexing question would be put to rest for ever. It seems, indeed, that Englishmen, even the most liberal amongst them, with one or two notable exceptions, have never been able to understand the needs of Ireland properly." Here were set the seeds which later blossomed into his ardent nationalism.

In autumn of that year he got a job as a mathematics teacher at Rockwell College, run by the Holy Ghost Fathers just outside Cashel, County Tipperary. The rather strange teenager who had gone to Blackrock five years earlier was returning south, this time as a young man on the verge of his twenty-first birthday, free for the first time in his life from the confines of home and the restrictive atmosphere of student life at Blackrock. He thoroughly enjoyed his new-found freedom and often referred to his two years at Rockwell College as the happiest period of his life. While there, Tom O'Donnell, one of his teaching colleagues, was the first to contract his name to "Dev," which duly stuck.

With classes in mathematics and physics, de Valera had a demanding teaching schedule. Some of his more famous students included the future president of University College, Galway, Monsignor Paddy Browne; the future politician and cabinet minister Fionan Lynch; and Michael Hillery, whose son Patrick would serve in a number of different cabinet posts during de Valera's final term as President of Ireland and would actually become President himself within three years of de Valera's death. Of course, all this was well into the future.

De Valera got on well at Rockwell with both the clerical and lay teaching staff and was liked by his pupils because he was not a very demanding taskmaster. He was, apparently, so enthusiastic about his subjects that he expected the students to be likewise and failed to notice those who were indifferent.

Earning a regular salary for the first time in his life, he was able to socialise in a way that he had never been able to afford before, even if the opportunities had presented themselves. He enjoyed the social life, and became particularly active in the local rugby club, which boasted two members of Ireland's Triple Crown winning side of three years earlier. He became particularly friendly with one of those men, Mike Ryan. Playing in the demanding position of full back on the first team, which reached the final of the Munster Senior Cup, de Valera was rated good enough to be considered for a place on the provincial team. Yet, as often happens, he would be better remembered for a ball he dropped than for any of his accomplishments on the field. On one particular occasion he fumbled a ball when he looked ready to score an easy try; an opponent picked up the ball and ran for an unforgettable try at the other end.

Back in 1903 de Valera was literally tall, dark and handsome. With his sallow complexion and Spanish features, he was fancied by many of the local girls, especially the daughter of the owner of the hotel frequented by the rugby players, but he shied away from her. He was deliberately avoiding amorous entanglements because he still harboured notions of entering the priesthood.

In the midst of his new-found freedom and his duties at Rockwell, de Valera's own studies suffered. At the end of the school year he returned to spend three months at Blackrock College, cramming for his final arts examination at the Royal University. As he awaited the results he went on a religious retreat to determine for once and for all whether or not he had a vocation for the priesthood. When he tried to talk about it to one of the Jesuit priests giving the retreat, the priest was more interested in other matters.

"But what about my vocation?" de Valera asked impatiently.

"Oh! your vocation," the priest replied. "You have what is known as an incipient vocation."

"If that is all I have after all those years," de Valera said, "it is time I forgot about it." He left the retreat, relieved at having finally made up his mind, but he was soon to have one of the bitterest personal disappointments of his life on learning that although he had graduated from the Royal University, he had done so with only a pass degree.

He returned to Rockwell for another year before deciding to move back to Dublin, where he hoped to continue his studies. It was a hasty, ill-considered decision, characteristic of youthful impetuosity. Although armed with the fulsome recommendation of the president of the college who gave him "the highest praise" for "success and zeal as a teacher," de Valera had made no arrangement to secure another job before quitting Rockwell and he was to have considerable difficulty. At one point, in desperation, he crossed the Irish Sea for an interview in Liverpool before eventually obtaining a temporary post at Belvedere College, Dublin. In the following years he was to depend on a whole series of temporary and part-time teaching positions at various colleges around the city, including Carysfort Teacher's Training College, Dominican College, Loreto College, and Holy Cross College.

For most of the first three years following his return to Dublin he lived within the confines of Blackrock College, which was unprecedented because he was neither enrolled as a student nor working as a member of the staff but, of course, he was very well-known there. He again involved himself in the debating society and was especially active in the college's past pupils union. He also continued to play rugby with the seconds team, which reached a cup final in 1908. Some people were never to forget de Valera's role in that game. Fancying himself as a place kicker, he insisted on taking all the penalty kicks, which he duly missed, with the result that he was blamed for losing the game. In later years some people would remember his misplaced self-confidence as a manifestation of a trait to hog the limelight without regard to the cost to his own team.

In late 1908 de Valera finally moved out of Blackrock College, and his intense interest in the college's activities was gradually replaced by another developing passion when he decided to learn Gaelic. At first his motivation was professional or mercenary. He had ambitions of lecturing at the National University, which was about to be set up. As there was a strong movement to make Gaelic an entrance requirement, he decided to join the Gaelic League in order to learn the language. One of his instructors was a primary school teacher, Sinéad Flanagan. She was already in her thirties and it has been suggested de Valera became infatuated with her because, as his first woman teacher, she provided the mother-figure he had always lacked. Whatever the case, he followed her to Tourmakeady, County Mayo, where she was teaching at the Irish summer school, and a romance blossomed. They were married on 9 January 1910.

Although they quickly started a family, he was never really a family man, which was hardly surprising in view of his own family background. Even though he was to have seven children, it is interesting to note that none was named after any of the Colls who had reared him.

Having grown up without a stable family life himself, he apparently did not know how to provide a proper one for his children. His authorised biographers later pointed to his children's subsequent careers as evidence of his role as a dedicated family man but, of course, this was not necessarily the case. He was really so involved in other matters that he had little time for his family. In the coming years he would be preoccupied with activities, first in the Gaelic

League, and then in the Irish Volunteers. With a pregnant wife and three young children, it seemed the height of irresponsibility for him to become involved in the rebellion of 1916, especially when he said he did not expect to survive the fighting. His family were left virtually destitute with little means of support. Following a brief jail term he entered politics and became preoccupied with the reorganisation of Sinn Féin and a series of newly formed organisations and institutions like Dáil Éireann, the American Association for Recognition of the Irish Republic, Cumann na Poblachta, Comhairle na dTeachtaí, and Fianna Fáil. Those activities were to land him in jail again and again and to take him away from his family for months and even years at a time.

The youngest of de Valera's children, Terry, recalled that one of his earliest memories was wishing his father would "go back to jail again." It was not until 1932 that Terry got to know his father. Before that, he said, the man "meant little more than the tall, dark-haired, bespectacled, severe figure who occasionally appeared on the home scene." By then, of course, the other children were at various stages of maturity.

In recounting their childhood memories, they mentioned frequent incidents indicative of just how little they knew their father. For instance, his oldest daughter, Máirín, recalled a conversation between her younger brothers, Eamonn and Brian. One asked the other who Dev was, only to be told by the brother that he was their mother's father.

"As a child, I feared my father, and resented his intrusion into our lives," the older of those two boys recalled. His father enforced a stricter discipline than Sinéad, and the boy found it hard to accept this. "Looking back," he continued, "I realise that he has never really appreciated the difficulties and shortcomings of minds less gifted than his own." It was of course quite natural for someone to think of his father as a brilliant intellectual, a characterisation readily accepted by his authorised biographers.

In later life as he developed real charisma, de Valera would be depicted as having one of the most brilliant minds. "Einstein said when speaking about his theory of relativity that there were only nine people in the world who really understood his theory and that de Valera was one of them," according to his son, Terry. Professor Donal McCartney noted that "more advanced admirers were known to claim that only two people, Einstein and de Valera, understood the theory." Yet there was nothing in de Valera's academic background to suggest he was one of the most brilliant minds of either of the centuries in which he lived.

While in the semi-cloistered atmosphere of Blackrock College, he did fare well scholastically, but once he discovered the freedom of the outside world, his performance suffered and he achieved only a pass degree and, despite some ten years of further courses working towards a Master's degree, he only managed to secure a diploma in education. Thus, while his son may have been content to excuse de Valera's paternal shortcomings on the grounds of some kind of eccentric brilliance, the explanation was far from convincing.

CHAPTER 2

"Ye Will Need Us"

Although de Valera had joined the Gaelic League primarily to further his ambition of becoming a professor at the new National University, he nevertheless became enthralled by the Gaelic language. He changed his first name to its Gaelic equivalent, Eamon, and even sought to Gaelicise his Spanish surname by spelling it Bhailéra for a time.

After obtaining a university diploma to teach Irish, he spent his summer vacations as principal of the Gaelic League's summer school at Tawim, County Galway, but he failed in his quest for professorships at the university colleges in both Galway and Cork. In 1912, however, he was appointed a part-time temporary professor of mathematics at an associate institution of the university, St Patrick's College, Maynooth, where courses were confined to the Roman Catholic clergy and students for the priesthood. While there he was to extend his already wide contacts with priests, many of whom were destined to become very influential, both in Ireland and abroad. Daniel Mannix who, as president of the college, invited de Valera to take up the post, soon emigrated and became the Cardinal Primate of Australia, while another member of the staff, Joseph MacRory, was to become the Cardinal Primate of Ireland towards the end of the following decade. Contacts like these were to prove very useful to de Valera during his subsequent political career, though at this time he had not yet shown any real interest in politics, other than the internal politics of the Gaelic League.

In 1910 he was elected to the executive committee of his branch, and he represented it at the Gaelic League's national convention the following summer. He even ran for election to the organisation's national executive at that convention, but was unsuccessful. His reaction to this defeat betrayed a certain vanity. He contended his failure to win one of the fifty seats on the national executive had been orchestrated by Sinn Féin, the radical nationalist political party. It was certainly vain of him to think in terms of that party trying to stop him rather than trying to get its own people elected. Anyway, he was wrong; it was actually the more militant Irish Republican Brotherhood (IRB), a secret oath-bound society, dedicated to the establishment of an Irish Republic, which had sought to orchestrate the election, as part of its policy of gaining control of all nationalist organisations by secretly permeating their executive branches with members of the IRB.

The Gaelic League professed to be non-political and its president, Douglas Hyde, strove to keep the organisation out of party-politics, but it was nevertheless highly politicised, with deep internal divisions. On the one side, there were conservatives like Hyde who tended to support the more moderate nationalistic aims of the Irish Parliamentary Party, while so-called progressives like Thomas Ashe, on the other side, publicly identified with Sinn Féin and secretly worked for the IRB.

The divisions came to a head at the Gaelic League's national convention at Galway in July 1913. Hyde denounced Ashe and five of his comrades as "disrupters" and tried to purge them from the leadership of the organisation by calling for their defeat and limiting the size of the national executive to twenty-five members. Ashe countered by proposing a thirty-five strong executive and de Valera, who was generally regarded as being in neither camp, played the role of peacemaker by suggesting the two sides split the difference and agree to an executive of thirty people. This amendment was accepted and de Valera acquired the reputation of a unifying moderate.

In the subsequent election five of the men whom Hyde had tried to purge lost their seats on the executive. With only Ashe hanging on, it looked like Hyde had been largely successful, but behind the scenes he had really lost out because almost two thirds of the new committee were secretly backed by the IRB, which effectively took control of the Gaelic League. Hyde remained as president but his influence was limited and he became a mere figure-head. On realising this, he quietly resigned from the organisation a couple of years later. By then de Valera's involvement had already waned as the focus of his energies turned elsewhere.

One of his branch colleagues in the Gaelic League had been Eoin MacNeill, who had been responsible for calling the meeting at the Rotunda at which the organisation was established in 1893. Now, twenty years later, writing in the League's official organ, *An Claidheamh Soluis*, he called for the formation of a nationalist force to counteract the influence of the Ulster Volunteer Force (UVF), set up in the north-east of the island to resist the introduction of Home Rule. A meeting was thus arranged for 25 November 1913 at the Rotunda.

Believing the British government would not carry through the introduction of Home Rule unless there was also a show of force from Irish nationalists to counter the UVF, de Valera attended the

21

Rotunda meeting and enlisted in the Irish Volunteer Force (IVF) established that night. The gathering was made up largely of members of the Gaelic League, Gaelic Athletic Association, Sinn Féin and the IRB. Though de Valera was comparatively unknown outside Gaelic League circles, he rose quickly within the ranks of the rapidly expanding IVF. When a new company was set up in the Donnybrook area of Dublin, he was elected captain, and he took charge of his men during the landing of arms at Howth, the following summer.

Faced with the problem of getting his men home with their new weapons, he ordered two of every three men to disperse and leave their weapons to the others, who were ordered to wait for him while he went home himself to get his motor cycle and side-car. In an operation lasting until the following dawn he then ferried the remaining men home, one by one.

Bolstered by the morale-building success of the Howth gun-running, the IVF expanded rapidly, especially after John Redmond, the leader of the Irish Parliamentary Party (IPP), threw his political weight behind the force. The Home Rule Bill for Ireland was duly passed at Westminster, but not before a hitch developed with regard to its implementation. In deference to the threat posed by the UVF, Home Rule was postponed until after the First World War, which began in August 1914.

When Redmond called on the IVF to come to the defence of the British Empire, the force split with the overwhelming majority supporting his call. Had Home Rule been implemented at the time, de Valera later said, he would "probably" have joined those who went to fight for the rights of small nations. But, under the circumstances, with Westminster vacillating in the face of Unionist intransigence, he felt the IVF would eventually be needed at home to insist on the implementation of Home Rule.

A meeting of the Donnybrook company of the IVF was held on 28 September 1914 to discuss the situation created by Redmond's call to arms. Unwilling to heed the call, de Valera walked out of the meeting and was joined by a majority of his men. "You will need us before you get Home Rule," was his departing cry. Although a majority of the company walked out, it was hardly right to say they followed him. Most of those men would probably not have joined in the first place if they had not been carried away by the enthusiasm which greeted the formation of the IVF. They had obviously joined without considering the ultimate implications of their actions. Now they seized on the opportunity to extricate themselves by leaving with de Valera, but when he then tried to reorganise the company, only seven of the men were interested.

The men who followed Redmond decided to call themselves the National Volunteers Force, so the breakaway minority was able to retain the original name. As one of the few remaining officers de Valera found himself in a more prominent position as the IVF began to reorganise, largely at the instigation of the IRB, which planned to stage a rebellion in the hope of establishing an independent Irish republic while Britain was preoccupied with fighting the Great War. Although de Valera was unaware of these plans at the time, he enthusiastically involved himself in the reorganisation and quickly came to the notice of the leadership.

In March 1915 he was promoted to the rank of commandant. As he was not in the IRB, which secretly controlled the IVF and usually ensured the appointment of its own members to top posts, his promotion was a testimony to his organisational ability. Before informing him of the promotion, however, the IRB leader, Patrick Pearse, satisfied himself about de Valera's likely attitude to the planned uprising. Posing a supposedly hypothetical question, Pearse asked how de Valera would react in the event the IVF leadership decided to stage a rebellion. De Valera replied he would follow orders, and this was good enough for Pearse, who promptly informed him of his promotion.

Two days later de Valera was invited to a meeting chaired by Pearse at which the plans were discussed for a rising in September 1915. The plans called for the seizure of the centre of Dublin which the IVF would then try to hold. Various battalions were assigned to defend the city against Crown forces stationed in the different barracks on the outskirts. As commandant of the third battalion, de Valera was to repel troops from Beggar's Bush Barracks.

Although the rising was postponed for several months, his ultimate role remained the same, and he familiarised himself thoroughly with the south-east section of the city that he had been assigned to defend. His enthusiasm was rewarded with his appointment as Adjutant of the Dublin Brigade under Thomas MacDonagh. In his new post de Valera soon realised that some of his subordinates knew more about what was going on than himself. He complained to MacDonagh, who explained that those men were members of the IRB. They were privy to secrets he could not be told unless he was prepared to take the organisation's oath of secrecy.

De Valera hesitated. He was not only uneasy because the Catholic Church disapproved of secret societies, but he was also

23

afraid that IRB membership might compromise his position within the IVF. What would he do, for instance, in the event of conflicting orders from his superiors in the IRB and Irish Volunteers?

MacDonagh assured him there would be no real conflict of interest because the IRB secretly controlled the IVF. De Valera therefore took the oath administered by MacDonagh, but made it clear from the outset that he would not attend IRB meetings. In short, he would keep its secrets but had no intention of being an IRB activist.

The story of the Easter Rebellion has already been told so often there is no need to go into detail here. De Valera had little to do with overall policy, which was decided by IRB leaders like Pearse, MacDonagh, and Thomas Clarke. The operation was timed to begin on Easter Sunday when the combined forces of the IVF and Irish Citizen Army would seize Dublin as well as other selected areas and set up a Provisional Government. Germany had promised arms, and these were to be landed near Tralee that day. But the plans were thrown awry by a sequence of unforeseen events.

It was only on the Thursday before the rising was due to begin that MacNeill, the official leader of the IVF, learned of the plans, and he threatened to call the whole thing off, but IRB leaders persuaded him to wait because Roger Casement had made arrangements in Berlin for German help. On Saturday, however, came news that Casement had been arrested near Tralee and that the arms ship was scuttled. The game was up as far as MacNeill was concerned. He ordered that the rising be called off and, to ensure his order reached all units, he inserted a notice in the Sunday Independent announcing the cancellation of all manoeuvres planned for the weekend.

Like other volunteers de Valera, who had already said his goodbyes to his family, was perplexed when he read the notice. Shortly afterwards he received a handwritten order from MacNeill confirming the cancellation, which was also subsequently confirmed by MacDonagh, but the latter advised him to be ready for further orders. The six main IRB leaders met along with James Connolly, the Marxist revolutionary, and decided to reset the date of the rebellion for the following morning. This caught not only the British, but also most of the Volunteers by surprise. The whole operation had been reset at such short notice that there was utter confusion in the ranks. More than half of the men who were due to take part did not show up, but the leaders decided to go ahead anyway.

The Easter Rebellion began with the seizure of the General Post Office in the heart of the city around noon on Monday, 24 April

1916. De Valera was assigned to hold the area around Boland's Mill, which was on one of the main roads that the British would use to bring reinforcements into the city. Once the real fighting began, he was almost totally cut off from news about what was happening in the city centre. In fact, Pearse had already surrendered a day before word would reach de Valera. Elizabeth O'Farrell, a member of Cumann na mBan, the women's auxiliary of the IVF, brought the surrender order but de Valera refused to accept it, because it had not been countersigned by his own commanding officer, MacDonagh. She therefore went off to get his signature. While waiting for her to return, de Valera discussed the situation with his Vice-Commandant, Joseph O'Connor, and, realising that the shooting around in the city had stopped, they concluded that the surrender message had indeed been genuine.

At this point de Valera was naturally afraid for the lives of himself and his men. He had heard stories of surrendering soldiers being shot at the battlefront in France, and now he feared the Volunteers might be summarily killed. He therefore tried to ingratiate himself with a British cadet they had been holding prisoner. He gave him his Browning automatic pistol with the request that the cadet would someday give it to his oldest son, Vivion. He then accompanied the cadet to Sir Patrick Dun's Hospital, where he surrendered to the British military. Thus de Valera did not actually surrender with his men. It was O'Connor who led them out of Boland's Mill a short time later. They were then joined by de Valera and were marched off, four abreast, to the Royal Dublin Society's show grounds at Ballsbridge.

Flanked by two British officers, de Valera was at the head of his men. He bitterly resented local people coming out with cups of tea for the British soldiers. He blamed the people of Dublin for the failure of the Rebellion because they had not helped. That they had no arms was no excuse as far as he was concerned. One of his men later said de Valera complained that the people should have come to the aid of the rebels even if they were armed only with knives and forks, but he disputed this. He contended that what he had actually said was that the people should have fought "though armed with hay forks only." Just where he thought the city dwellers of Dublin would get hay forks was another matter.

The real impact of his absurd remark was its betrayal of his tendency to blame others for something which, in the last analysis, was really the fault of the rebels themselves. Some of the leaders knew from the outset the rebellion was doomed, but they believed

25

their ultimate goals would be realised by others in the long run if they made a blood sacrifice at this time. They were right, but de Valera would only realise this later. He was one of those who had naively believed the rebellion might actually succeed in establishing an independent Irish republic, right then and there.

After two days in Ballsbridge, de Valera and the others were marched under a heavily armed guard across the city to Richmond Barracks. On the way they were jeered by onlookers. The people of Dublin clearly resented the Rebellion, but the British made the mistake of overreacting, and in the process antagonised the Irish people. The British rounded-up Irish nationalists indiscriminately and jailed them without trial. Many of those people had absolutely nothing to do with the rebellion; they were, in fact, critical of it as a foolhardy venture.

"Those wholesale arrests, dictated by panic, were a huge blunder from the British point of view," Piaras Beaslaí wrote. "They helped to convert many to sympathy with us; they provided a fresh grievance and a standing subject for agitation, and by bringing representative men from all parts of Ireland together in the intimacy of an internment camp they helped to strengthen our nucleus of future organisation, and to secure greater unity of thought and effort." But the summary executions of the principal leaders and other rebels did most to alienate the Irish people and win sympathy for those who had fought in the rebellion.

Pearse, Clarke and MacDonagh were shot by firing-squads in the early hours of de Valera's first morning at Richmond Barracks. He was sharing a cell with Count Plunkett, Seán T. O'Kelly, and others. In the following days eleven other leaders were executed.

Sinéad de Valera went to the office of the American Consul General in Dublin to get the United States government to plead for her husband's life, on the grounds that he was an American citizen. It was only then that anybody bothered to get a copy of his birth certificate and learned that he had been registered as George but subsequently christened Edward. He was asked about his American background when he was brought before the military court on 8 May, along with Thomas Ashe and four others. Among those who testified at the trial was the British cadet, whom his men had taken prisoner. He confirmed de Valera had been in command and added that he had been well treated himself as a prisoner.

Afterwards de Valera was taken to Kilmainham jail to await his fate. He expected the worst. From his cell he wrote a melodramatic note to Jack Ryan, his friend from his rugby-playing days at

Rockwell. "Just a line to say I played my last match last week and lost," he wrote. "Tomorrow I am to be shot—so pray for me—an old sport who unselfishly played the game."

De Valera was indeed sentenced to death, but the continuing executions had been causing so much revulsion among the Irish public that the British government called for a cessation. His sentence was duly changed to penal servitude for life, along with that of Thomas Ashe and others. He, Ashe, and Thomas Hunter were the only commandants to survive the Rebellion and the resulting executions. They were deported to English jails along with other survivors the following week.

While in jail de Valera won the reputation of being a kind of healing force among the Irish prisoners. One day, when some guards were leading MacNeill into a courtyard, de Valera called the Volunteers to attention and ordered them to salute their Chief of Staff. Though many of the men despised MacNeill for having tried to prevent the uprising, they nevertheless saluted him in the presence of the British guards. Thereafter de Valera was looked upon as having a unifying influence among the Volunteers. He was elected spokesman for the prisoners and he quickly showed the strange blend of leadership qualities that were to distinguish him throughout his years in politics. Robert Brennan, who was a fellow prisoner at the time and a lifelong supporter afterwards, noted that de Valera was a very good listener. He actually encouraged debate; yet in the end he would insist on having his own way.

"You can talk about this as much as you like, the more the better and from every angle," he would say. "In the last analysis, if you don't agree with me, then I quit. You must get someone else to do it."

From the outside world there were indications that the public odium in which the Volunteers were held following the Rebellion was waning markedly. In the United States, Irish-American groups exerted political pressure for the release of Irish prisoners. With Britain heavily dependent on American munitions to fight the war on the continent, the London government was anxious to court American favour. Consequently Lloyd George, who took over as Prime Minister in December 1916, announced a Christmas amnesty in which hundreds of Irish Volunteers, who had been interned without even a military trial, were freed. These men returned home to reorganise the shattered remnants of their movement.

The change in public attitude towards the rebels became apparent in February 1917 when Count Plunkett, the father of one of the executed leaders, was elected to Westminster in a by-election in Roscommon. He then announced he would not take his seat but intended to see that Ireland's claim to independence should be heard at the post-war peace conference.

While heartily approving of Plunkett's aims, de Valera had grave misgivings about the Volunteers becoming openly involved in politics, because he was afraid the movement's momentum could be irreparably damaged by an election defeat. He therefore advocated that Volunteers "should abstain officially from taking sides in these contests and no candidates should in future be officially recognised as standing in our interests or as representing our ideals." He opposed the idea of putting up one of his prison colleagues, Joe McGuinness, as a candidate in the next by-election, but young militants like Michael Collins, who had been released from internment, were not so cautious. They put forward the name of McGuinness in a Longford by-election, and he was narrowly elected, despite all the resources of the Irish Parliamentary Party.

Even though de Valera had been slow to appreciate the changes in Ireland during his absence, he was a better judge of the international political scene. After the United States entered the war in April 1917 with the avowed aim of making the world "safe for democracy," American pressure on the British was increased to force them to do something about the Irish question, so Lloyd George announced plans for a Convention in which people representing all shades of Irish opinion would be charged with drawing up a constitution for Ireland. Astutely perceiving that the British government might try to curry favour with public opinion by making the magnanimous gesture of releasing the remaining Irish prisoners, de Valera advocated a prison strike in order to deprive Britain "of any credit she may hope to gain from the release."

The prisoners began their campaign on 28 May 1917 by refusing to do prison work. When they were confined to their cells as punishment, they set about destroying the furnishings. These events were reported in the press and a public meeting to protest against prison conditions was arranged for 10 June 1917 in Dublin. Although the meeting was banned by the authorities, a sizeable crowd gathered, and there was a confrontation in which a police inspector was killed when struck with a hurley stick. Against this backdrop the British did indeed receive little credit for their magnanimity when they released the prisoners later that week. It seemed Lloyd George was simply trying to make a virtue out of necessity.

On the boat home de Valera headed a list of twenty-six recently released prisoners who drafted a formal appeal to President Wilson and the American Congress to keep an eye on Ireland. Observing that Wilson had recently proclaimed that the United States was fighting in Europe "for the liberty, self-government and undictated development of all peoples," they urged the American authorities "to take immediate measures to inform themselves accurately and on the spot about the extent of liberty or attempted repression which we may encounter." These were the words of buoyant, resolute people with high hopes, not a dispirited group of broken rebels.

CHAPTER 3

"Read *The Prince*"

Having been deported in disgrace little over a year earlier, the men returned to Ireland to a great welcome. De Valera was undoubtedly the hero of the hour; he was now the widely accepted leader of the men of Easter Week.

Nevertheless, the separatist movement was seriously fragmented at the time. The press erroneously depicted it as being under the control of Sinn Féin—the nationalist political party founded more than a decade earlier by Arthur Griffith—but Count Plunkett had actually been establishing a rival political organisation, the Liberty League. The whole movement was thus somewhat fragmented when de Valera was invited to run in a parliamentary by-election in East Clare shortly after his release.

From the outset he tried to act as a unifying force. He insisted, for instance, that Eoin MacNeill should be with him when he made his first appearance on an election platform. Some colleagues wanted to have nothing to do with MacNeill because of his role in trying to stop the Easter Rebellion, but de Valera brushed aside their objections. "The clergy are with MacNeill and they are a powerful force," he explained.

Adopting the tactics of a seasoned politician, de Valera remained as vague as possible during the campaign. He endorsed the idea of appealing to the post-war peace conference and the decision not to take part in the Irish Convention, in addition to stressing his own most cherished goal of reviving the Gaelic language. He also emphasised the necessity of not surrendering the rights of the majority to the Unionists in Ulster, but he relied most heavily on an emotional appeal associating himself with the ideals of the executed leaders of the Easter Rebellion. In fact, he went so far as to suggest the possibility of resorting to arms again in order to demonstrate his own commitment to those ideals. "To assert it in arms, were there a fair chance of military success," he said, "I would consider a sacred duty." Yet he avoided being too specific about those actual ideals.

"We want an Irish republic," he explained during the campaign, "because if Ireland had her freedom, it is, I believe, the most likely form of government." But he nevertheless emphasised he was not a doctrinaire republican. He was not firmly committed to any form of government. "So long as it was an Irish government," he said, "I would not put a word against it."

He was elected by a comfortable margin of more than two-to-one, following which he threw himself into the reorganisation of the separatist movement under the Sinn Féin banner by appearing at public meetings throughout the country. His message was basically the same during the months leading up to the Sinn Féin Árd Fheis (Convention) of October 1917.

While he advocated calling upon the post-war peace conference to ensure Ireland got her freedom, he realised the country would first need to assert her own nationhood in order to obtain a hearing at the conference. "To be heard at the Peace Conference," de Valera told a Dublin gathering on 12 July 1917, "Ireland must first claim absolute independence." It was as republicans, he said, they would have the best chance of enlisting the sympathetic support of such countries as the United States and France.

There was actually a difference of opinion between de Valera and Griffith over the most advantageous form of government for Ireland. For years the founder of Sinn Féin had been advocating the establishment of a Dual Monarchy between Britain and Ireland on Austro-Hungarian lines. But a few days before the Árd Fheis, de Valera managed to persuade him to accept a compromise formula, whereby Sinn Féin would pledge itself to securing a republic and once it had been achieved, the Irish people would then freely choose their own form of government by referendum. He also prevailed upon Griffith to withdraw from the race for the presidency of Sinn Féin and to propose him instead. At the last moment Plunkett also withdrew, so de Valera was elected unanimously.

He then proceeded to deliver a somewhat vague presidential address which seemed to have something for moderates and militants alike. "This is not the time for discussion of the best forms of government," he told the gathering as he explained the party was not irrevocably committed to a republic. "But we are all united on this—that we want complete and absolute independence. Get that and we will agree to differ afterwards. We do not wish to bind the people to any form of government." While all this seemed moderate enough, de Valera continued in contradictory terms, as he declared that it was "necessary to be united now under the flag for which we are going to fight for our freedom, the flag of the Irish Republic. We have nailed that flag to the mast; we shall never lower it."

Nobody could have been sure exactly where he stood, with the result that he was hailed as a born leader. Everybody was supposedly following him, even though none of them could have been sure of exactly where he was going. On the one hand he was outlining a political path, but in the same speech he also talked in the most militant terms of forcing Britain to resort to the sword: "We will draw the naked sword to make her bare her own naked sword, to drag the hypocritical mask off her face, and to show her to the world for what she is, the accursed oppressor of nations."

The following day the IVF held a separate convention at which de Valera was elected leader. Consequently, he was the head of the most important political and military wings of the separatist movement. The other principal organisation, the IRB, had recently lost its leading figure, Thomas Ashe, who had died after being force-fed while on hunger strike in jail. De Valera was therefore the undisputed leader of the separatist movement.

He began touring the country as a paid national organiser for Sinn Féin. Calling on the people to repudiate the so-called Irish Convention then sitting, he held out the hope that President Woodrow Wilson's announced war aims would lead to Irish freedom. With the Allies supposedly fighting for the rights of small nations, de Valera challenged them to name those countries concerned. Once earnest proof had been given that Ireland would be included among those nations, he promised that half a million Irishmen would be prepared to help the Allies. "Then they will find," he said, "that these half a million men will be ready to defend their own land, and ready, to give a helping hand to the oppressed."

De Valera was deliberately linking the Irish question with the most emotional international issue of the day—the First World War. The IVF was struggling for the principle of self-determination, he explained, so if Wilson was sincere, then the volunteers and the Americans were "genuine 'associates' in this war." De Valera was trying to depict the Irish cause in a favorable light for the Americans because, he explained, if Britain ignored Ireland's right to self-determination after the war, he intended to call on the "great bulk of the Irish in the States" to use their "weighty influence" to put pressure on the British.

There could be no doubt that he was questioning Wilson's sincerity. "If President Wilson is honest, he will easily pardon us for not trusting him with an implicit faith," the new Sinn Féin leader candidly explained. "If he is a hypocrite, if he is a meet partner for those who began this world war with altruistic professions of liberty and freedom, then the sooner America and the sooner mankind knows it the better." He astutely emphasised, however, that he was not pronouncing any judgement on Wilson. The Irish case could be used as the test to "prove to the world the sincerity or hypocrisy of the Allies and President Wilson when they declared that they were fighting for the self-determination of nations."

Meanwhile de Valera's efforts to bolster Sinn Féin initially ran into difficulties with three consecutive by-election losses to IPP candidates in early 1918. The first defeat was in south Armagh, where the Unionist community apparently supported the IPP candidate to the obvious infuriation of de Valera, who afterwards described the Unionists as "a rock on the road" to Irish freedom. "We must if necessary blast it out of our path," he added rather recklessly. Within three weeks of his inflammatory remarks, Sinn Féin suffered two further defeats—one in Waterford and the other in East Tyrone, where Unionists again apparently supported the IPP candidate. Sinn Féin seemed on the wane, but the British government soon undermined the IPP by authorising the extension of conscription to Ireland. Members of the IPP withdrew from Westminster in protest, which was tantamount to endorsing the abstentionist policy that Sinn Féin had been following all along.

The Lord Mayor of Dublin invited representatives of various shades of nationalist opinion to the Mansion House for a conference on what to do about conscription on 18 April 1918. A standing committee was established with de Valera and Griffith representing Sinn Féin, while John Dillon and Joe Devlin represented the IPP. There was also the mayor, three labour representatives and two independent members of parliament, William O'Brien and T.M. Healy. The uniformity of opinion bringing such a diverse group of Irishmen together was evidence of the unpopularity of conscription.

During the Mansion House deliberations de Valera stood out. "His transparent sincerity, his gentleness and equability captured the hearts of us all," according to O'Brien, who described the Sinn Féin leader's obstinacy as "sometimes trying," but it nevertheless "became tolerable enough when, with a boyish smile," de Valera would say: "You will bear with me, won't you? You know I am an old schoolmaster."

De Valera's influence was evident with the adoption of a declaration bearing the indelible imprint of separatist thinking. Basing the case against conscription on "Ireland's separate and distinct nationhood" and the principle that governments "derive their just powers from the consent of the governed," the conference denied "the right of the British government, or any external authority, to impose compulsory service in Ireland against the clearly expressed will of the Irish people."

At de Valera's suggestion the conference sought the support of the Catholic hierarchy, which responded by virtually sanctifying the campaign against conscription. The hierarchy called for a special mass to be celebrated the following Sunday "in every church in Ireland to avert the scourge of conscription with which Ireland is now threatened." It also asked the people to subscribe to an anti-conscription pledge drafted by de Valera.

During the conscription controversy de Valera sought to enlist American support by giving his first formal newspaper interview to a correspondent of the Christian Science Monitor. If Britain was really fighting for the principles enunciated by President Wilson, he contended "she could apply them without trouble and without delay" in Ireland's case. Under the circumstances he was not prepared to take the chance that the Irish people would be fairly treated, if they dropped their opposition to conscription. "Ireland cannot afford to gamble," he said. "Great powers strong enough to enforce their contracts can safely enter a combination, knowing their strength is a guarantee that the contract will not be violated and that what they stipulated for will not be denied them when success is achieved." A small nation like Ireland, however, would have no such guarantee.

De Valera also prepared a draft text for a formal appeal to the United States on behalf of the Mansion House Conference. While it was being circulated among the other members of the conference, he and some eighty prominent members of Sinn Féin were arrested for supposedly being involved in some kind of plot with Germany. The British never produced any convincing evidence of the existence of such a plot, much less that de Valera or any of the others were involved. Most Irish people assumed the British were just taking the Sinn Féin leaders out of circulation to pave the way for conscription. De Valera was certainly not involved in any German Plot, but he was deported and spent most of the next nine months in jail, without ever being brought before a court.

Sinn Féin made the most of the propaganda opportunities afforded by the arrests. An edited version of de Valera's appeal to the United States was published in pamphlet form. It ended in mid-sentence, as if he had been arrested with pen in hand while actually drafting the document. By arresting only members of Sinn Féin the British inevitably gave the impression they thought the party was primarily responsible for organising the widespread opposition to conscription, and as a result Sinn Féin profited most from the popular backlash generated by the issue. The series of by-election reversals was quickly ended with Griffith's victory in a Cavan by-election the following month.

When the First World War ended in November 1918, de Valera still hoped President Wilson would stand by his lofty wartime pronouncements. The American President had continued to speak in idealistic terms during the final year of the war. "Self-determination is not a mere phrase," he declared in February 1918. "It is an imperative principle of action, which statesmen will henceforth ignore at their peril."

"If America holds to the principles enunciated by her President during the war she will have a noble place in the history of nations," de Valera wrote to his mother from Lincoln jail on 28 November 1918. He believed those Wilsonian principles could be "the basis of true statecraft—a firm basis that will bear the stress of time—but will the President be able to get them accepted by others whose entry into the war was on motives less unselfish?

"What an achievement should he succeed in getting established a common law for nations—resting on the will of the nations—making national duels as rare as duels between individual persons are at present; if that be truly his aim, may God steady his hand."

Any remaining doubts about the tide of opinion sweeping Ireland since the Easter Rebellion were dispelled by the Sinn Féin landslide in the general election of 14 December 1918. Collins and two IRB colleagues, Harry Boland and Diarmuid O'Hegarty, were primarily responsible for selecting the Sinn Féin candidates. Relying on the successful formula used to secure the election of McGuinness in 1917, they selected a preponderance of men in jail. Many of them did not even know they were candidates until they were informed by prison authorities of their election to Westminster.

Sinn Féin had asked for a clear mandate, indicating in its election manifesto that its successful candidates would not sit at Westminster but would establish a sovereign, republican assembly in Ireland instead. The party won seventy-three seats against twenty-six for the Unionists, and only six for the once powerful IPP. Its leader, John Dillon, was trounced in East Mayo by de Valera, who received almost twice Dillon's support. De Valera's name was also put forward in East Clare, where he was unopposed, and in West Belfast, where he was defeated by Joe Devlin.

In the following weeks as it became apparent that the British were not about to release him, de Valera set about escaping. He regularly acted as a server at mass for the prison chaplain, and one day he managed to make an impression of the chaplain's master-key. He then got a colleague, Sean Milroy, to draw a Christmas card, showing Sean McGarry, the President of the IRB, holding a large key which he was trying to fit into a small keyhole, with a caption: "Xmas 1917 can't get in." Beneath was another drawing of McGarry looking through a large keyhole above the caption: "Xmas 1918 can't get out." Inside the card there was a note supposedly passing on best wishes from de Valera in Gaelic. In fact, however, the message explained that the key on the card was an exact drawing of the master-key, and the large keyhole provided a cross-section of the key's dimensions. There was a note to the effect, "Field will translate." Field was a code-name for Collins. It was a clever card which fooled not only the prison censor, but also McGarry's wife. It became necessary to get a separate message out to Collins explaining that the details of the key were on the Christmas card.

De Valera had hoped to be out by 21 January 1919—when the Sinn Féin representatives reaffirmed the Irish Republic, first proclaimed during the Easter Rebellion, and established Dáil Eireann, the promised national assembly—but there were a number of delays. The first two keys smuggled into the jail did not work, so a suitable blank key was delivered, along with cutting material to enable the prisoners to fashion a key inside the prison. Collins supervised the escape arrangements on the outside. He arranged to collect de Valera, McGarry and Milroy outside the jail and spirit them to hiding-places in England, where they would wait until he could arrange their safe passage back to Ireland.

On 3 February Harry Boland gave a pre-arranged signal that all was ready on the outside, using a flashlight in a field next to the jail. The prisoners responded from an agreed window by setting light to several matches at the one time, thereby making a small flare. The prisoners then made their way to the back gate, which they reached with little difficulty, only to find that the impetuosity of those outside threatened the whole venture. They had tried to open the outer gate with a key of their own, but it broke in the lock.

Fortunately de Valera managed to knock the broken piece out with his own key. The three prisoners then emerged, to the immense relief of those outside. Collins gave de Valera a jubilant thump on the shoulder, and they all made for a waiting taxi, which took them to the city centre. Collins and Boland took a train from there to London, while de Valera and the other two changed cars and set off for the Manchester area, where they went into hiding.

Collins was looking to de Valera to renew the military struggle because, in his presidential address at the Sinn Féin Árd Fheis, he had promised to "draw the naked sword" in order to make the British do likewise. "As for us on the outside," Collins wrote to an IRB colleague in jail, "all ordinary peaceful means are ended and we shall be taking the only alternative actions in a short while now."

But when de Valera returned, he had no intention of renewing the armed struggle, at least not for the time being. He announced he was going to the United States because he thought Ireland's best chance of success lay in enlisting American help, in view of President Woodrow Wilson's eloquent pronouncements about the rights of small nations for which Americans had supposedly gone to war in 1917. Collins tried, but failed, to persuade him to stay at home to direct military operations.

"You know what it is to try to argue with Dev," he told a friend afterwards. "He says he thought it all out while in prison, and he feels that the one place where he can be useful to Ireland is in America."

Despite his incarceration for almost nine months on trumped-up charges, de Valera gave the distinct impression of being comparatively moderate. From his hiding place in Dublin, for example, he endorsed Irish-American efforts to enlist President Wilson's help in Paris. Although some people were already saying the American President would not even try to get justice for Ireland, de Valera called for patience. "Pronounce no opinion on President Wilson," he advised. "It is premature, for he and his friends will bear our country in mind at the crucial hour."

De Valera was spirited back to Britain to await a ship to the United States. While he was in hiding the British released the other members of Sinn Féin who were being held for their supposed part in the so-called German Plot. He was therefore free to return to Ireland with the others without being apprehended, so he went back to attend a meeting of the Dáil.

Plans were made to stage a great public welcome. An announcement was made on behalf of Sinn Féin that de Valera would be given the kind of civic reception normally reserved for royalty. When British authorities proscribed the welcoming demonstration, Sinn Féin was faced with a dilemma, to risk a confrontation with the British, or suffer a damaging loss of face.

There was some serious soul-searching among party leaders. Although plans for the welcoming had been announced in the name of the party, the executive had nothing to do with the announcement. Collins had issued the statement himself and signed the names of the party's two national secretaries without authorisation. Still in his late twenties he was an arrogant, determined, young man. He was known as "the Big Fellow," not because of his physical size, seeing that he was less than six feet tall, but because, from the earliest days, he seemed to have a greatly exaggerated sense of his own importance. Even his friends considered him big-headed, and his conduct in the latest controversy certainly warranted the description.

Speaking "with much vehemence and emphasis," Collins made it clear to the party executive that he was looking for a confrontation with the British. "Ireland was likely to get more out of a state of general disorder than from a continuance of the situation as it then stood," he explained. "The proper people to take decisions of that kind were ready to face the British military, and were resolved to force the issue. And they were not to be deterred by weaklings and cowards." A heated argument ensued, and it was only resolved by deciding to consult de Valera himself.

On hearing of the controversy, he asked that the demonstration be cancelled rather than risk lives in an unnecessary confrontation. He was sure matters of much greater principle would arise in future. "We who have waited know how to wait," he explained. "Many a heavy fish is caught even with a fine line if the angler is patient."

When the Dáil met on 1 April 1919 de Valera was elected *Príomh Aire* (Prime Minister), and he then proceeded to name a cabinet which included people like Griffith, Plunkett, MacNeill, Collins, Cathal Brugha, and Constance Markievicz. The cabinet were truly representatives of the various factions within Sinn Féin.

With the Peace Conference deliberating in Paris, de Valera adopted a statesmanlike approach. "We are quite ready to take our part in a League of Nations which has as its foundation equality and right among nations," he declared. But he noted there were signs that France was demanding vindictive terms from the Germans, who would inevitably seek their own revenge in the not too distant future, just as the French had done as a result of the treaty ending the Franco-Prussian War in 1871. "We must try to save France from herself," he said. "If there is a peace imposed on Germany now, there will be a desire for revenge on the part of the German people later on." In fact, he said, "another war of revenge must surely follow." He was astutely predicting the outbreak of the Second World

War more than twenty years in advance.

Although de Valera portrayed a moderate internationalist outlook in his public speeches, he privately expressed antipathy towards conventional politics in conversations with people like Collins and Richard Mulcahy, the IVF chief of staff.

"You're a young man going into politics," he told Mulcahy. "I'll give you two pieces of advice, study economics and read The Prince"—Machiavelli's classical study of political duplicity. Mulcahy would later come to appreciate the advice, at least as a key to understanding de Valera, who was playing a crafty game of his own. He went along with the militants by talking tough, but when it came to action, he came down on the side of relative moderation.

His style of government, which allowed endless debate, gave a much greater role to the politicians within the movement. A special Sinn Féin Árd Fheis was held on 8 April at which a proposal by de Valera was adopted, debarring members of the cabinet from membership of the party's Standing Committee, which was now given a virtual veto over government action.

De Valera undoubtedly had Collins in mind when he explained the Standing Committee's consultative role. If, for example, a minister decided the Irish people should no longer pay income tax to the Crown, the proposal would first have to be referred for approval to the party's Standing Committee.

Collins had been arguing in favour of such a scheme within the new cabinet, but he had come up against the resolute obstinacy of Brugha. De Valera, as was his wont, had assumed an aloof position in the dispute, but his remarks at the Árd Fheis certainly leaned towards Brugha's more cautious position on the issue.

The militants were anxious to strike at the police forces, but de Valera was only prepared to go so far. In a forceful address to the Dáil on 10 April, he called for the ostracism of all policemen, because they were "the main instruments" in keeping the Irish people in subjection. "They are spies in our midst," he said. "They are the eyes and ears of the enemy." He added that their history was "a continuity of brutal treason against their own people."

Once de Valera made up his mind on any matter he was very difficult to shift, though he was usually prepared to allow others to make futile efforts to dissuade him on some point or other. Sitting through such arguments required an equal amount of patience on the part of other cabinet members, and this kind of patience was not one of Collins's strong points.

The Dáil agreed to float a National Loan by selling bonds as the

Fenians had done, and Collins, as Minister for Finance, drafted a prospectus for the loan and became rather irritated at de Valera's habit of mulling over every word. Collins wished to include a Dáil pledge to honour Fenian bonds floated in 1866, but de Valera had reservations and the reference was dropped from the prospectus.

De Valera also irritated him by agonising over the wording of the Irish submission to the Paris Peace Conference. "The damned Peace Conference will be over before he's satisfied," Collins grumbled in frustration.

Impatient for military action, Collins complained of "all sort of miserable little under currents," as de Valera and the politicians made things "intolerable" for militants like himself. "The policy now," he wrote, "seems to be to squeeze out anyone who is tainted with strong fighting ideas, or should I say the utility of fighting." As a member of the cabinet, he was now "only an onlooker" at meetings of the party's executive, which he described as "a Standing Committee of malcontents." They were "inclined to be ever less militant and more political and theoretical." When his IRB colleague, Harry Boland, went to the United States to make preparations for de Valera's forthcoming tour, for instance, the party replaced him as National Secretary with Hannah Sheehy-Skeffington, a sister of Fr Eugene Sheehy, the parish priest in Bruree. She was the wife of a pacifist murdered by a deranged British officer during the Easter Rebellion. This was all too much for Collins. "We have too many of the bargaining type already," he complained. "I am not sure that our movement or part of it at any rate is alive to the developing situation."

It was only after de Valera went to the United States in early June that Collins began to get his own way. In the following months he would gradually provoke that general state of disorder about which he spoke back in March.

CHAPTER 4

"The Trouble is Purely one of Personalities"

De Valera's American visit was primarily aimed at securing diplomatic recognition of the Irish Republic, but he also had some secondary goals, like collecting money for the cause, and also averting a threatened split within Irish-American ranks. He realised American officials would be reluctant to recognise the Irish Republic for fear of offending their wartime ally, Britain, but he still thought he could be successful if he exploited President Wilson's eloquent pronouncements about democracy and self-determination in order to enlist sufficient popular support to embarrass the American President into helping Ireland.

From the outset, therefore, de Valera saw his role in the United States as that of a propagandist. His aim, he told his first press conference in New York, was to arouse public opinion to exert pressure on President Wilson because "this pressure will show him that the people of America want the United States' government to recognise the Republic of Ireland."

"This is the reason I am eager to spread propaganda in official circles in America," he explained. "My appeal is to the people. I know that if they can be aroused, government action will follow." The Versailles Treaty was already generating political controversy in the United States, where there was uneasiness over the Covenant of the League of Nations, which had been incorporated into the treaty. Seizing on the propaganda potential of the situation, de Valera exploited the controversy in order to inject the Irish question "into international politics."

For six months he concentrated on the treaty issue as he travelled throughout the United States, speaking to public gatherings in at least thirty states, and traversing the three thousand mile breadth of the country four times. He was met by a crowd of some 25,000 at the railway station when he went to Boston and 50,000 crammed into Fenway Park, the city's premier baseball grounds, to hear his first public address on 29 June. Eight days later 17,000 jammed into Madison Square Gardens, New York, to hear him. This was estimated as the largest crowd ever in the arena, because the local police force—with its strong Irish presence—had permitted people to fill the aisles in blatant contravention of the city's fire regulations. There were 25,000 people in Soldier's Field, Chicago, three days later. He then proceeded to California. On his first coast-to-coast trip he delivered seventeen public speeches to an estimated total of half a million people. As the novelty of his appearances began to wear off, the crowds declined and his failings as a public speaker became more apparent.

He tended to read his speeches in a dull, halting manner but, as voice amplification was still rather primitive, this failing was of little consequence at the large gatherings. Even though he had been preceded by much better orators on the platform in Fenway Park, the *Boston Herald* reported that de Valera was nevertheless effective on the rostrum because he exuded the outstanding qualities of "passionate sincerity" and "utmost simplicity"—two characteristics that "bum their way into the consciousness of everyone who sees and hears him."

Throughout his travels he was careful to talk in terms which were consistent with America's war aims as outlined in President Wilson's famous fourteen points. Privately de Valera explained that his strategy was to let Wilson "know that if he goes for his fourteen points as they were and a true League of Nations, Irishmen and men and women of Irish blood will be behind him."

"Those of us who were fighting England were in reality fighting for those very principles for which Americans fought," he contended publicly, equating the motives of Irish rebels with those of the American soldiers who had fought in the First World War. If he had been an American, he said, he would have felt obliged to join the American forces and fight to make the world safe for democracy. Now this noble goal was in danger of being betrayed, however, unless something was done to rectify the situation.

"If America is determined to champion the cause of democracy in the world, that cause will triumph," he said. "If America leads the way towards true democracy, the democracy of England even, and of France and Spain and every country in the world will follow your lead." The United States should reject the Versailles Treaty with its existing Covenant for the League of Nations and then draw up a new covenant in Washington. "Now is the time to frame it," he declared. "It is not enough for you to destroy, you must build."

Although Ireland was not even mentioned in the treaty, de Valera cited its controversial Article X as grounds for calling on the United States government to recognise the Irish Republic without delay. Article X of the Covenant would commit members of the League of Nations "to respect and preserve" the territorial integrity of other member states "against external aggression." Thus, if the United States ratified the treaty without first recognising the

Irish Republic, Americans would be obliged to cut off support to Irish rebels because Ireland would be legally regarded as part of the United Kingdom. And to make matters worse, if some foreign powerer intervened militarily on Ireland's behalf—as France had helped the American colonies in their struggle for independence—the United States and other members of the League would be obliged to help Britain under the terms of Article X.

De Valera complained so much about the Covenant that he was popularly believed to be opposed to the League of Nations, whereas he actually favoured the concept and also approved of Article X per se. "If you are going to have a League of Nations, you must have some article in it like Article X, but it must be based on just conditions at the start," he stated In San Francisco. As things stood, Ireland was being dragged into the League as part of the United Kingdom and unless the United States recognised the Irish Republic, or at least made "an explicit reservation in the case of Ireland," Britain would hold that America's ratification of the Covenant amounted to formal recognition of England's claim to Ireland as part of her possessions, the integrity of which America must ever more lend her assistance in maintaining."

"Article X is the whole essence of the League," de Valera told a Denver gathering. "It is the preserving clause. If you preserve the conditions under which you start, then start right. It is wrong to preserve wrong: this is why we are against the League of Nations." In short, the real problem was not the Covenant, but Ireland's lack of recognition, and he was exploiting the controversy in an attempt to secure diplomatic recognition. "If the Irish Republic is recognised," he had already declared in Philadelphia, "the Covenant will be acceptable."

Wilson, a staunch Presbyterian of Scots-Irish parentage, was an anglophile with little or no sympathy for the Irish cause. He tried to ignore it for the longest time, but was eventually forced to speak out. He explained he had not been able to raise the Irish case at the Paris Peace Conference because those talks were concerned only with the territory of defeated nations. Once the treaty was ratified, however, he contended the United States would be able to take up Ireland's case at the League of Nations because Article XI of the Covenant provided that "every matter that is likely to affect the peace of the world is everybody's business."

"In other words," Wilson added, "at present we have to mind our own business. Under the Covenant of the League of Nations we can mind other people's business, and anything that affects the peace of the world, whether we are parties to it or not, can, by our delegates, be brought to the attention of mankind."

"Instead of relying on Article XI to undo the wrong of Article X, why not set up Article X in such a form that there will be no wrong to be undone?" de Valera responded. "If President Wilson was not sufficiently influential to get the Irish case before the Peace Conference, working in an unofficial way, he will not be influential enough to get the case of Ireland before the Council of the League of Nations."

Wilson was unwilling to allow any modification to Article X or any other parts of the Covenant. When the United States Senate adopted fourteen specific reservations, his supporters were instructed to defeat the treaty in November 1919.

De Valera's overall approach to the controversy over the League of Nations led to difficulties with the leadership of the influential Irish-American organisation, the Friends of Irish Freedom (FOIF). Its leaders, Judge Daniel Cohalan of the New York Supreme Court and John Devoy, the editor of the *Gaelic American*, resented his suggestion that the United States should renew efforts to make the world safe for democracy. That was sheer Wilsonian babble as far as Cohalan was concerned.

Born in upstate New York of Irish parents, he was a controversial figure, detested in Democratic Party circles as a political turn-coat. In the past he had been closely identified with the powerful Tammany boss, Charles F. Murphy, and had been a member of the New York delegations at the Democratic Party's National Conventions of 1904 and 1908. In 1910 he was appointed to the New York Supreme Court and, together with Murphy, spearheaded an unsuccessful attempt to block Woodrow Wilson's quest for the Democratic nomination on his way to the Presidency in 1912. Murphy soon made his peace with Wilson, but Cohalan did not. He bolted the party and supported Wilson's Republican opponent in 1916. Cohalan despised Wilson, and the feeling was quite mutual.

When the judge headed an Irish-American delegation which sought to make representations to Wilson before his departure for the Paris Peace Conference, the President insisted on Cohalan's exclusion. He gracefully withdrew and in the process greatly enhanced his own standing among Irish-American activists. He had not only stepped aside and borne Wilson's affront in the interest of the cause, but more importantly, he had been singled out as an opponent by the President himself, and this would become a valuable distinction in the coming months as Wilson's reputation plummeted in Irish-American circles.

Cohalan would undoubtedly have been delighted to use de Valera against Wilson, but the Irish leader was wisely unwilling to be used in such a way. He was anxious to be on friendly terms with both the Democrats and the Republicans, and he might have succeeded had he not tried to act as a power-broker, ready to deliver Irish-American support.

Cohalan and Devoy had already informed de Valera of their utter opposition to American membership of the League of Nations, even if Ireland were admitted to the organisation, so they therefore naturally resented his nationwide effort to depict "men and women of Irish blood" as being prepared to support the Versailles Treaty in return for Wilson's recognition of the Irish Republic. De Valera had no mandate whatever to speak for Irish-Americans and his intervention was resented as outside interference in American politics. Cohalan tried to keep him out of Irish-American affairs, and when de Valera asked "to be let into the political steps" the judge was planning, he was told not to "go near the political end at all."

"The trouble is purely one of personalities," de Valera explained. "I cannot feel confidence enough in a certain man [Cohalan] to let him have implicit control of tactics here without consultation and agreement with me." In short, de Valera was insisting on having the final say on policy matters, though he was prepared to consult with Irish-American leaders. "On the ways and means they have to be consulted," he conceded, "but I reserve the right to use my judgment as to whether any means suggested is or is not in conformity with our purpose."

Whether the United States decided to join the League of Nations or not, was basically none of his business. "The fight for the League of Nations was purely an American affair attacked from a purely American angle," de Valera admitted in a letter to the cabinet at home. He certainly had no right to say that people like Cohalan would support the Versailles Treaty under conditions that they had pronounced unacceptable. A clash was therefore virtually inevitable.

"I realised early," de Valera wrote, that "big as this country is it was not big enough to hold the judge and myself." Irish matters were only of secondary consideration to Cohalan. "I desired that Ireland's interest should come first," de Valera explained. "I held that the Irish here were organised not in their own interest here so much as to help Ireland. I held that the money contributed was obtained in the belief that it would be used as directly as possible for Ireland."

"It is sympathy for Ireland that has enabled such an organisation as the Friends of Irish Freedom to be built up," he contended. "That is why the vast mass of the rank and file have joined—that is why they have contributed, and I will not allow myself to be in any hobble skirts with respect to the doing of anything which we feel certain is for the good of the Cause."

Before de Valera went to the United States, FOIF had launched a Victory Fund to collect a million dollars, a quarter of which was earmarked for Ireland. He was convinced he could collect much more by selling Irish Republican bonds, but he felt Irish-American leaders adopted obstructionist tactics. They were opposed to any interference with the Victory Fund, which was due to be wound up in August 1919. This really did not matter because de Valera would not have been ready to launch the bond drive by then in any event, but he contended afterwards that Cohalan dragged his feet. The judge contended the proposed sale of bonds would be illegal unless the United States recognised the Irish Republic first. As a trained lawyer on the bench of the New York State Supreme Court, he knew what he was talking about—selling such bonds would have been a violation of the federal "blue sky" laws. De Valera, with no training in Irish, much less American, legal matters, was certainly presumptuous in pitting his own judgement against someone like Cohalan, but then the Irish leader was clearly touchy about having his judgement questioned on the bond issue.

While in the United States he decided to include a reference to honouring the Fenian bonds, which prompted Collins to write rather tactlessly that "it was worth going to America to be converted to that idea." The remark was just a passing comment, but to de Valera, for whom every written word was carefully calculated, the comment was fraught with significance.

"What did you mean it was worth going to America to be 'converted' to the idea of paying the Fenian bonds?" he asked indignantly. "Surely I never opposed acknowledging that as a National debt. You must mean something else. What is it?"

"I meant about the Fenian bonds, that it was worth going to America to be converted to my idea," Collins replied. "Honestly, I did not think the fact that I was practically forced to delete a certain paragraph from the prospectus looked much in favour of the idea. For God's sake, Dev, don't start an argument about its being from the prospectus only, etc. Don't please. It's quite all right."

Collins had done such an effective job in organising the National

Loan at home, that de Valera asked him to come to the United States to help organise the drive there, but Collins refused. Instead he sent out James O'Mara, a trustee of the Dáil, and O'Mara undertook the organisational work on a drive to sell bond certificates entitling purchasers to buy actual bonds of similar value once the Irish Republic was formally recognised. In this way it was possible to get around the American laws, and FOIF financed the drive.

Although Cohalan co-operated, this did little to stem the developing rift between himself and de Valera. There were, however, faults on both sides.

De Valera's own reports to the cabinet in Dublin left no doubt he had interfered in American affairs by presuming to speak for Irish-Americans during the controversy over the Versailles Treaty. On the other hand, the Cohalan faction interfered in Irish affairs when de Valera tried to reassure the public that Britain had nothing to fear from an independent Ireland. Many Americans had reservations about Irish independence because they felt an independent Ireland would pose security risks for Britain, their ally in the recent war. De Valera tried to allay their fears by indicating that Ireland would guarantee Britain's legitimate security needs.

In a *Westminster Gazette* interview in February 1920 he explained there were various ways of ensuring Britain's security. The British could declare a kind of Monroe Doctrine for the British Isles, he suggested, or they could conclude a treaty with Ireland on the lines of a 1901 treaty between the United States and Cuba, in which the Cubans guaranteed not to permit their independence to be compromised by allowing a foreign power to obtain "control over any portion" of their island. "Why doesn't Britain do with Ireland as the United States did with Cuba?" de Valera asked. "Why doesn't Britain declare a Monroe Doctrine for her neighbouring island? The people of Ireland so far from objecting, would co-operate with their whole soul."

The *Gaelic American* took exception to the use of the Cuban parallel, because the 1901 treaty specifically authorised the Americans to intervene in the island in order to ensure the preservation of its Independence, and there were also provisions granting the United States bases in Cuba. De Valera had only referred to Cuba's agreement to maintain her independence and, he explained, he had not been alluding to other aspects of the treaty, such as the granting of bases, which should have been apparent from a careful reading of his interview. But Devoy chose to disregard de Valera's clarification.

"When a part of a document is offered in evidence in court, or in negotiations," Devoy declared in an editorial, "the whole document becomes subject for consideration." He basically wanted to put de Valera on trial in the columns of the *Gaelic American*.

Instead of replying to Devoy, de Valera took the extraordinary step of complaining to Cohalan, by essentially demanding the judge disassociate himself from the editor's views. De Valera explained he was planning to use "the great lever of American opinion" as a wedge to achieve his aims in the United States and, as the Irish-Americans were to be the thin edge of this wedge, he was anxious to satisfy himself that the metal at the point was of the right temper. "The articles of the *Gaelic American* and certain incidents that have resulted from them, give me grounds for fear that, in a moment of stress the point of the lever would fail me," he continued. It was therefore vital he should know how the judge stood in the matter. "I am led to understand that these articles in the *Gaelic American* have your consent and approval. Is this so?"

De Valera's candid letter was an extremely naïve piece of insensitive arrogance. He was in effect telling the judge that he intended to use him without so much as asking if he was willing to be used in such a manner.

Understandably indignant, Cohalan replied he had no intention of being used as a lever for alien ends. And he warned that de Valera was making a serious mistake if he thought other Irish-Americans would allow themselves to be used in this way. "Do you really think for a moment that any self-respecting American citizen will permit any citizen of another country to interfere, as you suggest, in American affairs?" the judge asked. "If so, I may assure you that you are woefully out of touch with the spirit of the country in which you are sojourning."

De Valera was a novice as far as American politics were concerned, as was only too evident from his jubilant reaction to the United States Senate's adoption of a reservation to the Versailles Treaty on the Irish question in March 1920. The reservation, which expressed "sympathy with the expectation of the Irish people for a government of their own choice," stipulated that when such government was set up, "it should be promptly admitted as a member of the League of Nations."

"A Te Deum should be sung throughout all Ireland," de Valera cabled Griffith. "We thank Almighty God, we thank the noble American nation, we thank all the friends of Ireland here who have worked so unselfishly for our cause—we thank the heroic dead whose sacrifices made victory possible." In a covering letter he explained that it had been "what I had been always wishing for, and it came finally beyond expectations."

In his exuberance he totally misread the Senate's gesture, which was just a cynical congressional ploy to curry favour with the Irish-American electorate around St Patrick's Day, while at the same time ensuring that the overall reservations would be so unpalatable to supporters of the treaty that they would ensure its defeat. Next day sixteen of the senators who had voted for the Irish reservation proceeded to vote against the treaty with the reservations attached.

Speaking to a meeting of prominent Irish-Americans in New York that very evening, Cohalan complained that de Valera knew very little about American politics, yet consulted no one and by his arrogance alienated many people who had spent a lifetime helping the Irish cause. In the course of a thirty minute tirade, the judge accused the Irish leader of interfering in American affairs and causing "considerable friction" among Irish-Americans. He certainly had a valid point, but he continued in terms which showed that he himself was interfering in purely Irish affairs. He complained, for instance, that de Valera's controversial *Westminster Gazette* interview amounted to an offer of "a compromise to England which would put Ireland in the position of accepting a protectorate from England, and consent to an alliance with that country which would align the race with England as against the United States in the case of war" between America and Britain. Here Cohalan was clearly interfering in Irish affairs by assuming to say what the Irish people should do, just as de Valera had interfered in American affairs by telling the Americans what to do.

When de Valera was invited to explain his own position to this meeting, he tactlessly blurted out that he was not in the United States a month when he realised the country was not big enough for himself and Cohalan, which prompted the Roman Catholic bishop of Buffalo to remark that the judge could hardly be expected "to leave his native land just because the President had decided to come in."

The meeting, which dragged on for ten hours, was acrimonious in the extreme. At one point Harry Boland went into hysterics and had to retire from the room to compose himself. "De Valera's attitude was one of infallibility; he was right, everybody else was wrong, and he couldn't be wrong," one witness recalled. "I thought the man was crazy." In the end the bishop persuaded the two factions to agree to a truce. The meeting broke up on the understanding that henceforth de Valera would not interfere in purely American matters, and Cohalan and Devoy would keep out of essentially Irish affairs.

But de Valera had no intention of upholding his side of the agreement. Within a week he was writing to Griffith asking the Dáil to "secretly authorise him to spend between a quarter and a half a million dollars in connection with forthcoming elections in the United States." He wanted to keep the matter secret for the time being so as not to upset his fundraising efforts. "It is very important," he wrote, "that there should not be an open rupture until the Bond Drive were over at any rate."

In the following weeks de Valera concentrated on the recognition question as he toured the Deep South. He was trying to drum up public support to rescue a bill introduced in the House of Representatives some months earlier by Congressman William Mason. The latter had proposed that Congress allocate funds for a diplomatic mission to Ireland. Normally the President would first accord recognition and Congress would then authorise the funds for a diplomatic mission. In the case of the Mason Bill the procedure was being reversed, but the novel approach ran into such determined opposition that it was necessary to abandon it.

The poet, W.B. Yeats, attended one of de Valera's rallies in New York in May 1920, but he was disappointed. He described de Valera as "a living argument rather than a living man. All propaganda, no human life, but not bitter, hysterical or unjust. I judged him persistent, being both patient and energetic, but that he will fail through not having enough human life as to judge the human life in others. He will ask too much of everyone and will ask it without charm. He will be pushed aside by others."

In some respects the assessment was prophetic, but de Valera was no push-over, as Cohalan and Devoy were to learn in the coming months. The campaign for recognition had suffered a serious set-back with the failure of the Mason Bill, but de Valera did not despair. It was an election year in the United States and he was already working on a scheme to enlist the support of a presidential candidate for Irish recognition in return for Irish-American votes. Although the Irish-Americans were a distinct minority in the United States, they possessed an inordinate political influence because they were concentrated in the large urban areas of the most populous states and tended to block vote as directed by their leaders.

In New York, the state with the largest number of electoral votes for the Presidency, for example, the Irish-Americans were concentrated in New York City, where their support was crucial to any Democratic candidate, because upstate New York was heavily Republican. Thus, the Democratic candidate had to win well in New York City to carry the state, and this was highly improbable without the support of the Irish-American community. The "Irish vote" also tended to have the same kind of pivotal influence in other important states, hence the excessive influence exerted by the Irish-American political bosses within the Democratic Party.

De Valera hoped to enlist that influence to further his aims. "The Democrats will bid high for the Irish vote now," he explained. "Without it they have not the slightest chance of winning at the elections, unless something extraordinary turns up."

While he thought the Democratic Party was Ireland's best hope, he did not write off the Republicans. "Our policy here has always been to be as friendly with one of the political parties as with the other," he wrote. If the Irish-American vote was important to the Democrats, it could be just as valuable to the Republicans, seeing that solid Irish-American backing could guarantee the Republicans victory in a number of very important states because it would deprive the Democrats of their traditional support; they would then need to pick up twice as many votes from elsewhere just to offset the loss of the Irish-Americans.

Consequently, de Valera was just as optimistic about the possibility of being able to bargain with a Republican candidate. In fact, he considered Senator Hiram Johnson, the California Republican, to be "the best man available". "The only way to play the cards for Ireland," de Valera believed, was to get a firm public commitment from a candidate to recognise the Irish Republic. He hoped to get such a commitment from Johnson in order that "our people could start working for him," but the *Gaelic American* endorsed the California senator's candidacy without waiting for such a commitment.

De Valera resented Devoy's action; Johnson had been able to get what he was looking for without any commitment. "It is disappointing to see a clear nap hand played poorly," de Valera wrote. "Sometimes when I see the strategic position which the Irish here occupy in American politics I feel like crying when I realise what could be made of it if there was real genuine teamwork for Ireland alone being done. As far as politics is concerned, the position is almost everything one could wish for."

This amazing comment again betrayed his naïve view of the political situation. The Irish-Americans considered themselves Americans first; their "Irish" prefix was indicative of their ancestry, not their allegiance. To have engaged in "real genuine team work for Ireland alone" would have meant subordinating American interests to those of Ireland. He was actually trying to set himself up as a power broker in the selection of the President by getting Americans to vote strictly on the grounds of what the man would do for Ireland.

All this was clearly a violation of his agreement to stay out of American affairs but, as previously stated, he never really intended to uphold his end of the agreement anyway. Under the circumstances another clash with the Cohalan-Devoy faction was inevitable. The political truce collapsed in June 1920 when de Valera went to Chicago for the Republican Party's National Convention, despite being asked to stay away. He was hoping to influence the Republicans to adopt a plank calling for recognition of the Irish Republic in the party's election platform.

His people opened offices across from the convention centre and published a daily newsletter. On the eve of the convention they organised a torchlight parade involving some 5,000 marchers, who were afterwards addressed by de Valera. "The Republicans must promise to recognise the Irish Republic," he told them. "All of Chicago wants this—I know the entire country wants this—I have been all over the country and I know."

"There was no chance of offending America that we did not take," Patrick McCartan later recalled. Their actions were so glaring that the Chicago Daily Tribune carried a cartoon of the Irish leader with the comment: "De Valera is not really a candidate in this Convention." When he tried to get a personal hearing before the party's subcommittee on resolutions, he was refused and his plank calling for official recognition was heavily defeated by a vote of twelve to one.

Later Cohalan managed to persuade the subcommittee to adopt a resolution by seven votes to six calling for "recognition of the principle that the people of Ireland have the right to determine freely, without dictation from outside, their own governmental institutions and their international relations with other states and peoples." But on learning of the acceptance of the Cohalan plank, de Valera objected to it and demanded it be withdrawn. The chairman of the subcommittee was so annoyed at this foreign interference that he reversed his own vote and killed the plank.

Afterwards de Valera explained that he had undermined the Cohalan resolution because it was too vague. "It was positively harmful to our interests that a resolution misrepresenting Ireland's claim by understating it should have been presented," he said. The plank was supposedly an understatement because it called, not for recognition of the Irish Republic, but merely for recognition of the Irish people's right to self-determination.

Before going to the United States, de Valera had stressed that Ireland was only seeking the right of self-determination. After his arrival in New York, he endorsed this policy, and he subsequently emphasised this by dwelling on the point in many of his American speeches. "What I seek in America," he said on more than one occasion, "is that the United States recognise in Ireland's case, Ireland's right to national self-determination, that and nothing more." Upon his return to Ireland the following year he again emphasised the same theme in a whole series of interviews with foreign correspondents, as when he told a Swiss journalist that "the principle for which we are fighting is the principle of Ireland's right to complete self-determination." And on top of all this, he actually took umbrage when it was suggested to him that he should stop talking about self-determination and just call for recognition of the Irish Republic. His problem with the Cohalan plank was not therefore that it understated the Irish case. Rather, the whole controversy was part of a power struggle.

De Valera had already written home that he did not want anyone to think that he had "become a puppet to be manipulated" by the judge. He did not want American politicians to get the idea Cohalan was "the real power behind our movement—the man to whom they would have to go. Were I [to] allow myself to appear thus as a puppet, apart from any personal pride, the movement would suffer a severe blow. Those who hold aloof because of the plea that the Judge is running this movement would cry out that they were justified." It was noteworthy that he mentioned his personal pride before the interests of the movement.

In view of the manner in which he was denied normal parental affection, de Valera grew up with a deep yearning for distinction and a nagging sense of inferiority which was perversely stirred by his sudden fame, a fame which owed so much to chance that it provided little sense of security. Had he been more secure in his own mind, he might not have looked on Cohalan's actions as menacing, but as things stood he felt his position threatened, and he had to show he was no longer insignificant. He may well have convinced himself that he was acting in Ireland's interest, but then, as he would show in the coming years, he had a facility of being able to convince himself that his own self-interest was in the national interest.

Following the Chicago débâcle there were efforts to convene a conference to stop the feuding, but some of de Valera's own people wished to exclude him because he had been betraying "an unconscious contempt" for the opinions of others by doing most of the talking and not allowing others to speak. In this way he forced his own opinions and "thus thinks he has co-operation when he only gets silent acquiescence," according to McCartan.

De Valera also wanted a conference, but his aim was to reorganise Irish-Americans in order to inject the Irish question into the forthcoming national elections. In a letter to Bishop Michael J. Gallagher of Detroit, who was elected President of FOIF shortly after the Chicago incident, de Valera suggested a convention of the Irish race should be held in some central point like Chicago in order to make arrangements for a fresh campaign.

Chicago was suggested as the site in an obvious attempt to break the stranglehold which Cohalan's supporters—most of whom were based in the New York area—had on FOIF. But their resentment over Irish interference in American affairs was already very strong, and was further fuelled a few days later with the publication of some seized documents showing that the Dáil had authorised de Valera to spend a half a million dollars on the American elections. De Valera tried to take the mischief out of the report by issuing a statement emphasising that it was misleading to speak of the funds as intended for the American elections. "In public and in private I have been scrupulously careful to avoid even appearing to take sides in the party politics of this country," he declared. "Apart from any possible illegality, it would obviously be bad taste on my part and most inexpedient."

He seemed to be contending that he was staying above party politics by being prepared to back sympathetic candidates without regard to their party affiliation, but it was patently absurd for his authorised biographers to contend that he "could never be accused of interference with American internal politics." By his own admission he knew full well he was interfering in American politics in calling for the revision of the Versailles Treaty. Providing support for candidates in American elections would likewise have constituted an intervention in internal politics.

Cohalan's refusal to call another Race Convention before the

November elections was understandable. But he also had other grounds. FOIF leaders were not prepared to facilitate what Devoy believed was a blatant effort to remove them so that de Valera could "show that nobody in America amounts to anything and that he is the kingpin of the movement." They did agree, however, to call a meeting of the National Council of FOIF in New York on 17 September 1920. De Valera personally telegraphed each council member to attend, with the result that delegates from as far away as California came, but when he was unable to get his way, he walked out, trailed by supporters shouting, "follow the President."

Outside, de Valera announced plans to found a new organisation, which, he said, should be under the democratic control of members throughout the country, instead of being run by a cabal in New York. "We from Ireland simply ask this," he said, "that we should be accepted as the interpreters of what the Irish people want—we are responsible to them, they can repudiate us if we represent them incorrectly."

The American Association for Recognition of the Irish Republic (AARIR) was formally launched in Washington, D.C., on 16 November 1920. It prospered for some months and seemed to justify de Valera's belief that Cohalan's leadership was unacceptable to many Irish-Americans. In the following year FOIF suffered serious defections as its membership declined to about 20,000 members, while AARIR's soared to around half a million people in the same period.

But any chance of securing official American recognition had already been dashed with the election of Senator Warren G. Harding as the next President. There had been a noticeable shift among Irish-Americans toward the Republican candidate even though he made no effort to woo votes on the Irish question. In fact, when asked during the campaign about his attitude towards the Irish issue, he simply replied: "I would not care to undertake to say to Great Britain what she must do any more than I would permit her to tell us what we must do with the Philippines."

His election killed what little hope there was of securing American recognition. De Valera had failed dismally in his principal goal of securing official recognition, as well as in his secondary aim of helping to end the developing split within Irish-American ranks. The split was wider than ever when he returned to Ireland in December 1920, but he did leave behind a viable organisation which was primarily dedicated towards serving the Irish cause, rather than using the Irish situation to serve American ends. His mission had thus been a qualified success, because in addition he had collected over five million dollars and, by his clever exploitation of the opportunities afforded for propaganda, he had secured invaluable publicity for the cause. As a result of this publicity the British government came under enormous pressure to negotiate an Irish settlement, if only to avoid Anglo-American difficulties.

CHAPTER 5

"Ye Are Going Too Fast"

The situation in Ireland was very different from what it had been eighteen months earlier when de Valera went to the United States. He had left with the political wing of the movement in control at home, but in the interim Collins had managed to provoke that "general state of disorder" he had earlier talked about in March 1919. He had done so with his assassination Squad by systematically killing off and terrorising the most effective members of the Dublin Metropolitan Police Force.

The British administration in Dublin Castle over-reacted to the first shooting by banning Sinn Féin and the Dáil, thereby undermining the moderate, politically-minded people whom de Valera had left in control. In the following months the Dáil never even met, as Collins's Squad struck several times before the British instituted what Sir Maurice Hankey, the cabinet secretary, described as a policy of "counter-murder." They tried to beat Collins at his own tactics, adopting a shoot-to-kill policy in which undercover agents, often posing as Republicans, broke into the homes of members of Sinn Féin and killed them in front of their families. The police, mostly Irishmen, became demoralised and began to disintegrate in the face of ostracism by the people and the terrorism of the Irish Republican Army (IRA), as the IVF had become known during 1919. In March 1920 the British introduced paramilitary reinforcements, the infamous Black and Tans, a motley conglomeration of undisciplined misfits and malcontents who terrorised the country at large. The following autumn they were joined by the Auxiliaries, a supposedly elite corps of former army officers. They were the brainchild of the Secretary of War, Winston Churchill, who was clamouring for a more aggressive policy in Ireland.

The terror came to a head during the latter part of November 1920. On Bloody Sunday, 21 November, IRA assassination teams killed twelve undercover agents in various parts of Dublin, as well as two Auxiliaries who got in their way. That afternoon the Auxiliaries retaliated by raiding a football game in Croke Park and firing indiscriminately into the crowd, killing fourteen people, including one of the players on the field, and wounding some sixty others. In the aftermath Griffith was arrested and Collins became acting President in his place.

De Valera had planned to stay much longer in the United States and had received cabinet approval for the idea, but he quickly changed his mind on hearing the news from Dublin. In the following weeks Lloyd George sent out serious peace feelers and truce terms were agreed, but those suddenly fell through, apparently because the British decided the IRA was on the brink of collapse. Lloyd George suggested that Collins and Richard Mulcahy, the IRA Chief of Staff, should leave the country for a period and allow conditions more conducive for talks to develop. The British were aware that de Valera was returning, and the government actually issued instructions that he should not be arrested either when he landed in Liverpool or proceeded to Dublin.

De Valera arrived home on Christmas Eve and lost no time in complaining about the way the IRA campaign was being waged. "Ye are going too fast," he told Mulcahy. "This odd shooting of a policeman here and there is having a very bad effect, from the propaganda point of view, on us in America. What we want is one good battle about once a month with about 500 men on each side."

It was certainly insensitive of him to criticise the way the campaign had been run without, at least, waiting to consult a few people. Next, he tried to send Collins to the United States and persisted even after Collins had refused. De Valera got cabinet approval for the idea, and wrote a long letter to Collins on 18 January 1921 outlining a whole plethora of reasons for the trip. In fact, he gave so many reasons he seemed rather over-anxious, and Collins concluded the whole thing was just a ploy to get rid of him.

"That long whore won't get rid of me as easy as that," Collins remarked.

As *Príomh Aire*, de Valera's main function was basically to supervise the other ministers, some of whose departments were little more than notional. Count Plunkett was Minister for Foreign Affairs, for instance, but he had never set up a department, so de Valera undertook the function himself. He essentially took over the duties and merely advised the secretary to consult Plunkett once in a while.

All representatives sent abroad by the Dáil were primarily engaged in propaganda in their futile efforts to secure diplomatic recognition. The only country which had ever shown any real inclination to recognise the Irish Republic had been the Soviet Union, whose representatives in Washington had actually agreed to draft terms for a recognition treaty, but de Valera was afraid to proceed for fear the agreement with the Bolshevik government would damage the possibility of securing official American recognition. He therefore delayed, but tried to keep the Soviet representatives interested by secretly loaning their financially embarrassed mission some $20,000. In return, he received jewels as collateral, and the whole transaction remained a closely guarded secret for more than a quarter of a century.

De Valera looked on the whole area of Foreign Affairs and the main function of the new department as primarily a matter of propaganda. "It is in fact what I have called the 'Statistical' or permanent-value department of propaganda," he wrote.

As part of this propaganda de Valera deliberately portrayed himself as a moderate. In written statements and a number of interviews which he gave to foreign correspondents, who were spirited to his hiding place, he cultivated a moderate image. But in his personal contacts with members of the IRA, he talked about engaging the British in major battles in a way that could be best exploited for propaganda purposes in the United States. While it may have seemed strange that he should have been anxious to wage war in order to influence American opinion, his judgement was astutely based.

Lloyd George was deeply concerned about American opinion in January 1921. He privately voiced disquiet over the effect of his Irish policy on Anglo-American relations, especially after the British ambassador in Washington gave him "a most gloomy account" of the American situation. "In the interests of peace with America," the Prime Minister said, "I think we ought to see de Valera and try to get a settlement."

With the British sending out peace feelers offering a settlement on the lines of Dominion Home Rule, de Valera showed a keen interest in the whole dominion concept and indicated the real status of the dominions would be acceptable to Ireland, seeing that Bonar Law, the Canadian-born leader of the Conservative Party, had said the dominions had "the right to decide their own destinies."

"Thus," de Valera declared, "the British Dominions have had conceded to them all the rights that Irish Republicans demand. It is obvious that if these rights were not being denied to us we would not be engaged in the present struggle." He went on to stress that, notwithstanding its name, Sinn Féin was not an isolationist movement. The Dáil had already proved this by advocating the country's willingness to join the League of Nations. "We are thoroughly sane and reasonable people, not a coterie of political doctrinaires, or even party politicians, Republican or other," he emphasised.

Before going to America de Valera had taken a hard line on

the Ulster question, as he spoke about kicking the Unionists out or blasting them out of the way, but since the Partition Act had become law in December 1920, he modified his tone and talked about accepting a form of partition. "There is," he said, "plenty of room in Ireland for partition, real partition, and plenty of it." He suggested the island could be divided into administrative units associated in a confederation like Switzerland. "If Belfast—or for that matter, all Carsonia as a unit—were a Swiss Canton like Berne, Geneva, or Zurich, it would have more control over its own affairs, economic, social, and political, than it is given by the Westminster Partition Act. The real objection to that Act—prescienting from the question of its moral and political validity—is that it does not give Belfast and Ulster enough local liberty and power. In an Irish confederation they ought to get far more."

On the issue of Britain's security, de Valera repeatedly emphasised—as he had been doing since his famous *Westminster Gazette* interview—his government's willingness to satisfy Britain's legitimate needs. "Time after time," he declared in March 1921, "we have indicated that if England can show any right with which Ireland's right as a nation would dash, we are willing that these be adjusted by negotiations and by treaty." After recognising Ireland's independence, he said, Britain could "issue a warning such as the Monroe Doctrine, that she would regard any attempt by any foreign power to obtain a foothold in Ireland as an act of hostility against herself. In case of a common foe Ireland's manpower would then be available for the defence of the two islands."

Some people thought de Valera should declare that the Dáil's republican position was not negotiable, but he felt he was putting more pressure on the British to negotiate by making moderate pronouncements. "In public statements," he explained, "our policy should not be to make it easy for Lloyd George by proclaiming that nothing but so and so will satisfy us. Our position should be simply that we are insisting on only one right and that is the right of the people of this country to determine for themselves how they should be governed. That sounds moderate, but includes everything and puts Lloyd George, the Labour Party and others on the defensive, and apologetic as far as the world is concerned."

When Seán T. O'Kelly, the Irish representative in Paris, advised against the moderate approach, de Valera resented the advice. "I wish," the President wrote, "he would confine himself to his own country, and I am sending him a message to that effect." O'Kelly's wife, Cáit, was going to Paris, so de Valera asked her to explain the advantages of advocating a settlement on the lines of his *Westminster Gazette* interview, but her husband was still not persuaded.

"I have not the least wish or intention to make myself trouble-some," O'Kelly wrote to de Valera on 17 April 1921, "but lest you should have to say later, why did not people protest in time, I hold seriously—and I shall be astonished if some others will not be found who think as I—I hold that the firm stand we take 'on an Irish Republic or nothing' needs not *change* but *development*."

The President was so impressed with his own ideas that he did not seem to understand how somebody like O'Kelly could disagree with him, except that his proposals had not been explained properly. He therefore sent an insolent letter to Cáit O'Kelly, rebuking her for apparently distorting what he had told her. If it were not for the pos-sibility of such misrepresentation, he wrote, "I would have regarded his letter as incomprehensible, and even worse. Considerable fric-tion and very serious misunderstanding might have resulted. I can never allow such risks to be run again." At the same time he sent a stern letter to O'Kelly himself telling him that all representatives abroad "must carry out the instructions of the Department, whether they personally agree with the policy or not." He added that "it is only by resignation that the representatives can find a way out."

Shortly afterwards de Valera did receive a resignation, and his handling of the whole affair was certainly of little credit to him. He had offered the post of ambassador to the United States to James O'Mara, but the latter declined because, as he explained privately, he could no longer "hold any official position under the govern-ment of the Irish Republic whose President claims such arbitrary executive authority, and in whose judgement of American affairs I have no longer any confidence." He not only refused the post but also resigned as one of the Dáil's three trustees and announced he would not stand for re-election to the Dáil Itself. Instead of just accepting the resignation, de Valera sent O'Mara a petulant tel-egram announcing he was being fired. It was a blatant example of de Valera's presumption of the arbitrary authority about which O'Mara had already complained. Even if O'Mara had not already resigned, de Valera did not have the authority to remove him, see-ing that he had been appointed by the Dáil.

A number of people within the movement were clearly worried by de Valera's conduct. Both Tom Barry and Ernie O'Malley, two of the IRA's more active field commanders, feared he was tend-ing towards calling off the military campaign, so they both deliberately exaggerated the strength of the IRA when they met him for the first time. He, on the other hand, surprised them by taking a different line from what he had been saying publicly. Privately he was still talking about taking on the British in major engagements. O'Malley remarked afterwards that the President was very poorly informed about the real military situation, which was hardly surprising seeing that he had just been exaggerating the position himself. Collins and Mulcahy later joked about some of de Valera's foolish questions.

This ridiculing of the President was symptomatic of a growing rift between de Valera and Collins. Just when the President became aware of the other man's attitude is not clear. But he told his authorised biographers that from April 1921 onwards, "Collins did not seem to accept my view of things as he had done before and was inclined to give public expression to his own opinions even when they differed from mine."

Of course, on the other side, de Valera had begun questioning Collins's judgement on the very day of his return from the United States when he complained about the way the IRA campaign was being run. Collins might have expected better because he had supported de Valera strongly in his troubles in the United States. He had accepted, without question, de Valera's assumption of the title of President of the Irish Republic, even though this was one that Collins could have claimed himself as President of the IRB. When Cathal Brugha and Constance Markievicz were critical of the *Westminster Gazette* interview, Collins sided with Griffith to close down cabinet debate on the matter, and he could not have been more forthright in his support of the President against Cohalan and Devoy. In fact, even though Devoy had been lauding him in the columns of the *Gaelic American*, Collins severed the IRB's connections with Clan na Gael, which was the power base of the two Irish-American leaders. "Let it be clearly understood finally," Collins wrote to Devoy on 16 October 1920, "that we all stand together, and that here at home every member of the Cabinet has been an ardent supporter of the President against any and every group in America who have either not given him the co-operation which they should, or have set themselves definitely to thwart his actions."

Collins had also taken a keen interest in the welfare of de Valera's family at their home in Greystones, County Wicklow. Despite being the most wanted man in the country, he regularly risked life and limb bringing Sinéad money and news from America, and while at the house he would take time to play with the children. In later life she would go out of her way to tell members of the Collins family how much the visits had meant to her. Collins also arranged for her to visit the United States during 1920, though in this instance de Valera probably resented the gesture, because he told Sinéad her place was at home with the children and he sent her away. She had actually come at a time when there were some ugly rumours circulating about his relationship with his secretary, Kathleen O'Connell. They had been travelling about the country together, and rumours that they were having an affair had found their way into the press. Organising Sinéad's visit would not therefore have been one of Collins's more helpful gestures in de Valera's eyes.

Now, while the President was trying to sound moderate in public statements, Collins took an uncompromising line in a couple of well-publicised interviews with American correspondents. As a result the British concluded there was a power struggle going on, with de Valera looking for peace while Collins wished to fight on for a military solution. Lloyd George was anxious to negotiate but he felt it would be pointless talking to de Valera and he was afraid of the political repercussions if he talked with Collins. "The question is whether I can see Michael Collins," he explained. "No doubt he is the head and front of the movement. If I could see him, a settlement might be possible. The question is whether the British people would be willing for us to negotiate with the head of a band of murderers."

Very few people realised at the time that Lloyd George was actually in a precarious political position. He was at the head of a coalition government in which his own party was in a distinct minority, while his Conservative partners enjoyed an overwhelming majority of their own within parliament. They were therefore in a position to bring down his government and form one of their own, almost at will.

Working behind the scenes British agents arranged a secret meeting in Dublin on 5 May between de Valera and Sir James Craig, who was shortly to become the first Prime Minister of Northern Ireland, but nothing came of the meeting. Each of them had been led to believe the other had asked to see him, so they waited for each other to begin.

"Well?" said de Valera.

"Well?" replied Craig.

A brief silence followed as they eyed each other across a table. "I'm too old at this political business to have nonsense of this kind: each waiting for the other to begin," de Valera said. "And," he later

63

recalled, "I started putting our case to him."

Craig, who interjected to say that northern Unionists consid-ered the Union with Britain sacred, had difficulty getting a word in edgeways.

"Do you know how the Union was brought about?" de Valera asked, according to himself. "And I started telling him about it."

"After half an hour he had reached the era of Brian Boru," ac-cording to Craig. "After another half hour he had advanced to the period of some king a century or two later. By this time I was get-ting tired, for de Valera hadn't begun to reach the point at issue." Craig therefore seized on an opportunity to suggest they draft a press release to the effect that they had met and exchanged views.

On 12 May 1921 the British cabinet discussed the possibility of negotiating with Sinn Féin. Churchill, who had been one of the most vocal proponents of the British terror, now favoured a truce, because Britain was "getting an odious reputation" in the United States. Lloyd George said that "de Valera does not agree with the gun business" but could not stop it because Collins was "against compromise." Austen Chamberlain, the new Conservative leader, argued that there was no point in negotiating "as long as de Valera is at the mercy of Michael Collins." As a result the cabinet divided with five of the Liberal ministers voting for a truce, while Lloyd George sided with the Conservative majority to continue to pursue the existing policy.

Within a fortnight, however, Brigadier General Frank Crozier, who had recently resigned as head of the Auxiliaries, went public with a blistering attack on the conduct of his men and the Black and Tans. He admitted they had fired into the crowd without provoca-tion on Bloody Sunday. Maybe the pressure on the British govern-ment would not have been as great if the Crown forces were making progress, but the reverse was evident. On 25 May the IRA attacked the Custom House in the Irish side's largest single operation since the Easter Rebellion. It was a calculated military risk, deliberately taken for its politcal effect, which was really devastating because it made a mockery of repeated British assertions that the IRA was on the brink of collapse. As a result the British government decided it had to change its policy.

Initially the decision was to intensify the campaign, but Lloyd George was prevailed upon by the South African Premier, Jan Christian Smuts, with discreet support from King George V, to seek a negotiated settlement first. The King foreshadowed the peace ini-tiative in his opening address to the new parliament of Northern

Ireland on 22 June, but the whole thing was almost scuppered next day when de Valera was arrested by British troops in the house in which he and Kathleen O'Connell were living in Blackrock. The troops apparently did not realise their government had issued orders not to arrest him.

Austin Stack was designated to take over as acting President, which was clearly a demotion for Collins, who had taken over the previous December. To make matters worse, he despised Stack, who had a reputation for being a bit of a bungler, but Stack never really got the chance to take over because de Valera was released within a matter of hours and asked to await a communication from the British government. This was an invitation from Lloyd George for himself and anyone he wished to accompany him to come to London for talks with himself and Craig "to explore to the utmost the possibility of a settlement."

De Valera saw the simultaneous invitations to himself and Craig as a trap. Meeting with Craig on an equal basis would, for one thing, afford tacit recognition to partition. Anyway, he was afraid Lloyd George would use the inevitable differences between Belfast and Dublin to blame the Irish for the failure of the talks. Before responding to the actual invitation, therefore, de Valera said he would have to consult with the Irish minority, and he invited Craig and four Unionists, elected for Trinity College, to meet him.

Smuts also came to Dublin for secret talks on 5 July, and de Valera explained to him that he would not take part in tripartite talks which included Craig, and he demanded a truce before the talks could begin. The South African leader, who was anxious to be able to give the British some idea of the kind of peace settlement the Dáil wanted, questioned de Valera. "What do you propose as a solution of the Irish question?"

"A republic," de Valera replied.

"Do you really think that the British people are ever likely to agree to such a republic?"

Such a status was so desirable, de Valera explained, the Irish side would agree to be bound by treaty limitations guaranteeing Britain's legitimate security needs, but he emphasised they would not be prepared to accept any limitations on dominion status. In short, he insisted the Irish people should have the choice between a "republic plus treaty limitations and dominion status without limitations."

"We want a free choice," de Valera emphasised. "Not a choice where the alternative is force. We must not be bullied into a decision."

"The British people will never give you this choice," Smuts replied. "You are next door to them." He then talked about the difficulties in South Africa following the Boer War and noted that when the people were subsequently asked if they wanted a republic, "a very large majority" preferred free partnership with the British Empire. "As a friend," Smuts added, "I cannot advise you too strongly against a republic. Ask what you want but not a republic."

"If the status of dominion rule is offered," de Valera replied, "I will use all our machinery to get the Irish people to accept it."

Smuts reported on his Irish visit to a cabinet level meeting in London next day. It was decided to accede to de Valera's demands for both a truce and the exclusion of Craig from the conference, but it was left to de Valera to take the initiative for Craig's exclusion. He did this by agreeing to meet the Prime Minister to discuss "on what basis such a conference as that proposed can reasonably hope to achieve peace."

De Valera invited a delegation consisting of four cabinet colleagues, Griffith, Stack, Plunkett, and Barton, as well as Erskine Childers, the acting Minister for Propaganda, to accompany him. Collins was anxious to go but the President flatly refused to have him, and there were some bitter words between them.

Having been demoted in favour of Stack, of all people, Collins was now being ignored for people like Laurence O'Neill, the Lord Mayor of Dublin, and the Dáil deputy, Robert Farnan, who had been invited along with his wife. In addition, there were two secretaries, one of whom was Kathleen O'Connell. The delegation set up headquarters at the Grosvenor Hotel, but de Valera and Kathleen stayed with the Farnans in a private house that had been acquired for them.

When de Valera intimated to the British he would prefer to meet Lloyd George "alone," the Prime Minister jumped at the opportunity, and they had four private meetings during the next seven days. The traditional account of the first meeting had de Valera lecturing the Prime Minister on ancient Irish history and only reaching the time of Cromwell by the end of the two-and-a-half-hour meeting, but in his own account Lloyd George actually observed that the Irish leader had an agreeable personality and "listened well."

De Valera was quite prepared to listen because he wanted to show as little of his own hand as possible. He was therefore willing to let Lloyd George do most of the talking.

"You will be glad to know that I am not dissatisfied with the general situation," de Valera wrote to Collins after the second meeting next day. "The position is simply this: Lloyd George is developing a proposal, which he wishes me to bring in my pocket as a proposal to the Irish Nation for its consideration. The proposal will be theirs. We will be free to consider it without prejudice."

Collins realised the offer was unlikely to be acceptable, but he warned the President not to reject the proposals without allowing the Dáil to consider them, because this would afford the Irish side the opportunity of demanding the release of all imprisoned members of the Dáil so that they—the democratically elected representatives of the people—could consider the offer. Several deputies had already been released since the truce, but Collins was particularly anxious to secure the release of Seán MacEoin, who was under sentence of death. "No matter how bad the terms are, " he wrote, "they would be submitted to a full meeting" of the Dáil.

There was widespread press speculation about de Valera's willingness to compromise, so he decided to speak out. "The press give the impression that I have been making compromise demands," he said. "I have made no demands but one—the only one I am entitled to make—that the self-determination of the Irish nation be recognised." He was particularly anxious to deny a report in the Paris newspaper, *Le Matin*, which quoted him as having supposedly said he would drop the word republic provided Ireland was given "the substantial equivalent" to it. This was basically his position, but he denied making the statement or anything like it.

At their third meeting on 18 July, Lloyd George remarked that the notepaper on which de Valera had written to him was headed "Saorstát Eireann," which literally translated as "Free State of Ireland." He therefore asked what "Saorstát" meant.

"Free state," replied de Valera.

"Yes," remarked the Prime Minister, "but what is the Irish word for republic?"

De Valera was taken aback. Although his own command of the Gaelic language was not nearly as complete as he liked to pretend to non-speakers, he must have known that the leaders of the Easter Rebellion had used the term *Poblacht na hÉireann* (Republic of Ireland), but he now played dumb, possibly because he had no convincing explanation as to why the original term had been dropped and Saorstát adopted instead in 1919.

"Must we not admit that the Celts never were Republicans and have no native word for such an idea!" Lloyd George exclaimed triumphantly. He was quite content that *Saorstát Éireann* could be used in any agreement, provided the literal translation—Irish Free State—was used.

The formal British proposals, which were delivered to the Irish delegation on the night of 20 July, offered to give the twenty-six counties a form of dominion status which would be limited by defence restrictions curtailing the size of the Irish army, prohibiting a navy, and insisting upon guarantees that Britain could obtain whatever facilities she might desire during a war of international crisis. The proposals, which included an insistence on free trade between Britain and Ireland, also stipulated that the new Irish state should "allow for full recognition of the existing powers and privileges of the parliament of Northern Ireland, which cannot be abrogated except by their own consent."

Denouncing the British terms next day, de Valera noted they did not even amount to an offer of dominion status, because the restrictive conditions meant Ireland was being offered less than the status of existing dominions like Canada and South Africa. As he had with Smuts in Dublin a fortnight earlier, he indicated a willingness to accept "the status of a dominion sans phrase," according to Lloyd George, "on condition that Northern Ireland would agree to be represented within the all-Ireland parliament. Otherwise, de Valera insisted that the only alternative was for the twenty-six counties to be a republic."

"This means war," the Prime Minister warned.

But de Valera refused to be intimidated. He became so dismissive of the offer that at one point he actually said he would not "be seen taking these things home." That stunned the Prime Minister, who had been threatening to publish proposals despite an agreement do so only by agreement.

"Aren't you going to give me a considered reply?" Lloyd George asked.

"I'll give you a considered reply if you keep your part of the bargain."

With that de Valera departed, leaving the document behind him. He later sent word to Downing Street to forward the proposals to him in Dublin, in effect, he not only called Lloyd George's bluff but also made good his own threat not to be seen carrying the proposals home with him. If the Prime Minister wanted a considered reply he was going to have to wait for it.

The British proposals were a significant advance on anything previously offered to Ireland, so de Valera had to be careful that his reply would not give the British the opportunity of enlisting the popular support thought necessary to suppress the Irish Sinn Féin movement. Unless the Irish people were given some alternative other than "continuing the war for maintenance of the Republic," he later admitted, "I felt certain that the majority of the people would be weaned from us." Hence he had to come up with an alternative for which the Irish people would be prepared to fight.

Lloyd George, of course, was more concerned with international opinion than with what the Irish people thought. He was not optimistic about de Valera coming up with an acceptable alternative. "There is, I fear, little chance of his counter-proposals being satisfactory," the Prime Minister wrote to King George V that day, "but I am absolutely confident that we shall have public opinion overwhelmingly upon our side throughout the Empire and even in the United States when our proposals are published."

De Valera knew the Irish side could not win an actual war with Britain, so he hoped to persuade all concerned to agree to a settlement in which Britain would acknowledge Ireland's freedom and the Irish would then freely accept the same *de facto* status as the dominions, without formally being a member of the British Commonwealth. He had not yet worked this out fully in his own mind when he presented his idea to the cabinet on 25 July. In fact, he had not even thought of a name for the plan.

It was a particularly thorny meeting, and things were not helped by his poor chairmanship. His cabinet meetings lacked discipline. Instead of considering one thing at a time, he tended to deal with everything together in the hope of reaching a general consensus. This would have been extremely difficult at the best of times, but it was almost impossible in a cabinet of eleven headstrong ministers, who were often joined by obstinate understudies. As a result the discussions tended to ramble and were usually quite inconclusive. Ministers frequently came away with conflicting opinions about the outcome of discussions.

At the meeting on 25 July Griffith and W.T. Cosgrave said the British offer was better than they had expected and MacNeill welcomed it, while Collins described it as "a step forward," but Stack was very critical. Childers was also hostile. J.J. O'Kelly, the Minister for Education, suggested that the documents should be circulated so that everyone could give the issues more consideration, and Constance Markievicz, the Minister for Labour, agreed with him.

Brugha sat silently until de Valera asked him for his views after everyone else had spoken. A normally quiet, reserved man, he nevertheless had definite views and did not believe in mincing words. Resolute and utterly fearless, he was prone to obstinacy. When he spoke everybody knew exactly where he stood. "I haven't much to add," Brugha now said looking straight at de Valera, "except to say how glad I am that it has been suggested that we circulate these documents and consider them fully before we meet again, if for no other reason than to give you and the great masters of English you keep at your elbow an opportunity of extricating us from the morass in which ye have landed us."

"We have done our best," de Valera replied, "and I have never undertaken to do more than my best."

"We have proclaimed a Republic in arms," Brugha reminded him. "It has been ratified by the votes of the people, and we have sworn to defend it with our lives."

"The oath never conveyed any more to me than to do my best in whatever circumstances might arise."

"You have accepted a position of authority and responsibility in the Government of the Republic," Brugha said, striking the table with his fist, "and you will discharge the duties of that office as they have been defined. I do not want ever again to hear anything else from you."

The meeting adjourned almost immediately afterwards and did not resume until two days later. By this time de Valera had decided to call his plan External Association. In accordance with it, Ireland would not actually be a member of the British Commonwealth, but externally associated with the various dominions. He presented his colleagues with a memorandum arguing that "the Irish people would be ready to attach themselves as an external associate to that partial league known as the British Commonwealth of Nations." With this he overcame Brugha's objections, and the members of the government unanimously agreed that External Association would be acceptable.

Although Collins had been showing moderation within the government, he remained uncompromising in public. Indeed he made another of his unauthorised pronouncements on 6 August when the British announced the release of all members of the Dáil with the exception of MacEoin. Without as much as consulting anyone, Collins issued a statement warning "there can and will be, no meeting of Dáil Éireann" without the release of MacEoin.

De Valera had hoped to work quietly behind the scenes, believing it would be easier to secure MacEoin's release if the British were not forced to back down publicly, but Collins's intervention destroyed those efforts, so he abandoned his own low-keyed approach and declared publicly that he could "not accept responsibility for proceeding further in the negotiations" unless MacEoin was freed. The British cabinet promptly reversed its earlier decision and released him.

In view of the fuss kicked up over MacEoin, it was ironic that de Valera did not bother to consult the Dáil proper or even MacEoin himself before formally rejecting the British offer in a letter to Lloyd George on 10 August 1921. "On the occasion of our last interview," he wrote, "I gave it as my judgement that Dáil Éireann could not and the Irish people would not accept the proposals of your Government. I now confirm that judgement." But the Dáil had not even met, and did not convene until the following week when it was presented with a *fait accompli* and simply asked to endorse this reply.

In his letter to the Prime Minister, de Valera stated that the restrictive conditions, which were unheard of in the case of the dominions, would be an interference in Irish affairs. "A certain treaty of free association with the British Commonwealth group, as with a partial league of nations, we would be ready to recommend," he wrote, "had we an assurance that the entry of the nation as a whole in such an association would secure it the allegiance of the present dissenting minority, to meet whose sentiments alone this step could be contemplated." The Irish factions would settle partition among themselves without resorting to force, if the British would just stand aside. "We agree with you," he added, "that no common action can be secured by force."

Back In 1918 de Valera had concluded that the British undermined the Irish Convention by assuring Ulster Unionists that they would not be coerced. Bolstered by the assurance, the Unionists insisted on having their own way, and when the Nationalists balked, the Convention inevitably ended in failure. "It was evident to us," de Valera wrote shortly after the Convention, that "with the 'coercion-of-Ulster is unthinkable' guarantee, the Unionists would solidly maintain their original position." Thus when he gave Lloyd George a similar assurance on 10 August 1921, he was obviously accepting that some form of partition would be a part of any settlement.

CHAPTER 6

"No Road is Barred"

The Dáil convened in the Round Room of the Mansion House on the morning of 16 August. The hall was crammed and the atmosphere stifling when de Valera entered ceremoniously, followed by the rest of his ministry in Indian file. The gathering rose to give them a rapturous welcome. The President sat facing the general body as the Speaker read out the Republican oath in Gaelic, allowing the deputies to repeat it after him. For some, Including de Valera, it was the first time they took the oath, obliging them to "support and defend the Irish Republic, which Is Dáil Éireann, against all enemies, foreign and domestic."

De Valera delivered a short presidential address in which he spoke "with great emphasis and obvious sincerity," according to one experienced reporter. Speaking off the cuff he caused a bit of a stir when he talked about the unmistakable answer given by the people in the recent general election. "I do not say that the answer was for a form of government so much, because we are not Republican doctrinaires, but it was for Irish freedom and Irish independence, and it was obvious to everyone who considered the question that Irish Independence could not be realised in any other way so suitably as through a Republic," he explained.

In another speech next day he elaborated by emphasising his personal readiness to compromise on partition and defence, as well as on the issue of association with the British Commonwealth. "I would be willing to suggest to the Irish people to give up a good deal in order to have an Ireland that could look to the future without anticipating distracting internal problems," he said. The Unionists in the six counties were "Irishmen living in Ireland," so he would be prepared to give up a lot to win them over. "We are ready," he emphasised, "to make sacrifices we could never think of making for Britain."

Having publicly indicated his willingness to compromise, he went even further in the following days when the Dáil met in private session. In the course of a rather rambling discussion on 22 August, he told deputies to realise that if they were determined to make peace only on the basis of recognition of the Republic, then they were going to be faced with war, only this time it would be a real war of British reconquest, not just a continuation of limited military coercive measures "in support of the civil police" to force some people to obey the law. In short, he was saying the War of Independence had not been a real war at all.

Although de Valera's remarks were couched in terms of outlining stark realities so the Dáil could decide the best course for itself, there was absolutely no room for doubt about his readiness to compromise, even on important issues like the partition question. He now gave the private session an idea of what he had meant when he talked publicly about making sacrifices for a secure settlement.

"The minority in Ulster had a right to have their sentiments considered to the utmost limit," he explained, according to the official record. "If the Republic were recognised he would be in favour of giving each county power to vote itself out of the Republic if it so wished." The only choice would be to coerce Northern Ireland, and he was opposed to such coercion because, for one thing, it would not be successful and, anyway, he warned, attempting to coerce the majority in Northern Ireland would be to make the same mistake the British had made with the Irish people as a whole. On the issue of Commonwealth membership, he told deputies "they could not turn down what appeared to be, on the face of it, an invitation to join a group of free nations provided it was based on the principles enunciated by President Wilson." And he also indicated they would have to make concessions to satisfy Britain's security requirements.

"It was ridiculous of course to say that because Ireland was near Britain she should give Britain safeguards," de Valera admitted. "But," he continued, "America demanded such strategic safeguards from the small island of Cuba." If security concessions were refused, Britain would depict the Irish as unreasonable, America would agree, as would the international community generally, and then "England would be given a free hand to deal with Ireland." The Irish people's natural moral right to their own island would be eradicated, just as the rights of the American Indians had been trampled on in North America. "Look at America," he said ominously, "where are the natives? Wiped off the face of the earth." The same thing could happen in Ireland. "Unfortunately," he added, "they were very far away from living in a world where moral forces counted;" it was "brute force" which mattered. If the deputies insisted on securing recognition of the Republic as a totally independent country, they would be acting like prisoners in jail going on hunger-strike to secure their freedom. If they won, they would have their freedom, but if they lost, they would be dead and have nothing. His choice of allusion was particularly significant because he was personally opposed to hunger-strikes.

De Valera gave only a vague outline of the kind of compromise alternative he had in mind. He demanded what amounted to a blank cheque to negotiate whatever agreement he thought fit, subject only to its subsequent approval by a majority of the Dáil. With the latter due to go back into public session for the formal election of the president, he told the secret session he wanted his own position clearly understood before allowing his name to be put forward.

"I have one allegiance only to the people of Ireland and that is to do the best we can for the people of Ireland as we conceive it," he declared. "If you propose me I want you all to understand that you propose me understanding that that will be my attitude." All questions would be discussed, he said, "from the point of view absolutely of what I consider the people of Ireland want and what I consider is best from their point of view."

One deputy interjected to object to the President's stated willingness to allow each of the six counties to vote itself out of the Irish Republic, but de Valera reaffirmed his position. He would be ready to consider allowing counties or provinces to vote themselves out.

"I do not feel myself bound to consider anything," he emphasised. "I feel myself open to consider everything." He would not be confined. "I will not accept this office if you fetter me in any way whatever," he declared. "I cannot accept office except on the understanding that no road is barred, that we shall be free to consider every method." The policy of his government would be to do what he thought best for the country and "those who would disagree with me would resign."

Brugha had said at the cabinet meeting of 25 July that the President had no right to consider anything which was not in line with allegiance to the Irish Republic, so the latest remarks were a patent effort to ensure such an argument would have no validity in future. De Valera concluded by proposing the Dáil adjourn for the day. No time was allowed for any debate on what he had said; there was no room for discussion, as far as he was concerned. If the deputies wanted him as President they had to accept his terms; otherwise, they should elect somebody else.

Before the election for President, however, there was a discrepancy to be cleared up about his actual title because, as de Valera himself admitted, "no such officer had been created." Back in 1919 he had simply assumed the title of President without the authority of the Dáil, which had only elected him *Príomh Aire*. Now the discrepancy was somewhat obliquely tackled by slipping the term "President" into a constitutional amendment limiting the size of the cabinet to seven specified officers—"the President who shall also be Prime Minister" and the Ministers for Foreign Affairs, Home Affairs, Defence, Finance, Local Government, and Economic Affairs. De Valera was then duly elected President and he nominated Griffith, Stack, Brugha, Collins, Cosgrave, and Robert Barton to the respective cabinet posts.

One of the President's first acts following the appointment of his government was to release the text of a letter he sent to Lloyd George the previous day confirming "the anticipatory judgement" of the Dail's rejection of the British offer. Exploiting the occasion with some theatrics to bolster his own carefully cultivated image of passionate sincerity, de Valera explained it had been agreed with the British to publish the communication at noon and, as it was two minutes short of the appointed time, he waited in silence for the two minutes. He then read the letter which concluded by intimating that the British should convene a conference to negotiate a democratic peace settlement. "To negotiate such a peace, Dáil Éireann is ready to appoint its representatives, and, if your Government accepts the principle proposed, to invest them with plenary powers to meet and arrange with you for its application in detail."

The British responded with an invitation to a conference. It was generally assumed that de Valera would lead the Irish delegation but he refused.

Mindful of strong-arm tactics attempted by Lloyd George in July, he contended the delegation could always use the necessity of consulting him as an excuse to prevent it being forced to make hasty decisions. But there were really much broader considerations. "There seemed, in fact, at the time to be no good reason why I should be on the delegation," he wrote. "There was, on the other hand, a host of good reasons why I should remain at home. One had, above all, to look ahead and provide for the outcome of the negotiations. They would end either in a 'make' or 'break'—in a settlement based on the accepted cabinet policy of External Association, or in a failure of the negotiations with a probable renewal of war. In either case I could best serve the national interest by remaining at home.

"If the outcome were to be the settlement we had envisaged, that based on External Association," he continued, "it was almost certain that it would be no easy task to get that settlement accepted wholeheartedly by the Dáil and by the Army." He had already got a taste of the kind of bitterness such a proposal could generate, not only from Brugha's vitriolic outburst at the cabinet meeting on 25 July, but also during the controversy following his *Westminster Gazette* Interview In the United States. External Association was essentially a more developed version of his Cuban proposals first suggested in that controversial interview.

By not taking part in the negotiations, therefore, de Valera believed he would be in a better position to influence radical republicans if he were to campaign for the acceptance of a compromise agreement. "My influence," he argued, "would be vastly more effective if I myself were not a member of the negotiating team, and so completely free of any suggestion that I had been affected by the 'London atmosphere'." In emphasising this point an allusion was made to Woodrow Wilson's failure to get the United States Senate to ratify the Versailles Treaty following his involvement in the Paris peace talks.

Those negotiating would inevitably have to compromise, but even this might not be good enough in the last analysis. Consequently, by staying at home, he would be in a position to rally both moderates and radicals to fight for an absolute claim, instead of a less appealing compromise. "Were there to be a 'break' with any substantial section of our people discontented and restless, the national position would be dangerously weakened when the war resumed. I was providing for this contingency much better by remaining at home than by leading the delegation."

Throughout the struggle he had tried to be all things—a moderate among moderates and a radical among militants. His real strength within the movement at home had always been his unifying role. And, as he wished to maintain that role, it made good sense not to get too involved in the nitty-gritty of the negotiations. In the last analysis his decision to stay in Dublin was based on sound, selfish, political reasons. He knew that those who went were likely to become scapegoats—with the radicals if they compromised, and with the moderates if they did not. "We must have scapegoats," he admitted.

Later in trying to justify his decision, he sought to rationalise his selfish considerations by cloaking his actions in the national interest, but here he argued a little too much. He contended, for instance, that by staying at home he could play his part "in keeping public opinion firm" and also "in doing everything possible to have the Army well organised and strong." These reasons sounded rather hollow coming from someone who had spent most of the

Black and Tan period in the United States.

Griffith, Collins and Cosgrave were not impressed by his arguments. They felt he should be the head of the delegation, but Stack, Brugha, and Barton supported him, so he was able to use his own vote to exclude himself when the cabinet voted on the issue. He then proposed Griffith to lead the delegation, with Collins as his deputy.

Stack objected to their appointment. According to himself, he made "a weak kind of objection" on the grounds that "both gentlemen had been in favour of the July proposals." At least, he explained amid protests from both men, he got the impression that Griffith only wanted some modifications.

"Yes," said Griffith, "some modifications!"

Griffith himself agreed to act as chairman of the delegation, but the President had trouble persuading Collins.

"I was somewhat surprised at his reluctance for he had been rather annoyed with me for not bringing him on the team when I went to meet Lloyd George earlier on in July," de Valera recalled. "I now considered it essential that he should be on the team with Griffith."

"They by themselves alone, it seemed, would form a well balanced team," the President continued. "Griffith would, I thought, have the confidence of the 'moderates' and Collins that of the IRB and the Army." He added that "with these two as the leaders no one could suggest that the delegation was not a strong and representative one."

In arguing for his own exclusion Collins made some of the same points as de Valera had already made for not going himself. In effect, Collins argued, he was seen as the real leader so he would be in a better position to influence Republicans to accept a compromise if he was not involved in the negotiations. The British considered him a treacherous gunman, so the delegation could always delay in order to consult him or demand further concessions to placate him. The Irish delegation would thereby be able to get the best possible terms from the British.

"For three hours one night, after the decision had been made to send a delegation to London, I pleaded with de Valera to leave me at home and let some other man take my place as a negotiator," Collins recalled. "The point I tried to impress on de Valera was, that for several years (rightly or wrongly makes no difference)— the English had held me to be the one man most necessary to capture because they held me to be the one man responsible for the smashing of their Secret Service organisation, and for their failure to terrorise the Irish people with their Black-and-Tans." It really did not matter whether the legend was true, or was simply the product of press sensationalism. "The important fact," Collins emphasised "was that in England, as in Ireland, the Michael Collins legend existed. It pictured me as the mysterious active menace, elusive, unknown, unaccountable, and in this respect I was the only living Irishman of whom it could be said."

De Valera listened but was not impressed. From his own standpoint, it was vital for Collins to be intimately involved in any settlement because he was too influential and too volatile to be left out, especially when he had been questioning the President's judgement on military and political matters in the lead up to the truce. Since then Collins had bitterly resented his exclusion from the group that went to London in July, and he had deliberately stampeded the President in the matter of demanding MacEoin's release. On top of all this, de Valera, with his acute sensitivity to criticism, was no doubt suspicious of the implied criticism in Collins's fulsome praise of James O'Mara in the Dáil on 26 August. O'Mara, it will be remembered, had resigned as a Trustee of the Dáil and had refused to stand for re-election as a deputy in May because of his differences with de Valera, who made little more than a passing reference in his report to O'Mara's contribution in organising the American fund-raising. Collins, on the other hand, singled out O'Mara for his pioneering fund-raising work without which, he said, they would not have been nearly so successful. The best way de Valera had of ensuring Collins would not undermine any settlement terms was to have him negotiate them.

"It is not a question of individuals now," the President told Collins. "It is a question of the nation and you and I and the cabinet know that the British will not make their best offer in your absence." Despite his own better judgement, Collins decided to go because, as he said himself, "it was a job that had to be done by somebody." In the past he had never shirked responsibility when a job needed to be done, and now was no different. "I had no choice," he said. "I had to go."

Three others were then selected, in de Valera's words, "to work in well with Griffith and Collins." His first thought was to send Brugha and Stack, but they had rejected the idea when Collins challenged them to go, which was probably just as well because they would not have formed a good team with the others. "Cathal is the honestest and finest soul in the world, but he is a bit slow at seeing fine differences and rather stubborn, and the others would not seek to convince him, but would rather try to outmanoeuvre him, and there would be trouble," de Valera explained some months later. "If I were going myself I would certainly have taken him with me." Griffith and Collins would not work with Stack either, so he "was equally out of the question," according to the President.

From the two other cabinet members, Barton was chosen. He felt the choice had been been made for propaganda purposes because he was a wealthy Protestant landowner. Two lawyers, George Gavan Duffy and Eamon Duggan, rounded off the team as "mere legal padding," according to the President.

When the Dáil was asked to ratify the selection of the delegation Cosgrave tried unsuccessfully to have de Valera included, but his motion was defeated. The Dáil then voted to confirm each of the five members of the delegation individually, and the delegation was accorded full plenipotentiary powers. Gavan Duffy, although a member of the delegation himself, tried to have its powers limited, but de Valera was adamant. He had twice previously threatened to resign as President if full plenipotentiary powers were denied to the delegation, and he again emphasised he would not stand for any restrictions. "Remember what you are asking them to do," he said. "You are asking them to secure by negotiations what we are totally unable to secure by force of arms." With that the motion was withdrawn.

Although the conference was initially due to meet in Inverness, Scotland, on 20 September, a wrangle developed over the Irish letter of acceptance. Lloyd George cancelled the conference and there followed a protracted exchange of letters and telegrams as he and de Valera sought to find an agreeable basis for the conference.

There were essentially two points at issue in their correspondence. Initially de Valera stated that the conference should consider Ireland's right to self-determination, while Lloyd George insisted that it could only consider the detailed application of his July offer. De Valera promptly modified his demand to a request that the scope of the discussions be unconditional, but Lloyd George held his ground. In six of his seven communications he stressed that only the July proposals could be considered, but in his final telegram he backed down and agreed the conference could "explore every possibility" of settlement "with a view to ascertaining how the association of Ireland with the community of nations known as the British Empire may best be reconciled with Irish national aspirations." This formula was essentially a compromise on their original positions, but de Valera seemed to get the better of the dispute because he had taken the more flexible stand.

The second point at issue involved recognition of Irish sovereignty. "Our nation has formally declared its independence and recognises itself as a *sovereign* state," de Valera wrote, in accepting the initial invitation to the Inverness conference. "It is only as the representatives of that State and as its chosen guardians that we have any authority or powers to act on behalf of our people." It was the publication of this letter which prompted Lloyd George to cancel the conference. Although de Valera explained he was only stating that the Irish representatives recognised their own government, Lloyd George wanted no confusion on the point. There could be no question of his government affording recognition to the Dáil regime or even acknowledging that the Irish recognised their own regime as sovereign. He stressed this point in his telegram on 29 September when he extended another invitation for the Irish side to send representatives to a conference, this time in London.

De Valera's acceptance of this invitation involved dropping the self-recognition stand, though he did try to confuse the issue by stating that "our respective positions have been stated and are understood." This was an attempt to give the impression he was still holding to his earlier position, but his remarks were not a condition. They were a statement of fact, which could only be logically interpreted as an admission that he understood and accepted Britain's insistence that there could be no conference if he formally persisted with his claim of self-recognition.

"The communication of September 29th from Lloyd George made it clear that they were going into a conference not on the recognition of the Irish Republic, and I say if we all stood on the *recognition* of the Irish Republic as a prelude to any conference we could very easily have said so, and there would be no conference," Collins later contended. "What I want to make clear is that it was the acceptance of the invitation that formed the compromise. I was sent there to form that adaptation, to bear the brunt of it."

He clearly had misgivings, but these were probably mollified by de Valera's candid acceptance of the necessity for compromise. The President had courageously confronted the Dáil hard-liners by emphasising his unwillingness to exclude the possibility of any kind of settlement. Moreover, he had sent Harry Boland to the United States to prepare opinion there for a compromise settlement.

Friends of Collins tried to persuade him to back out of the delegation. Some members of the Supreme Council of the IRB "thought there was something sinister" afoot, and they warned him that he was in danger of being made a scapegoat. "Let them make a scapegoat or anything they wish of me," he replied. "We have accepted the situation as it is, and someone must go."

In appointing Griffith and Collins, de Valera and his cabinet colleagues knew they were selecting their more moderate members. The two of them were more favourably disposed to the July proposals than any of the other ministers.

"That Griffith would accept the Crown under pressure I had no doubt," de Valera admitted to a friend shortly afterwards. "From the preliminary work which M.C.[Collins] was doing with the IRB, of which I had heard something, and from my own weighing up of him I felt certain that he too was contemplating accepting the Crown." The President looked on them as a kind of fishing bait, which he thought he could use to lure the British. He actually described them as "better bait for Lloyd George—leading him on and on, further in our direction. I felt convinced on the other hand that as matters came to a close we would be able to hold them from this side from crossing the line."

De Valera had Erskine Childers appointed chief secretary to the delegation, because he would have a strong influence over Barton, who was like a younger brother to him. They were double first cousins, and Childers had actually been reared by Barton's parents. The President believed Childers, supported by Barton, "would be strong and stubborn enough as a retarding force to any precipitate giving away by the delegation."

But, if he really suspected that Griffith and Collins would be so weak, why did he not include Childers in the delegation proper? It would have been idiotic to think a secretary could control the delegation through his influence with a younger cousin, especially when there were some questions about that cousin's stability. Shortly before the truce de Valera wrote that he thought Barton was on the verge of a breakdown, and now he was supposedly depending on him to hold Griffith and Collins with the aid of a secretary! Under the circumstances it is difficult to avoid the conclusion that Childers had been sent with the delegation, not so much as to hold Griffith and Collins, as to keep an eye on them for de Valera, who made the mistake of assuming he could get them to hold out for whatever settlement he wanted even though he had saddled them with the full responsibility of negotiating a settlement by insisting they be given plenipotentiary powers.

Members of the delegation were furnished with credentials

stipulating that they had full plenipotentiary powers "to negotiate and conclude on behalf of Ireland with the representatives of his Britannic Majesty, George V, a Treaty or Treaties of Settlement, Association and Accommodation between Ireland and the community of nations known as the British Commonwealth." De Valera thought, however, that he could prevent them from signing anything that he did not want by having the cabinet issue them with the following secret instructions:

(1) The Plenipotentiaries have full powers as defined in their credentials.

(2) It is understood however that before decisions are finally reached on the main questions that a despatch notifying the intention of making these decisions will be sent to the Members of the Cabinet in Dublin and that a reply will be awaited by the Plenipotentiaries before the final decision is made.

(3) It is also understood that the complete text of the draft treaty about to be signed will be similarly submitted to Dublin and reply awaited.

(4) In case of a break the text of final proposals from our side will be similarly submitted.

(5) It is understood that the Cabinet in Dublin will be kept regularly informed of the progress of the negotiations.

Since the Dáil had already conferred full plenipotentiary powers, the instructions from the cabinet, an inferior body, were not legally binding in any instance in which they limited the powers of the delegation. Indeed, from the instructions themselves, it would seem that they were not intended to limit those powers because the first of the instructions basically reaffirmed that the delegation had the full authority "to negotiate and conclude" a treaty. It was, of course, morally obliged to try to comply with the instructions, which had been accepted as a kind of informal understanding. In fact, the word "understood" was used in each of the three instructions that might be seen as limiting the delegation's authority to sign an agreement.

De Valera had apparently issued the instructions as a safeguard to ensure his own ultimate control over the delegation. "I expected to be in the closest touch with it," he wrote. "In fact, it was my intention to be as close almost as if I were in London."

Before the plenipotentiaries left Dublin de Valera furnished them with an incomplete document known as Draft Treaty A, which outlined External Association in treaty form. In accordance with it Ireland would be recognised "as a sovereign independent state" and Britain would renounce "all claims to govern or to legislate" for the island. In return, Ireland would become externally associated with the British Commonwealth, enjoying equal status with the dominions and being separately represented at imperial conferences. Instead of the common citizenship of the dominions, however, External Association envisaged reciprocal citizenship— the subtle difference being that Irish people would be Irish citizens rather than British subjects, but they would enjoy the same rights and privileges as British subjects while residing within the British Commonwealth, and British subjects would enjoy reciprocal rights with Irish citizens while resident in Ireland. De Valera had thought it necessary to seek reciprocal rights because he was afraid of losing the sympathy of Irish people throughout the British Empire if the Dáil looked for a settlement which would make Irish immigrants aliens within the Commonwealth. In many respects the distinction between reciprocal and common citizenship represented on a personal level the distinction between External Association and dominion status at the national level.

De Valera's controversial *Westminster Gazette* interview was the inspiration for another aspect of Draft Treaty A, which called for the British Commonwealth to guarantee "the perpetual neutrality of Ireland and the integrity and inviolability of Irish territory." In return Ireland could commit "itself to enter into no compact, and take no action, nor permit any action to be taken, inconsistent with the obligation of preserving its own neutrality and inviolability and to repel with force any attempt to violate its territory or to use its territorial waters for warlike purposes." Once ratified by the respective parliaments the Treaty would be registered with the League of Nations at Geneva and the dominions would try to get "the formal recognition of Ireland's neutrality, integrity and inviolability by the League of Nations in conformity with the similar guarantee in favour of Switzerland."

Draft Treaty A was not really a serious effort to draw up a draft treaty, as has often been contended; it was strictly a negotiating document which the Irish delegation would present in response to the British proposal of 20 July. De Valera proposed the Irish side should draw up a series of contingency documents. Draft Treaty B would be the document the delegation would publish as the Irish alternative in the events the negotiations collapsed, and Draft Treaty S would be the document the plenipotentiaries would use for internal purposes as their prospective treaty. De Valera gave Duffy and Childers partially completed copies of Draft Treaties A and B, but he did not attempt to advise them on Draft Treaty S. "We must depend on your side for the initiative after this," he explained to Griffith. The choice of the term "your side" was indicative of the division within the cabinet even at this early stage.

As far as negotiating tactics went, de Valera's advice was to try to ensure that the most difficult issue, the question of the Crown, would be left until last.

"Supposing they refuse to do this?" Griffith asked.

"Well, you can put it to them that we ought first of all discuss the things there will be no great dispute about."

"But supposing they insist on considering the question of the Crown first?"

"You can only use your powers of persuasion. After all, they cannot want to have a break on the first day."

Griffith pressed for further advice. "Well," said de Valera rising from the table at which they were sitting, "there you have the situation. You'll have to make the best of it."

"Oh, wait now," cried Griffith. "That won't do!"

"Why?"

"It's not enough to say 'make the best of it'."

"I'm not talking about a settlement," de Valera explained. "I'm talking about the method of handling the negotiations. You see, if we get them to concede this and this and this and this, and then come to a stumbling-block, like the question of the Crown, which they say is a formula, then we can put the question before the world and point out that they want to renew the war on us for a formula."

CHAPTER 7

"There is Obviously a Misunderstanding"

The conference was little over a week old when de Valera provoked a minor crisis by reviving the self-recognition issue without even telling the delegation. He did this by publishing an open telegram which he sent to Pope Benedict XV in response to an exchange of telegrams between the Pope and King George V.

In acknowledging the Pope's best wishes, the King had expressed the hope that the negotiations would "achieve a permanent settlement of the troubles in Ireland and may initiate a new era of peace and happiness for my people." According to de Valera, the King's message implied that the strife in Ireland was merely a domestic British problem and that the Irish people owed allegiance to the British Crown, whereas he wished to make it clear to the Pope that it was an international struggle because the Irish people had already declared their independence. Of course, he could quite easily have chosen to interpret the King's telegram differently because it was diplomatically worded. The President explained to Griffith that it was the Pope's telegram which was the irritating one from the Irish standpoint because in addressing the British King in the first place, "the Vatican recognised the struggle between Ireland and England as a purely domestic one for King George, and by implication pronounced judgement against us."

Thus the whole affair was really a backhanded attempt to chide the Pope by insulting the British King. In the circumstances Griffith and Collins were understandably annoyed that while they were involved in delicate negotiations the President had revived the recognition controversy not only without consulting them but even without having the courtesy of forewarning them. Collins, already uneasy, became deeply suspicious. To him it looked like de Valera was preparing the ground to blame the delegation for any compromise by covering up the fact that the acceptance of the British invitation to the conference had basically involved at least the temporary abandonment of even self-recognition. A further particularly irritating feature of the whole affair was that it brought the question of the Crown, which the Irish delegation had hoped to leave until last, to the forefront of the negotiations.

Under instructions from the delegation, Childers wrote to de Valera for advice on the best way to handle the subject. The plenipotentiaries felt they could respond with an outright refusal to consider any kind of association with the Crowm, he explained, or they could "obtain a field of manoeuvre and delay the crucial question" by stating that "they would be prepared to consider the question of the Crown," if agreement were reached on all other issues. But the President never replied.

With no advice forthcoming, the delegation decided on the latter of the two approaches outlined by Childers. Although no role had been envisaged for George V in line with External Association, Griffith held out the possibility for some kind of accommodation. "If we came to an agreement on all other points," he explained, "I could recommend some form of association with the Crown." This was too much for de Valera; he warned the plenipotentiaries on 25 October that there could be no question "of our asking the Irish people to enter an arrangement which would make them subject to the Crown, or demand from them allegiance to the British King. If war is the alternative we can only face it, and I think that the sooner the other side is made to realise that the better."

Griffith and Collins were furious. The President had not answered when they asked for advice on the matter; they therefore considered his latest letter an impertinent and unwarranted interference. "Obviously, any form of association necessitates discussion of recognition in some form or another of the head of the association," they protested. Indeed they felt so strongly that they insisted the whole delegation sign their letter of protest.

"There is obviously a misunderstanding," de Valera replied. "There can be no question of tying the hands of the Plenipotentiaries beyond the extent to which they were tied by their original instructions. These memos of mine, except I explicitly state otherwise, are nothing more than an attempt to keep you in touch with the views of the Cabinet in Dublin."

Maybe the President's warning would not have seemed so ominous, if it had not been for the circumstances surrounding the papal telegram and a number of other little things, like the ostentatious displays of the IRA, which had enjoyed a massive influx of volunteers since the beginning of the Truce. With numbers jumping from just a few thousand to more than seventy thousand, de Valera had set about reorganising the army, and he toured the country, visiting training camps and reviewing parades. When he tried to impose Stack as Assistant Chief of Staff at IRA headquarters, many insiders felt he was making a concerted effort to weaken Collins's hold on the IRA. In addition, he had recently asked Griffith for an explanation as to why people advising Collins on defence matters had not been summoned through Brugha as Minister for Defence. He added that any legal or constitutional advisers should be summoned through Stack. Collins was understandably uneasy because both Brugha and Stack passionately detested him, and his uneasiness was aggravated by a suspicion that Childers was, in effect, spying on him in London by sending secret reports to Dublin. Childers—who had, of course, been planted by de Valera to keep an eye on Griffith and Collins—was indeed sending secret reports. When it came to conspiring, however, Collins was no slouch himself. He decided to cut Childers out of the negotiations, but to do this it was also necessary to exclude Barton, and he did both by quietly suggesting to the British that the conference break up into smaller sub-conferences at which the leaders of the two delegations would meet informally without any secretaries. The British jumped at the suggestion and even facilitated Collins by assuming responsibility for the idea. The two full delegations never met again for the remaining five weeks of the eight week conference.

Gavan Duffy and Childers both protested to de Valera about the suspension of the plenary sessions of the conference, but he refused to act. For one thing, he approved of the way Griffith was conducting the negotiations, in holding out the possibility of accommodation on the Crown and Empire in return for an assurance of an end to partition.

"I have been of the opinion from the very beginning of the negotiations," the President wrote to Griffith on 9 November, "that if the Conference has to break the best issue to break on would be 'Ulster'; provided we could so manage it that 'Ulster' could not go out with the cry 'attachment to Empire and loyalty to the Throne.' The difficulty, of course, was to secure this without jeopardising our own fundamental position." In return for Griffith's agreement to recommend an unspecified form of association with the Crown and Empire, Lloyd George was trying to get Craig to agree to Irish unity. "There can be no doubt whatever that the Delegation has managed to do this admirably," de Valera wrote. "The danger now is that we shall be tempted, in order to put them more hopelessly in the wrong, to make further advances on our side. I think, as far as the Crown-Empire connection is concerned, we should not budge a single inch from the point to which the negotiations have now led us."

That was a prophetic piece of advice, but unfortunately Griffith did not heed it. When Lloyd George was unable to move Craig, he came to Griffith. He wanted to threaten the Ulster Unionists with a Boundary Commission which would cut off the nationalist areas of Northern Ireland, but his own position would be undermined if—after he threatened Craig—the Irish delegation publicly repudiated the proposal. Griffith assured the Prime Minister he would not repudiate him. To make sure there was no confusion on the point, Lloyd George had his assistant cabinet secretary, Thomas Jones, draw up a short memorandum on the Boundary Commission idea, and Griffith assented to its contents. He apparently did not realise that in agreeing not to repudiate Lloyd George in the matter, he was actually accepting the poposal, if no other agreement could be found on the issue.

De Valera got full cabinet approval for the idea of recognising the British King as head of the proposed External Association between Britain and Ireland. In their talks with the British, Griffith and Collins depicted External Association as simply a means of ensuring Ireland would have "dominion status *sans phrase*," which de Valera had insisted on during his meetings with Lloyd George in July. The problem was that the British King was an absolute monarch in theory and had the legal right to veto all legislation in Britain and the dominions. Under the unwritten British constitutional system, the King's veto power had long since been eroded and no longer existed in fact, because even if the British parliament wished to instruct him to use his theoretical authority to veto dominion legislation, the existing dominions were too far away for Britain to enforce such a veto. But Ireland was so close that the British would have little difficulty acting in the name of the Crown to interfere in Irish affairs. For the Irish representatives, therefore, it was essential to eliminate the Crown from the Internal affairs of Ireland, in order to avoid any confusion. In this way Ireland's domestic independence would thus be protected from outside intrigue, while Britain's legitimate needs would be assured at the same time. In essence the Irish were contending they were only trying to ensure Ireland would have the *de facto* status of the dominions. Lloyd George eventually undermined this argument by offering to include in a treaty any phrase the Irish wished to "ensure that the position of the Crown in Ireland should be no more in practice than it was in Canada or in any other dominion."

"With this offer," Griffith wrote, "they knocked out my argument." He might just as well have written that they had demolished de Valera's argument because the delegation had been following the President's line in the matter.

At this point the negotiations were coming to a conclusion. The

British announced that they would present their final terms in the form of a draft treaty on the following Tuesday, 6 December 1921. They apparently intended to follow the same practice as with the Versailles Treaty, which had been published the same day as it was given to the German delegation. The Germans then had some weeks to consider the document before signing it. Lloyd George explained he would be presenting the draft terms to the Stormont government in Belfast on the same day.

The Irish, of course, were not in the same position as the Germans, seeing that they had not capitulated. Griffith and Collins insisted that they should be allowed to see the draft treaty and show it to their colleagues in Dublin before the document was given to Craig. Otherwise, they warned, there could be complications. Lloyd George agreed to this informal arrangement.

There was no doubt, however, that the final terms would be presented by the following Tuesday. "By Tuesday next," Craig told Stormont, "either the negotiations will have broken down or the Prime Minister will send me new proposals for consideration by the Cabinet."

A cabinet meeting was arranged in Dublin to discuss the British draft treaty on Saturday, 3 December 1921. Gavan Duffy and Barton had not wanted to return to Dublin, but Griffith insisted the whole delegation be present to comply with their instructions to consult the cabinet "before a grave decision was made."

Subject to certain specified exceptions, the British offered the Irish Free State, as Ireland would be known, the same status as the dominions in "law practice and constitutional usage." The exceptions, which limited Irish freedom in comparison with the dominions, were in matters of defence and trade. The British insisted on free trade between the two countries and demanded the coastal defence of Ireland "be undertaken exclusively" by Britain, which would retain control of four specified Irish ports and any other facilities desired "in time of war or of strained relations with a foreign power." Moreover, the size of the Free State's army could not be proportionately larger than the British army in relation to the two countries' populations.

Members of the Irish parliament would also have to take a different oath of allegiance to the British Crown from other parliamentarians throughout the dominions, but this had been at the insistence of the Irish delegation. Instead of swearing direct allegiance to the King, the Irish had demanded merely an oath to uphold the Irish constitution. The British therefore came up with a compromise proposal in accordance with which members of the Dublin parliament would swear "allegiance to the Constitution of the Irish Free State; to the Community of Nations known as the British Empire; and to the King as Head of the State and of the Empire."

On the Ulster question the draft treaty gave fleeting recognition to Irish unity in that it would apply to the whole island even though Northern Ireland representatives were not even consulted, but Unionist interests were protected by a stipulation allowing Northern Ireland to vote itself out of the new state and keep its existing status. In that event, however, a Boundary Commission would be set up to redraw the border of Northern Ireland "in accordance with the wishes of the inhabitants, so far as may be compatible with economic and geographic conditions."

The meeting to consider the draft terms was held at the Mansion House. It included the seven cabinet members, the two plenipotentiaries who were not members of the cabinet, Childers as secretary of the delegation, Kevin O'Higgins, the Assistant Minister of Local Government, and Colm Ó Murchada, the acting cabinet secretary in the absence of Diarmuid O'Hegarty in London. At the outset each of the plenipotentiaries gave his views on the draft treaty. Griffith explained that he was in favour of the proposals, and Duggan supported him, though Childers noted "Collins was difficult to understand—repeatedly pressed by Dev but I really don't know what his answer amounted to." Stack later recalled that "Collins did not speak strongly in favour of the document at all," but Ó Murchada described him as being "in substantial agreement" with Griffith and Duggan in arguing that rejecting the "Treaty would be a gamble as England could arrange a war in Ireland within a week." Collins did advocate, however, that the oath should be rejected, and he believed further concessions could be gained on the trade and defence clauses.

At the President's Invitation, Childers criticised the proposals. Confining himself to the defence clauses, he denounced them, saying they meant the country's status would be even less than that of a dominion. "I said," he recalled, "we must make it clear that we had a right to defend ourselves." This right was being denied by the stipulation giving Britain the exclusive right to defend Irish coastal waters.

De Valera interjected, according to Childers, saying that "exclusively' clearly meant a prohibition on us which could not be admitted. He said he differed *from me* in that he thought it natural for them to demand facilities on our coast as being necessary."

Brugha then created what Childers termed "an unpleasant scene." The Defence Minister asked who was responsible for the sub-conference set up in which Griffith and Collins had been doing most of the talking for the Irish side. When told that the British had initially invited the two of them, Brugha remarked that the British had selected "their men."

Griffith was furious, he stood up and went to where Brugha was sitting and demanded the slanderous accusation be withdrawn, but Brugha refused at first.

Although angry, Collins contained himself. "If you are not satisfied with us," he said, "get another five to go over."

At that point Barton came to the defence of his two colleagues by saying that they had been negotiating with the "knowledge and consent" of the full delegation. Brugha then asked for his remark to be withdrawn but the damage was already done. Griffith insisted it be recorded, and an air of tension prevailed throughout the rest of the day's discussions.

De Valera avoided personalities in criticising the draft treaty, which he rejected mainly on the grounds that the oath was unacceptable. "The oath," he later wrote, "crystallised in itself the main things we objected to—inclusion in the Empire, the British King as King of Ireland, Chief Executive of the Irish State, and the source from which all authority in Ireland was to be derived." He was also critical of the terms relating to Northern Ireland. While he could understand accepting dominion status in return for national unity, he said the draft treaty afforded neither one nor the other. The plenipotentiaries should return to London, he said, and try to have the document amended and, if they failed, face the consequences, even if it meant war.

Arguing that it was unfair to ask Griffith to break on the Crown when he was unwilling to fight on the issue, Barton suggested de Valera should return to London with the delegation. The President later said that he was seriously considering the suggestion when Griffith declared his own attitude. After as many concessions as possible had been gained, he said he would sign the treaty and allow the Dáil to decide whether or not to accept it, or resume the armed struggle.

"Don't you realise that, if you sign this thing, you will split Ireland from top to bottom?" Brugha interjected.

"I suppose that's so," replied Griffith, apparently struck by the implication of Brugha's words. "I'll tell you what I'll do. I'll go back to London. I'll not sign the document, but I'll bring it back and submit it to the Dáil and, if necessary, to the people."

Satisfied with this, de Valera decided there was no need for himself to join the delegation. He later indicated that he "probably would have gone" to London had it not been for Griffith's undertaking not to sign the proposed treaty. It never seemed to have occurred to him that he did not have the authority to join the delegation without the prior approval of the Dáil which had ratified the selection of each of the plenipotentiaries at his insistence.

Though various objections were raised to specific points in the draft treaty during the daylong discussion, the oath was the single item which evoked most criticism. With the exception of Griffith, every member of the cabinet advocated its rejection. About thirty minutes before the meeting broke up, Cosgrave declared he would not "take that oath." A discussion ensued in which the cabinet was asked to suggest an alternative.

Brugha objected to having any oath unless the British were willing to swear to uphold the treaty themselves. De Valera also questioned the necessity for an oath, and on being told that the British were insisting on one as a political necessity, he sought to find an acceptable formula to replace the oath in the draft treaty.

"It is obvious that you cannot have that or anything like 'and the King as head of the State and the Empire'," he said. "You could take an oath of true faith and allegiance to the Constitution of Ireland."

"I started trying to get some sort of oath," he told the Dáil afterwards. "Here is the oath I refer to, 'I, so and so, swear to obey the Constitution of Ireland and to keep faith with His Britannic Majesty, so and so, in respect of the Treaty associating Ireland with the states of the British Commonwealth'."

"Nothing doing," declared Brugha, "there is going to be no unanimity on such an oath as that."

"Surely, Cathal," de Valera said, "you can't object to taking an oath if you agree to association."

Stack agreed with the President, so he, too, tried to persuade the Defence Minister that such an oath would be acceptable.

"Well," Brugha sighed in resignation, "you may as well swear."

"At the end of the discussion on the oath," Childers recalled, "I expressly raised the point myself as to whether scrapping the oath in the draft meant scrapping of the first four clauses of the British draft, that is to say the clauses setting out dominion status."

"Yes," replied the President.

Childers was satisfied. But neither Griffith nor Collins heard the exchange. The meeting was winding up and some decisions were taken hurriedly.

It was decided that the plenipotentiaries should return to London with the same powers and instructions. If the oath was not amended, they were to reject it regardless of the consequences. If this led to a breakdown of the conference, Griffith was advised to say that the matter should be referred to the Dáil, and he was to try to put the blame on Ulster. The plenipotentiaries were authorised to negotiate with Craig if they desired, but de Valera was unable to get unanimity on this point. Brugha and Stack held out and a hurried vote was taken. It was also decided that the trade and defence clauses should be amended. Instead of the four Irish ports the British were demanding, the President said they should be given "*two ports* only."

"All this amendment business was too hurried," Childers noted in his diary, "but it was understood by RCB [Barton], GD [Duffy], and me that amendments were not mandatory on [the] delegation." They were "only suggestions." De Valera later emphasised the same point in the Dáil himself. "I did not give, nor did the cabinet give, any instructions to the delegation as to any final document which they were to put in."

Back in London next morning Childers and Barton began drafting alternative proposals. They were soon joined by Gavan Duffy. On seeing their document, Collins immediately objected to the inclusion of External Association. He thought the cabinet had been satisfied with the guarantee of the *de facto* status of the dominions; there had not even been any discussion about External Association in Dublin the previous day. He was right, but the President had responded affirmatively when Childers asked if the suggested alterations to the oath also applied to the association question.

Neither Collins nor Griffith had any recollection of that exchange, but Duggan confirmed Childers's account. Collins was furious. Such an important issue—indeed, what would ultimately prove to be the vital issue—should not have been left to a monosyllabic response to an almost throw-away question from a secretary.

Collins's confusion was understandable when one considers that de Valera actually proposed two different alternative oaths that were consistent with dominion status. One of those has already been quoted. Griffith, Collins and Duggan also noted that the President had suggested that they could take an oath recognising "the King of Great Britain as Head of the Associated States," which could be interpreted to mean that the King would be the head of each state individually as well as head of the combined association of states.

Barton and Childers argued that de Valera had proposed recognising the King only as "Head of the Association." Barton looked at the notes he had taken at the meeting, but those were not conclusive. Childers, on the other hand, had recorded in his pocket diary that the President had said "King of the Associated States," while the version recorded by Ó Murchada was identical to that remembered by Griffith, Collins and Duggan.

A fortnight later de Valera contended that he must have said Association" not "Associated States," but he was undermined by his own recollection as he proceeded to tell the Dáil: 'I do swear to recognise the King of Great Britain as Head of the Associated States.' That is the way I expressed it verbally meaning the association of the states." This form of the oath was rejected by the British, so it was not that important from the standpoint of the negotiations, except that it does illustrate how Collins could have questioned whether those in Dublin were trying to instruct him or confuse him.

Collins was actually so annoyed that he refused to present the new document to the British, but not before adopting obstructionist tactics within the delegation. He deliberately tried to make the new document "unreasonable" by insisting that "Dev had said that only two ports [and] nothing else" could be conceded to the British, according to Childers. "I protested against making Dev's words ridiculous."

Meanwhile de Valera had returned to Munster to continue his tour of IRA units. He was in Limerick on Tuesday morning when he heard a treaty had been signed. "I never thought they would give in so soon!" he exclaimed. In view of Griffith undertaking not to sign the draft treaty, he assumed the British must have conceded what he wanted, so he was delighted. "I felt like throwing my hat in the air."

That evening he returned to Dublin as he was to preside at an academic symposium in his new capacity as Chancellor of the National University of Ireland, to which he had been elected the previous month. Having failed to get a full-time post as an academic, he had jumped over the heads of those who had passed him over and been elected to the lifetime position as head of the whole university system. He was already in his academic robes when Eamonn Duggan and Desmond FitzGerald arrived at the Mansion House with a copy of the Treaty, which Duggan handed to him. When he showed no interest in the document, Duggan asked him to read it.

"What should I read it for?" de Valera asked.

"It is arranged that the thing be published in London and Dublin simultaneously at 8 o'clock and it is near that hour now," replied Duggan.

"What, to be published whether I have seen it or not?"

"Oh well, that's the arrangement."

While he had clearly shown little enthusiasm for the agreement before reading it, he was despondent afterwards. He summoned a meeting of the available cabinet members for the following morning and said that he intended to demand the resignations of Griffith, Collins and Barton from his government upon their return, but he was persuaded to hold his hand by Cosgrave, who argued that the plenipotentiaries should be allowed to explain what had happened in London.

A full cabinet meeting was called for the following day, 8 December 1921, and de Valera prepared a press release. "In view of the nature of the proposed treaty with Great Britain," the release read, "President de Valera has sent an urgent summons to members of the cabinet in London to report at once so that a full cabinet decision may be taken."

Desmond FitzGerald, the Minister for Publicity who had just returned from London where he had been helping the delegation, was surprised at the tone of the statement. "This might be altered, Mr President," he said. "It reads as if you were opposed to the settlement."

"And that is the way I intended it to read," replied de Valera. "Publish it as it is."

"I did not think he was against this kind of settlement before we went over to London," FitzGerald whispered to Stack in surprise.

"He is dead against it now anyway," replied Stack. "That's enough."

The ensuing cabinet meeting on Thursday lasted throughout the day and late into the evening, with three short breaks. The main topic of discussion was the circumstances leading up to the signing of the Treaty.

Barton said he had signed because he had been threatened by Lloyd George with "immediate and terrible war." Griffith, on the other hand, refused to admit duress in his decision. He had felt his position had been undermined when Lloyd George produced the memorandum he had approved concerning the Boundary Commission. He had promised not to repudiate that proposal, so he could not break on the Ulster question and, as he had already made it clear that he would not break on the issue of the Crown, he had actually agreed to sign before Lloyd George ever issued his infamous ultimatum. Collins said that "if there was duress it was only 'duress of the facts'."

"There was not, and could not have been, any personal duress," as far as Collins was concerned. Lloyd George did not take out a gun and personally threaten anyone. "The form of duress he made use of," Barton explained, "was a more insidious and in my opinion, a more compelling duress, for Mr Lloyd George, knowing already from Mr Griffith himself that he was prepared to sign, demanded that every other delegate should sign or war would follow immediately, and insisted that those who refused to sign must accept responsibility." And Barton was not prepared to "accept the personal responsibility for the slaughter to ensue."

Barton blamed de Valera for the mess because of his refusal to go to London when asked the previous weekend. In fact, at different times de Valera had rejected appeals from all three cabinet members on the delegation, and he had also turned down similar appeals from Childers and Gavan Duffy. Moreover the President had been instrumental in conferring the full responsibility for negotiating a settlement on people he knew were more moderate than himself. "The disaster was," Barton said, "we were not a fighting delegation."

The cabinet was fairly evenly divided on the Treaty. The President had apparently hoped for majority support; he knew he could depend on the support of Brugha and Stack, but Cosgrave sided with Griffith and Collins. Thus it all came down to Barton's decision. Although the latter disliked the Treaty, he supported it because he had committed himself to do so by signing it in the first place.

De Valera said he had worked for a settlement that radicals like Brugha could accept. Indeed he had done a good job in bringing the rather stubborn Brugha to the point where there was very little difference between what he was prepared to accept and what the British were offering. Now, the President charged, the chance of securing a united cabinet had been wrecked by the plenipotentiaries signing the agreement without consulting the cabinet. It was obvious he took as a personal affront the delegation's failure to consult him again before the actual signing. In a letter to Joe McGarrity a few weeks later he described this failure as "an act of disloyalty to their President and to their colleagues in the Cabinet such as is probably without parallel in history."

None of the delegation had thought it necessary to consult Dublin before signing. They believed they had fulfilled their instructions by placing the draft treaty before the cabinet on Saturday. Once they had done that they were free to do as they thought fit. "Now I would like everybody clearly to understand," de Valera told the Dáil afterwards, "that the plenipotentiaries went over to negotiate a Treaty, that they could differ from the cabinet if they wanted to, and that in anything of consequence they could take their decision against the decision of the cabinet."

That was the way things were supposed to be, but de Valera secretly had other ideas. If he did not like what they intended doing, he obviously intended to take over himself. Had Griffith not said on Saturday that he would not sign the draft treaty, de Valera would have assumed responsibility himself. "I would have gone and said 'go to the devil, I will not sign'," he explained.

He still had high hopes of defeating the Treaty, and he told the cabinet he would be putting forward his own alternative in the Dáil.

After the meeting de Valera issued a statement to the press condemning the Treaty, which he contended was "in violent conflict with the wishes of the majority of the nation." He added that "the greatest test of our people has come. Let us face it worthily without bitterness, and above all, without recriminations. There is a definite constitutional way of resolving our political differences—let us not depart from it, and let the conduct of the cabinet in this matter be an example to the whole nation."

Privately next morning he expressed confidence "of winning better terms." Childers was amazed. De Valera actually seemed "certain of winning" in the Dáil.

CHAPTER 8

"That Little Sentimental Thing"

Although the cabinet had voted in favour of the Treaty, de Valera insisted that the document could not be submitted to the Dáil "as a cabinet measure." Instead, Griffith would have to propose the motion for ratification as Chairman of the delegation.

When the Dáil convened on 14 December 1921, de Valera opened the discussion with a distinct lack of candour. Starting with a few perfunctory words in Gaelic, he explained he was going to speak in English because his command of Irish was not good enough, but on breaking into English he gave an entirely different reason. "Some of the members do not know Irish, I think," he said, "and consequently what I shall say will be in English."

It was a bad start to the debate, but was fairly typical of his overall attitude. At times when talking to a smaller, more exclusive group, he was quite candid, but then when he spoke to a broader audience, he would change the emphasis to a point of distortion. For instance, he was amazingly candid with deputies after he persuaded the Dáil to go into private session from which the press and public were excluded. The transcript of the session, which lay unpublished for more than half a century, provides a valuable insight into his thinking on the whole controversy. He admitted that there was only a small difference between the Treaty and what he would accept. Some people said those differences were only shadows, and he did not seem altogether sure that the depiction was inaccurate. "There are differences that may be regarded as shadows, but they are more than shadows," he said. The British considered such things important. "If they are mere shadows, why should they be grasping for the shadows and not we?" he asked. "I wanted to clear these shadows because they meant an awful lot."

De Valera was so convinced and enthusiastic about the validity of his own position that he explained it in minute detail, producing his own alternative in the form of a draft treaty, which became known as Document No. 2. It differed from the actual Treaty in a number of respects. There was no oath, for example, in Document No 2; it merely stated that "for the purposes of association, Ireland shall recognise his Britannic Majesty as head of the Association." The Treaty oath to which de Valera took such exception read:

I … do solemnly swear true faith and allegiance to the Constitution of the Irish Free State as by law established, and that

I will be faithful to H.M. King George V, his heirs and successors by law, in virtue of the common citizenship of Ireland with Great Britain and her adherence to and membership of the group of nations forming the British Commonwealth of Nations.

De Valera candidly explained to the private session that, at the last cabinet meeting before the Treaty was signed, he had proposed an oath on the following lines:

I, so and so, swear to obey the Constitution of Ireland and to keep faith with his Britannic Majesty, so and so, in respect of the treaty associating Ireland with the states of the British Commonwealth.

He added he would still "be quite ready" to take that oath, if he was satisfied with the form of the association to which Ireland would belong.

Those two oaths were comparatively similar except that what de Valera was referring to was External Association, not membership of the British Commonwealth. Hence his main objection to the Treaty really centered on the question of association. In both oaths the first allegiance would be to the Irish constitution and fealty would be sworn to the British King in virtue of Ireland's association with Britain and the dominions, but each oath envisioned a different form of association. The Treaty oath involved "common citizenship" and dominion status, while the President was thinking of reciprocal citizenship and External Association. He had no problem with swearing to be "faithful" to the King because he realised the word "faithful" had been used instead of the word "allegiance" in order to denote equality between those taking the oath and the British King. "I take it to mean that 'faithful' is as regards a bargain made in the faithfulness of two equals who show it in keeping the bargain," he explained. His main difficulty with the Treaty oath was in swearing "allegiance to the constitution of the Irish Free State *as by law established.*"

The constitution would be drawn up by a Provisional Government which, under the terms of the Treaty, would be established by those elected to the Southern Parliament in accordance with the terms of the Government of Ireland Act (1920), which had been passed by Westminster in the name of the King. It therefore followed that the Free State constitution would be drawn up in the King's name. "The point is," the President emphasised, "that the oath contained in the Treaty actually and unequivocally binds the taker to 'allegiance' to the English King, for under the terms of the Treaty the constitution of the Irish Free State 'as by law established' is the King of England and nobody else." If the Irish side accepted a constitution drawn up in the name of the British King, it would be tantamount to acknowledging the ultimate authority of the British Parliament. In theory, therefore, under the terms of the Treaty the British parliament would, in the name of the King, be legally entitled to interfere in Irish affairs. In line with Document No. 2, on the other hand, Ireland would be clearly an autochthonous state—that is a state deriving its authority to govern from its own people rather than from some outside agency like the British parliament.

The first clause of de Valera's alternative emphasised that "the legislative, executive, and judicial authority of Ireland shall be derived solely from the people of Ireland." There followed a clause stipulating that Ireland would associate with the British Commonwealth on matters of common concern and would enjoy the same privileges as the other dominions, with the respective citizens of Ireland and the dominions enjoying reciprocal rights. Matters of common concern were defined as:

Defence, Peace and War, Political Treaties, and all matters now treated as of common concern among the States of the British Commonwealth, and that in these matters there shall be between Ireland and the States of the British Commonwealth "such concerted action founded on consultation as the several Governments may determine."

In other words Ireland would enjoy the same *de facto* freedom as the dominions and would assume the same responsibilities.

The defence clauses of Document No. 2 were basically the same as the Treaty except that de Valera stipulated that the facilities granted to Britain should be returned after five years if no other arrangement was made, whereas the Treaty merely stipulated the situation would be reviewed after five years. The President's stand in regard to the Ulster question was identical to the Treaty for all practical purposes. Document No. 2 stated that the Dáil would not recognise "the right of any part of Ireland to be excluded from the supreme authority of the National Parliament and Government," but it then went on to Incorporate the Treaty clauses on the Boundary Commission verbatim.

In short, he was saying he would not recognise that Northern Ireland had a right to secede but he would nevertheless recognise the actual secession for the sake of "internal peace, and in the desire to bring no force or coercion to bear upon any substantial part of the province."

He was not really concerned about the partition issue. "The difficulty is not the Ulster question," he explained. "As far as we are concerned this is a fight between Ireland and England. I want to eliminate the Ulster question out of it." Thus, he said, he was ready to accept the partition clauses of the Treaty even though they contained "an explicit recognition of the right on the part of Irishmen to secede from Ireland." In short, Document No. 2 did recognise the right of the Unionists to secede, notwithstanding its empty declaration to the contrary. De Valera would later admit that the Treaty provided a better chance of ending partition because Unionists would find dominion status less objectionable than External Association.

Collins flatly rejected de Valera's alternative, which he honestly felt was even worse than the Treaty. While the British King would have the theoretical right to interfere in Irish affairs, such interference would be a violation of Britain's unwritten constitution and would also violate the Treaty's stipulation that the Free State would have the same *de facto* status as Canada and the other dominions. If Britain was going to violate the Treaty, it would be even easier to violate Document No. 2, because the latter would not afford the protection of the dominions, which under the Treaty would have a vested interest in ensuring Britain did not violate Irish sovereignty, because such a violation would set a precedent for similar interference in their own affairs.

Even de Valera himself made the startling admission that his alternative was little better than the Treaty. "It is right to say that there will be very little difference in practice between what I may call the proposals received and what you will have under what I propose," he explained. "There is very little in practice but there is that big thing that you are consistent and that you recognise yourself as a separate independent State and you associate in an honourable manner with another group." If the Dáil stood by Document No. 2, the British would "not go to war for the difference," he contended. "I felt the distance between the two was so small that the British would not wage war on account of it. You say if it is so small why not take it. But I say, that small difference makes all the difference. This fight has lasted all through the centuries and I would be willing to win that little sentimental thing that would satisfy the aspirations of the country." In short, he was arguing that the British would not fight for the difference, while Collins was contending they would fight even though the difference was not worth fighting over.

De Valera soon realised he had made a tactical mistake in producing Document No. 2 because, on the one hand, it tended to alienate radical Republicans and, on the other hand, it strengthened

Collins's argument that it was not worth fighting for the difference between it and the Treaty. He was really outlining a very complicated thing, and most deputies were not interested in complications. He therefore withdrew his proposal at the end of the private session, and demanded that nobody should refer to it during the ensuing public session.

When the Dáil reconvened in public, Griffith formally proposed the ratification of the Treaty, and he was seconded by Seán MacEoin. De Valera then called for its rejection. "I am against this Treaty because it does not reconcile Irish national aspirations with association with the British Government," he declared. "I am against this Treaty, not because I am a man of war, but a man of peace. I am against this Treaty because it will not end the centuries of conflict between the two nations of Great Britain and Ireland." In the course of his speech he never even alluded to the partition question; he kept his remarks general and avoided specific references to the Treaty, with the exception of the oath. He contended that the Treaty was "absolutely inconsistent with our position; it gives away Irish independence; it brings us into the British Empire; it acknowledges the head of the British Empire, not merely as the head of an association but as the direct monarch of Ireland, as the source of executive authority in Ireland." If deputies approved the agreement, he concluded, they would be "presuming to set bounds on the onward march of a nation."

When Collins spoke, he explained that he had planned to compare the Treaty with Document No. 2 but in deference to the President's desire for secrecy, he did not do so. Instead he confined himself to the merits of the Treaty. "I do not recommend it for more than it is," he emphasised. "Equally I do not recommend it for less than it is. In my opinion it gives us freedom, not the ultimate freedom that all nations desire and develop to, but the freedom to achieve it." Before winding up, however, he referred to his own Irish background in a way that subtly questioned the background of de Valera and some of his leading supporters. Few people could have failed to notice that leaders on the other side of the floor, like the American-born de Valera with his Spanish father, or the English-born Childers, or Brugha with his English father, or Markievicz, were not able to boast of such a strong Irish ancestry.

Behind the scenes a number of attempts were made to avoid a Dáil division on the Treaty. One suggestion was for the Dáil to transfer the necessary authority for the Provisional Government to function. In this way the Irish people could claim the Dáil as the ultimate authority for the Free State Constitution, so there would be no question of the Irish side acknowledging the King as the source of the Free State's authority. De Valera dismissed the idea because, he said, Griffith and Collins would not accept it. When they did, he rejected it anyway. He also dismissed comparatively similar suggestions put forward by both Collins and a group of back-bench deputies who included some of his own supporters like Seán T. O'Kelly and Paddy Ruttledge.

As the debate dragged on de Valera did irreparable damage to his own reputation as a practical moderate by acting as if he had a right to determine Dáil procedure. He intervened repeatedly and spoke more than two hundred and fifty times during the thirteen days of public and private debate. Although many of those interruptions were just short interjections, some were quite lengthy. The latitude he was given testified to his standing within the Dáil, though his opponents did eventually become somewhat exasperated.

Griffith and Collins had complied with what, they believed, was his unreasonable request that they not refer to Document No. 2 during the public sessions, but they balked when he tried to introduce a revised version of that document at the close of business on 4 January 1922. Having already agreed that no amendment could be entertained until the Treaty had been voted upon, he seemed to be splitting hairs when he argued he was not proposing an amendment to the Treaty but an amendment to the resolution calling for the Dail's approval of the Treaty. "I am responsible for the proposals," he told a stunned Dáil, "and the House will have to decide on them. I am going to choose my own procedure."

"I submit it is not in the competence of the President to choose his own procedure," Griffith replied in a cold, intent manner. "This is either a constitutional body or it is not. If it is an autocracy let you say so and we will leave it."

"In answer to that I am going to propose an amendment in my own terms," de Valera replied defiantly. "It is for the House to decide whether they will take it or not." The atmosphere was tense and he seemed to be about to say more, but he was calmed by one of the deputies on the bench behind him tapping him gently on the shoulder. The undignified spectacle was thus mercifully ended as the Dáil recessed for the evening.

Afterwards de Valera issued a "proclamation" to the Irish people. "Do not enter upon a compact which in your hearts you know can never be kept in sincerity and in truth," he began. "No matter how worthy, they are neither good friends to Ireland nor to England nor to humanity who advise you to take that course. Be bold enough to say No to those who ask you to misrepresent yourselves."

Next morning the *Freeman's Journal* was scathing in its criticism of the President's conduct. He was accused of "arrogating to himself the rights of an autocrat," by the newspaper's political correspondent. "It seems as though he wanted to wreck the Dáil before a vote could be taken, and then carry the devastating split as far as his influence could reach, throughout the length and breadth of the land. The worst disaster which has befallen Ireland since the Union is imminent, and can only be averted by the deputies who love their country more than they love Mr de Valera, refusing to share his terrible responsibility." The same issue of the newspaper carried a vitriolic editorial denouncing the President for his "criminal attempt to divide the nation" by pressing "an alleged alternative" that contained "all the articles for which the Treaty had been assailed by the 'ideal orators of Dáil Eireann'." The editorial went on to accuse Erskine Childers of being the architect of the President's proposals. "It is the curse of Ireland at this moment that its unity should be broken by such a man acting under the advice of an Englishman who has achieved fame in the British Intelligence Service." The editorial continued:

THESE ARE THE MEN FOR WHOM THE NATION IS TO PUT ASIDE ARTHUR GRIFFITH, MICHAEL COLLINS, AND RICHARD MULCAHY.

WHEN THE FIGHT WAS ON MR DE VALERA AND MR ERSKINE CHILDERS FELL ACCIDENTALLY INTO THE HANDS OF THE MILITARY.

THEY WERE IMMEDIATELY RELEASED.

THAT WAS THE TIME THERE WAS £10,000 FOR THE CORPSE OF MICHAEL COLLINS.

THE IRISH PEOPLE MUST STAND UP, AND BEGIN THEIR FREEDOM BY GIVING THEIR FATE INTO THE HANDS OF THEIR OWN COUNTRYMEN.

In the face of the uproar caused by his gaffe about choosing his own procedure, the President changed his tactics on 6 January. This time he did not even try to use a hair-splitting technicality. He told a secret session of the Dáil that morning of his intention to resign at the public session in the afternoon. Deputies therefore convened in an air of expectation.

"Even in his happiest moments Mr de Valera has scarcely surpassed himself in declaratory power," one reporter noted. The President began slowly and deliberately, but his voice became charged with emotion when he started to defend his alternative proposals. "Now, I have definitely a policy," he explained, "not some pet scheme of my own, but something that I know from four years' experience in my position and I have been brought up amongst the Irish people. I was reared in a labourer's cottage here in Ireland."

The Dáil applauded. This was obviously the President's answer to the snide questioning of his credentials as an Irishman by the *Freeman's Journal*. "I have not lived solely amongst the intellectuals," he continued. "The first fifteen years of my life that formed my character were lived among the Irish people down in Limerick; therefore, I know what I am talking about; and whenever I wanted to know what the Irish people wanted I had only to examine my own heart and it told me straight off." Now he knew the Irish people did not want the Treaty, so he was going to wreck it. He announced his resignation as President and said the Dáil would have "to decide before it does further work, who is to be the Chief Executive in this Nation." And he was going to stand for re-election.

"If you elect me and do it by a majority," he said, "I will throw out that Treaty." This was a naked attempt to turn the whole Treaty issue into a personal vote of confidence. His manoeuvre evoked so much criticism that he felt compelled to withdraw his resignation, but not before making some self-righteous remarks.

"I am sick and tired of politics—so sick that no matter what happens I would go back to private life. I have only seen politics within the last three weeks or a month. It is the first time I have seen them and I am sick to the heart of them." Depicting himself as straight and honest in the face of the twisted dishonesty of his opponents, he continued. "It is because I am straight that I meet crookedness with straight dealing always," he said. "Truth will always stand no matter from what direction it is attacked."

"One of the most irritating features of Mr de Valera's behaviour at this time," Piaras Beaslaí wrote, "was that, having used every device of a practical politician to gain his point, having shown himself relentless and unscrupulous in taking every advantage of generous opponents, he would adopt a tone of injured innocence when his shots failed, and assume the pose of a simple sensitive man, too guileless and gentle for this rough world of politics." Of course, it was debatable just how generous his opponents were, but Griffith and Collins did forego the opportunity of criticising Document No. 2 publicly, and in doing this they surrendered a magnificent opportunity of demonstrating to the public early in the debate the extent to which the cabinet had been committed to a compromise settlement. This would have forced de Valera and his supporters on the defensive and would probably have driven a wedge between them and the die-hard Republicans. Whatever about all that, there could be no doubt de Valera was less than candid with his feigned innocence about the seamier side of politics. He had been up to his neck in such politics while in the United States and, arguably, he had more political experience than anyone else in the Dáil. In fact, he refuted his assertion of innocence in the same speech by referring to his American experiences.

"I detest trickery," de Valera said. "What has sickened me most is that I got in this House the same sort of dealing that I was accustomed to over in America from other people of a similar kind." It was particularly significant he should compare his critics in the Dáil with his opponents in the United States, because there was a remarkable similarity between his attitude towards the Treaty and his actions during the Republican Party's National Convention at Chicago in June 1920. "It was a case of Cohalan and his machine over again," he wrote to McGarrity.

Just as he knew there was no realistic chance of securing diplomatic recognition in the United States, he knew no British politician would be prepared to accept his alternative proposals in Document No. 2., "No politicians in England would stand by them," he admitted. "It would be a document that would give real peace to the people of Great Britain and Ireland and not the officials. I know it would not be a politicians' peace. I know the politician in England who would take it would risk his political future, but it would be a peace between peoples."

De Valera had undermined the platform plank suggested by Cohalan in Chicago to demonstrate that he, not Cohalan, was the real spokesman for the Irish in America. Now he seemed determined to show that he was the real leader at home, not Collins or Griffith. For the Dáil to have accepted the President's suggestion that the Treaty be rejected and Document No. 2 presented to the British instead would have been as foolhardy as he was naïve if he really believed that the propaganda campaign advocated by him had any more chance of success than the pathetic failure of his comparatively similar effort to win over the American electorate in 1920 after the Chicago debacle. A successful campaign in 1922 would have needed the sympathetic understanding of at least some sections of the press, and there was little chance of securing this, seeing that the only organs which opposed the Treaty had done so on the grounds that the agreement was too generous towards Sinn

Féin. Not one Irish daily newspaper supported de Valera's position, and there was little prospect of getting international support because even American opinion was strongly in favour of the settlement.

On the day of the actual vote the *New York Times* carried an editorial that was bitterly critical of de Valera:

Apparently he essayed a Napoleonic or Cromwellian stroke in resigning, at the same time that he demanded re-election with all power placed in his hands; but when this failed, he talked and acted like a hysterical schoolgirl. Whatever happens in Ireland, de Valera seems to have hopelessly discredited himself as a leader. Narrow, obstinate, visionary and obviously vain, he has now, in his representative capacity, wrought immense harm to the Ireland of his professed entire devotion.

Harry Boland, who had just returned from the United States to vote against the Treaty, admitted that "the great public opinion of America is on the side of this Treaty." Indeed, he added, the American press had adopted "a unanimous attitude in favour" of it. There was even strong support among some of de Valera's supporters in the United States.

The President of AARIR had come out in favour of the agreement, as had Boland himself initially. He had praised the Treaty as "an agreement which restores Ireland to the comity of nations." He explained he had issued his statement before the Treaty was published in the United States. He had made the mistake of assuming the Treaty would be favourable because de Valera had assured him nothing less than External Association would be acceptable. But this did not explain why, after the terms were published, he actually denounced Cohalan and the secretary of FOIF for criticising the agreement. The pair of them had, ironically, been among the first to denounce the Treaty publicly, but they subsequently supported it after they learned de Valera was opposed to it. Such vicissitudes certainly lent credence to the idea that personalities figured largely in the controversy.

Stripped of its polemical distortions and insinuations, the debate centred on bizarre irrelevancies. Despite the national significance and momentous implications of the Treaty, it was painfully obvious that personalities were playing an inordinate role in determining how people were lining up on the issue. On the one side people were backing de Valera, while on the other side they were gathering behind Collins.

As in Chicago, de Valera would again pretend to stand on an

issue of principle but his actions were a matter of tactics; he was trying to show that he was the real leader and not allow others to usurp what he believed was his rightful authority. "I was captaining a team and I felt that the team should have played with me to the last and that I should have got the last chance which I felt would have put us over and we might have crossed the bar in my opinion at the high tide," he told the Dáil. "They rushed before the tide got to the top and they almost foundered the ship."

"A captain who sent out his crew to sea, and tried to direct operations from dry land!" Collins remarked to those about him.

"I am excusing myself to the Dáil as the captain of the ship and I can only say it is not my fault," de Valera continued. "Had the Chairman of the delegation said he did not stand for the things they had said they stood for, he would not have been elected." Here the President's argument was patently distorted. He knew well where Griffith stood when he proposed him for the delegation, and that was why he sent Childers to keep an eye on him.

As the proposer of the resolution calling for the Dáil's approval of the Treaty, Griffith was supposed to have the last word before the vote was taken, but de Valera again violated the procedure. "Before you take a vote," he said, "I want to enter my last protest—that document will rise in judgement against the men who say there is only a shadow of difference". He was obviously calling on deputies to reject the Treaty in favour of his own Document No. 2.

De Valera was not entitled to the last word, and Collins was not about to let him have it. "Let the Irish nation judge us now and for future years," cried Collins.

The clerk of the Dáil began calling the role in the order of constituencies. It took about ten minutes to complete the voting and another couple of minutes before the announcement was made that the Treaty had been approved by sixty-four votes to fifty-seven. There was no real demonstration within the hall, but when news filtered outside there was a wave of enthusiastic cheering in the street, where a crowd of some hundreds had gathered. The cheering continued for some minutes and seemed to stir those inside the chamber.

"It will, of course, be my duty to resign my office as Chief Executive," de Valera said. "I do not know that I should do it just now."

"No," cried Collins.

"There is one thing I want to say," the President continued. "I want it to go to the country and to the world, and it is this: the Irish people established a Republic. This is simply approval of a certain resolution. The Republic can only be disestablished by the Irish people. Therefore, until such time as the Irish people in regular manner disestablish it, this Republic goes on."

Collins called for a committee of public safety to be set up by both sides of the Dáil to preserve order. Some people thought de Valera was going to respond favourably until Mary MacSwiney intervened to denounce the vote just taken "as the grossest act of betrayal" that Ireland ever endured. "There can be no union between representatives of the Irish Republic and the so-called Free State," she declared.

De Valera announced he would like to meet "all those who voted on the side of the established Republic" the following afternoon, and Collins repeated his appeal for "some kind of understanding" between the two factions "to preserve the present order in the country."

"I would like my last word here to be this," de Valera responded. "We have had a glorious record for four years, it has been four years of magnificent discipline in our nation. The world is looking at us now—"

At this point he broke down, buried his head in his hands, and collapsed sobbing into his chair. It was a very emotional scene; women were weeping openly, while men were visibly trying to restrain their tears.

CHAPTER 9

"No Right to Do Wrong"

On learning the details of the Anglo-Irish Treaty de Valera announced it was a matter for the cabinet, and when the cabinet approved the agreement, he said it was a matter for the Dáil. And when the Dáil approved, he contended the Treaty could only be ratified by the Irish people.

On the morning after the Dáil approved the Treaty, the fifty-seven deputies who voted against the motion met and decided to form their own organisation, Cumann na Poblachta (Association of the Republic). At this point they did little other than agree upon a name. Instead, they concentrated on their next move in the Dáil. De Valera planned on resigning as President when the Dáil reconvened next day, and they decided to try to have him re-elected. If successful, he would exclude all pro-Treaty people from his cabinet and would not cooperate with efforts to implement the agreement.

Nobody should have been surprised on Monday morning when he formally resigned his presidency. Collins immediately proposed he be replaced by a committee of public safety drawn from both sides of the House, but de Valera rejected the idea on supposed constitutional grounds. "I have tendered my resignation and I cannot, in any way, take divided responsibility," he stated. "You have got here a sovereign assembly which is the government of the nation. This assembly must choose its executive according to its constitution and go ahead."

On being challenged to outline his policy, de Valera said he would "carry on as before and forget that this Treaty has come." Once the Irish people understood its implications he predicted they would not stand for it. "When that Treaty is worked out in legislative form and put before them," he said, "then they will know what they have got."

Critics accused him of making a mockery of normal democratic procedure by trying to give power to the minority rather than the majority who supported the Treaty, but de Valera defended his stand. "I am thinking of it as the better and the constitutional and the right and proper way to do the work," he explained. "Remember, I am only putting myself at your disposal and at the disposal of the nation. I do not want office at all. Go and elect your President and all the rest of it. You have sixty-five. I do not want office at all."

Responding with a cold, reasoned attack depicting the

President's proposition as a twisted appeal to the emotions of deputies in order to undermine the Treaty, Griffith noted there had been no need for the President to resign in the first place. "We suggested that Dáil Éireann might continue until the Free State election came into effect," he said. By resigning and then running for re-election, de Valera was personally seeking the endorsement of the Dáil to ignore the Treaty. As no other candidate was initially proposed, some supporters argued he should be deemed to have been re-elected unanimously, but he refused to hear of this. He wanted a formal vote.

Collins tried to nominate Griffith, but the Speaker ruled the Dáil would have to vote on de Valera's nomination first. When the vote was taken de Valera did not vote, in an apparent effort to dramatise that he was not personally seeking office but only putting himself at the disposal of the nation. His arrogance could easily have proved costly because he was defeated by only two votes, sixty to fifty-eight. One deputy, Thomas O'Donnell—the man who had first coined the name "Dev" when he and de Valera were teaching colleagues at Rockwell—had voted for the Treaty and for the President's re-election. As a result, if only one of those who had voted against de Valera actually voted the other way, his own vote would probably have made the difference between victory and defeat.

Griffith immediately rose to pay a generous tribute. The vote, he said, had not really been against de Valera; it was for the Treaty. "I want to say now, that there is scarcely a man I have ever met in my life that I have more love and respect for than President de Valera. I am thoroughly sorry to see him placed in such a position. We want him with us."

"I voted, not for personalities, but for my country," one deputy shouted. "Dev has been made a tool of."

"I want to assure everybody on the other side," de Valera replied, "that it was not a trick. That was my own definite way of doing the right thing for Ireland. I tell you that from my heart. I did it because I felt it was still the best way to keep that discipline which we had in the past." Mindful of the dangers ahead, he continued, "I hope that nobody will talk of fratricidal strife. That is all nonsense. We have got a nation that knows how to conduct itself."

His opponents certainly thought his actions were part of a calculated ploy designed to destroy the Treaty. Maybe they misjudged his sincerity, though in time he would give them plenty of grounds for questioning his sincerity on this occasion. He would become the person who would talk most about the fratricidal strife which he had described as nonsense.

In the following weeks de Valera did virtually everything possible to frustrate the implementation of the Treaty. The Treaty stipulated that the Parliament of Southern Ireland, established under the Government of Ireland Act (1920), would appoint a Provisional Government to take over from the British administration in Dublin Castle. This should have posed little problem because Sinn Féin had used the elections for the Southern Parliament to elect Dáil deputies, so the members of the two bodies overlapped for all practical purposes. Whether the new executive was called the Provisional Government or Dáil cabinet mattered little to Collins, but de Valera insisted the Dáil should preserve its separate identity because it had no authority to do anything about implementing the Treaty without the prior approval of the Irish people.

When Collins proposed the election of Griffith as "President of the Provisional Executive," he was basically only suggesting a change of title, but de Valera refused to hear of it. It was ironic that he, of all people, should be so obstinate, seeing that he had changed the title from *Príomh Aire* to President back in 1919 without even consulting his Dáil colleagues, and he waited for more than two years before asking them to regularise the constitutional position in August 1921.

The wrangle over the title was left unresolved overnight, before de Valera won his point. If elected, Griffith told the Dáil next morning, he would occupy whatever position de Valera had occupied.

"That is a fair answer," de Valera replied. "I feel I can sit down in this assembly while such an election is going on." But within minutes he changed his mind and announced he was walking out of the Dáil "as a protest against the election as President of the Irish Republic of the Chairman of the Delegation who is bound by the Treaty conditions to set up a State which is to subvert the Republic." Accompanied by supporters, he then walked out. It was a contemptuous act, especially by someone who professed to consider the Dáil the sovereign assembly of the Irish people.

Collins was enraged. "Deserters all!" he shouted as they walked out. "We will call on the Irish people to rally to us. Deserters all!"

"Up the Republic," one of the departing deputies cried.

"Deserters all to the Irish nation in her hour of trial. We will stand by her," Collins continued.

"Oath breakers and cowards," said Madame Markievicz.

"Foreigners—Americans—English," cried Collins.

"Lloyd Georgeites," Markievicz shot back, as the vulgar absurdity was mercifully ended with the final departure of de Valera's supporters.

Outside, the former President emphasised his determination to do everything possible to prevent the implementation of the Treaty. "We have a perfect right to resist by every means in our power," he told journalists.

"Even by war?" asked a reporter.

"By every means in our power to resist authority imposed on this country from outside," he replied.

Under the terms of the Government of Ireland Act, the Lord Lieutenant was supposed to convoke the Southern Parliament in the name of the Crown, but this was not done. Instead President Griffith, acting in his capacity as chairman of the Irish plenipotentiaries, called on members of the parliament to meet on 14 January 1922, when they dispensed with the oath of allegiance to the British King prescribed for members of the parliament. Strictly speaking therefore, the body was not the Southern Parliament at all but an adjunct of the Dáil. But the British let matters stand and handed over power to the Provisional Government under the chairmanship of Collins. He appointed a cabinet which included most of the members of the cabinet appointed by Griffith. Ever since the founding of the Dáil there had been two governments in the country, but now the two were being run by Sinn Féin. However, the whole thing was of little consequence seeing that most of the ministers held parallel posts in both governments. As a result the dual arrangement was essentially a symbolic gesture to facilitate de Valera's objections.

Collins was arguing the Treaty would provide a stepping stone to the desired freedom, while de Valera refuted this. "It is not a stepping-stone," he told an American journalist, "but a barrier in the way to complete independence. If this Treaty be completed and the British Act resulting from it accepted by Ireland, it will certainly be maintained that a solemn binding contract has been voluntarily entered into by the Irish people, and Britain will seek to hold us to that contract. It will be cited against the claim for independence of every future Irish leader."

Collins tried to give a practical demonstration of the stepping-stone theory by incorporating aspects of External Association in the new constitution being drawn up by the Provisional Government. He said, for example, that the constitution could incorporate the clause at the very heart of External Association stipulating that the legislative, executive and judicial authority should be derived solely from the Irish people. He also contended the Treaty-oath pre-scribed for members of the Free State Parliament could be omitted from the constitution so that deputies would not have to take it. The pro-Treaty people had already avoided taking the oath prescribed for members of the Southern parliament, so there were grounds for believing he could deliver on this latest promise also.

De Valera was, of course, highly sceptical. He challenged the pro-Treaty people to make good their boasts by framing the con-stitution and presenting it to the people so "they would know what they were voting on."

Although out of government, he was by no means in the politi-cal wilderness. He was still president of Sinn Féin, and he appar-ently enjoyed the support of a majority of party members at the grass-root level, even though the party's executive was pro-Treaty. He used his influence at the party's annual Árd Fheis, which con-vened on 21 February 1922, to extract an agreement from Griffith and Collins to delay the proposed elections for three months and to publish the new constitution beforehand. In return, he used his influence to shelve a resolution which would have prohibited those who had voted for the Treaty from standing as Sinn Féin candidates in the next election.

Initially de Valera seemed happy with the agreement as he called on the Irish people to reject the Treaty at the polls, but he soon changed his approach and demanded the electoral register be updated, which would have necessitated an even longer delay than the three months agreed at the Árd Fheis. "The register on which you proposed to hold the elections," he wrote to Griffith, "contains tens of thousands of names that should not be on it, and omits sev-eral tens of thousands that should be on it—the latter mainly those of young men who have just attained their majority, who were the nation's most active defenders in the recent fight, and whose voice should certainly not be silenced in an election like the pending one, in which the fate of their country and the ideals for which they fought are to be determined."

Exasperated by de Valera's tactics Griffith refused a further de-lay. He felt the call for a new electoral register was not motivated by a concern for the democratic rights of the unfranchised, but was merely a ploy to stall the elections in order to avoid certain defeat. And de Valera's actions in the following weeks—after the formal launching of his new party, Cumann na Poblachta, on 15 March 1922—certainly raised questions about his commitment to democ-racy. Speaking in Thurles on St Patrick's Day he told a crowd which included a contingent of armed IRA, that they would have "to wade through Irish blood, through the blood of the soldiers of the Irish government, and through, perhaps, the blood of some members of the government in order to get Irish freedom," if the Treaty was ratified.

The speech was widely interpreted as threatening civil war or attempting to incite one, though de Valera indignantly refuted any such notion. He said he was merely assessing the situation realistically, and he accused his critics of using his words to do the very thing of which they were accusing him.

"You cannot be unaware," he wrote to the editor of the *Irish Independent*, "that your representing me as inciting the civil war has on your readers precisely the same effects as if the inciting words were really mine."

De Valera was, in fact, rapidly losing his influence over the IRA, which was showing signs of great internal stress. Most of the headquarters staff—controlled by Collins and the IRB—were pro-Treaty, while divisional commanders and the rank and file volunteers were strongly anti-Treaty, especially in those areas that had been most active in the struggle against the British. Some of the more militant, like Rory O'Connor, the Director of Engineering, had little time for de Valera.

"Some of us are not more prepared to stand for de Valera than for the Treaty," O'Connor told the press. He wanted an IRA convention called to elect a new leadership, but the headquarters staff—realising their own position was tenuous at best—refused. De Valera tried to make the best of his own weak position by siding with those asking for a convention. He even suggested that the IRA should split on Treaty lines.

"I have sufficient faith in the Irish people to believe that they can divide without turning on one another," he said, adding that it would be better to have two united, disciplined armies than one divided and powerless force. Many people mistakenly thought de Valera was the actual instigator when O'Connor—claiming to represent eighty per cent of the IRA—announced an Army Convention would be held on 26 March 1922 in defiance of the government and headquarters staff. O'Connor told the press that the IRA had freely submitted to the authority of the Dáil but was now withdrawing its allegiance because the Dáil had betrayed the Republic by recommending the Treaty. "The holding of the convention means that we repudiate the Dáil," he said.

"Do we take it we are going to have a military dictatorship

then?" he was asked.

"You can take it that way if you like."

The convention, which convened three days later, was attended only by anti-Treaty volunteers who elected an executive of their own, thus splitting the IRA along Treaty lines. Under the new executive the anti-Treaty IRA quickly became active, conducting raids for arms, as well as bank robberies, to finance their operations.

De Valera later wrote that he "heartily disagreed" with O'Connor's repudiation of the Dáil, but he nevertheless publicly defended the action in a whole series of press interviews at the time. Having stoked radical Republican passions, he was no longer able to control them. He was pretending to lead while he was, in fact, being dragged along by his supposed followers. He made approving statements which concealed his differences with them, and he soon found himself compelled to serve the folly he had approved. He was like a man floundering in a bog, sinking deeper every time he tried to move. He would try to assume a position of real leadership with his approving statements only to find himself outmanoeuvred as they moved on inexorably towards war. In the process he became a model of infuriating inconsistency.

Speaking in Dun Laoghaire on 6 April, for instance, he said the Irish people had a right to ratify the Treaty, even with the British threat of war hanging over their heads. That weekend, however, he defended the anti-Treaty IRA's repudiation of the Dáil as quite natural. "If the Irish people were allowed a free choice," he said, "they would choose by an overwhelming majority exactly what these armed forces desire." As far as he was concerned it was a misnomer to talk about free elections with the British threat of war hanging over the electorate.

"The threat of war from this government," he declared, "is intimidation operating on the side of Mr Griffith and Mr Collins as sure and as definite as if these gentlemen were using it themselves, and far more effective, because indirect and well kept in the background. Is our army to be blamed if it strives to save the people from being influenced by, and from the consequences of, giving way to this intimidation?"

On Good Friday, 14 April, Dublin awoke to find that the anti-Treaty IRA had seized some prominent city-centre buildings, including the Four Courts, where they established their headquarters. The similarity with the start of the Easter Rebellion, six years earlier, was unmistakable. Although de Valera had not even been informed, much less consulted beforehand, it was still widely assumed he was behind the move and he did little to disabuse the notion.

A Labour Party deputation which called on him found him particularly unreceptive. "We spent two hours pleading with him, with a view to averting the impending calamity of civil war," one member of the deputation later recalled. "The only statement he made that has abided with me since as to what his views were was this: 'The majority have no right to do wrong.' He repeated that at least a dozen times in the course of the interview." He refused to accept he had a "duty to observe the decision of the majority until it was reversed." Some years later he explained his attitude: "What appeared to be an obvious wrong was being justified by the idea that it was backed by the majority vote of the people. I said that that did not justify wrong. That never justified wrong. If you got a unanimous vote of the people telling you to go and shoot your neighbour, you would be quite in the wrong in carrying out that majority will. You would not be right. Therefore the majority rule does not give to anybody the right to do anything wrong, and I stand by the statement."

In the purely abstract sense he was correct, but he had not been talking in the abstract on Good Friday 1922. Taking his remarks in their proper context, he was contending that the anti-Treaty IRA had a right to ignore the wishes of the majority of the Irish people. He actually issued an inflammatory proclamation that weekend which ended with an emotional appeal to the youth of the country. "Young men and young women of Ireland," he concluded, "the goal is at last in sight. Steady; all together; forward. Ireland is yours for the taking. Take it." It is hard to see how such a statement could have been interpreted as other than an appeal for young people to support the anti-Treaty IRA which had just seized the Dublin buildings.

Faced with imminent civil war the Roman Catholic archbishop of Dublin made a desperate attempt to avert the impending disaster by inviting de Valera, Brugha, Griffith and Collins, as well as some Labour leaders, to a conference at the Mansion House. Again progress proved virtually impossible because of the bitter personality differences between the Sinn Féin leaders.

At one point Brugha accused Griffith and Collins of being British agents. When the archbishop demanded the accusation be withdrawn, Brugha agreed but proceeded to explain that he considered those who did the work of the British government to be British agents.

"I suppose we are two of the ministers whose blood is to be waded through?" Collins snapped.

"Yes," replied Brugha quite calmly. "You are two."

For months vile accusations had been hurled at Griffith and Collins, while de Valera stood by indifferently, depicting himself as having consistently tried to maintain the Republican position. He never denied his willingness to compromise with the British, but now he contended the compromise would always have had to be consistent with the Republican ideal.

"Was that your attitude?" Griffith asked. "If so a penny post-card would have been sufficient to inform the British government without going to the trouble of sending us over."

De Valera began to explain but Griffith interrupted. "Did you not ask me to get you out of the strait-jacket of the Republic?"

"Oh, now gentlemen, this won't do any good," the archbishop interjected.

"I would like to explain," de Valera said, "because there is a background of truth to the statement." He said he was thinking of the strait-jacket of the isolated Republic when he asked Griffith to go over.

There was so much bitterness between Griffith and Collins on the one hand, and de Valera and Brugha on the other, that the two sides had to withdraw to separate rooms while others vainly tried to mediate.

Few people realised then that de Valera was largely impotent when it came to negotiating on behalf of hardline Republicans. "If de Valera were on your side," Mary MacSwiney wrote to Richard Mulcahy on 24 April 1922, "we should still fight on. We do not stand for men but for principles, and we could no more accept your Treaty than we could turn our backs on the Catholic Faith."

She was in for a rude awakening a couple of days later when the Catholic hierarchy issued a blistering condemnation of the "immoral usurpation and confiscation of the people's rights" by those in the Four Courts "who think themselves entitled to force their views upon the nation." The bishops added that "the one road to peace and ultimately to a united Ireland, is to leave it to the decision of the nation in a general election, as ordered by the existing government, and the sooner the election is held the better for Ireland."

O'Connor's faction was determined to prevent elections, however, and de Valera publicly supported them. From a purely democratic standpoint there were valid reasons for opposing an election. The electoral register was out of date, and the British were making a mockery of the democratic process by using their threat of war to bolster support for the Treaty.

The Colonial Secretary, Winston Churchill—who was charged with dealing with Irish affairs—was, in his own words, deliberately exploiting "the fear of renewed warfare" as a means of getting the Irish electorate to "go to the polls and support the Treaty." The Republicans realised this, so they threatened to resort to intimidation of their own if the elections were held.

De Valera rejected several suggestions put forward by Griffith and Collins to prevent intimidation at the polls. They even offered to arrange a referendum in which all adults could participate-whether their names were on the electoral register or not. The people would meet at the same time in designated localities throughout the country and would vote by passing through barriers where they would be counted, but he refused to consider such "Stone Age machinery." Anyway, he complained, the proposed referendum would only be held in the Twenty-six Counties, instead of throughout the island.

Northern Unionists were bitterly opposed to the Treaty, so the inclusion of the Six Counties could significantly alter the result of a referendum, but this was only a debating point. De Valera simply did not want any election at the time, and he publicly justified his refusal to co-operate on the grounds there were "rights which a minority may justly uphold, even by arms, against a majority." He was the one who had earlier insisted that the Treaty should be put to the people, now when his opponents were trying to do this and it was obvious he was going to lose, he wanted the vote postponed for a further six months. "Time would be secured for the present passions to subside," he argued, "for personalities to disappear, and the fundamental differences between the two sides to be appreciated—time during which Ireland's reputation could be vindicated, the work of national reconstruction begun, and normal conditions restored."

"We all believe in democracy," he told a correspondent of the *Chicago Tribune*, "but we do not forget its well-known weaknesses. As a safeguard against their consequences the most democratic countries have devised checks and brakes against sudden changes of opinion and hasty, ill-considered decisions." In America a treaty needed the approval of a two-thirds majority of the United States Senate for ratification. As the Irish system had "not yet had an opportunity of devising constitutional checks and brakes," he intimated it was legitimate for the anti-Treaty IRA to do so. "The

Army sees in itself the only brake at the present time, and is using its strength as such," he said.

For one who had championed the right to self-determination for years, de Valera had drifted into an untenable position in his efforts to obscure his own differences with Republican militants. Later he would regret his failure to speak out against them at this time, but he did seem to be proffering an olive branch while speaking in the Dáil on 17 May. Having consistently refused to recognise the Provisional Government, he now declared that "they could use any machinery" setup under the Treaty, provided they did not depart from fundamental principles. In short, he was ready to co-operate with the Provisional Government in matters which advanced the cause of Irish freedom.

Collins, who had pleaded with him to adopt such an attitude both before and after the Dáil voted on the Treaty, agreed to explore further the possibility of an agreement with him, and they concluded their famous election pact on 20 May 1922. In accordance with the pact, which was ratified by the Dáil, the two wings of Sinn Féin would put forward a united panel of candidates in ratio with their existing strength in the Dáil, and in the likely event the party was successful, they would form a kind of coalition government in which ministerial positions would be allocated on a five to four ratio in favour of the pro-Treaty wing, and the IRA would elect the Minister for Defence. In short, the Treaty would not be an election issue at all.

The British were furious on learning of the arrangement. Churchill complained it would be a violation of a Treaty provision stipulating that every member of the Provisional Government should signify acceptance of the Treaty. Although Griffith also had serious reservations, he defended what Collins had done as a means of advancing the Treaty.

"Does it matter if de Valera is in charge of education?" O'Higgins asked the British. "Are we bound to take steps which would wreck the Treaty?"

Without the pact, Collins contended, the anti-Treaty IRA would disrupt the elections by preventing balloting. Other parties and individuals were free to contest the election and as some of them were likely to defeat anti-Treaty Sinn Féin candidates, Collins confidently expected a pro-Treaty majority. This would not only be tantamount to endorsing the agreement, but would also undermine the existing argument that the Dáil had been elected on a platform to uphold the Irish Republic and did not therefore have the authority to implement the Treaty.

After mollifying Churchill's fears about the pact, Collins tried to use the election deadline to rush the British into accepting a constitution compatible with Document No. 2. The draft constitution excluded the Treaty-oath and incorporated an autochthony clause stipulating that "the legislative, executive, and judicial authority of Ireland shall be derived solely from the Irish people." There was also a clause stipulating that only the Free State parliament could declare war on behalf of the country. If the British parliament ratified such a constitution for the Irish Free State, this would be tantamount to acknowledging the right to neutrality—that prized right which de Valera had contended would make "a clean sweep" of the whole defence question during the Treaty negotiations.

Although the British accepted the bulk of the draft constitution, they balked at the exclusion of the oath. They insisted its omission would be a violation of the Treaty. After pressing hard for its exclusion, Collins finally relented. The oath was incorporated into the constitution and the Treaty itself was scheduled to the document, with the stipulation that in any conflict between the Treaty and the constitution, the Treaty would take precedence.

The text of the constitution was only released on the eve of the election. As a result the Irish people did not have a chance to see it until it was published in the daily newspapers on election day. While this fulfilled the strict letter of the Árd Fheis agreement to publish the constitution before the election, it effectively denied critics the chance of explaining the document before polling. By then Collins had also run rough-shod over the spirit of the election pact.

Speaking in Cork just two days before polling, he virtually asked voters to support others rather than vote for anti-Treaty candidates on the Sinn Féin panel. "I am not hampered now by being on a platform where there are coalitionists, and I can make a straight appeal to you, to the citizens of Cork, to vote for the candidates you think best of, whom the electors of Cork think will carry on best in the future the work that they want carried on," he said. "You understand fully what you have to do, and I will depend on you to do it."

There was no doubt this was a violation of the spirit, if not the actual letter, of the election pact. Of course, it should be pointed out that the anti-Treaty faction had already violated the pact by engaging in some blatant intimidation to prevent pro-Treaty independents and candidates of other parties contesting the election.

Even though Sinn Féin had deliberately avoided making the Treaty an election issue, there was no doubt the electorate favoured the Treaty. Of the sixty-five pro-Treaty Sinn Féin candidates, fifty-eight were elected, while only thirty-five of the anti-Treaty people were successful. But even those figures exaggerated the anti-Treaty support because 16 of them were returned without opposition. Where the seats were contested, forty-one of forty-eight pro-Treaty candidates were successful, while only nineteen of forty-one of the party's anti-Treaty candidates were elected.

The popular vote painted an even bleaker picture for the anti-Treaty side, which received less than twenty-two per cent of the first preference votes cast. Even though its forty-one candidates were more than double the number fielded by the Labour Party, their combined vote was a mere 1,353 votes more than the total of Labour's pro-Treaty candidates, who won seventeen of the eighteen seats they contested. There was absolutely no doubt that the Irish electorate favoured acceptance of the Treaty, at least as a short-term measure.

Nevertheless, some people had no intention of accepting the verdict. Two days after the election, the anti-Treaty IRA held another convention at which it was proposed to give the British government seventy-two hours notice that the Truce was being terminated. Although twelve of the sixteen-man executive supported the motion, it was vigorously opposed by the Chief of Staff, Liam Lynch, and also by Cathal Brugha. When the matter was put to a vote, the proposal was narrowly defeated by 118 to 103 votes.

Rory O'Connor and others refused to accept the decision. They returned to the Four Courts, where they locked out those who had voted against their motion. The twelve dissident members of the executive repudiated Lynch and elected a new Chief of Staff of their own, Joe McKelvey.

De Valera played no part in the machinations of those in the Four Courts. He concentrated instead on political matters. Confidently expecting to be a member of the new cabinet in line with the election pact, he planned to oppose the ratification of the new constitution in the Dáil, but the whole political climate was further poisoned with the assassination of Field Marshall Sir Henry Wilson in London on 22 June by two members of the IRA. The assassination sparked a chain of events which were to have tragic consequences for the nation.

Believing that those occupying the Four Courts were responsible for Wilson's murder, the British demanded the Provisional

Government put an end to the occupation without delay. "If it does not come to an end, if through weakness, want of courage, or some other even less creditable reason it is not brought to an end, and a speedy end," Churchill told the House of Commons, "then it is my duty to say, on behalf of His Majesty's Government, that we shall regard the Treaty as having been formally violated, that we shall take no steps to carry out or legalise its further stages, and that we shall resume full liberty of action in any direction that may seem proper."

It was Ireland's great misfortune at this time that the man at the helm of Irish affairs in Britain was someone as volatile and tempestuous as Churchill, who prided himself as a man of action, but whose judgement was suspect, to say the least. The British commander in Ireland, General Sir Neville Macready, was actually ordered to attack the Four Courts but astutely delayed, while those in the Four Courts forced the pace of events themselves. They planned to restart the struggle with the British in Northern Ireland. On 27 June they raided the premises of a Dublin car dealer and seized sixteen cars in which they planned to convoy a small force to the Six Counties. Forces of the Provisional Government managed to arrest some of the raiders, and those in the Four Courts retaliated by seizing "Ginger" O'Connell, the deputy Chief of Staff of the Provisional Government's army. Collins then retaliated with an ultimatum to those in the Four Courts to withdraw by the early hours of 28 June. When the time limit expired, the forces of the Provisional Government bombarded the Four Courts. In view of Churchill's comments in the House of Commons, the Republicans concluded that the attack was launched at the bidding of the British, who provided the heavy artillery. Just as the attack of Fort Sumter marked the opening of the American Civil War, the attack on the Four Courts has generally been considered the start of the Irish Civil War.

CHAPTER 10

"Principle and Expediency"

On learning of the assault on the Four Courts, de Valera condemned the pro-Treaty forces for attacking their former comrades in arms "at the bidding of the English." Those in the Four Courts "would most loyally have obeyed the will of the Irish people freely expressed," he contended and went on to ask the Irish people to rally to their assistance: "Irish citizens, give them support! Irish soldiers, bring them aid!"

He then enlisted in the IRA and joined those occupying the Gresham Hotel in the city centre. In spite of press reports to the contrary, he was never one of the recognised military leaders, though he did take an active part in trying to stop the hostilities. After the fall of the Four Courts his comrades at the Gresham were prepared to stop fighting and allow the whole issue to be settled by the Dáil, which was due to meet on 30 June 1922, but their offer was ignored.

De Valera sent messages to both Griffith and Collins who refused to talk unless the men would lay down their weapons. "Let them lay down their arms," the pro-Treaty leaders insisted, "and then we'll talk to them."

"Had the offer been accepted," de Valera later contended, "the whole civil war would have ended with the Four Courts incident and terms would have been arranged before the war had properly commenced." Griffith and Collins were apparently determined to force the IRA into line for once and for all. When they refused to talk, de Valera slipped out of Dublin and headed for Munster. He characterised as a *coup d'état* the government's decision to postpone the inaugural meeting of the new Dáil until 15 July 1922.

Although the Irish people had undoubtedly supported the Treaty at the polls, this did not mean that the pro-Treaty wing of Sinn Fein was given *carte blanche*. It had no authority to prorogue the new Dáil, especially as it comprised only a minority in the new assembly. Yet Griffith and the members of the Provisional Government took it upon themselves to ignore the new Dáil. Without even attempting to consult a majority of the new assembly, W.T. Cosgrave took over as chairman of the Provisional Government from Collins in July, and as acting President a fortnight later, following Griffith's death.

There was no legal basis for these actions, and de Valera was further irritated that they had never even asked for his nominees for the new cabinet, as they should have done in accordance with the Pact, which was legally binding because it had been passed by the second Dáil.

Instead of spotlighting the usurping activities of the Provisional Government, however, the press rounded on de Valera, whom it characterised as the Republican leader, and saddled him with the brunt of the responsibility for the Civil War, even though he really had little influence with the Republican leadership. "The newspapers are as usual more deadly to our cause than the machine guns," he complained.

While on the run in Munster de Valera was preoccupied with the thought of arranging peace. He had no doubt the majority of the people were critical of the IRA. "In Fermoy, Mallow, and other towns, the people looked at us sullenly, as if we had belonged to a hostile invading army," Robert Brennan recalled. "Dev had seen all this, as had I, and that was one of the reasons he was so desperately trying for peace while he still had some bargaining power."

Many good men had fallen. Brugha had been killed, as had Harry Boland. On the other side Griffith died following a massive stroke on 9 August. De Valera, who spoke kindly of the dead President, feared Collins would try to set up a military dictatorship after he took over as Commander-in-Chief of the Free State Army. "Any chance of winning?" de Valera asked himself. He was convinced the Irish people would have to be won over "to the cause before any successful fighting can be done," so he felt a duty to persuade "the men to quit—for the present."

"Dev says 'we should surrender while we are strong'," Childers wrote at the time. But Liam Lynch, who had become the undisputed Chief of Staff of the Republican forces following the fall of the Four Courts, had no intention of surrendering, and he instructed his Deputy Chief of Staff, Liam Deasy, to give the former President no encouragement.

De Valera met Deasy in Gurranereagh, County Cork, on 21 August. "We discussed the war situation far into the night," Deasy recalled. "His main argument was that, having made our protest in arms and as we could not now hope to achieve a military success, the honourable course was for us to withdraw." Deasy agreed to an extent but pointed out that the majority of the IRA "would not agree to an unconditional cease fire."

Next morning Deasy accompanied de Valera to the cross at Béal na mBláth, where they learned Collins had just passed through the area. When de Valera asked what the IRA intended to do, Deasy replied they would prepare an ambush in case Collins returned by the same route. One of those present remarked that Collins might not leave his native county alive.

"I know," replied de Valera, "and I am sorry for it. He is a big man and might negotiate. If things fall into the hands of lesser men there is no telling what might happen."

Next day de Valera learned Collins had indeed returned by the same route and had been killed in the ensuing engagement. The former President did not share the elation of the man who brought the news. "It's come to a very bad pass when Irish men congratulate themselves on the shooting of a man like Michael Collins," he said. It seemed as if he momentarily forgot that he personally held Collins largely responsible for the Civil War.

Collins must indeed share some of the blame for the conflict, because in his efforts to avoid it, he compromised himself by trying to do the impossible. He worked tirelessly to placate both the Republicans and the British. In the process he tried to reconcile the irreconcilable and opened himself to the charge of duplicity by making contradictory commitments that he could not possibly keep. Professor T. Desmond Williams concluded that both de Valera and Collins were largely to blame for the Civil War because, he wrote: "Collins tried to do too much, de Valera too little."

Once the fighting began, however, de Valera did try to persuade his side to stop. After failing to persuade Lynch and Deasy, he asked to be allowed to address the IRA Executive, but Lynch refused to call a meeting. De Valera went so far as to meet secretly with Collins's successor, Richard Mulcahy, on 6 September. He told Mulcahy he did not agree with what was being done by the Republicans and had no responsibility for it, but he added that the IRA leaders believed in what they were doing, and he would follow them as a humble soldier as long as they continued. He asked about finding some kind of basis for peace in a revision of the Treaty, but Mulcahy insisted the Treaty terms were not negotiable.

The former President was despondent afterwards. "We have all become involved in the most hateful of conflicts—Civil War—in which there can be no glory and no enthusiasm, unless one allows himself to be mastered by the spirit of party faction. Worst of all, there seems to be no way out of it. I am convinced that there is the will for peace on both sides, but no basis is discoverable on which it can be made." He added:

IF THE REPUBLICANS STAND ASIDE AND LET THE TREATY COME INTO FORCE, IT MEANS ACQUIESCENCE IN THE ABANDONMENT OF THE NATIONAL SOVEREIGNTY AND IN THE PARTITION OF THE COUNTRY—A SURRENDER OF THE IDEALS FOR WHICH THE SACRIFICES OF THE PAST FEW YEARS WERE DELIBERATELY MADE AND THE SUFFERINGS OF THESE YEARS CONSCIOUSLY ENDURED.

IF THE REPUBLICANS DO NOT STAND ASIDE, THEN THEY MUST RESIST, AND RESISTANCE MEANS JUST THIS:—CIVIL WAR AND ARMED OPPOSITION TO WHAT IS UNDOUBTEDLY, AS I HAVE SAID, THE DECISION OF THE MAJORITY OF THE PEOPLE.

FOR REPUBLICANS THE CHOICE IS, THEREFORE, BETWEEN A HEARTBREAKING SURRENDER OF WHAT THEY HAVE REPEATEDLY PROVED WAS DEARER TO THEM THAN LIFE AND THE REPUDIATION OF WHAT THEY RECOGNISE TO BE THE BASIS OF ALL ORDER IN GOVERNMENT AND THE KEYSTONE OF DEMOCRACY—MAJORITY RULE.

IS IT ANY WONDER THERE IS, SO TO SPEAK, A CIVIL WAR GOING ON IN THE MINDS OF MOST OF US, AS WELL AS IN THE COUNTRY (WHERE WE HAVE BROTHER ACTUALLY PITTED AGAINST BROTHER)?

When the third Dáil eventually convened on 9 September de Valera decided to stay away for reasons of "principle and expediency." He felt justified in principle because his opponents were "guilty of every sort of unconstitutional and illegal action." He argued that the IRA Executive could justifiably assert that the new Dáil was "an illegal assembly in as much it was summoned by the illegal junta called the 'Provisional Government'." Since the second Dáil had not met as it should have done after the June elections in order to dissolve formally before the third convened, Republicans could contend that the second Dáil was still the country's legitimate parliament.

Although the Treaty had not been an election issue, de Valera privately admitted that the election results left no room for doubt that the majority of the Irish people clearly favoured the Treaty. He thought it would be expedient, however, for the Republicans to stay away from the Dáil, because they could not be effective there, as they would be greatly outnumbered and, to make matters worse, the divisions within their own ranks would be exposed. "Our presence at the meeting would only help to solidify all other groups against us," he wrote. "We would be the butt of every attack. We could not explain—we would be accused of obstructing the business and 'talking' when we should 'get on with the work."

He personally toyed with the idea of repudiating the Dáil and setting up a Republican government instead. Some IRA leaders called on Republican members of the Dáil to meet separately as the legitimate parliament. Even if it proved impossible to muster the necessary quorum of twenty members, they argued that the requirement could be fulfilled by deeming any deputy who was prevented from attending to be present "in spirit."

"This is no use," de Valera declared. It was not that he disliked the idea of setting up such a government, but he did not believe it would be possible to sustain it. "If the Army Executive were at hand and would definitely give allegiance to the government, I'd think it wise to try it," but he knew this was not going to happen. Without the unconditional allegiance of the IRA Executive, the proposed Republican government "would be a farce," he argued. And the IRA Executive had already repudiated all political control. "Rory O'Connor's unfortunate repudiation of the Dáil, which I was so foolish as to defend, even to a straining of my own views in order to avoid the appearance of split, is now the greatest barrier that we have," de Valera wrote.

The Republican politicians had placed themselves in an invidious position by accepting the IRA Executive's repudiation of political control. "Our position as public representatives is impossible," de Valera complained. "The position of the political party must be straightened out. If it is the policy of the party to leave it all to the army, well, then the obvious thing for members of the party to do is to resign their positions as public representatives. The present position is that we have all the public responsibility and no voice and no authority." In an effort to pressurise Lynch, he even threatened to resign. "If I do not get the position made quite clear, I shall resign publicly."

"I am almost wishing I were deposed," de Valera wrote to McGarrity, "for the present position places upon me the responsibility for carrying out a programme which was not mine." The IRA was trying to destroy the Treaty and all that it stood for, whereas he only wanted to revise it. "The programme 'Revise the Treaty' would be mine," he added, "and I could throw myself into it heart and soul. I am convinced it is the only way for the present to keep the Republican idea alive."

He knew the armed struggle was doomed to fail and he was already thinking of the lines he would pursue afterwards. "If the Free State should become operative, and the present physical resistance fails," he wrote, "I see no programme by which we can secure independence but a revival of the Sinn Fein idea in a new form. *Ignoring England.* Acting in Ireland as if there was no such person as the English King, no Governor-General, no Treaty, no oath of allegiance. In fact acting as if Document [No] 2 were the Treaty. Later we could act more independently still. Whilst the Free State were in supposed existence would be the best time to secure the unity of the country. That is my one hope out of the situation. If we can get a single state for the whole country, then the future is safe."

Although he had contended during September that any Republican government established without the "unconditional allegiance" of the IRA would only be "a farce," he actively partook in such a farce the following month after the Roman Catholic hierarchy condemned the IRA for waging "what they call a war, but which, in the absence of any legitimate authority to justify it, is morally only a system of murder and assassination." Calling for the virtual excommunication of all those fighting on the Republican side, the bishops appealed to the people to support the government: "We desire to impress on the people the duty of supporting the national government, whatever it is, to set their faces resolutely against disorder, to pay their taxes, rents, and annuities, and to assist the government in every possible way to restore order and establish peace."

The Republican side had no government so there was no doubt the bishops had come out solidly behind the Provisional Government. Under the circumstances, de Valera changed his mind about setting up a Republican regime. At least it afforded him the opportunity of regaining some say over the Republican forces. "I do not care what Republican government is set up, so long as one is," he explained, "only I will not take responsibility if I do not get the corresponding authority to act in accordance with my best judgement. If the Army think I am too moderate, well let them get a better President and go ahead."

Of course, he was convinced it was not possible to get a better President than himself, so he went ahead and secretly convened a meeting of six members of the second Dáil in Dublin on 25 October to set up an "Emergency Government." They elected him President and he appointed a twelve member Council of State to advise the cabinet, which he subsequently selected.

In the following weeks the Republican government issued a series of proclamations renouncing all debts contracted by the Provisional Government, rescinding the Dail's approval of the Treaty, outlawing the existing courts, but few people were impressed, because the Republican regime was surrounded by an air of sheer unreality. It was supposed to be advised by the Council of State, for instance, but the advisory body was unable to meet because many of its members were arrested before they could get together. On top of that, some of de Valera's cabinet choices were already in jail, but he chose them anyway so that they would be regarded as nominally filling the positions.

Many of the people he hoped would support the new government refused to have anything to do with it because, even though they sympathised with Republican aims, they did not approve of fighting their fellow countrymen against the will of the majority of the people. Thus, in order to enlist their active support, it was going to be necessary to win over the Irish people, but the press was so hostile that there was little chance of getting the Republican message across to them. "Poor 'people'," de Valera wrote, "how one begins almost to despair of democracy when one realises how little of the truth is allowed to reach them and how misleading the information on which they must form their judgments."

There were some developments in November that seemed to provide propaganda opportunities, such as Mary MacSwiney's decision to go on hunger-strike to protest her imprisonment. Comparisons would inevitably be drawn with the stand taken by her late brother, the Lord Mayor of Cork, Terence MacSwiney, who had received enormous international publicity for the Republican cause two years earlier when he died after a protracted hunger-strike in protest against his imprisonment by the British. Once she began her fast, however, it was imperative that she should persevere to the bitter end, or her protest would prove counter-productive.

"When Terry was dying, knowing how conscientious he was and how good, I feared that he might have some scruples about what he was doing, and intended giving him an official order to continue, as I might to a soldier running great risks on the battle-field," de Valera wrote to her. "For him to surrender having begun would have been not personal defeat, but defeat for his cause. Your case is the same and may the God of Calvary give your spirit the necessary strength to endure to the last if need be and take you to Himself when your ordeal is ended."

The propaganda potential of the protest was enhanced after eleven days when her sister, Annie, went on a sympathy hunger-strike outside the gates of Mountjoy Jail, but before the whole protest was able to capture the public imagination, the Provisional Government released Mary MacSwiney and transferred her to hospital. She had won, but her victory was completely overshadowed by other events during her three-week fast.

Following the bishops' pronouncement the Provisional Government had made a concerted effort to break the back of the Republican resistance by offering an amnesty to anyone giving up the fight, but at the same time it made the possession of any arms a capital offence. On 10 November Childers was captured in possession of a small pearl-handled revolver given to him by Collins during the Black and Tan period. "The gun he had in his possession," de Valera wrote, "was an automatic that Mick gave, telling him to defend the Republic. I saw it with him myself—a tiny automatic, little better than a toy and in no sense a war weapon."

"They may ill-treat him," de Valera wrote to Childers's wife, "but I do not think they will dare execute him." Nobody had been executed yet, and de Valera was not worried for the safety of Childers, at least not at first. In fact, he advocated that Childers retain legal counsel and use the trial for propaganda purposes. "The trial would educate our people as nothing else would," de Valera wrote. But the Republican regime had already decided not to recognise the courts, especially the military tribunals established for the duration of the Civil War. Childers therefore put up no real defence on 17 November. Through his counsel he merely demanded he be treated as a prisoner of war, and he rejected the tribunal's right to try him, but by then it was obvious the Provisional Government meant business because four members of the IRA were executed that day after being found guilty of possessing weapons by a military tribunal. Next day the tribunal duly found Childers guilty and sentenced him to death.

De Valera decided Childers should appeal, even though this meant recognising what were legally the Crown courts of the Provisional Government. "These wretches," he wrote, alluding to the members of Cosgrave's cabinet, "are now desperate, and cruel with the cruelty of desperation, and they have by their infamous propaganda so prepared the way for the dark deeds they contemplate that it is necessary to dispute every inch of the way with them by every available means. Erskine's name is so much better known than any of the others that the case will rouse the conscience of all the best of our people." It was, in short, a good propaganda opportunity; Childers, who first came to international prominence as a bestselling author almost two decades earlier, was so well-known that his appeal would be covered by the press and the Irish people would therefore get to hear of his plight whereas "the case of an unknown person would be passed over in silence and not reach them."

Although the subsequent appeal, lasting four days, received extensive publicity, the court rejected the defence contention that the military courts were illegally constituted, and it dismissed the appeal on the grounds that "once a state of war arises, the civil courts have no jurisdiction over the acts of the military during the continuance of hostilities." With those words Childers's fate was sealed. He was executed early the following morning.

"Of all the men I have ever met Childers was the noblest and the best," de Valera wrote to Sinead. "I never met a man with whom I would have changed personalities except him and I only wish I could hope for as high a place in heaven as I am sure he will occupy."

One particularly infuriating aspect of the execution was the injustice of picking on Childers who, de Valera felt, was in "no way responsible" for the Civil War. "Well may God forgive them," he added. "I would not like to let myself write what I feel." Even though he had been thinking in terms of surrendering only weeks earlier, there was now a distinct hardening in his attitude. "We must win now," he declared. "I am glad that we have the government formed before this. It is so much easier to die for a definite positive programme."

But not everybody on his side believed in what de Valera considered positive. Liam Lynch reacted to the executions by warning that unless IRA captives were treated properly as prisoners of war, his men would "adopt very drastic measures" to protect themselves. Henceforth, the IRA announced, all those who had voted for capital punishment were legitimate targets.

On 7 December 1922, the day after the Irish Free State was formally established and Provisional Government replaced by a new government with Cosgrave as President of its cabinet, or Executive Council as it was called, the IRA shot two members of the Dáil outside Leinster House. The new Free State government promptly retaliated next morning by summarily "executing" four of its most prominent Republican prisoners—Rory O'Connor, Joe McKelvey, Liam Mellows, and Dick Barrett, all of whom had been held without trial since the fall of the Four Courts. The following week the IRA reacted by burning the homes of a number of Dáil members and in the process killed the young son of one deputy.

These tit-for-tat killings were too much for de Valera, who thought such reprisals were counter-productive. "The policy of an eye for an eye is not going to win the people to us, and without the people we can never win," he complained to Lynch. "The recent burnings were, in my opinion, peurile and futile from a military or any other point of view." While believing it was perfectly legitimate to burn Free State offices, de Valera drew the line at burning family homes. "Terrorist methods may silence those of our opponents who are cowards," he wrote, "but many of them are very far from being cowards, and attempts at terrorism will only stiffen the bold men among them. I am against such methods on principle, and believe we will never win in this war unless we attach the people to our government by contrast with theirs."

He thought the only hope the Republicans had of victory was to win over a large segment of the Free State Army, or else secure the overwhelming support of the people. Hence he was very conscious of matters showing Republican forces in an unfavourable light. He did not want to tie their hands in defending themselves against outrageous behaviour by their opponents, but, he warned Lynch, "the other side is dragging us and the country step by step into the mire with itself. I want to break the vicious circle somewhere, if I can."

The Republicans suffered a serious psychological setback in late January following the capture of Deasy, their Deputy Chief of Staff. He signed a document calling on all his colleagues to agree to an "immediate and unconditional surrender." This appeal, which was quietly circularised to Lynch, de Valera, and others, was published when no response was forthcoming. With the Republican position apparently crumbling, de Valera's determination to salvage something from the struggle became most apparent.

"Some of our good men are falling by the way," he wrote to McGarrity. "The critical moment here has just arrived. Both sides are strained to the utmost, but I think we can bear it better than our opponents can, tho' at this very moment we received the biggest blow we have got since we started. If they find that it doesn't knock us out they will despair, I think. Already they are divided into a war party and a peace party, almost of equal strength, I am told. We are a far more homogenous body than they are. If this war were finished Ireland would not have the heart to fight another war for generations, so we must see it through."

In view of the Deasy affair, "the biggest blow" to which de Valera alluded, it was important for Republican forces to dispel the impression that they were on the verge of collapse, with the result that de Valera enthusiastically supported an IRA plan for a campaign of sabotage in Britain. "Were we to abandon the Republic now," he wrote, "it would be a greater blow to our ideals and to the prestige of the nation than even the abandonment on December 6th, 1921. In taking it upon ourselves to be champions of this cause we have incurred obligations which we must fulfil even to death." He therefore advised Lynch to make sure the initial operation in Britain was a big, concerted one followed by a series of other blows.

Just as in the Black and Tan period de Valera was thinking in terms of a military campaign conducted to exert political pressure on the other side to seek a negotiated settlement. He even seemed to think that the Republicans might still be successful, especially with outside help. "We are at the critical stage now," he wrote to J.J. O'Kelly, a Republican emissary then in the United States. "If our friends everywhere made one big effort we could win and smash the others. It must be death or glory for us now."

There was no military evidence to justify de Valera's melo-dramatic optimism, but he was thinking in terms of the political situation. On 7 February he wrote to Lynch suggesting they take the initiative to find "a constitutional way" out of the impasse. "If we make a decent peace offer which will command the support of reasonable people the others can't proceed and we shall have a victory."

The Free State authorities were coming under strong political pressure to seek peace. Looking back on the civil war some months later, Cosgrave noted the "worst moments had been in February" when some senators had "shown a tendency to buckle, and had come to tell him that he must make terms with de Valera."

"De Valera hopes to bring about negotiations which will en-able him to make a dignified escape from his present position," Cosgrave declared publicly at the time, "but we are not going to help anybody in that way." O'Higgins made it clear the govern-ment was determined to pursue its campaign with full vigour. "The people who continue to act with Mr de Valera in his criminal con-spiracy against the life and future of the Irish nation, will have no cause for complaint if the Irish nation, acting on its instincts of self-defence and self-preservation, deals with them in a very summary and very ruthless fashion," O'Higgins declared.

He had become a particular hate figure of the Republicans be-cause of his outspoken support of the government of which he was both Vice President and Minister for Justice. In the latter post he was nominally responsible for the executions which included that of his good friend, Rory O'Connor, who had been the best man at his wedding barely a year earlier. Even though he had been per-sonally opposed to the execution, he felt duty bound to preserve cabinet unity and endorse the action publicly. As a result he would never be forgiven by the Republicans, who extracted a murderous revenge. On 11 February 1923 O'Higgins's father was shot at his home in front of his wife and teenage daughter. Such actions, of course, only made de Valera's quest for peace much harder.

He considered issuing a personal statement suggesting all disputed issues be submitted to a vote of the Irish people, with the will of the majority forming "the ultimate court of appeal," not because the majority would necessarily be right or just, but because this would afford a peaceful, democratic alternative to force. But he ran into strong Republican opposition when he sent a copy of his proposed statement to Mary MacSwiney.

Warning that the statement would "be a bigger blow than Liam Deasy's and do more harm," she insisted he did not have the authority to make proposals without the approval of the IRA Executive. She was adamantly opposed to the idea of recognising the people as the ultimate court of appeal. "If that is granted," she complained, "our civil war has no sanction; the bishops are quite justified; and so is everything the F[ree] S[taters] have said to us. And if it is right now to submit to majority rule on this point, it was equally right last July. What have all the lives been lost for?"

Faced with this hardline opposition, de Valera backed away from his proposed initiative and proceeded to take a very different line the following week when he answered some questions submitted by a correspondent of the International News Service. He listed four reasons why Republicans could not agree to be bound by the will of the majority in the Irish Free State. One, he said the people had no right to vote away any part of the national heritage, as it belonged to "all generations." Two, the whole thirty-two counties of Ireland would have to be consulted, not just the twenty-six of the Free State. Three, no vote could be free so long as the British threat of war remained. Four, Republicans had no means of getting their views across to the people because the press was so hostile. "One cannot submit to the judgement of a court which cannot be informed of the facts," he concluded.

Blocked in his effort to make a new peace initiative, de Valera resorted to an old one, resurrecting his Document No 2. "The way to peace is to remove the threat of war," he told a representative of the Press Association. "Let England signify her willingness to accept the proposals which I put forward as an alternative to the 'Treaty,' January a year ago, and if there are any who prefer the 'Treaty,' let the Irish people decide as between the 'Treaty' and these proposals." Even though some Republicans were not satisfied with Document No 2, he said they would not resist it in arms. He was personally prepared to sponsor his proposals "as a basis of an honourable peace" at any time, he said. "The fact that these proposals, and my statements have been 'twisted by knaves to make a trap for fools' doesn't take away from the truth that is in them."

De Valera was in an unenviable position. "I have been condemned to view the tragedy here for the last year as through a wall of glass, powerless to intervene effectively." His opponents were holding him responsible for the civil war, while some of his own side were frustrating his efforts to secure a negotiated settlement. "Miss MacSwiney would probably feel justified in taking the initiative in starting this war," he wrote, "I would not." She was insisting he secure the approval of the IRA Executive for any peace proposals, and Lynch was refusing to convene the Executive. He even took exception to de Valera talking about Document No. 2, which, he complained, was having "a very bad effect" on Republican soldiers. "Generally they do not understand such documents," he wrote to de Valera. "We can arrange peace without referring to past documents."

De Valera was furious. "I will take no further responsibility for publicly handling the situation if I have, at every turn, to account for what I say to people who have not given a moment's thought to the whole question," he wrote to Lynch. Many good men had already come to the conclusion that there was no hope of victory, "and if you were to hold that the objective was the 'isolated' Republic, I would say they were right." He also wrote a frank, rather insulting letter to Mary MacSwiney complaining that while she tended to overestimate Republican strength and underestimate that of the Free State, he tended to do the opposite. "Of the two," he continued, "I have no doubt that an omniscient being would rate my error as but a very small fraction of yours—vanity?" It was indeed ironic that he should assume the insight of an omniscient being to accuse somebody else of vanity!

Meanwhile the military position of the Republicans continued to deteriorate. Plans for the sabotage campaign in Britain were undermined with the arrest and deportation of those who were to carry out the campaign. At the same time Free State forces began acting in the "summary and very ruthless manner" that O'Higgins had talked about even before his father was killed. During early March there were three separate horrific incidents in Kerry involving the Free State Army. On 7 March 1923 nine Republican prisoners were taken from Tralee to Ballyseedy Cross, where they were tied to the stump of a tree in which a mine had been placed. The mine was then detonated, killing eight of the men and so mutilating their bodies that the perpetrators failed to realise that one of the men had been blown clear and survived to tell what had happened. There was a relatively similar incident near Killarney the same day in which another man survived, but the following week Free State troops in Cahirciveen shot five prisoners in each leg to make sure that none could escape before blowing them up with a mine. In this instance, one of the Free State soldiers was so revolted by the behaviour of his colleagues that he defected and told the story. The war had degenerated to greater depths of depravity than even in the Black and Tan period.

Lynch was no longer able to resist calls for a meeting of the IRA Executive. When it eventually convened in the Waterford mountains on 23 March, de Valera had to suffer the indignity of having to wait outside for three-quarters of an hour, while those inside argued over whether or not to admit him. When he was finally admitted, he was told he would have no vote but could speak in favour of a motion advocating that continued resistance would "not further the cause of independence."

Lynch was strongly opposed to the motion, and he managed to carry the day by six votes to five. Nevertheless de Valera was authorised to investigate prospects of securing a settlement which would not be inimical to his own announced principles. The meeting then adjourned until 10 April 1923.

In the following days Free State authorities, who were determined—in the words of O'Higgins—that the war was "not going to be a draw with a replay in the autumn," showed little interest in de Valera's peace overtures. But he was nevertheless convinced that the Republicans should quit the armed struggle and turn to political methods. "To me our duty seems plain, to end the conflict without delay," de Valera wrote to Paddy Ruttledge on 9 April. "Those who would continue working for our independence must gird themselves for a long patient effort of reorganisation and education."

That same day Lynch was shot and fatally wounded, so the IRA Executive cancelled its proposed meeting for the following day. In the wake of Lynch's death, de Valera professed an emotional desire to continue the struggle but contended it would not be justifiable. "I am afraid," he wrote, "we shall have to face the inevitable sooner or later, bow to force and resort to other methods, either ourselves or those to whom we leave the future of the cause."

While privately arguing for peace, de Valera adopted a very different approach publicly in order not to undermine whatever negotiating position the Republicans had. "It is better to die nobly as your chief has died than live like a slave," he declared in an address to Republican forces, adding that their cause was immortal—"defeats may defer but cannot prevail against its ultimate triumph."

On 27 April de Valera was finally able to put forward the terms he had wanted to offer back in February. He publicly offered to call off the Republican campaign on condition that the sovereign rights of the nation were recognised as "indefeasible and inalienable" with all legitimate legislative, executive, and judicial authority being derived from the Irish people, who would be "the ultimate court of appeal." He further stipulated that no citizen should be debarred from the government or parliament because of a refusal to take an oath. To show his good faith, he announced all Republicans were being ordered "to suspend aggressive action" by not later than noon of the last day of April.

Next day he met two senators, Andrew Jameson and James Douglas, with a view to having them act as intermediaries. They contacted Cosgrave, who authorised them to present the Free State's terms, which demanded that the Republicans accept that all issues should "be decided by the majority vote of the elected representatives of the people," and that they should give up their weapons. Cosgrave reportedly said he was not interested in the weapons themselves. "They can be delivered up to a bishop anywhere," he said. "Let them be burned, but these arms cannot, and will not, if I have any responsibility for the government of this country, remain in the hands of those who are not subject to the authority of the people's parliament." In return all military action against the Republicans would be suspended, and they would be free "to canvass for the votes of the people at the next general election, provided they undertook to adhere strictly to constitutional action." Cosgrave would not undertake to negotiate with the British in regard to the oath, so the Republicans would have to subscribe to it, if they were to sit in the Free State Dáil.

The terms were basically quite liberal, but de Valera rejected them. The question of surrendering arms had been the issue on which his peace initiative had foundered when he was in the Gresham Hotel at the start of the civil war, and he had always insisted no conscientious Republican could take the Treaty-oath. If he surrendered on those issues now, it would mean the whole civil war had been for nothing. He therefore reissued his terms on 7 May with the added stipulation that pending an election, a suitable building would be furnished in each province so "Republican arms shall be stored up, sealed up, and defended by specially pledged Republican guards—these arms to be disposed of after the elections by reissue to their present holders, or in such other manner as may secure the consent of the government then elected." In publishing those terms the anti-Treaty weekly, *Éire*, noted that the conditions "were intended simply as a basis for discussion." It was obvious that de Valera was looking desperately for some way for the Republican soldiers to save some face, but Cosgrave insisted that his government's terms were not negotiable.

Some years later de Valera contended that the government's intransigent attitude was personally motivated to ensure he would not be able to get back into public life. "It is a terrible thing to think," he said, "that men could be animated in big things by such mean motives." Blinded by his own self-righteous conviction, he failed to appreciate any views other than his own. Cosgrave's main point was that the Republicans should accept the majority wishes of the people. De Valera personally accepted this himself, but he was so busy trying to save face that he was not willing to accept it openly without clouding the issue.

In mid-May he outlined the situation for the IRA Executive and the available members of his Emergency Government at a secret meeting in the Dublin suburbs. He contended that the only alternatives open to them were of surrendering unconditionally or else just dumping their weapons and quitting the fight without any kind of surrender. He favoured the latter course, and those present agreed with him. On 24 April, therefore, Frank Aiken, the new Chief of Staff of the IRA, simply ordered the Republican forces to dump their arms and accept that the enemy had "for the moment prevailed." De Valera issued a simultaneous statement emphasising that there was no longer any hope of military success. "Further sacrifice of life would now be vain and continuance of the struggle in arms unwise in the national interest and prejudicial to the future of our cause," he declared. "Military victory must be allowed to rest for the moment with those who have destroyed the Republic."

CHAPTER 11

"Publicity Before All"

Following the cessation of hostilities the struggle moved back into the political arena from which de Valera never really believed it should have strayed, notwithstanding some of his own public pronouncements to the contrary. He again came to the fore on the Republican side, having embarked on the enormous task of rebuilding his political influence. His eventual recovery from the disastrous mistakes of the past two years was unquestionably one of the greatest feats in the democratic politics of the twentieth century.

De Valera believed the best way of achieving ultimate Republican objectives was to pursue the policy he had outlined to McGarrity in September 1922, before setting up the so-called Emergency Government. "I have been thinking whether it would not be possible to devise some scheme by which the real power of the nation would reside in some assembly outside any kind of parliament elected by their F[ree] S[tate] machinery—but I do not think anything of the kind is feasible," he wrote. The only policy likely to succeed was, he wrote, to ignore any aspect of the Treaty inconsistent with independence and squeeze "England out by a kind of boycott of Gov. General, etc." This would entail violating the Treaty and breaking the oath and "then compelling England to tolerate the breaches or bring her to a revision which would lead to something like the Doc[ument No]. 2 position."

Since the Republicans had avowedly only called off their military campaign "for the moment," they were still liable to arrest, and de Valera had to stay in hiding and rely on statements to the press to get his message across to the public. In one of these, on 28 June 1923, he announced that Sinn Féin candidates would contest the next general election to "give the people an opportunity to put on record by their first preference votes their detestation of allegiance to a foreign king, their repudiation of partition, and their desire for a government which would really be obedient to their own will, and not an instrument of British domination." Since the Boundary Commission had not met and the financial issue had not yet been finally settled, he contended the people had "not yet come to realise the humiliation of it all."

"But," he added, "they soon will. The fate of the North East boundary clause and the amount of Ireland's share of the Imperial burden will be determined sometime. When it is, and the boundary clause has been waived, or some new ignominious bargain has been struck to evade it, and when, in addition, the full weight of an Imperial contribution of some ten to fifteen millions annually is being pressed upon their shoulders, the people will surely wake up, become conscious of the full extent of the deception that has been practiced upon them, and learn what it is that those who gave their lives to prevent the consummation of this 'Treaty' hoped to save them from."

After Cosgrave called a general election for August, de Valera gave his first firm, public indication of his determination to follow a political path and rule out further military activity. In an interview with an American correspondent, he emphasised that the Republicans were serious about adopting a political approach. "It is not the intention," he said, "to renew the war in the autumn or after the elections. The war, so far as we are concerned, is finished."

"We intend to devote ourselves to social reform, and to education, and to developing the economic and material strength of the nation," he added. "Politically we shall continue to deny the right, and to combat the exercise, of any foreign authority in Ireland. In particular we shall refuse to admit that our country may be carved up and partitioned by such an authority." If Sinn Féin won a majority in the election, he said his government would refuse "to co-operate with England in any way until England was ready to make with us an arrangement as would make a stable peace possible—that is, an arrangement consistent with independence and unity of our country and people as a single state."

Although de Valera had virtually ignored the partition issue during the Treaty debate, he now began raising it with increasing emphasis in his public statements—and often with a distinct lack of candour. In a letter to the *Irish Independent* he implied that the partition clauses were under discussion when Griffith made the famous promise not to sign the Treaty. He went on to state he had "never been able to understand" how Griffith had "allowed himself to be deluded by the Boundary Commission idea." But de Valera should have understood this better than anyone because he had accepted the same scheme himself and actually included the relevant Treaty clauses verbatim in Document No. 2.

While de Valera was in hiding, members of Cumann na nGaedheal campaigned openly about the country. Cosgrave and Desmond FitzGerald were in Tralee when someone in the crowd shouted: "What about de Valera?"

"De Valera is on the run, because he acted as an enemy of this country," FitzGerald replied. "As long as we are in power, de Valera and every other enemy of the country will have to be on the run."

Next day de Valera responded with another statement, this time asserting that he and his colleagues had no intention of remaining in hiding indefinitely. "Living or dead, we mean to establish the right of Irish Republicans to live and work openly for the complete liberation of our country," he declared. "Our opponents make a mistake if they imagine that we are going to remain on the run. If the people of Clare select me as their candidate again, I will be with them and nothing but a bullet will stop me."

He was duly selected to stand by the Sinn Féin organisation in Clare, and he announced he would address a public meeting in Ennis on 15 August 1923. He realised his life would be in danger if he fell into the hands of Free State troops, because Noel Lemass—whose younger brother, Seán, would one day succeed de Valera—had recently disappeared after being arrested, but de Valera thought the personal danger would be minimised and the political advantage maximised if he could get on the platform so his arrest would be witnessed by a crowd. In that event the Free State authorities would be placed in the position of appearing to oppose free speech, and they would be clearly seen to be responsible if anything happened to him subsequently.

Taking care to avoid detection, he made his way to Ennis by a circuitous route, and managed to make it to the platform in the town's square undetected. It was about 2.30 in the afternoon when he took off his coat and cap and walked to the front of the platform.

"There he is!" someone shouted. "My God, 'tis himself."

A great roar went up as he stood there looking unmoved. He seemed calm but looked pale and drawn, having only, the night before, shaved off the beard and moustache he had used for disguise since the start of the civil war. He began with a few perfunctory words in Gaelic before breaking into English, but he had only barely begun when Free State troops surrounded the platform. Friends gathered around him. "I have to go," he shouted to the crowd, "but I am glad it is in Clare that I am being taken."

Suddenly the soldiers began firing and elements of the crowd stampeded. Amid the confusion de Valera was knocked and was wounded in the leg by a small bullet fragment. He made it clear to the Free State officer in charge that he had no intention of resisting arrest and the soldiers should therefore have some consideration for the crowd. A number of those on the platform tried to cling to him as he limped off with the troops.

"We have arrested the man who called up anarchy and crime, and who did more damage than anyone could have conceived, or than was ever done by the British," O'Higgins declared next day in Rathmines. "Through him, and at his instigation, a number of young blackguards had robbed banks, blown up bridges, and wrecked railways, and that in the name of an Irish Republic." O'Higgins added, "The real issue in the election is—anarchy versus law and order, and the government candidates stand for law and order and decency."

While O'Higglns probably believed what he was saying, Republicans could hardly be blamed for seeing things differently. It was a strange kind of law and order the government was standing for when no one was ever brought to justice for the barbaric excesses of Free State troops in Kerry, nor were any charges brought against de Valera, who would have welcomed the chance to defend himself in court.

The Cosgrave government decided to prosecute him "with the least possible delay," but the Attorney General was only able to put together a pathetic case. The only "real evidence" that could be found to substantiate any charge of misconduct during the civil war was an inflammatory letter de Valera had written to the secretary of Cumann na mBan on 5 January 1923. In view of the enormity of the accusations made by members of the government, it would have been utterly ludicrous if he was charged only with inciting Cumann na mBan, of all organisations! Yet the government ordered he should be held indefinitely as a danger to "public safety."

Throughout the civil war many Republicans had looked on de Valera with deep suspicion and distrust. They did not agree with his Document No. 2 and they were suspicious of his obvious lack of enthusiasm for the actual fighting, but with his arrest all this was forgotten. He "was captured just in time to escape oblivion," according to one editorial. He might have faded out in ridicule had the government freed him "as a political curiosity," because there were deep divisions in the Republican ranks over his role in calling off the civil war. Mary MacSwiney, for instance, was highly critical of him, but he assumed a tragic grandeur in the eyes of Republicans following his arrest. When the Sinn Féin Árd Fheis met in October, she presided in his absence and, despite her own private reservations, paid him—"our beloved President"—a moving tribute. "There is nobody but Eamon de Valera himself who can fill the place of Eamon de Valera," she said. He was propelled back into the forefront of the movement, and the vituperation of the Free State authorities merely enhanced his stature in the eyes of Republicans.

On the weekend following his arrest he was supposed to appear at a public rally in Dublin, so his twelve-year-old son, Vivion, took his place. "My father promised that he would speak to you here today," the boy began, "and he is a man who would keep his word if he could. But he cannot speak to you today, for *giollaí na nGall* (servants of the foreigners) seized him in County Clare the other day and they have him in prison now. I know not what they will do with him."

Young de Valera was followed by the teenage son of the late Erskine Childers. The two boys provided a strong emotional appeal to people to support Republican candidates, especially when the ruling Cumann na nGaedheal was acting with what Alfred Blanche, the French Consul-General, called the "même odieux arbitraire" (same odious highhandedness) which had characterised all its actions since coming to power. Blanche, who had been in Dublin since 1917, described the former British regime as heavenly in comparison with the Cosgrave government. Perhaps this explained the surprisingly good showing made by Republicans at the polls.

Sinn Féin candidates ran unexpectedly well, with over twenty-seven per cent of the votes. They won forty-four seats, which was more than anyone had anticipated. Although Cumann na nGaedheal, which won sixty-three of the 153 seats, was denied a majority, it had no difficulty forming a government when Sinn Féin deputies declined to take their seats at Leinster House.

For six months de Valera was held in solitary confinement and allowed only to see an American lawyer in January 1924 after the Free State government sued for control of the money deposited by de Valera in the United States in 1920. As the Republicans wished to contest the case, the lawyer was admitted to de Valera but their meeting was bugged by the prison authorities. Some of the reports make fascinating reading, especially for the meetings held on 3 and 4 January when de Valera outlined events since the Easter Rebellion. He and the lawyer then became suspicious of being bugged, and they began to take precautions, with the result that much of what they said was missed, and the verbatim transcripts which General Michael J. Costello forwarded to the Minister for Defence, Richard Mulcahy, were littered with blanks.

It was "wholly for propaganda" that de Valera wanted to press ahead with the legal battle for the American funds. "The vital weakness of the Free State Government was that it knew nothing of the psychology of the people," he told the lawyer. "They are incapable of feeling the nation's pulse. They have no publicity department worth talking of. Any government that desires to hold power in Ireland should put publicity before all."

Believing the Republicans were back to where they had been in the aftermath of the Easter Rebellion, de Valera said they would have to rebuild virtually from scratch. He had the lawyer smuggle out a note to P.J. Ruttledge, the acting President of the Emergency Government. "We must stand for fair play and justice between all classes, and push co-operation and such enterprises as will be of advantage to all," he wrote. "The more we lean to the economic side the better it will be for the political objective but it must be a national programme for the common good not a class programme."

The Republican prisoners were gradually released, with de Valera being freed in July 1924, eleven months after his arrest. One of his first tasks was to do something about the Emergency Government, which had supposedly been set up by "the faithful members" of the second Dáil. A number of new Republican deputies had been elected in the general elections of June 1922 and August 1923, but they had no legal standing within the Emergency set up, because the second Dáil was still supposedly the *de jure* parliament.

Faced with the difficulty of finding a proper role for the new deputies, de Valera proposed replacing the Council of State which was supposed to advise the Emergency Government with another advisory body, Comhairle na dTeachtaí (Council of Deputies) in which members of the second Dáil would sit with those who had been elected subsequently. At the first meeting of the new council on 7 August 1924 he explained that his cabinet colleagues were unanimous that the Emergency Government—which included not only the cabinet but all members of the second Dáil—should be maintained, but they would authorise Comhairle na dTeachtaí to function as "the actual government of the country." In short, the second Dáil would be the *de jure* government, while Comhairle na dTeachtaí would, in theory, be the *de facto* one. Yet de Valera personally accepted the Free State Dáil as the *de facto* government of the country, with the result that what he was really saying was that Republicans should consider Comhairle na dTeachtaí as the *de jure de facto* government, and the Free State parliament at Leinster House the *de facto de facto* Government.

The complexities of the situation in which the Republicans were involving themselves were such that one can only wonder if anybody present really understood what de Valera meant when he summarised their difficulties by concluding: "The material point is whether the second Dáil should meet now and hand over its powers and authorities to the body that was subsequently elected, and whether they should meet afterwards and hand over to the body recently elected the powers they subsequently had."

When questioned by those present, de Valera explained he did not envision the Emergency Government operating as a rival to the Free State parliament but "simply a preparatory government, getting ready to take over the work of Government." In essence it would operate as a shadow cabinet, except it would claim to be the *de jure* government, or, as he put it, "the proper authority to be obeyed by the mass of the citizens if they were willing to obey it."

Eventually, he predicted, the Irish people would realise he had been right about the Treaty, and the country would then turn to the Republicans, who would be in an advantageous position if they could form a government able to trace its origins directly from the two Dáils of the 1919-1922 period. His basic public approach was to harp on what he believed were the deficiencies of the Treaty. In the course of his remarks to Comhairle na dTeachtaí he made one very perceptive observation about what he called the "ridiculous" Boundary Commission clause of the Treaty. "It was meant to fool and could be used at any time to get out of anything on the grounds that the taking away of portions of the Six Counties might be uneconomical," he noted astutely. But he did not explain this publicly because, of course, to have done so would have left himself open to the charge of having undermined the Free State's case, and he was keenly aware of the danger of being made a scapegoat for the unfavourable report he expected from the commission. "The object of the Free State," he warned his colleagues "was to make it appear that we by our opposition had smashed the possibility of the North coming in. We have to be very careful."

Henceforth in his speeches attacking the Treaty, he would concentrate on the partition question, but he did so in broad, general terms, such as when he told a meeting in Ennis that he had entered politics to help prevent partition. He had gone to Ennis on 15 August 1924 for a rally on the spot where he had been arrested exactly a year earlier. It was an emotional occasion, ideal for a demagogue, but he knew his limitations as a public speaker.

"I am afraid," he began, "I would disappoint a number here if I were not to start by saying, 'Well, as I was saying to you when we were interrupted'." The crowds laughed, despite his rather clumsy introduction. Yet, in a way, it was this kind of thing which provided him with his effectiveness as a speaker, because it gave the impression he could not act and thus created the illusion of passionate sincerity which so many people thought they perceived in his speeches, even though he was often deliberately twisting the truth, such as in Dundalk the following week when he said he had refused to take his seat in Leinster House because it was a partition parliament.

When a general election was called in Northern Ireland in the autumn of 1924 de Valera announced Sinn Féin would put forward candidates to allow the northern people to demonstrate "their detestation" of partition. He defended the seat he had won himself in south Down in May 1921, but when he went to speak in Newry, he was arrested, served with an exclusion order, and put back over the border. The following day he ignored the order and crossed the border to speak in Derry, but he was again arrested. This time he was taken to Belfast and brought before a court, charged with violating the exclusion order.

When asked to plead before the court, he refused. "I decline to plead before this court," he replied, "because I don't recognise that this court has authority, seeing it is the creature of a foreign power and is therefore not sanctioned by the Irish people." This was the extent of his defence. The magistrate found him guilty and sentenced him to a month in Crumlin Road jail.

The publicity generated by his actions and his harping on the partition issue helped to create the mistaken impression that the partition issue had been a major consideration in his opposition to the Treaty. Indeed this impression would eventually become quite widespread, even though it had not been a real factor in his decision to oppose to the Treaty. He had indicated a willingness to accept partition before the Treaty negotiations, and he had already explained that taking his seat in Leinster House "would be a matter purely of tactics and expediency," if the oath were dropped. In short, he was merely using the partition issue to cloak political expediency in the hypocritical garb of principle.

Although he had accepted the Boundary Commission idea back in December 1921, he did become critical of the scheme long before the commission began its deliberations, and he astutely anticipated its eventual outcome. As a result he benefited politically from the backlash following the ensuing debacle.

People had been led to believe that the Boundary Commission would carve off large areas of the six counties. On a number of occasions Collins had publicly predicted that so much territory would be given to the Free State that Northern Ireland would become an unviable economic entity and would therefore be forced to unite with the rest of the island. Consequently there was amazement in late November 1925 when the *Morning Post* leaked the draft terms of the commission's report, envisaging a two way transfer of territory, with parts of Counties Donegal and Monaghan being given to Northern Ireland, which would lose about the same amount of territory elsewhere. Ironically, the commission had concurred with Collins's assessment about the economic consequences of transferring the Nationalist areas of Northern Ireland, but it went on to conclude—as de Valera had privately predicted—that this would violate the provision in the Treaty stipulating that the transfer of territory should be made in accordance with economic and geographic considerations. The phrase in question had been included in the Treaty, according to Lloyd George, simply to prevent the transfer of isolated areas such as Unionist areas of Dublin or Nationalist areas of Belfast. The Boundary Commission's findings were therefore a violation of the spirit of the Treaty.

Eoin MacNeill, the Free State's representative, resigned from the Boundary Commission and a delegation from Dublin tried to contain the political damage by concluding an agreement in which the commission's findings were set aside. The Free State dropped its claim to territory and, in return, the British released the Irish government from its obligations under the Treaty to assume a portion "of the Public Debt of the United Kingdom."

De Valera denounced the settlement. "Secession ought not to be tolerated and, if it can be prevented, ought to be prevented, and on no account whatever should the national consent be given to it," he declared. He was particularly critical of the abandonment of Nationalist areas adjacent to the border. "To abandon these communities for any consideration whatever," he added, "is not merely an act of unpardonable injustice but a national disgrace."

The whole thing was a grave injustice which undoubtedly played into the hands of de Valera, who had been exploiting anti-British sentiment for all it was worth. Only in June he had invoked the name of Wolfe Tone to denounce the British connection as "the never-failing source of all Ireland's political evils." Although some financial concessions had been made by the British to soften the disappointment of the boundary setback, de Valera dismissed these. "Let no Irishman think," he said, "that we have gained any-thing more than avoiding the possibility of being cheated further."

Strong pressure was exerted on de Valera and his colleagues to take their seats in the Dáil. Even hardliners like Stack toyed with the idea of entering Leinster House to vote against the agreement. "Would there be sufficient opposition to enable us to turn the scale?" he asked de Vaiera. "Oath and all I would be inclined to favour the idea (tho' my mind is not quite made up), if our going in would defeat the proposal. Would it not be the end of the Free State?"

The Labour Party, the official Opposition in the Dáil, invited Sinn Féin deputies to a meeting in the Shelbourne Hotel, Dublin, on 8 December 1925 in the hope of organising a united front to defeat the boundary agreement in the Dáil. When the Sinn Féin deputies met privately afterwards, de Valera vacillated and declined to take a stand one way or another. "Much as I loved Dev," Gerry Boland recalled years later, "there were times when he could not just make up his mind."

This was one such occasion, but he had to move very cautiously because it was far from sure that the Opposition would be able to muster enough support to defeat the government, and a miscalculation of that kind could prove politically disastrous for de Valera, who was well aware of signs of a developing split within the Republican ranks. Little over a fortnight earlier, the IRA had severed its connection with Sinn Féin after Frank Aiken admitted the party was considering entering Leinster House. At the Sinn Féin Árd Fheis four days later de Valera was confronted with a particularly embarrassing resolution calling for the formal abandonment of Document No. 2 "as a basis for any future treaty" because it "would not now be an equitable settlement between this nation and England." Although he had managed to get that motion withdrawn, he must have been mindful of the fragility of his own leadership position when the question of entering the Dáil came to the fore at the Shelbourne Hotel, especially when the majority there decided against taking their Dáil seats.

They decided instead on their own rather futile gesture—a protest meeting at the Rotunda. Thus, while the controversial boundary agreement was being ratified in Leinster House, Sinn Féin deputies could only make a rather pathetic denunciation at a public meeting. As it turned out, the Cosgrave government would have had sufficient support to ensure ratification, even if the Sinn Féin deputies had taken their seats and voted against the measure.

Although de Valera went along with the majority of Sinn Féin deputies on this occasion, he was under strong pressure from others within the party to get off the political fence, and to take a decisive step. "There are some who would have us sit at the roadside and debate abstruse points about a *de jure* this and a *de facto* that," Sean Lemass noted, "but the reality we want is away in the distance—and we cannot get there unless we move." He believed that de Valera wanted to be seen to be pushed, so his remarks were really not as critical of him as outsiders might have thought. In January 1926 de Valera announced publicly that he would personally favour entering the Dáil if he could do so without taking the oath, and he persuaded the Sinn Féin Executive to call an extraordinary Árd Fheis in March to consider the whole question.

Prior to his arrest in 1923 de Valera had informed Mary MacSwiney that the oath was the only matter of principle on which he was in favour of abstaining from Leinster House, but while he was in jail she managed to persuade the party to adopt the more radical policy of refusing to recognise the Free State government, its legislature, or institutions. Her policy had taken a firm root by the time of his release, and now when he wished "to bring the policy back to the point it should never have changed from," he ran into strong opposition from those who looked on his approach as "a complete change of front."

People like Mary MacSwiney, Count Plunkett and Father Michael O'Flanagan thought compromise and betrayal were exactly the same. They were only interested in preserving the purity of their policy, and they could never reconcile themselves with anyone who believed in achievement. They were unwilling to abandon abstentionism, even if the oath were abolished.

Others like Seán Lemass, Gerry Boland and Sean MacEntee were more pragmatic; they believed in getting things done. But they were very different kinds of men with strong differing views, and they looked to de Valera to provide the leadership necessary to harness their diverse talents. He formally proposed at the special Árd Fheis on 9 March "that once the admission of oaths of the twenty-six county and six county assemblies are removed, it becomes a question not of principle but of policy, whether or not Republican representatives should attend these assemblies."

In the course of the ensuing debate Father Michael O'Flanagan, the long-time Vice-President of Sinn Féin, proposed an amendment to prohibit representatives of the party from entering "into any usurping legislature set up by English law in Ireland." This amendment was passed narrowly by 223 to 218, but when the full amended resolution was then moved, it was defeated by 179 to 177 with eighty-five abstentions. As a result, matters were really left at where they were before the Árd Fheis. While some people might argue nobody had won, de Valera had undoubtedly lost. He therefore resigned as President of Sinn Féin (but not as President of the so-called Emergency Government) at the end of the meeting on 11 March 1926.

Afterwards he left the hall with Seán Lemass. "Well, Seán," he said according to himself. "I have done my best, but I have been beaten. Now that is the end for me. I am leaving public life."

"But you are not going to leave us now Dev, at this stage," Lemass reportedly argued. "You cannot leave us like that. We have to go on now. We must form a new organisation along the policy lines you suggested at the Árd Fheis. It is the only way forward."

"We discussed it further," de Valera recalled, "and at last I told him that I could not but agree with the logic and said I would do all the necessary things." Although Lemass has usually been credited with persuading de Valera to take the step in deciding to establish a new party, it was most unlikely it all happened in this way. De Valera was not the kind of man who made such momentous decisions on the spur of the moment. He accepted the decision of the Árd Fheis with such equability, that he had probably already decided on his future course beforehand and he only pretended to allow Lemass to persuade him, because it suited his political purposes. He could still play the role of the reluctant politician, ever ready to return to private life, but compelled by his sense of duty to remain in politics in the national interest.

Of course this does not mean that Lemass did not have a profound influence in the weeks and months leading up to the actual decision. He believed the Republican cause was being hurt by "various cranks of one kind or another" who had attached themselves to Sinn Féin. The public image of the party "was being affected by this galaxy of cranks," Lemass explained, with the result that "the foundation of a new movement which could cut clear of this accumulation of queer people was not unattractive."

"The new situation is full of hope, if only it can be maintained without developing into a bitter split," de Valera was writing to McGarrity within forty-eight hours. "I have been convinced that the programme on which we were working would not win the people in the present conditions. It was too high and too sweeping." Sinn Féin had been standing aloof, offering not alternative policies but a whole alternative system of government. It was all or nothing, and "the people could only see us as offering them the fire as a retreat from the frying pan," he explained. People wanted a parliamentary alternative, and if the Republicans did not supply one, they would turn to class interest groups, like the Labour Party or a farmers' party. "The national interest as a whole will be submerged in the clashing of the rival economic groups," he warned. It was "now or never" for the Republicans.

De Valera wanted to offer the electorate a realistic alternative with a more gradual approach. "The oath," he wrote, "is a definite objective within reasonable striking distance. If I can mass the people to smash it, I shall have put them on the march again, and once moving, and having tasted victory, further advances will be possible." To achieve their ultimate objectives, however, the Republicans first needed to win the support of a majority of the electorate. "Until the majority of the people can be shown to be on the side of the Republican cause," he continued, "England will always be able to misrepresent the position, to win the support of the Church and maintain a barrier of Irishmen as her shield against us. We are in constant danger of being anglicised into a mere British province under a continuance of these conditions." If only the militants would "hold firm without violently obstructing" his plans, he was convinced he could win over the electorate.

This was essentially what Collins had been asking for back in January 1922 when de Valera had led the hardliners in refusing to accommodate him. Now people like Mary MacSwiney were no more prepared to cooperate with de Valera than they had been with Collins.

When Comhairle na dTeachtaí met a fortnight later, the debate was quite acrimonious. "It was horrible, MacSwiney noted. She and the hardliners were insisting the second Dáil was the *de jure* government; they were prepared to allow de Valera and his supporters to take their seats in Leinster House, provided they refused to take the oath and agreed, in the event of securing a majority, to scrap the existing Free State Constitution and draw up a new one on an all-Ireland basis. In short, he could go ahead and if he was successful, he would set up the alternative form of government which they had been advocating, and they would then dissolve the second Dáil. If he failed, on the other hand, they "would still be holding the fort," and could still claim the second Dáil as the *de jure* government of the whole island.

These conditions were unacceptable. "It was clear that the mentality of Dev and his party had changed considerably, and they were no longer willing to contemplate our holding the government position, and letting them carry on without any risk of compromising that position," she wrote. He now wanted to relegate the second Dáil "to a mythical region where it might get some formal recognition, but with a clear understanding it should claim no rights, nor try to exercise any."

"Honestly," MacSwiney wrote to Seán T. O'Kelly in the United States, "I cannot see why that should have annoyed them. It was exactly the point of view expressed by Dev himself a few months before." If he had the support of a majority, she thought he would have welcomed strong opposition, but he resented it when he was in a minority. "Anyhow, be that as it may," she continued, "the other side took the same poor attitude to my poor self as the Treaty people did a few years ago. Even Dev was as nasty as he could be. He has given me some surprises in these past months I can tell you."

She felt she and her colleagues were following the exact same line they had all adopted in 1922, while he now seemed ready to adopt the policy of "accepting the Treaty position but not the Treaty," which had been advocated by those she called "the Traitors" four years earlier. "If he is taking risks as he says," she continued, "he may call and think us who will not take those risks 'cowards' if he likes, but one does not like to see him doing the very thing he was the first to blame others for—try to pull down and belittle the very thing he helped to build."

In order to bring matters to a head, a resolution was proposed calling on Comhairle na dTeachtaí "not to approve of the policy as outlined by the President." This motion of virtual censure was carried by nineteen votes to eighteen, and de Valera thereupon resigned as President of the Emergency Government. His break with Sinn Féin was now complete. He had failed to get his own way, so he moved to set up his own organisation, as he had done in America in 1920, in Dublin in the aftermath of the Dáil's acceptance of the Treaty in 1922, and now again in the wake of Sinn Féin's rigid adherence to the policy of abstentionism.

CHAPTER 12

"I Am Not A Communist"

Shortly after resigning as President of the "Emergency Government" de Valera announced he would be forming a new party, Fianna Fáil (The Republican Party). The bracketed name had been added at the insistence of Seán Lemass, who was afraid the populace might confuse the Gaelic word *Fáil*, which meant "destiny," with the English word "fail." While Fianna Fáil literally translated as "Soldiers of Destiny," it really had a broader connotation; it was derived from Inis Fáil (island of the warriors), an allegorical name for Ireland. The name therefore had a certain literary and cultural appeal, which was not insignificant in a country able to boast of such contemporary literary giants as George Bernard Shaw, William Butler Yeats and James Joyce.

The party was formally inaugurated at La Scala Theatre in Dublin on 16 May 1926, and de Valera was elected its first president. His immediate aim, he said, was to remove the oath and once this had been accomplished, to advance the national cause by "cutting the bonds of foreign interference one by one until the full internal sovereignty of the twenty-six counties was established beyond question."

"With a united sovereign twenty-six counties," he said, "the position would be reached in which the solution of the problem of successfully bringing in the North could be confidently undertaken." He acknowledged that entering the Free State Dáil would entail recognising partition, but he emphasised this did not mean acquiescing to it. "We have been in no way a party to the partition of our country," he declared. "We have not accepted it and do not accept it. We shall at all times be morally free to use any means that God gives us to reunite the country and win back the part of our Ulster province that has been taken away from us."

Much of the detailed organisational work was left to Seán Lemass and Gerry Boland, the joint National Secretaries of Fianna Fáil, while de Valera travelled about the country helping to boost the nascent local branches with morale-boosting appearances to explain the party's overall goals. Even though he had previously contended the "Emergency Government" was *de jure* and the Irish Republic was still in existence, he now said it was necessary to face realities. "If we do not recognise the facts," he declared in Ennis on 29 June, "we cannot make progress. For the moment we have been driven out of the citadel and I am asking our people to attack it again and retake it. I cannot rally the people to a fresh attack if I keep on shouting that I have got the citadel already."

Although he tried to play down the significance of his break with Sinn Féin, Mary MacSwiney publicly accused him of moving dangerously close to the stand he had refused to take when invited by Collins in 1922. "The policy now adopted by Fianna Fáil," she asserted in a letter to the press, "seems to be just that which we refused four years ago—'accepting the Treaty position, but not accepting the Treaty.' If that was not a proper policy for Republicans in 1922, how can it be right in 1926?"

De Valera formally recognised the Free State's authority and its British connection later that year by applying for an Irish passport to go to the United States, where he hoped to embarrass the Cosgrave government by frustrating its ongoing efforts to get hold of the two-and-a-half million dollars he had deposited in the name of the Irish Republic in 1920. He had already suggested using the money for some non-political purpose like preserving the Gaelic language, but the government had contemptuously dismissed his suggestion. He knew there was little chance of regaining control of the money himself, but he felt it would be a worthwhile propaganda exercise if he could get the American courts to rule against the Free State government.

"These funds can be legitimately disbursed only for the purposes of an all-Ireland government functioning independently without any acceptance of British interference or control," he contended upon his arrival in New York on 5 March 1927. After testifying in the court case, de Valera toured the United States raising funds for Fianna Fáil which, he explained, needed to win the support of the majority of the Irish people before it could achieve its Republican goals. "We can rally and reorganise the Irish people," he told an overflow crowd at Carnegie Hall, "but we cannot obtain the support of world opinion against England, our real enemy, until a majority of the people's representatives are with us." He regularly exploited the anglophobia of his Irish-American audiences in his speeches.

"Some of those listening to me," he told a gathering in St. Paul, Minnesota, "believe, no doubt, the story that the British army have evacuated Ireland. When I left Cobh on this trip I passed out between the forts which guard Cork harbour. By whom were these forts manned? By Irish troops? By Free State troops even? Not at all. They are held by British troops and the British flag flies over them." While speaking in Boston he contended Britain's retention of Irish bases had implications even for America, because if England went to war with the United States, "we would be obliged to submit to seeing our land used as a base to fight our best friend." Ireland could not therefore be considered free while her territory could be used in this way. "We only ask," he said, "that our people be permitted to choose, without hindrance and interference, the form of government they desire."

Given his own approach to events in 1922, it was unlikely he won over many people with his democratic expressions now, but in the following months and years his message would gradually get through, especially when his opponents, mesmerised by their hatred of him, went to undemocratic and even treasonous lengths in their futile attempts to undermine him. His first real success after becoming leader of Fianna Fáil was when the New York Supreme Court ruled that the disputed money deposited by him in 1920 should be returned to subscribers because the Republican government of 1919-1922 had never been officially recognised. The ruling was widely seen as a victory for him because he had secured an eminent independent judgment that the Irish Free State was not the legitimate successor of the Irish Republic, notwithstanding the result of the general election of June 1922.

The American visit provided both a propaganda victory and some much needed funds for Fianna Fáil, but his reception in the United States bore little resemblance to the welcome he was given during his earlier visit. Some 5,000 people did come out to hear him speak in Boston just before his return home, but this crowd paled into insignificance when compared to the 50,000 people who thronged Fenway Park to see him in June 1919.

Shortly after returning to Ireland de Valera had a chance to test his new party's strength at the polls when Cosgrave called a general election for June 1927. Fianna Fáil made a very impressive showing in its first outing, winning 44 seats, just three short of the ruling Cumann na nGaedheal, which lost heavily at the hands of small parties. Even without the abstentionists in Fianna Fáil and Sinn Féin taking their seats, Cumann na nGaedheal still did not have a majority in the Dail.

On 23 June de Valera and his Fianna Fáil colleagues tried to claim their seats, but they were stopped and told they would first have to subscribe their names to a book containing the Treaty oath, which they refused to do. Afterwards they issued a statement emphasising that "under no circumstances whatever" would they subscribe to the oath. They planned, instead, to collect the 75,000 signatures necessary to call a referendum to amend the constitution by abolishing the oath. De Valera contended that the Cosgrave government was deliberately retaining the oath as a political means of ensuring that conscientious Republicans would not enter the Dáil. In ancient times the walls of Bandon bore the inscription, "Beggar, Jew, atheist may enter here, but not a Papist." Now, he said, the authorities of the Free State were essentially inscribing their own slogan over government buildings: "Unionist, Orangeman, anarchist may enter here, but not a Republican." He was clearly taking the offensive but was suddenly thrown back on the defensive when the political climate was devastated with the assassination of Vice-President Kevin O'Higgins in Dublin on 10 July.

"The assassination of Mr O'Higgins is murder and is inexcusable from any standpoint," de Valera declared. "It is a crime that cuts at the root of representative government, and no one who realises what the crime means can do otherwise than deplore and condemn it. Every right-minded individual will deeply sympathise with the bereaved widow in her agony."

Following the assassination the Cosgrave government exploited the popular indignation to rush through legislation forcing Fianna Fáil deputies to swallow their pride and take the oath, or face extinction as a political party. The new legislation required all Dáil candidates to sign an affidavit to take their seats within two months of being elected. Any candidate refusing to comply would be disqualified.

De Valera publicly reaffirmed his determination not to take the oath on 24 July, but indicated that if Thomas Johnson, the leader of the Labour Party, managed to form a coalition government and then did away with the oath, Fianna Fáil deputies would take their seats and would not attempt to "press any issues involving the Treaty to the point of overthrowing such a government during the normal lifetime of the present assembly." But the Labour Party had little chance of forming a government without the active help of Fianna Fáil.

Behind the scenes de Valera was wavering. The assassination of O'Higgins had provoked a backlash in favour of the government, and there was a danger Fianna Fáil's momentum would be irreparably damaged unless he now moved decisively. "Short of a miracle, or a successful armed conflict," he concluded, there was no way of achieving Republican goals if the party continued to abstain from the Dail. He therefore seized a way out provided by opponents who had consistently maintained, ever since the signing of the Treaty, that the oath was just a formality.

"I asked myself, whether in a crisis like that I would be justified in staying outside if it were, in fact, true that this thing was a mere formality," he explained.

In return for Fianna Fáil support for Thomas Johnson as President, the Labour Party leader promised, if elected, to take immediate steps to have a constitutional referendum held on the question of abolishing the oath.

Next day Fianna Fáil formally decided to subscribe to the book containing the dreaded oath, but first the party issued a statement explaining it considered the oath merely an empty political formula. The statement, signed by forty-two deputies, emphasised that they proposed "to regard the declaration as an empty formality and repeat that their only allegiance is to the Irish nation, and that it will be given to no other power or authority."

On entering Leinster House, de Valera presented the clerk with a copy of the signed statement. "I am not prepared to take an oath," he declared in Gaelic. "I am not prepared to take an oath. I am prepared to put my name down in this book in order to get permission to go into the Dáil, but it has no other significance." He then picked up a Bible from the table in front of him and moved it to the other side of the room. "You must remember," he stressed upon returning, "that I am taking no oath." Then placing some paper over the oath at the top of the page he signed his name as if it was a blank sheet of paper. "I signed it in the same way as I would sign an autograph in a newspaper," he said afterwards. "If you ask me whether I had an idea what was there, I say 'yes'." But, he added, "it was neither read to me, nor was I asked to read it."

The first vote in which de Valera and his Fianna Fáil colleagues participated was a momentous one. The Labour Party had tabled a motion of no confidence in the government. Johnson was confident of winning, and Cosgrave had already resigned himself to defeat. Fianna Fáil deputies kept a very low profile during the debate. Only Seán T. O'Kelly spoke, and he said just a few words in Gaelic to the effect that everybody knew where Fianna Fáil stood on the issue. The National League, made up of supporters of the old Irish Parliamentary Party, was pledged to support the motion of no confidence, but at the last moment one of its nine deputies, John Jinks, absented himself from the house, apparently because he feared the consequences of supporting the Fianna Fáil backed motion. As a result the vote was tied, and the Speaker cast his vote to save the government.

Had the motion been carried, Johnson would undoubtedly have been able to form a coalition government because in accordance with established practice the Dáil would have had to vote for its own dissolution, so there was little chance of Cosgrave being able to call a general election, especially so soon after such an election. Following the vote the Dáil adjourned for the rest of the summer, and during the recess Cosgrave took the unprecedented step of asking the Governor-General to dissolve parliament without the approval of the Dáil and call another general election in September. Cumann na nGaedheal, which gained twenty-one seats, was able to form a stable government with the help of the Farmers' Party. Fianna Fáil, on the other hand, consolidated its own position as the second largest party in the Dáil by increasing its representation by thirteen seats.

As Leader of the Opposition during the next four and a half years de Valera used every opportunity to appeal to the nationalistic instincts of the Irish people, especially when he was able to offset his own position against what he believed was the weak, subservient approach of the Cosgrave government in its relations with Britain. The Fianna Fáil leader thereby skilfully exploited the anti-British sentiment still rife in the country.

No issue was too remote or too trivial to be exploited. When the United States invited the Irish Free State to sign the Kellogg-Briand Pact, a treaty outlawing war, de Valera was one of the few politicians in the world to express democratic reservations. "I have no doubt whatever," he said, "that the people of this country would be anxious to see a genuine treaty arrived at between the nations by which war would be outlawed." Just as he had criticised Article X of the Versailles Treaty back in 1919, he now criticised the Kellogg-Briand pact because, he contended, Britain would be able to use it to hold people in subjugation by insisting that signatories of the pact should not support struggles of national liberation within the British Empire. "We want to be disassociated from any form of reply that would imply that we recognise Great Britain's right either to hold this country or any other country," he declared. In short, he was insisting that the Irish people should have the right to resort to war to bring about Irish unity, if necessary.

De Valera deftly managed to create the impression of a real difference between his attitude towards partition and that of the Cumann na nGaedheal government. And authorities in Northern Ireland helped to boost the impression by arresting him again for ignoring the exclusion order when he crossed the border to open a bazaar in Belfast in February 1929. He then engaged in some nationalistic grandstanding by insisting on speaking Gaelic in court, much to the amusement of Irish Nationalists and the annoyance of the baffled judge, who sentenced him to a month in jail.

The land annuities controversy was probably the area in which Fianna Fáil did most political damage to the government, because de Valera was able to make a good case against the Free State paying annuities arising out of the land purchase legislation from around the turn of the century. He contended that a considerable amount of money was being paid to Britain without any obligation to do so.

The Government of Ireland Act (1920), the British legislation which had partitioned Ireland, had specified that the land annuities would be handed over to the respective governments in Dublin and Belfast. At the time Lloyd George said the annuities were being given "as a free gift for the purpose of development and improvement of Ireland."

Admittedly, Article 5 of the Treaty had subsequently acknowledged that the Free State would "assume liability for the service of the public debt of the United Kingdom," but it specified that "any just claims on the part of Ireland" would be taken into account. The Irish signatories had not admitted a responsibility to pay any money; they had agreed to consider the question separately at a later date and to pay, if it could be shown anything was owed. Collins, who did the bulk of the negotiating on the financial issues, had argued that the British actually owed money to Ireland as a result of overtaxation during the nineteenth century. This overtaxation had already been acknowledged by a Royal Commission.

If the land debts had been reassumed under Article 5 of the Treaty, they would have been cancelled again under Article 2 of the Boundary Commission agreement of 1925, which released the Free State "from the obligation under Article 5" of the Treaty. Thus, de Valera contended that even if the land annuities had been owed prior to 1925, they were not thereafter, notwithstanding the blunder by Cosgrave's Minister for Finance in apparently agreeing to pay the annuities as part of the so-called Ultimate Financial Settlement of 1926. De Valera refused to accept this agreement as binding because it had never been submitted to the Dáil for ratification. As a result, he contended it was not worth the paper on which it was written.

"No minister can assign national property away by his own signature," de Valera declared. "This has never got statutory sanction, and every sum paid out in virtue of that agreement without collateral statutory sanction is being paid out without the proper authority." His arguments had a certain vicarious appeal for many Irish people aggrieved that the Boundary Commission's interpretation of the Treaty had robbed the Free State of the contiguous Nationalist areas of Northern Ireland. Now it seemed that the same kind of selective interpretation of the Boundary agreement should work in the Free State's favour.

The annuities controversy also afforded de Valera more scope to exploit economic issues. While in jail in 1924 he had advocated using economic policies to further his political aims, and Fianna Fáil quickly implemented such a policy, though it was always of secondary consideration to himself. Economics were largely a means to a political end.

During the late 1920s the world was in the midst of one of the greatest economic booms, and *laissez-faire*—the doctrine which called for governments not to interfere in economic matters—was very much the maxim of those Roaring Twenties. As the boom was largely industrial, the Irish Free State missed out on most of the benefits, and de Valera began questioning the *laissez-faire* attitude before it became fashionable to do so. "Surely," he told the Dáil in July 1928, "there is no excuse for raising that maxim to a dogma when things are going badly, for, if you do, it only means that you are letting things get worse. You must actively interfere. We hold, unlike Ministers opposite, that active interference is necessary by the Ministry if you are going to get the country out of the rut in which it is at present."

He personally espoused an economic nationalism aimed at making "Ireland as self-contained and as self-supporting as possible." His economic outlook was influenced by a kind of late eighteenth or nineteenth century romantic concept derived from the philosophies of the cultural nationalism which had blossomed in Germany and England. He subscribed to the ideal of people living in frugal comfort, providing for themselves their own food, clothing and shelter, and cherishing the spiritual values and cultural heritage above the material luxuries available in some of the wealthy industrial nations.

As things stood, the country's existing economic role was essentially providing food for Britain. To him Ireland was like a servant faced with the choice of staying in a comfortable, well-furnished mansion where he was being mistreated by his master, or moving out into a meagre cottage where he can be his own master.

"If he goes into the cottage he has to make up his mind to put up with the frugal fare of that cottage," de Valera explained. "As far as I am concerned, if I had the choice to make, I would say, 'We are prepared to get out of that mansion, to live our lives in our own way, and to live in that frugal manner'."

To more materially-minded people, de Valera's vision was sentimental twaddle, but it was a romanticised vision which appealed to a large segment of the electorate living in rural poverty. Their expectations had been stirred by independence but emigration—with all its uncertainties—had still seemed like the only means of escape from their poverty trap. For them, there was something compelling about de Valera, who spoke with the certainty of a prophet. He said he knew how to solve the country's problems, and he seemed so certain of himself. He was a man with vision and a realistic dream that they could understand—not of luxurious mansions, but of frugal cottages. He was a man who cared about their problems and who held out hope for them of a better life in their own country. In short, he was a man they could follow.

Fianna Fáil appealed strongly to the underprivileged by advocating the redistribution of unutilised land and a more equitable distribution of the country's wealth. "One evening after one of these debates," de Valera told the Dáil, "I happened to be walking along Merrion Square about five or six o'clock and there I saw little children with their hands stuck down in the bins that are put outside doors." They were looking for scraps of food, or pieces of coal. He rightly denounced such scenes, and blamed the government for not alleviating such conditions. Fianna Fáil found ready support among people who believed the government could do more, especially when de Valera complained about the wasteful extravagance of the office of Governor General, and the overpaying of higher civil servants while other people did not have enough to live on.

"I would review every salary of over a thousand pounds a year," he said. "I hold that it is unjust that such salaries should be paid by the community whilst a large section of it are unable to find employment or to get bread." A thousand pounds a year, he said, should suffice even for government ministers.

While de Valera generally dealt with economic matters in broad, simplistic terms, Seán Lemass—the real architect of the party's economic approach—was more specific. He called for steps to build up domestic investment, by taxing exportable capital and providing income tax concessions on money invested at home. "Until we get a definite policy decided on in favour of industrial and agricultural protection and an executive in office prepared to enforce that policy," Lemass argued, "it is useless to hope for results." It was ironic that Lemass was borrowing heavily from the economic views of Arthur Griffith, in much the same way as de Valera would adopt the stepping stone approach advocated by Collins, while Cumann na nGaedheal leaders allowed their own vision to be distorted by their hatred of the man they blamed for the Civil War.

Much of the government's reactions to Fianna Fáil's growing influence was negative; it tried to exploit the fears of the electorate by predicting all kinds of gloom and doom—economic disaster and war with Britain. Government spokesmen said Fianna Fáil would dismiss all existing civil servants on taking office and introduce a spoils system to reward its own supporters. It was easy to play on the fears of the civil servants, who largely owed their jobs to the Cumann na nGaedheal government. But de Valera adamantly refuted any intention of adopting a spoils system. He promised that Fianna Fáil would not victimise civil servants who had worked for the Free State authorities during the Civil War. "I believe in justice for every man, friend or opponent, and I am going to assume that those who took service in the Free State did it believing they were right," he declared.

Fianna Fáil was confronted with all kind of nasty rumours. On 22 November 1928 de Valera took the unusual step for a politician of publicly denying some particularly unseemly stories about his own private life. "My wife was supposed to have had to leave the country and live abroad because she could not live with me," he told the Dail. "I was supposed to be living with two or three other women."

"I never heard that before," Cosgrave interjected.

"Let us get down to it," de Valera continued. "It was part of a campaign—everybody knows it was part of a campaign. We may talk as much as we like about democracy, but as long as people pander to that sort of thing, and inspire it, you are not going to have any respect here for the so-called will of the people. It went on not merely from platform and in private, but it was spoken from the pulpit; it came from the altar. I myself was told by a lady in Chicago that a bishop told her that my wife had to go over to America in order to keep me straight there because I was associating with women."

The daily press was unanimously opposed to Fianna Fáil, so de Valera felt seriously handicapped in his efforts to get his party's policies across to the electorate. "There is nothing so important for

Ireland as a newspaper that will champion her freedom," he told a press conference on arrival in New York on 21 December 1927. He was on his way to Rochester, New York, to spend Christmas with his mother, whose husband had only a week to live. During the six weeks de Valera spent in the United States on this visit, he managed to raise $80,000 for a new national newspaper. He returned the following December and spent almost six months touring the country raising further funds. In the course of his travels he again played on the anglophobia of Irish-Americans by stressing anti-British themes.

"The circulation in Ireland of British newspapers such as the *Daily Mail*, the *Daily Express*, and *Daily Chronicle* has been rapidly increasing," he said. "The whole thought and philosophy behind these newspapers is entirely alien." His appeal was to Irish-Americans to save the Irish people from the contamination of the pernicious British press, and help him to destroy the Treaty which bound Ireland to help Britain in the event of an Anglo-American war. He also criticised Britain for extracting exorbitantly high land annuity payments, which he compared to the comparatively modest war debt payments Britain was making to the United States. In proportion to their population, he said, the Irish were paying sixty-six times more to Britain annually than the British were paying to the United States.

The American tour was a financial success, especially as the United states was already in the early throes of the Great Depression. He returned home in late May 1930 with sufficient funds to establish the *Irish Press* in September of the following year, a particularly propitious time, as there was a general election due within the next twelve months.

In June 1931 de Valera involved himself in a controversy over the appointment of a Protestant librarian in County Mayo. Letitia Dunbar-Harrison, the woman at the centre of the controversy, was a graduate of Trinity College, Dublin. She had been selected by the Local Appointments Commission, but Mayo County Council ignored its legal obligations and refused to confirm the appointment, ostensibly because she could not speak Gaelic, but the real reason had more to do with her Protestant background and her Trinity College education. If de Valera had wanted the opportunity to demonstrate that the majority had no right to do wrong, then this could have been a case. The majority in Mayo had no right to discriminate against the unfortunate woman on religious grounds. But de Valera tried to have it both ways. He denounced religious discrimination, and then proceeded to endorse it in this instance.

"I believe that every citizen in this country is entitled to his share of public appointments, and that there should not be discrimination on the ground of religion," he told the Dáil. "Religion should not be made an excuse for denying a person an appointment for which he or she was fully qualified." Here was the rub. "What are qualifications?" he asked.

As far as he was concerned, a Protestant librarian was not properly qualified to deal with Catholics, any more than a Protestant doctor would be qualified to deal with Catholic patients. "If I thought that the principle that the librarian in a Catholic community should be Catholic was a new principle introduced merely to deny a Protestant an appointment, I should vote against it, but I know from my youth that it is not so," he continued. Catholic communities were entitled to insist on Catholic librarians and Catholic doctors and the likes, he contended. "I say that if I had a vote on a local body, and if there were two qualified people who had to deal with a Catholic community, and if one was a Catholic and the other a Protestant, I would unhesitatingly vote for the Catholic." Carried to its logical conclusion, his argument could have meant Protestants being banned from virtually every position dealing with the public.

Fortunately, when he came to power he never tried to implement these views, which raises the question whether, on that day in June 1931, he actually believed what he was saying, or was just cynically exploiting the controversy for political gain. Party strategists might well claim he was acting from legitimate expediency, because politics in those days was a dirty and, indeed, deadly business.

Likewise his reaction in October when the government introduced a new Public Safety Bill, innocuously titled the Constitution (Amendment No 17) Bill. He denounced the legislation, which would authorise the government to proscribe certain organisations and introduce military tribunals to deal with politically motivated crime. In recent months there had been an upsurge of militant Republican activity, and the Garda Commissioner, General Eoin O'Duffy, was particularly worried about Saor Éire, a militant, Marxist splinter group of Republicans. De Valera opposed the measures as unwise and unnecessary. They were, he said, an attempt by the government to create national anxiety "in order to prepare a favourable atmosphere for the coming election."

In the Dáil there was a free ranging debate, which became quite bitter and very personal at times. It was largely symptomatic of the period, and indicative of the residual Civil War bitterness. The Fianna Fáil leader accused Cosgrave of rejecting his peace overtures to end the Civil War just to keep him out of politics, and then much to de Valera's indignation, someone on the government side accused him of deliberately staying out of harm's way in the United States during most of the Black and Tan period.

"I came here the moment the Acting President was put in jail," de Valera replied. "I came over here when Cork at the time was burned. I came here at the beginning of the Black and Tan regime proper. I stayed in Dublin through it. I went to meetings of our cabinet that we held when your present President of the Executive ran away to England. I called him back. I saved him from the cabinet that would have kicked him out."

All of this had happened more than a decade earlier and had nothing to do with the bill under discussion, but the intensity of de Valera's indignation indicated a sore spot had been touched. Cosgrave, who was not in the chamber at the time, returned later to refute the charge against him. He had only missed one cabinet meeting during the Black and Tan period and that was while de Valera was in the United States.

"I want to say I am guilty of hastily retorting and imputing cowardice," de Valera explained. "But that I did that, knowing myself that the charge I made was false, I deny." In short, he made the charge because he was provoked, but he would stand by it. By "imputing cowardice" in this instance, de Valera raised questions about his own conduct. If, as he now said, he believed Cosgrave had "deserted his duty" in 1921, why did he reappoint him to the rationalised cabinet in August of that year? Secondly, in making the charge of cowardice was de Valera employing what psychiatrists call "projection"—the technique in which the ego of an individual denies certain undesirable characteristics in himself while attributing them to others? This is not to say that de Valera was guilty of cowardice, but rather, that his touchiness on the subject raises questions about his own confidence in the matter.

Despite the acrimony in his relations with Cosgrave, de Valera was careful not to take issue with everything the President had said during the debate. In particular he endorsed Cosgrave's pronouncements on private property, which were of special interest to the Catholic Church. Having been outflanked by Cosgrave for Church support during the Civil War, de Valera had no intention of being outflanked again. "The right of private property is accepted as fundamental," the Fianna Fáil leader said, "and, as far as Catholics are concerned, there has been definite teaching upon it."

The government had been in touch with the Catholic hierarchy, and it was preparing a pastoral letter condemning the organisations being targeted by the government. In order to ensure the Church said nothing to hurt Fianna Fáil, de Valera made a personal call on his old teaching colleague at Maynooth, Joseph Cardinal MacRory.

Throughout its period in power the Cosgrave government had sought to demonstrate the Irish Free State was independent, even though still a dominion. In view of Collins's contention that the Treaty provided the "freedom to achieve freedom" the government felt a psychological need to provide visible manifestations of the country's independence, which was done in various ways, the most important of which was the enactment in 1931 of the Statute of Westminster, which formally recognised the dominions as masters of their own destinies and in no way subservient to Britain. It made the *de facto* status of the dominions *de jure*. De Valera had maintained during the Treaty controversy that Britain would never accord the *de facto* status to the Free State, and some British politicians, most notably Winston Churchill, actually tried to have the Irish Free State specifically excluded from the Statute of Westminster because the country did not enjoy the real status of a dominion, seeing that Britain retained Irish bases and enjoyed defence concessions provided by none of the other dominions. But Churchill's arguments were ignored when Cosgrave insisted that the Treaty specifically guaranteed that the status of the Free State would be no less than that of Canada or the other dominions.

De Valera later admitted that the enactment of the Statute of Westminster showed he had underestimated the real significance of the Anglo-Irish Treaty. And when one considers that even while underestimating the Treaty he had admitted there was only a small difference between it and what he wanted, then his subsequent admission meant, in effect, that he had been making a fuss all those years over something less than a small difference over a "little sentimental thing." Although the government still had nine months of its term to run, Cosgrave apparently decided to exploit the benefits of the Statute of Westminster by going to the country. He called a general election for 16 February 1932.

But the Irish electorate never looked on the 1931 Statute in the same way as the Cosgrave government, which seemed to expect the people to be impressed by Britain's formal acknowledgment that the Treaty conferred the freedom claimed by Griffith and Collins.

Neither of them had ever contended that the Treaty was an end in itself; it was a means to an end, a stepping stone to an independent Irish republic. What the people needed therefore was definite proof in the form of constitutional change, not just another document affirming what had already been claimed ten years earlier.

Cumann na nGaedheal had come to power in the first flush of the country's newly won independence and suffered as a result by being lumbered with unrealistic popular expectations. On top of this, the government ran an inept election campaign, offering the people only the status quo with the austere financial policies it had been pursuing with an almost masochistic zeal. It tried to depict this as a preferable alternative to the catastrophe which would ensue if de Valera came to power.

During the months leading up to the election Fianna Fáil had been offering constitutional, social and economic changes. The oath would be abolished, the land annuities withheld from Britain, tariffs introduced to foster native industries, tillage encouraged—in the form of wheat and sugar beet production—to keep more people on the land. In addition, Fianna Fáil promised to increase the number of individual landowners by distributing unutilised land and increasing the number of homesteads. The party also promised a big urban housing program, which would not only rehouse people in suitable accomodation, but also provide employment in the construction industry. People like Seán Lemass proudly depicted the party's policy, especially its programme for industrialisation, as the radical solution necessary to overcome the country's chronic unemployment, which was aggravated just before the elections by the stemming of emigration as a result of the world-wide economic depression. He called for "the same vigour and enthusiasm as the Russian government is now applying to the five-years' programme in operation in that country."

In the emotional atmosphere of the campaign it was not long before de Valera was accused of being a Communist, or at best a weak Kerensky who would be toppled by Communists in Fianna Fáil once the party came to power. Even Cosgrave stooped to such insinuations when he told a public meeting in Tralee that Cumann na nGaedheal was "against Communism and Russianism"—the obvious implication being that Fianna Fáil was not opposed to them.

De Valera issued an election manifesto on behalf of Fianna Fáil promising not to exceed its requested mandate "without again consulting the people." The manifesto went on to stress that the party had "no leaning towards Communism and no belief in communistic doctrines."

"I am not a Communist," de Valera declared on campaigning in Tralee, next day. "I am quite the reverse."

While de Valera did not specify in detail in the election manifesto how his party's programme would be paid for, he did promise to economise by eliminating "waste and extravagance" in the public service, and by scaling down "the higher salaries till they are more in keeping with the means of the taxpayer and the frugal living that all sections of the community must be content with until every one who is able and willing to work is given a fair opportunity to earn his daily bread." What he did not say was that he intended to use the land annuity payments to offset the cost of the programme. Many farmers had mistakenly thought Fianna Fáil was promising to cancel their land payments, whereas, in fact, de Valera still planned to collect them.

Some 30,000 people gathered to see de Valera wind up the Fianna Fáil campaign in Dublin on the eve of the election. He said a "comparatively moderate" programme had been adopted by the party "because a large section of our people have to be convinced we can do the things we set out to do. We want them to be convinced. We are giving them our pledge that we will keep exactly to the mandate we have asked for, until we come before them again. And, when we do, we know we will come before a people who will have renewed courage and who will not be frightened by any stories of bogey men."

His appeal obviously worked because Fianna Fáil gained enough seats to become the largest party in the Dáil. As the Labour Party, with its seven seats, was offering to support Fianna Fáil, it was obvious that de Valera was going to be elected President of the Executive Council when the Dáil reconvened the following month, though it was far from clear that his enemies would allow the democratic will of the people to be implemented.

CHAPTER 13

"They Left it to Me"

There was little over a fortnight between the general election and the convening of the new Dáil to elect a government. It was a tense and uncertain period. Although Fianna Fáil were virtually certain of victory, there were fears that elements in the security forces might stage a *coup d'état*.

For the past six months General Eoin O'Duffy, the Garda Commissioner, had been sounding out colleagues and Army officers about the possibility of a joint Garda-Army takeover in the event Fianna Fáil were voted into office. General Michael Brennan, the Army Chief of Staff, refused to have anything to do with the scheme and actually had those officers who might be interested, transferred out of harm's way. David Neligan, the head of the Garda's Special Branch, also refused to be a party to O'Duffy's machinations, but the Commissioner still had posters secretly printed calling on the public to support his government in the event he went ahead with the coup. Cosgrave had absolutely nothing to do with the scheming, but he did get wind of the Commissioner's activities and asked Neligan about the rumours, only to be told the situation was under control. At this point Cosgrave and his colleagues decided to replace O'Duffy if they were returned to power.

In the days before the new Dáil met de Valera was very interested in getting his message across to people in the United States. On 22 February he gave an interview to John Steele of the *Chicago Tribune*, in which he outlined his proposed programme for government. He was going to tackle the oath and the Public Safety Act, and if the opportunity arose, he would try to do something about partition. Steele asked if he intended to set up an independent republic and take the country out of the British Commonwealth.

"That will come in its own good time," he replied. "Meantime our mandate does not extend so far."

On 4 March de Valera made a broadcast to the United States in which he seemed to be preparing public opinion for Anglo-Irish difficulties. "Mischief makers wish to represent our efforts to secure fair play for the people of Ireland as a policy of antagonism to England," he said. "My desire has always been to bring about the friendliest relations between Britain and Ireland, but I know that the only sure foundation for such relations, and for lasting peace, is justice and the recognition of the right of our people to be free."

When the Dáil convened five days later, several of the Fianna Fáil deputies, fearing trouble, went into the chamber with hidden pistols. De Valera was unarmed, but his oldest son, Vivion, accompanied him to Leinster House with a pistol in his pocket. Realising the outcome of the vote was a foregone conclusion, Cosgrave did not speak against de Valera's nomination. With the support of the Labour Party, Fianna Fáil was assured of victory, and de Valera was elected by eighty-one votes to sixty-eight, with additional support from three independents, including James M. Dillon, the son of the last leader of the IPP. Fianna Fáil supporters engaged in wild, enthusiastic cheering. They were cheering for the election of their man, but the Irish people had something much more important to cheer about that day—the victory of democracy at a time when the lights of freedom were going out throughout Europe. What would have happened if O'Duffy, who later temporarily succeeded Cosgrave, had been in power that day?

"Nothing so became Cosgrave in office as his manner of leaving it," Professor J.J. Lee has written. While the comment was probably made flippantly, the professor's excellent study of twentieth century Ireland ably charts Cosgrave's many accomplishments, and the dignified manner in which he handed over power to his civil war enemies was certainly one of them, because in doing so he made an invaluable contribution to democracy in Ireland, every bit as much as de Valera did in accepting the restraints of his own mandate in the coming months.

Following his election de Valera left the chamber to receive his commission from the Governor-General, James MacNeill, who had taken the unprecedented step of coming to Leinster House to save the newly elected President the indignity of going to the Vice-Regal Lodge to have his appointment confirmed by the representative of the British King. De Valera announced his new ministers without consulting them beforehand. For this and every other one of his governments he always seemed more influenced in his choice of ministers by "his own personal regard for them rather than his assessment of their capacity to do that particular job," according to Seán Lemass, his new Minister for Industry and Commerce. "He made up his own mind, and certainly, to my mind, he was not the best of judges of the capacity of individuals to do particular categories of work." Seán T. O'Kelly was appointed Vice-president of the Executive Council and placed in charge of Local Government, Seán MacEntee became Minister for Finance, Frank Aiken Minister for Defence, and James Ryan, Minister for Agriculture. The most surprising appointment was James Geoghegan as Minister for Justice. He was a former member of Cumann na nGaedheal, and his selection was obviously intended to reassure the police force that there would be no victimisation.

The new government included many strong-willed individuals, but de Valera, who retained the portfolio of External Affairs for himself, was able to instil an extraordinary cohesiveness. Most of his ministerial colleagues had been through so many splits together—beginning with the split in the Irish Volunteers in 1914, the Treaty-split in 1922, and the Sinn Féin split in 1926—that they undoubtedly shared his general outlook, at least on what he considered the most important issues. Yet, as their records indicated, they were men who were not afraid to stand against the majority, so keeping them together was going to be a difficult task.

Part of de Valera's secret undoubtedly lay in a combination of his own tremendous patience and his magnetic charm, which even some of his bitterest political opponents freely acknowledged. His public image was of a dour, austere individual. "He dresses habitually in black and so appears with his rather stern countenance to be in perpetual mourning for a nation in bondage," one diplomat reported. "No cleric ever lived a more austere life than did de Valera," the Papal Nuncio told a newly arrived diplomat in 1937. "He never smoked, never took a drop of any alcoholic drink except in public when as a matter of courtesy he forced himself to gulp down a few swallows of wine." This was presumably the image the President wished to portray, but it was wide of the mark. Although he gave up smoking while in jail in 1916, he continued to take a social drink in private throughout his life.

One of the striking features of the new government was the excellent working relationship it soon developed with the public service, even after reducing the salaries of senior civil servants. But, of course, de Valera had led by example in this matter. He had reduced his own salary by £1,000 to £1,500 and the salaries of other ministers by £500 to £1,000. The civil servants have been praised for the loyal, professional way in which they served the new government, but the new President and his colleagues deserve considerable credit for resisting Republican taunts to dismiss those who had loyally served the previous governments. Many were fearful for their jobs. Seán Collins, Michael's older brother, was particularly anxious. He had a young family and only a temporary civil service job. Before the change of government, he made frantic efforts to have his position made permanent, but was unsuccessful. In desperation his wife explained their plight to Sean T. O'Kelly's wife, who attended the same church. A few days later de Valera sent word that the appointment was being made permanent. He scrupulously adhered to his election promise not to engage in any victimisation, and he personally formed excellent relations with the Permanent Secretaries of his own two departments—Seán Moynihan in the Office of the President, and Joseph P. Walshe in External Affairs.

De Valera's staff found him an easy man to work for, and they stayed with him for years. Walshe, who became acting secretary of the Department of External Affairs in 1922 and was later made Permanent Secretary, only moved in 1946 to fulfil a lifelong ambition to serve in the Vatican, when he became the country's first diplomat to be appointed to the rank of ambassador. Sean Moynihan did move to the Department of Finance in 1937, but he was replaced by his brother, Maurice, who had been de Valera's Private Secretary since coming to power in 1932. He remained in his new position until 1959 when de Valera retired from active politics. Kathleen O'Connell, who joined de Valera as Personal Secretary in the United States in 1919, stayed with him until her death in 1956, when she was replaced by her niece, Marie O'Kelly, who remained with him until his death, a couple of decades later.

Those who knew de Valera personally, found him a charming individual with a disarming sense of humour. He had the Irishman's ability of being able to laugh at himself and even make light of some of his own failings. This was a side of his character which never came across to outsiders because of his unwillingness to admit any failings in public. He defended everything he did and every decision he ever made with the fierce intensity of a prophet, indignant at having his judgment questioned, which led many people to conclude he believed he was never wrong. Yet he was personally without ostentation. He usually answered the front door and the telephone himself when he was at home, thereby privately projecting a straightforward simplicity, despite being the most complex of individuals. All his colleagues were on a first name basis with one another, but he always remained that bit aloof. He was always "Mr de Valera" or "Chief" to his ministers. It was said his wife was the only one who called him "Dev" to his face.

His style of leadership was to seek agreed decisions on overall policy by relying "upon the force of physical exhaustion to get agreement," according to Lemass. The President frequently found himself presiding over intense battles between his ministers, vigorously pursuing the interests of their own departments. He rarely

173

allowed consideration of any subject to end with a vote. Instead, he sought, "unanimity by the simple process of keeping the debate going—often till the small hours of the morning, until those who were in the minority, out of sheer exhaustion, conceded the case made by the majority." As de Valera personally possessed an almost inexhaustible store of patience, it meant he usually got his own way. He was—to use the title of one of his earlier biographies—a Unique Dictator.

Before long the opposition was accusing his ministers of being mere political sheep, blindly following his lead. This was because they usually kept their differences within the cabinet, or Executive Council, as it was called. Under his watchful eyes, the competing ministers conducted themselves with discretion, and even party insiders were unaware of the intensity of ministerial differences. Once the government decided on a policy, those with reservations—having conceded to the cabinet consensus—would loyally support the decision in public. "When we have discussed and differed and come to a conclusion in advance as we do, it is easy to suggest, because they are loyal—having accepted a decision—that in putting it into effect they are only 'yes men'," de Valera explained. "Some of these men were in the movement before I was. They are men of independent mind and character."

Much of his own time was taken up with foreign policy matters, especially relations with Britain. From the outset his aim was to follow the course he had outlined in 1923 of "squeezing England out" by boycotting the Governor-General and "breaching the Treaty"—by discarding the oath and "then compelling England to tolerate the breaches or bring her to a revision which would lead to something like the Doc. 2 position."

Members of the government refused to attend functions to which the Governor-General had been invited. While there was no formal announcement of this policy, it quickly became apparent when the *Irish Press* reported that the Vice-President and the Defence Minister, O'Kelly and Aiken, had walked out of a social function at the French Legation when the Governor-General arrived. MacNeill protested over the snub, and de Valera expressed regret. He promised a similar occurrence would not happen again if MacNeill informed him of his "public social engagements" in advance. In other words, members of the government intended to boycott the Governor-General but would do so discreetly, if he co-operated.

In April 1932 the government introduced legislation to abolish the oath. The British contended it was an integral part of the Treaty and could not therefore be abolished unilaterally, but de Valera did not look on the Treaty as morally binding because the Irish side had been forced to sign it under a threat of immediate and terrible war. "Whether the oath was or was not an integral part of the Treaty made ten years ago is not now the issue," he informed the Dominions Office. The real issue was that most people wished to get rid of the oath, and he contended the Statute of Westminster, which recognised the dominions as masters of their own domestic affairs, provided the authority to remove the oath from the Free State Constitution. As a result, he explained, the Free State had virtually secured the status he was seeking in 1921 when he proposed Document No. 2.

"The twenty-six counties," he told the Senate, "had practically got into the position—with the sole exception that instead of being a republic it was a monarchy." In this speech de Valera came as near to admitting publicly that he had been wrong in the whole Treaty controversy as he would ever come. "I am prepared to confess," he continued, "that there have been advances made that I did not believe would be made at the time."

"The only" way in which the Free State could be precluded from enacting the proposed legislation, he said, "would be if the Treaty had fixed a position for all time out of which it could not advance from the point of view of status." Back in 1921 he had argued that the country's status would be fixed forever, while Collins and Griffith disagreed. Now he adopted their position while those who never tired of evoking the memory of Griffith and Collins assumed his old stance. The Senate deliberately frustrated the government's efforts to abolish the oath by invoking its suspensory powers, allowing it to delay the final enactment of the legislation for up to eighteen months.

Meanwhile de Valera moved ahead with his other plans. He approached the British about revising the Treaty to bring it into line with External Association. The first British official who talked to him after his election as President was William Peters, his country's trade commissioner in Dublin. The new President was "most cordial throughout," Peters reported. "I was pleasantly surprised by his readiness to take or make a point, by his clearness of expression and perhaps more than anything else by the absence of heaviness and the glint of humour in his eye." But the Dominions Secretary, J.H. Thomas, had no intention of allowing himself to be impressed. He had already closed his mind to making any concession to de Valera in matters relating to the Treaty. "In our own interests and also in loyalty to others, namely, those who, like Mr Kevin O'Higgins, have given their lives for the Treaty, and those who, like Mr Cosgrave, have risked, and are still risking, their lives and political fortunes for it, we should stand absolutely by the sanctity of the Treaty," Thomas wrote in February. "On this there can be no compromise: our attitude should be clear and definite."

No politician in the Irish Free State would dare support the Treaty-oath openly as a good thing, so when de Valera moved to get rid of it, members of the opposition found themselves in difficulty.

They accused the government of wasting time on the bill instead of tackling the country's unemployment, but de Valera dismissed their charge.

"Not a single member of the Ministry was occupied for ten minutes either on that bill, or anything else connected with it," de Valera told the Dáil on 29 April. "They left it to me and to the lawyers, as it was a legal question."

Cumann na nGaedheal actively resorted to underhanded and, indeed, treacherous, if not treasonous, methods. In late April 1932 Senator John McLoughlin, the leader of the Irish Senate, brought Thomas a secret message from Cosgrave encouraging the British to adopt an intransigent attitude towards de Valera, and he asked for "a firm and early statement" from the British government. A couple of days later Dónal O'Sullivan, the clerk of the Senate, told the Dominions Secretary that Cosgrave was anxious for the British to outline the actions they would take if the oath bill was passed.

The "firm and early" statement asked for by Cosgrave was drafted by the Chancellor of the Exchequer, Neville Chamberlain, approved by the government and read to parliament by Thomas on 11 May. It basically warned that Britain would not negotiate any further agreement with the Dublin government if the Treaty were violated by the abolition of the oath. The British hoped their warning would have a salutary influence, and their hopes were encouraged when de Valera asked for talks on the land annuities dispute. They responded by sending two cabinet ministers, Thomas and Lord Hailsham, the Minister for War, to Dublin on 7 June. Presumably the choice of the Minister for War was intended as a subtle threat, but for Irish people the minatory implications were all but lost in the significance of the actual visit. Throughout the 1920s when Irish ministers had anything to discuss with the British, they invariably went over to London, so having the British come to Dublin, for a change, was seen as a victory for national dignity, and this enhanced de Valera's prestige.

For the talks, which lasted only an hour and a half, he was accompanied by Geoghegan, his Minister for Justice. The British had come essentially to listen, and they were not impressed. Though they accepted the President's "complete personal sincerity," they described him as "a complete dreamer, and with no grasp of realities." Their colleagues were not any more impressed three days later when the talks reconvened in London. This time de Valera was accompanied by O'Kelly and the secretaries of his two departments, Seán Moynihan and Joseph P. Walshe, as well as John Dulanty, the Irish High Commisioner in Britain. They met with Prime Minister Ramsay MacDonald, together with Thomas, Hailsham, and two other senior cabinet colleagues—Stanley Baldwin, the Conservative Leader and Herbert Samuel, the Home Secretary.

During the discussions de Valera said he was anxious for amicable relations with Britain, but the only basis for lasting friendship would be if Ireland were recognised as a thirty-two county republic. Once this had been done, he said, the island would probably agree to be freely associated with Britain, but the British were no more interested in this than their predecessors had been a decade earlier, though this time there was no threat of war.

"Don't think, Mr President, that the day you declare a republic you will be met by British guns and battleships," Thomas said. "You will be faced with the possibility of all your people in England being aliens—with the return to your country of thousands of civil servants and thousands of unemployed people now receiving public assistance. That will be Great Britain's answer, and it is for you to realise it."

Although de Valera considered the oath an internal Irish question which was none of Britain's business, he was amenable to discuss financial matters. In fact, he seemed eager to negotiate, which was understandable because he had a fairly good case, especially on the land annuities question. The British case rested on two agreements, a secret one signed in 1923, and the so-called Ultimate Financial Settlement of 1926. De Valera had already refused to accept the latter because it had never been ratified by the Dáil, but he had never even heard of the 1923 agreement until the British referred to it. If there was any valid agreement obligating the Free State to pay the annuities, he said it would be "scrupulously honoured." He therefore ordered a search for a copy of the 1923 agreement.

The Irish copy was in very poor condition when found. "It is literally in tatters," the President told the Dáil, "half-pages, parts of pages not typed, interlineations and so on. Honestly, I never saw a contract of any kind presented in such a form. There is not even an Irish signature to it." Cosgrave had signed the British copy, but de Valera refused to accept it as binding because the Dáil had never ratified the agreement. In fact, the only kind of ratification to which the British could point was Thomas' rather extraordinary contention that the agreement had been popularly ratified by Cosgrave's return to power following the subsequent general election. It was, of course, preposterous to contend that the Irish people had ratified the agreement when they were ignorant of its very existence, not to mention its details.

Although the Ultimate Financial Settlement had never been submitted to the Dáil, its terms were published in 1926, but these now took on a different significance in the light of the earlier agreement. The relevant clause of the 1926 agreement read: "The Government of the Irish Free State undertakes to pay to the British Government at agreed intervals the full amount of the annuities accruing due from time to time under the Irish Land Acts, 1891-1909, without any deduction whatsoever whether on account of income tax or otherwise." It now became apparent to de Valera that the 1926 document only dealt with the land annuities indirectly by exempting them from Irish taxes. Even if ratified, it would only have committed Dublin to pay the amount due in accordance with the 1923 agreement, which was nothing because, he contended, the 1925 agreement doing away with the Boundary Commission had cancelled the obligation by specifically releasing the Dublin government from any obligation to service the British public debt. "Since we came into office with the responsibility which it involves," de Valera told the Dáil, "we have given more detailed study to these matters than was possible when we were in Opposition, and the more we study them, the more we are satisfied that the position we took up in regard to them was sound both in law and justice."

From the outset the British realised the Dublin government had a legal case. Neville Chamberlain, the Chancellor of the Exchequer, privately admitted to his colleagues in March 1932 that de Valera had "an arguable point," because the wording of the Boundary Commission agreement absolved the Dublin government "from liability for the service of the Public Debt of the United Kingdom, and that the Irish annuities form part of the Public Debt." As a result Chamberlain felt there was "a certain risk that an arbitrator might hold that Mr de Valera is right from a purely legal and technical point of view, and it would seem most undesirable that we should expose ourselves to such a decision."

There was no doubt in Chamberlain's mind that the Irish were morally obliged to pay the land annuities, and he believed the Dublin government had implicitly agreed to do so in the spirit of the Ultimate Financial Settlement. After all, if no money was owed, they would never have bothered to exempt non-existent payments from taxes in 1926. But de Valera felt equally strongly that there was no moral obligation because the land for which the British wanted payment had been stolen from the Irish people in the first place by British invaders over the centuries. To the British he was a kind of crank harping on the centuries of British misrule and abuse and utterly out of touch with current realities. Having been nurtured on the virtues of Imperialism, they could not understand his attitude, which really challenged the very foundations of their glorious Empire. If they had no moral right to the land annuities, they had no moral right to the Empire.

De Valera offered to submit the issue to the international court in The Hague, but the British insisted on the arbitration of a Commonwealth tribunal. He agreed to this but demanded that the personnel of the tribunal not be restricted "solely to citizens of the States of the British Commonwealth." The British were unwilling to agree to this. The whole question was becoming inextricably linked with the broader constitutional question of the Free State's membership of the British Commonwealth. Since all the other dominions looked to Britain as their mother country, the President contended that such a commission would be biased in favour of Britain. "The dice would always be loaded against Ireland," he told the Dáil. Convinced the Free State had been wronged by the Boundary Commission—presided over by a South African judge—de Valera was not about to take the chance of being wronged again.

He was insisting a formal agreement be properly concluded before his government would hand over any more money. In addition to the land annuities amounting to about £3 million a year, he also included a further £2 million worth of other annuity payments for such things as British pensions for Irish civil servants. He was not disputing a moral obligation to contribute towards the matters covered by each and every one of the annuity payments, he was just insisting that the arrangements be negotiated again and this time properly formalised. But the British felt renegotiating such things with de Valera would hurt Cosgrave politically, not to mention be prejudicial to their own existing position. They, therefore, held tough.

If Dublin did not hand over the money due by 16 July, they announced they would collect the money by other means; they would implement a twenty per cent tariff on imports from the Irish Free State. On the eve of the imposition of the new tariff, de Valera went over to London in a last ditch effort to persuade the British to agree to international arbitration. This time he went without any of his cabinet colleagues. He wanted a private meeting with MacDonald, but the latter was reluctant. As a result they met privately for only fifteen minutes before MacDonald was joined by the Lord Chancellor.

There was really very little room for empathy between de Valera and MacDonald. The latter, a resolute pacifist who had gone to jail as a conscientious objector during the First World War, had no regard for the hero of the Easter Rebellion. He saw him as someone who gloried in the idea of a violent struggle for national ideals. "Behind it all is the romance of force and of arms—shooting, murdering and being murdered," MacDonald wrote. "It is the gay adventure of the fool put into a china shop in hobnail boots with liberty to smash."

Under the circumstances, he found de Valera very trying: "He begins somewhere about the birth of Christ and wants a commission of four picked solely to give individual opinions to explore the past centuries and all he demands is a document, a manifesto, a judgement as from God himself as to how the world, and more particularly Ireland, should have been ruled when they were cutting each other's throats and writing beautiful missives at the same time. It makes one sick."

"So long as de Valera is there," MacDonald stated, "there is no way out." The two sides held their ground on the annuities dispute, though de Valera offered to pay the disputed money into a suspensory account pending international arbitration. However, the British still insisted on a Commonwealth tribunal. They noted Cosgrave had cited the views of six Irish lawyers who believed Dublin was violating its obligations, but de Valera dismissed this as election propaganda. He accused the British of trying to bring him down and warned that they were making "a profound mistake." The Irish people were in a resolute mood to support him, and anyway he had no intention of calling an election. He asked them to suspend the "marching orders" for an economic war, or he would stir up trouble for the British government. He actually mentioned the many Irish miners working in the coal fields of Lancashire. Not surprisingly, at this point the meeting broke up, and de Valera stormed down the hall of 10 Downing Street with MacDonald calling after him that he hoped they would meet again.

"I don't think so," the President replied.

Next day the Dublin government withheld the annuity payments, and the British retaliated by introducing a twenty per cent tax on Irish imports. Dublin, in turn, imposed similar levies on British imports. This was the start of the Economic War, which was to last for almost six years.

CHAPTER 14

"IT WILL BE HAIR-SHIRTS ALL ROUND"

As Britain and Ireland were each other's best customer, the dislocation in trade caused by the Economic War was significant to each. Of course, the impact was felt most by the Irish because Britain was virtually their only customer. In fact, ninety-six per cent of all Irish exports went to Britain at the time.

From the Fianna Fáil standpoint, however, the Economic War was a kind of mixed blessing. Cattle exports were most seriously affected, and farmers were compelled to turn increasingly to tillage—one of the party's more cherished goals. In addition, the government was able to adopt protectionist policies in order to foster Irish industries in the hope of building an economy sufficiently strong and viable to stand independently of Britain. "The present situation if rightly handled, can prove of permanent benefit to the Free State," Lemass noted. De Valera realised that the drastic action taken by the British made it easier for his government to implement a stringent policy of self-sufficiency. He told the Senate it was possible to make a virtue out of necessity and reap the benefits of the Economic War. "The suffering," he said, "is going to be made up by the foundation here of the sort of economic life that every Irishman who thought nationally in the past has hoped for."

De Valera travelled throughout the country to organised rallies, appealing to the strong nationalistic instincts of the Irish people to support his government's policies in the economic struggle against Britain by buying Irish-made goods. While the British were fighting with economic weapons, which he was unable to match, de Valera fought back with propaganda and made inroads, even among people who had no time for him. Jan Christian Smuts, the former South African leader, thought "with a mad fellow like de Valera" leading Ireland to bankruptcy and even civil war, the British should back down. "What is the sense of forcing things to such fatal issues?" Smuts asked. "Surely Great Britain must be the strong friend and elder brother." He called for "patience and magnanimity."

The difficulties over the annuities were not the main problem as far as Britain was concerned. Thomas Inskip, the British Attorney-General, publicly admitted there would be little difficulty in resolving the differences between the two governments, were it not for the constitutional implications of de Valera's overall policy. "If there could be a clear and sincere declaration of the desired intention of the Irish Free State to stay within the Empire on the basis of their constitutional position and in a spirit of loyal partnership," Inskip said, "no annuities or debts could cloud the prospect."

While de Valera had been making last minute efforts to stave off the Economic War, O'Kelly, Lemass and Ryan went to the Imperial Conference in Ottawa, where they informally explored the possibility of a settlement with Thomas, with whom O'Kelly and Lemass got on much better, because they socialised with him. Thomas and Lemass, both inveterate gamblers, got involved together in long card-playing sessions, with each jocosely vowing to win the land annuities off the other. Thereafter there was a noticeable softening in Thomas' attitude towards the whole dispute. If the British did agree to negotiate, he told O'Kelly, they would need assurance that de Valera would not try to use the occasion as a stepping-stone to a republic. In response de Valera wrote a letter for O'Kelly to show Thomas, explaining that "acceptance of a position within the Commonwealth was implied" in the limited mandate which Fianna Fáil had asked for at the polls. "The present government will respect the limitations of its mandate," he added, "but, like every other government, can only speak for its own lifetime."

Nothing came of these discussions because de Valera clearly had no intention of being satisfied with the Free State's existing imperial trappings. He was already involved in an escalating dispute with the Governor General, who was taking umbrage at being boycotted by the government.

MacNeill had refused to accept de Valera's expression of regret for the incident at the French Legation; he demanded a formal apology from both O'Kelly and Aiken, as well as the President himself. When the apology was not forthcoming, the Governor-General sent an ultimatum to de Valera on 7 June, threatening to publish all his correspondence in the matter "within three days unless I receive apologies here from you and the other Ministers who have sometimes openly and sometimes otherwise sought to behave with calculated discourtesies to the Governor-General from whom you accepted confirmation of your appointments." De Valera replied instructing MacNeill not to publish the confidential correspondence, but the Governor-General carried out his threat when the deadline expired. With the annuities dispute coming to a head, de Valera did not retaliate immediately; instead, he waited until 9 September before demanding MacNeill's removal. At first the British asked for details of the dispute, but the President refused to explain his motives. He simply insisted his government was acting within its rights in demanding MacNeill's dismissal. John Dulanty, the Irish High Commissioner in London, quietly arranged for MacNeill to tender his resignation to the King on 3 October.

At this point de Valera asked the British to do away with the office. He proposed that the Chief justice should act in the Governor General's place, but the Chief Justice, Hugh O'Kennedy, was unwilling. De Valera next proposed taking over the duties himself, but the British argued that this would be a violation of both the Treaty and the Free State Constitution. To have pursued the matter under the circumstances would have meant violating his election promise not to exceed his party's requested mandate, so he nominated a new Governor-General, Dónal O Buachalla, a member of Fianna Fáil. Instead of moving into the Vice-Regal Lodge in Phoenix Park, O Buachalla took up residence in the Dublin suburbs, where his only official function was to sign acts of the legislature. In this way de Valera successfully diluted the significance of the office and would abolish it altogether before very long.

Although O Buachalla was essentially a political nonentity, who had failed to win a seat at the last general election, his appointment was not intended as an insult to the British government. Had the President wished to do this, he could have appointed some cleaning woman, as some of his supporters suggested. O Buachalla's salary of £2,000 per year was dramatically down on the £28,000 that MacNeill got in salary and expenses, but it was still higher than the President's own salary, which was a way of preserving the dignity of the office.

De Valera's hand was no doubt strengthened during this controversy by the way in which he distinguished himself at the League of Nations in Geneva that September. It was a particularly critical time for the League. The Japanese had been flouting the Covenant with their invasion of Manchuria, which was the first real test of the League's ability to prevent war. It was the Irish Free State's turn to provide the President of the Council, in line with the practice of rotating the position every three months. De Valera was therefore presented with an international stage and he took it with relish.

There had been speculation about whether he would even bother to attend the session. He had acquired the reputation as an enemy of the League as a result of his supposed activities in the United States during 1919. It was ironic because he had not actually been opposed to the Covenant; he had merely exploited the controversy in an attempt to secure American recognition. It will be remembered that he had infuriated Irish-American leaders like Cohalan and Devoy by saying the Covenant would be acceptable, if the Irish Republic was recognised. Later, upon his return to Ireland, he managed to foster the myth that one of his aims had been to get the United States Senate to reject the Covenant. Indeed, when he addressed the Dáil in January 1921 he actually listed the defeat of the League of Nations as the first of his objectives in going to the United States. Hence, his arrival in Geneva in September 1932 was greeted with a certain amount of scepticism.

But de Valera confounded his critics by attending the opening session of the Council on Saturday, 24 September, and made a good impression by presiding forcefully at what was a particularly thorny meeting. He agreed to a six-week postponement of the Council's consideration of the Manchurian crisis, pending the presentation of a commissioned report, but he resolutely rebuffed Japanese efforts to secure a longer delay. He insisted the Council should meet to consider the report by mid-November at the latest.

As President of the Council, it fell to de Valera to deliver the opening address to the Assembly two days later. The secretariat as usual drafted the opening speech, but he discarded it and delivered one he had prepared himself instead. It was a remarkably simple straightforward speech, spotlighting the League's shortcomings and emphasising the need to strengthen the organisation in order to provide it with the necessary influence to achieve its worthy goals.

"Out beyond the walls of this Assembly," he said, "there is the public opinion of the world, and if the League is to prosper, or even survive, it must retain the support and confidence of that public opinion as a whole." There was widespread criticism that little more than lip-service was being paid to the principles of the Covenant because influential national interests seemed capable of paralysing the actions of the League, with the more powerful among them being able to smite the organisation with apparent impunity, he added. The only effective way of silencing the criticism was to enlist the support of millions of apathetic people by showing the Covenant was indeed "a solemn pact, the obligations of which no state, great or small, will find it possible to ignore."

"No state should be permitted to jeopardise the common interest by selfish action contrary to the Covenant," de Valera continued, "and no state is powerful enough to stand for long against the League if the governments in the League and their peoples are determined that the Covenant shall be upheld." While he judiciously avoided mentioning Japan by name, there was no doubt he was alluding to the Japanese when he talked of the necessity of ensuring no aggressor profited from aggression.

When he finished the Assembly seemed dumbfounded. He sat down to "a stony silence unbroken by a single note of applause," according to the *Irish Times*. While that newspaper had been no admirer, it nevertheless warmly welcomed his speech: "We cannot be surprised that Geneva received this unwelcome homily in silence; but for once at least, the world will be inclined to applaud Mr. de Valera."

The *Irish Times* had relied on an agency report, and there were similar reports in the *New York Herald Tribune*, *Manchester Guardian*, and *Daily Express*. The latter headlined its story: "Geneva Stunned by de Valera Onslaught." All gave the unmistakable impression that the speech had been strongly resented by the diplomats present.

"There is a touch of rather bitter irony in the spectacle of Mr de Valera, of all people in the world, thrusting aside the conventional words prepared for him in order to tell the League of Nations those grim truths about itself which are only too apparent," noted a *New York Herald Tribune* editorial. "It was all true enough, but the words come with a strange sound from Mr de Valera—himself the flaming embodiment of that excessive nationalism which more than any other single force has been responsible for the League's present state."

Despite reports to the contrary, the speech was actually well-received by the diplomats present. The gathering had apparently not realised de Valera had finished for some moments, which accounted for the stunned silence at the end of his address; this was followed by a burst of genuine applause. "In the lobbies the speech received nothing but praise," noted the correspondent of the *London News Chronicle*. "It was the most candid piece of criticism that within my recollection any League chairman has ever dared to utter. Yet the speech was moderate in tone, entirely without bitterness and, indeed, indicative of the speaker's sympathy with the work and aims of the League."

The international press warmly applauded the speech. "This morning Mr de Valera made the best speech I ever heard from a President of the League," wrote the correspondent, of the *London Daily Herald*. "That is not only my own judgement. It is the opinion of almost every League journalist with whom I have spoken." The prestigious *New York Times* devoted an extensive report and a favourable editorial to the address. "Rarely has Geneva heard such a speech," the newspaper reported on its front page. "It is Mr de

Valera's personal work, and together with the way he presided over the Council on Saturday, it unquestionably made him the outstanding personality of this session."

On his way back from Geneva, de Valera stopped off in London with his Attorney General, Conor Maguire, and they had a meeting with Thomas, Chamberlain, Hailsham and John Simon, the Foreign Secretary. It was agreed to reopen the negotiations on the disputed financial issues the following week in London. This time de Valera brought Maguire, Geoghegan and Seán MacEntee with him. His choice of colleagues was noteworthy. It was the first time he had included MacEntee in any talks. The other two had been with him before, but they were both party lightweights. Maguire was not even a member of the Dáil.

On first meeting the British in Dublin in June, de Valera had been accompanied by Geoghegan and Maguire, but he brought Seán T. O'Kelly to London when the talks resumed a few days later. He sent O'Kelly, Lemass and Ryan to Ottawa, and he took Joseph Connolly to Geneva to act as head of the Irish delegation in the Assembly of the League of Nations while he presided over the Council. Then on his way home he called on the British with Maguire. By involving so many ministers in the discussions, de Valera was able to assure cabinet members they were being kept fully informed, yet none of them was given the opportunity of gaining enough expertise to be regarded as competent to challenge de Valera's authority in External Affairs.

O'Kelly and Lemass had personally got on well with the British in Ottawa, and they would have seemed a logical choice for the delegation that went to London in October, though it was most unlikely they would have made any difference because the British were determined to make no concessions. The cabinet committee dealing with Irish affairs had already decided "it would be unthinkable in Mr Cosgrave's interests, as well as our own" to concede on the financial issues. De Valera realised Britain's intransigence was being encouraged by Irish elements.

"I have come to the conclusion," he told the Dáil upon his return, "that the British government, pressed forward as it is by certain anti-Irish feeling in Britain and supported by the attitude of a minority in this country, is not prepared to examine this position on its merits or to yield to claims of simple justice." He implied the Cosgrave opposition was implicated, and he was right.

During September MacDonald's parliamentary Private Secretary, Ralph Glyn, had visited Ireland, where he met several prominent members of Cumann na nGaedheal, including Cosgrave and his former Minister for Agriculture, Patrick Hogan. They expressed fears about rumours that the British were about to make a settlement with the Fianna Fáil government. This would "be quite disastrous and would mean the end of their constitutional party and all hope of working harmoniously with Great Britain," Glyn reported. As a result MacDonald felt it would be wrong to make any concessions to de Valera. He hoped the economic dislocation in Ireland would lead to the downfall of the Fianna Fáil government and its replacement by Cosgrave's party, which would undoubtedly be more accommodating to the British.

The opposition had not only been secretly encouraging British obstinacy, but had also been adopting obstructionist tactics at home. Even though Michael Collins had advocated accepting the Treaty as a mere stepping-stone to more complete freedom, some of his followers were invoking his name in 1932 as if the agreement had been intended as a permanent settlement. The bitterness engendered by the Civil War was still so intense that Cumann na nGaedheal supporters were now opposing policies they had supported in the past, simply because de Valera and Fianna Fáil now espoused them.

The British were confidently expecting the Irish government to collapse under its economic pressure. Unemployment was soaring and, with the world-wide depression, the safety value of emigration was shut off. In fact, for the first time since the Great Famine of 1847, more people returned to Ireland than emigrated in 1932. Seán Lemass painted an extremely gloomy picture for his colleagues in early November.

"I do not think it can be denied that we are facing a crisis as grave as that of 1847 and I feel strongly that our present efforts are totally inadequate to cope with it," he warned. "We have reached the position where a collapse of our economic position is in sight." He engaged in some informal discussions with the British in the following weeks, presumably with de Valera's approval, though without any real authority. "You must remember," an Opposition senator told Thomas, "that the President is as vain as a peacock and that he is not going to allow any of his Ministers to negotiate on their own."

The people of the Free State were, on the whole, undoubtedly worse off, but the burden was being spread more equitably. De Valera's opponents accused him of being in favour of a "hair-shirt policy." But the government's introduction of more compassionate welfare policies helped to alleviate some of the worst conditions. The opposition had been pursuing a "silk-shirt policy for some and the hair-shirt policy for others," he complained. "If there are to be hair-shirts at all," he added, "it will be hair-shirts all round."

De Valera had a handy scapegoat in the old bogeymen, the British. He blamed them for the economic difficulties, accusing them of waging an Economic War to keep Ireland in subjugation. Now he was calling on the Irish people to play a part in what could be the last round of the seven centuries-long struggle for independence. "If the British Government should succeed in beating us in this fight," he warned the Fianna Fáil Árd Fheis on 8 November 1932, "then you would have no freedom, because at every step they could threaten you again and force you again to obey the British. What is involved is whether the Irish nation is going to be free or not."

In the heightened atmosphere of political tension there was growing unrest throughout the country as Republican elements showed signs of intensifying militancy. The Fianna Fáil government had dissolved the military tribunals in March and freed those convicted under them, with the result that the Republicans were enjoying a freer hand than at any time since the Civil War, and they were flexing their muscles in a number of ways. They exploited the anti-British sentiment being aggravated by the Economic War. Walls throughout the country were daubed with the slogan, "Burn everything British but their coal." Bar owners were threatened not to sell British beer, and the IRA raided public houses throughout the country, destroying stocks of Bass Ale. On 14 December a consignment of Bass was hijacked on the way from the Dublin docks and dumped in the River Liffey. "The Dublin Beer Party," as it was dubbed by Republican propagandists, was intended as a symbolic re-enactment of the Boston Tea Party at the start of the American Revolution. An Phoblacht adopted the slogan, "No free speech for traitors," to call on Republicans to disrupt the meetings of Cumann na nGaedheal, which reacted by turning for protection to the Army Comrades Association, a quasi-military organisation of former Free State soldiers.

In his Árd Fheis speech, de Valera called on Fianna Fáil supporters to disassociate themselves from disruptive tactics. "I want everyone in our organisation to have nothing to do with intimidation of other people or with interference at public meetings," he said. "Every person has the right to their point of view."

But this message was lost on radical Republicans like Frank Ryan. "No matter what anyone says to the contrary, while we have fists, hands and boots to use, and guns if necessary, we will not allow free speech to traitors," he told a meeting in Dublin on 10 November. To him, everybody who backed the Treaty, supported the Free State, or even wore poppies commemorating the dead of the First World War, was a traitor.

In the face of such irrational militancy, Fianna Fáil was in danger of being squeezed by both sides, especially with the economy deteriorating at an alarming rate. De Valera was hoping the United States would come to his government's economic rescue once Franklin D. Roosevelt, the new President-elect, moved into the White House in March 1933. Back in 1919 when Roosevelt was practising as a lawyer, de Valera had consulted him about the legality of the bond certificates and there were now grounds for hoping that Ireland was going to have a friend in the White House. But the British organised a propaganda stroke on the annuities controversy before the end of the year.

In December, when France, Belgium, Poland and Hungary defaulted on the war debt payments to the United States, Neville Chamberlain announced Britain would be paying her $95 million on time, even though it meant asking parliament for a supplementary estimate to cover the loss of the Irish annuities and increased unemployment benefits. Next day *The New York Times* had a front page headline: "Irish land issue and relief put Britain out £21,420,955." The headline had grossly exaggerated the impact of the withholding of the land annuities on the British economy, because those annuities amounted to less than fifteen per cent of the sum mentioned, and anyway the British exchequer had recouped the money with the tariffs on Irish imports.

The report cast the British in a most favourable light and was, by implication, extremely damning of the Dublin government, which was now being lumped among the defaulting nations at a time when the whole issue was a particularly touchy subject for the American people, already in the grips of the Great Depression. For de Valera, who was always deeply conscious of American opinion, the whole thing was particularly disturbing, especially at this time, but it did not take him long to pull a propaganda stroke of his own. Within a week he announced that the Irish Free State was repaying the Republican loan which he had launched in the United States during the War of Independence. Although the money would not become due until Ireland was recognised as an independent republic, he announced it was being repaid immediately with a twenty-five per cent premium added. The timing of his gesture was impeccable.

While the furore was still raging over the other nations defaulting on their war debt payments, the Irish were moving to pay their debt in full, even before it was due. As a result, the story made front page news throughout the country.

This was not the only piece of astute timing. As the year came to a close the constitutional opposition at home was showing signs of coming together. James Dillon, the independent member of the Dáil who had supported de Valera's election as President, had become very critical and helped to found the National Centre Party, which was gaining significant support in the farming community, where there was considerable discontent on account of the disastrous drop in cattle exports and a misunderstanding over the land annuities. Many farmers had mistakenly thought de Valera was promising to abolish the annuities, instead of merely withholding them from Britain. Much to their annoyance the Land Commission still collected the payments for the Irish exchequer. Feelings were running so high that the National Centre Party entered negotiations with Cumann na nGaedheal in the hope of uniting politically, but before they could combine, de Valera moved decisively. On 2 January he called a snap general election, apparently without even consulting his government.

The ensuing campaign was probably the bitterest in the State's history. The opposition was more positive this time out, as it tried to outflank Fianna Fáil by proposing modifications to the President's own policies. Cosgrave promised, if he got back into power, to cancel the arrears of land annuities, declare a moratorium on their payment for 1934, and negotiate to have them reduced thereafter. He also promised to end the Economic War, arrange a trade agreement with Britain, and secure a revision of the previous financial settlements by "courageous negotiations." No doubt this was intended to insinuate that the Fianna Fáil government had not been courageous, but the electorate was just as likely to infer that Cosgrave was inadvertently admitting he had not negotiated courageously himself during his ten years in power.

Fianna Fáil had been in office less than ten months and, if anything, people would have been inclined to say that de Valera had been a little too ambitious and too courageous in his negotiating. If Cumann na nGaedheal had stood on a similar platform the previous year Cosgrave might have had a better chance, but now his promises seemed like an endorsement of de Valera's approach. "Even Cosgrave admits that Fianna Fáil was right all the time," the government declared in its election advertising.

CHAPTER 15

"My Father and Mother Were Married"

De Valera's timing in calling the general election proved impeccable. Fianna Fáil won seventy-seven of the 143 seats to become the first party in the history of the Free State to win an overall majority in the Dáil. He was duly re-elected as President of the Executive Council, and there followed one of the most productive periods of his life. As President and Minister for External Affairs, he was involved in a wide variety of important areas, making momentous decisions on constitutional, security, and economic matters, in addition to fulfilling his parliamentary duties. He also took an active part in representing the Free State at the League of Nations in Geneva, where—as will be seen in the next chapter—he secured an enviable reputation for himself as a statesman.

Throughout 1933 discontent over the deteriorating economic situation continued to grow. The economic war was not even six months old when de Valera called the general election, so its impact was not really appreciated and his government was still confidently holding out the possibility of finding new markets to replace those lost in Britain. He hoped the United States would come to his rescue, especially Franklin D. Roosevelt about to move into the White House in March, but the new President had strong anglophile tendencies, and he would not be in office a year before it would become apparent that he had no intention of helping the Irish in their dispute with Britain. When asked at a press conference about the possibility of concluding a trade agreement with the Free State, Roosevelt dismissed the idea.

"No," he replied. "Tell me, can we enter into a trade agreement with Ireland without the consent of Great Britain?"

"I think so," the reporter replied. "Ireland claims they can." This brought a laugh from the President and assembled reporters. It was typical of the frivolous way in which Roosevelt got his message across without engaging in any politically hazardous elaboration. As usual the reporters facilitated him by not asking any more questions on the subject.

The countries of Europe showed little interest in an economic deal with the Free State either, because they thought the Anglo-Irish difficulties would soon be resolved and the Irish would then return to their old markets in Britain. It was probably to impress the continentals as much as to frighten the British that de Valera talked publicly about the Irish market in Britain being "gone forever" during the summer of 1933. "We have to face the fact," he said, "that the market that we have enjoyed in the past, Economic War or no Economic War, will never be there for us again."

The government's efforts to extend industrial employment met with some success, though this was always more associated with the ablest of de Valera's ministers, Seán Lemass, while the President was more popularly associated with the rural scene, where his policy was little short of disastrous from the economic standpoint. As the British tariffs began to bite hard into the Irish economy, the government was forced to introduce export subsidies. A bounty was paid on cattle being sent to Britain to offset the tariff being collected by the British. As a result the Dublin government was effectively paying the annuities in the form of export subsidies, and the British were collecting them in the form of tariffs, while the economy of each country suffered due to the loss of business brought about by the penal taxes.

De Valera still thought the way to alleviate rural unemployment was to increase tillage, so he was not all that disturbed by what was happening to the cattle trade. Even if the cattle market in Britain disappeared altogether, he said he was satisfied it would "work out, ultimately, for the best interests of this nation." The government provided subsidies to farmers to grow wheat and sugar beet, but the policy had little effect on the employment situation. The overall acreage under tillage did not change much. In the province of Leinster, where there was a slight increase in tillage, there was a decrease in the size of the population engaged in the agricultural sector, while in Connaught, where the amount of tillage decreased, agricultural employment rose. Tillage was obviously not the panacea de Valera believed. The main impact of the subsidies was to prompt farmers who had previously been growing other cereals, such as oats and barley, to switch to wheat. This led to a rise in the price of oats and barley, and as the Irish climate was not really conducive to growing wheat, consumers ended up paying more for an inferior product.

While large agricultural exporters were the hardest hit by the drop in the cattle trade, the small farmers were also hurt and, as many of them were already living at a subsistence level, the government came to their aid by extending unemployment assistance to them. Thus de Valera's economic policy undermined his own dream of self-sufficiency by encouraging dependency on state welfare. He had to endure Opposition gibes that his policy would, in effect, leave the Irish people without a shirt on their backs. But he was unapologetic.

"That is the policy that is going to reduce us to the hair-shirt and báinín," he said. "If we did come in here in báiníní, we would not be a bit colder than we are and we might look just as well." As far as he was concerned, economic matters were never more than a secondary consideration to him, because he was always more interested in the constitutional implications of his overall programme.

The British admitted the Economic War was inextricably linked with the constitutional controversy over the the Free State's relationship with the British crown, so when de Valera talked *ad nauseam* of Ireland's centuries of struggle, he was effectively reminding the Irish people that their current plight was really nothing new. It was part of the same process endured by their forefathers, only now there was a much greater chance of success. He exploited historical tradition to instil in the people a pride in their Irishness and a sense of their own greatness, which had a distinct appeal to many of those reared as part of the British Empire. They grew up in a society fostering a kind of national inferiority complex as it constantly looked to London for leadership and enlightenment. The Cumann na nGaedheal government had tried to emphasise the country's distinct nationality in many ways, especially in the area of foreign policy, but it contributed to the feelings of inferiority by looking to Westminster for permission to act on matters which should have been none of Britain's business, and also by invariably sending ministers to London for talks without ever insisting on any reciprocal visits from the British. De Valera had started to rectify this trend in 1932 but he was inhibited by his promise to respect the limited mandate sought by Fianna Fáil. Following his re-election in 1933, however, he was free to accelerate the process by various means.

He had never shown any real interest in—or appreciation of—cultural matters other than the Irish language, but this did not deter him from speaking on the subject at the opening of the radio station in Athlone on 6 February 1933. "The Irish theatre movement has given us the finest school of acting of the present day," he declared. "The strange fitfulness of the lamentations and love songs, the transition from gladness to pathos, have thrilled the experts and made them proclaim our music the most varied and most poetical in the world."

De Valera used a kind of refined cultural demagoguery to incorporate Ireland's past, both real and mythical, in his current struggle. In effect, he called on the Irish people to forget their current economic difficulties in the interest of something much greater than provincial considerations or material things. "The Irish genius has always stressed spiritual and intellectual rather than material values," he said in his Athlone broadcast. "That is the characteristic that fits the Irish people in a special manner for the task, now a vital one, of helping to save western civilisation." He wanted people to look beyond "narrow and intolerant nationalism." He was not just calling for Ireland's restoration to what he considered her rightful place among the nations, but was also enlisting the Irish people in a kind of crusade to save the world. "Ireland today has no dearer hope than this," he said, "that true to her holiest traditions, she may humbly serve the truth and help by truth to save the world."

Well might his foreign critics think he was lost in the celtic mists. His opponents at home, who would not credit him with anything positive anyway, thought he was talking tosh, but for many people he was redressing the balance of centuries and dispelling the notion of national inferiority. While the armies of Europe were preparing to march, the Irish people sent a veritable army of their own abroad to save the world, in the form of thousands of missionaries. De Valera would skilfully align himself with the worthy ideals of those people.

The strength of his appeal was not found in magnetic oratory or in the logic of his message, but in the passionate sincerity he projected. He did not engage in theatrics or grand eloquent rhetoric but kept his approach apparently simple. Those who did not believe in what he was saying were nevertheless convinced he believed it himself. As a former teacher he knew the value of simplicity and repetition, and he used his own political calendar of anniversaries to trot out again and again various myths about Ireland's past glories, cultural greatness, spiritual resilience and the indomitable determination of her people to secure their freedom against overwhelming odds. No doubt individual examples could have been used to justify such arguments in specific instances, but it was pure mythology to attribute such characteristics to the Irish people as a whole, as if they were some kind of chosen race. These myths provided emotional support for his message, and they were repeated so often that people began to look on them as truths. Occasions like St Patrick's Day, Easter and Christmas were particularly favoured for such speeches, because they helped to add a religious overtone to his message, with the result that his personal outlook seemed to have about it a mystical quality rooted deeply in Irish history and

Catholic values.

His Cumann na nGaedheal opponents meanwhile made the dreadful mistake of flirting with fascism, an ideology that was totally foreign to the Irish people. It was not that they were fascist themselves, but they were so blinded by their hatred of de Valera that they went to irrational lengths in opposing him. He stood aloof, endorsing decent, moral, democratic values and distancing himself from the militancy of his opponents on both the right and the left of the political spectrum. In the process he entrenched himself in the centre ground of Irish politics.

The attention of the electorate was frequently diverted from economic problems to security considerations, as the government trod a delicate path between rival factions which threatened the institutions of the State. From de Valera's standpoint the most immediate threat came from his old Civil War opponents, who were immediately suspicious when he appointed Patrick Ruttledge Minister for Justice in place of Geoghegan in his new government in February 1933. They saw this as an indication that the President no longer felt any need to placate the police force with the likes of Geoghegan, the former Cumann na nGaedheal supporter, and those suspicions were fuelled with the removal of the Garda Commissioner, General Eoin O'Duffy.

On 22 February 1933 de Valera summoned O'Duffy to his office and, in company with Ruttledge, informed the Commissioner he was being relieved of his post. He offered him another position in the civil service with the same salary, but O'Duffy declined and was dismissed. David Neligan, the head of the Special Branch, who had been suspended on full pay in December on a disciplinary matter, was also given a similar choice, and he took up a position in the Land Commission. Eamonn Broy, who had been a close colleague of Michael Collins, was appointed Commissioner, but O'Duffy's removal was still viewed by many as an indication that Fianna Fáil was going back on its promise not to victimise people who had the served the Cumann na nGaedheal government. As a result, the former Commissioner was hailed as a kind of martyr within Opposition circles.

De Valera refused to be drawn on the reasons for O'Duffy's removal. "In the opinion of the Executive Council," he said, "a change of Commissioner was desirable in the public interest." Cosgrave had obviously thought the same thing a year earlier because he had personally planned to remove O'Duffy, but he now sought to exploit the issue to embarrass the government by charging it with victimisation. When the Dáil debated the dismissal, de Valera explained that the government wanted a Commissioner in whom it would "have full confidence." He had heard rumours of O'Duffy's efforts to organise a coup the previous year, so the government's lack of full confidence was not only understandable but, in this instance, fully justified, as would become painfully evident to people on both sides of the political divide before very long.

O'Duffy was elected leader of the Army Comrades Association in July and promptly began remodelling it on fascist lines. He changed the organisation's name to the National Guard, and moved about the country on a massive recruiting drive, opening up the organisation to all "citizens of Irish birth or parentage who professed the Christian faith" and who were not members of any secret society. The size of the membership increased dramatically, but probably never reached the 100,000 claimed by him at the end of the year.

The National Guard—or the Blueshirts as they were called because they had adopted a blue shirt as their uniform, just as the fascists had adopted the black shirt in Italy, and the Nazis the brown shirt in Germany—found considerable support among pro-Treaty elements, who felt a need for such an organisation to protect themselves from the disruptive tactics of the IRA, because the government seemed rather indifferent to their plight. De Valera genuinely feared a fascist-style *coup d'état* when O'Duffy called on Blueshirts throughout the country to march to the lawn outside Leinster House for a demonstration commemorating Griffith and Collins on Sunday, 13 August. In view of O'Duffy's outspoken admiration of Mussolini, many people assumed he was trying to imitate the fascist leader's infamous March on Rome.

Faced with the danger of a coup, the government revived Article 2A of the constitution to ban the march, and little over a week later went a step further and proscribed the National Guard itself. Critics were beside themselves with frustration. This was another of de Valera's many political u-turns. He had vociferously denounced the same public safety legislation when it was introduced in 1931, and he had suspended it after coming to power the following March, but he had never formally repealed it. Now he just resurrected the act and re-established the military tribunals for use mainly against the Blueshirts and their supporters, who were already deeply concerned about another of his inconsistencies.

The President was insisting that people like O'Duffy and former Cumann na nGaedheal ministers should surrender weapons they had for their personal protection. As things stood, the Blueshirts and the IRA were arming and preparing to take on one another. "The government would not be worthy of the confidence of the people if it permitted any such thing as that to go ahead," de Valera explained. "We are hoping to see that people who have arms that we can get, will not retain them in these circumstances. In talking about "the arms that we can get," he was referring mainly to licenced weapons, which were held almost exclusively by those on the Cumann na nGaedheal side. Hence the Blueshirts felt the revived public safety legislation was being applied unevenly against them, while the IRA was being given a degree of latitude it had not enjoyed for years.

De Valera, who was understandably reluctant to act against his former Civil War colleagues, apparently felt his government was redressing a long-standing imbalance. Those now complaining were mostly former Free State soldiers or police, but they were not suffering anything like what some of them had inflicted on the IRA in the past decade. "During those ten years every act of indiscipline was condoned," the President contended. That was an exaggeration, but no real effort was ever made to bring to justice those soldiers responsible for the heinous atrocities in County Kerry in 1923.

Some of the Blueshirt element had literally got away with murder, at least as far as de Valera was concerned, and he was now determined they were not going to continue flouting the law, because if they were not stopped, the competition between them and the IRA would ultimately lead to catastrophe. "We should have rapidly developed here into a position similar to the position that we have had on the continent before either fascism or communism triumphed," he explained a few years later. He did not engage in a witch-hunt against his former enemies; he did not even seek to prosecute those responsible for the Civil War atrocities, but he did call on the police to enforce the laws being flouted by the Blueshirts.

The latter posed the most immediate threat to the government, and it made strategic sense to tackle them first in order to demonstrate that the police would enforce the laws impartially, even against their former colleagues from Civil War days. Critics—no doubt sincerely but nevertheless mistakenly—accused de Valera of giving the IRA a free hand in order to make way for a complete Republican takeover, but he was determined to follow a constitutional path and he quietly made resolute efforts to persuade the IRA to take the same path. He would eventually succeed in persuading most Republicans. Ironically, his task was probably made easier by the hostility of the Blueshirts, because in the face of their threat, Republicans naturally identified with him and sided with Fianna Fáil.

In September Cumann na nGaedheal and the National Centre Party merged with the Blueshirts to form what was officially called "the United Ireland Party—Fine Gael." Initially it was generally known as the United Ireland Party, but gradually the name Fine Gael took over.

O'Duffy was elected president of the party, with Cosgrave, Dillon and MacDermot included among six vice-presidents.

After the banning of the National Guard, the Blueshirts changed their name to the Young Ireland Association and when this was banned, they became the League of Youth. Each time they retained the blueshirt uniform, so banning them under the circumstances had little effect. The government therefore moved to ban their uniform with the Uniforms (Restriction) Bill. With the Opposition trying to frustrate his every move, de Valera astutely advised Fianna Fáil deputies to keep as quiet as possible about the bill and allow the Opposition to do most of the talking as this would have a better "effect on public opinion outside." In effect, he was giving the Opposition enough political rope to hang themselves, and some of them duly obliged.

John A. Costello, a moderate and thoroughly decent man, was among those who had already got carried away in the debate. "The Blueshirts will be victorious," he predicted just as "the Blackshirts were victorious in Italy" and "the Hitler shirts were victorious in Germany." Such remarks did more to associate Fine Gael and the Blueshirts with fascism than anything de Valera could have said. Although the legislation passed all stages of the house within three weeks, the Senate invoked its suspensory powers to delay the bill's enactment for eighteen months.

This was too much for de Valera, who retaliated by introducing a bill to abolish the Senate. It passed the Dáil on 24 May but, as expected, the Senate also used its suspensory powers to delay its enactment.

Throughout all of this Fine Gael had a very high profile, as it sought to exploit economic discontent and make political capital out of every controversy, especially in the run up to local elections of June 1934. O'Duffy predicted Fine Gael would win twenty of the twenty-three county councils being contested, and his predictions were taken seriously because these elections were still conducted on a limited franchise based on the rates. He deliberately tried to turn the local elections into a referendum on the government's performance, but this rebounded on him badly when Fianna Fáil fared much better at the polls. His predictions turned out to be wildly extravagant; Fine Gael won only three of the county councils. In the process O'Duffy's political reputation suffered irreparable damage and, under pressure, he resigned as leader of the party, and was replaced by Cosgrave.

Although de Valera managed to win the support of most Republicans, there was still a recalcitrant minority, and it controlled the IRA. He had a number of secret meetings with IRA leaders—like Seán Russell, George Gilmore, and Seán MacBride—in order to persuade them to support his programme of systematically dismantling the Treaty. He was basically asking them to do what Collins had asked in 1922, and they were no more prepared to heed his call than they had been to follow Collins. They, in turn, tried to persuade him to join with them.

"He is a very hard person to argue with," MacBride wrote after five lengthy meetings with de Valera. "He spent a tremendous amount of time reiterating his position and justifying his actions in 1921-22-23 and 27 and I found it extremely hard to get him to consider anything but his own point of view." MacBride demanded the removal of most of the senior civil servants, whom he described as "merely British secret service agents." He also wanted to act to end partition, but the President was ruling out the use of force.

"The only policy for abolishing partition that I can see," he explained, "is for us, in this part of Ireland, to use such freedom as we can secure to get the people in this part of Ireland such conditions as will make the people in the other part of Ireland wish to belong to this part."

When he argued that the IRA should respect the majority will of the people, MacBride reminded him of his earlier statement about the majority having no right to do wrong. Eventually the President lost his temper, or pretended to do so, at any rate. "He got excited and said that he would maintain law and order even if it cost him his life and no matter what he did to maintain it," according to MacBride.

Unable to persuade the IRA leaders himself, de Valera looked for help from McGarrity in the United States. Knowing that McGarrity was a bitter anglophobe, the President blamed the British for all his problems. "The pressure of the British must begin to tell at some time," he explained. "It is, I fear, beginning to tell now and nothing can save the situation except united action and almost fierce

The childhood home of Eamon de Valera at Bruree, Co. Limerick.

De Valera in Holyhead with some of those who accompanied him to London to meet Lloyd George in July 1921. From left to right, Robert Barton, Eamon de Valera, Count Plunkett, Arthur Griffith and Erskine Childers.

Harry Boland, Michael Collins and Eamon de Valera.

de Valera inspecting the Western Division of the Irish Republican Army at Six Mile Bridges, Co. Clare.

First Fianna Fail Party to enter Dail Eireann, 11th August 1927. Eamon de Valera, seated centre, with Countess Markievicz to his right.

Eamon de Valera and Sinéad on their wedding day, 9th January 1909.

Eamon de Valera and Seán T. O'Kelly outside 10 Downing Street, 10th June 1932.

Eamon de Valera taking the salute at a march-past of troops of the Irish Free State, Dublin 1934

The new Taoiseach Eamon de Valera receives the seal of office from President Seán T. O'Kelly in 1951.

Pope Pius XII with Eamon de Valera, whom he received in audience at his summer residence at Castelgandolfo, 5th October 1957.

President de Valera visits
Kilmainham Jail in 1961.

Eamon de Valera with
John F. Kennedy.

Eamon de Valera, right,
with John A. Costello
– they twice succeeded
each other as Taoiseach.

Sinéad de Valera in Aras an Uachtarain.

The de Valera family and relatives, led by his eldest son Major Vivion de Valera entering St. Patrick's Hall, where lay the remains of Mr de Valera.

organisation on the part of everyone who wants to win this fight. If our friends over there could be got to bring pressure on the IRA to throw in their weight behind the government tremendous progress could be made." He asked McGarrity to use his influence to do two things. One, to organise public opinion in the United States by explaining how Britain was using economic pressure in an effort to crush the Irish people. Two, to "get the IRA lads to see a little bit of sense," and stop their "damn foolacting business such as the Bass raids." If excluding Bass Ale would do any good, he would do it, but he believed the British would retaliate by excluding Guinness from Britain "and we would suffer ten times as much."

But McGarrity's sympathies were clearly with the IRA. "We have all been vexed and alarmed here on reading that the government has acted against the people [at] home who are trying to stop the use of English goods in Ireland," he replied. "We feel the sooner you exclude everything English the quicker you will win the fight. Lord Guinness is one of their own and will not be taxed by the English nor have his product excluded."

It was just a matter of de Valera sitting down with the IRA and ironing out their differences, as far as McGarrity was concerned. "To be frank," he continued, "it is apparent that an agreement between your forces and the forces of the IRA is a national necessity. They can do things you will not care to do or cannot do in the face of public criticism, while the IRA pay no heed to public clamour so long as they feel they are doing a national duty. You both profess to desire the same goal, why in God's name do you hesitate to sit down and try to find a working agreement? It is the extreme, the fanatical thing as the English call it, that frightens them and causes them to seek for peace."

"I don't think I ever got a letter which required such patience to read through," de Valera explained. "There was a pain in every line." Indeed, he was so upset, he took almost four months to respond, and then every line of his own reply was permeated with frustration.

"You talk about coming to an understanding with the IRA," he wrote. "You talk of the influence it would have both here and abroad. You talk as if we were fools and didn't realise all this. My God!"

Ever since 1921, de Valera contended he had been doing everything he could to maintain Republican unity. "How can you imagine for one moment that I don't realise what division in the Republican ranks means at a time like this?" he asked. "But is this need and desire for unity to be used as a means of trying to blackmail us into adopting a policy we know could only lead our people to disaster? It has taken us ten long years of patient effort to get the Irish nation on the march again after a devastating Civil War. Are we to abandon all this in order to satisfy a group who have not given the slightest evidence of any ability to lead our people anywhere except back into the morass?"

What de Valera was really looking for was not so much Republican unity as Republican support. He was still determined he should be the leader and that he should call the shots. "We desire unity," he wrote, "but desires will get us nowhere unless we can get some accepted basis for determining what the national policy shall be and where leadership shall lie. What is the use of talking any more with people who are too stupid or too pig-headed to see this. A nation in its struggle can no more be successful than an army can without a plan of campaign and an accepted leadership to see it through." His programme now was based on the cease fire terms, which the Republicans had offered to the Free State government towards the end of the Civil War. Those terms, which he had prepared himself, were the only basis the Republicans could agree on in 1923.

Had those proposals been accepted by the Cumann na nGaedheal government, much of the subsequent bitterness would have been avoided, he contended, because the IRA as a whole would have accepted the terms at that time. Now, however, some of the more militant were making impossible demands. He now blamed the whole mess on Cosgrave because the latter had rejected his terms out of personal spite in order to destroy him politically. Here was another example of that arrogance which de Valera's critics found insufferable. He had the audacity to contend, in effect, that the terms he drew up in 1923 were the only terms of reconciliation which could be devised by any human being. "I do not believe the wit of man will discover any other basis," he wrote.

Republicans had initially welcomed de Valera's election in 1932, but the enthusiasm of their more militant members gradually waned, just as his patience with them eventually wore thin, though all the time he had been weaning Republicans away from the IRA and into the Fianna Fáil fold. Some were impressed by the way he tackled and virtually emasculated the Blueshirts, while others, often in strident circumstances, were won over when his government introduced pensions for veterans of the War of Independence. On 12 March 1936 he explained his policy to a British visitor in terms of "disarming the gunmen by a peaceful process." Within a fort-night, however, he would have grounds to reconsider when the IRA murdered Boyle Somerville, a seventy-year-old retired Royal Navy admiral, at his home in Castletownshend, County Cork. His sup-posed crime was having obliged some local men seeking references to join the British navy. On 25 April there was a further killing in County Waterford, when the IRA killed one of its own members for allegedly informing. De Valera denounced the crimes and his government outlawed the IRA, much to the annoyance of his own former colleagues.

"You govern the Free State as it was when Cosgrave held your office," Mary MacSwiney wrote. Back in 1922 he had denounced Cosgrave's insistence that there should be only one army and one government; now he was taking the same stand himself.

He ignored this letter at first "because," he wrote, "to reply to it in full would have meant engaging in a futile controversy on mat-ters of past history at a time when the problems of the present and the future claim my attention." It was only after she wrote to him again that he responded.

"Are you not aware that defenceless citizens have been mur-dered in the most cowardly manner within the last few months in Co. Cork and Co. Waterford?" he wrote. "Is it not obvious to you that the murders were the work of an organisation? Do you approve of them? Do you not admit that in every community there must be some authority to prevent and punish murder? Or do you suggest that the protection of life and the prevention of crime must wait until the community is satisfied with its political status?"

"You are a fool—a criminal fool!" she replied. "And you might have been so great!!"

In 1931 when the Cumann na nGaedheal government intro-duced the public safety legislation after a Garda superintendent had been shot by the IRA, de Valera had denounced the government. "Every word you are saying now—with such attempted sacrosanc-tity—they said then," she wrote. "The IRA was outlawed, banned, proclaimed in the best British style which you are copying very faithfully today. You took a different stand then. Read your own speeches of 1931, on this selfsame coercion act passed in the self-same circumstances, and then face your own sincerity."

Notwithstanding the contradictions, de Valera pressed ahead with his efforts to suppress the IRA. "If one section of the commu-nity could claim the right to build up a political army," he explained in Enniscorthy on 2 August 1936, "so could another, and it would not be long before this country would be rent asunder by rival military factions." He added that "if a minority tries to have its way by force against the will of the majority it is inevitable that the majority will resist by force, and this can only mean Civil War."

His opponents on both sides were quick to point out that he was talking now in very different terms from 1922 when he had maintained that the minority had a right to uphold its views with arms. Even though Cosgrave agreed with the suppression of the IRA, he could not allow the opportunity to pass without accusing de Valera of being a recent convert to democracy.

De Valera persistently maintained, however, that he had played an honourable role in the events leading to the Civil War. Although he had refused to get into a debate about the past with Mary MacSwiney, he turned around and challenged Cosgrave to agree to an historical commission to look into the causes of the Civil War. He proposed that Cosgrave and himself should each nominate three people such as a judge, a constitutional lawyer, and a professor, or a recognised student of history to serve on the commission and to ask the Catholic hierarchy to nominate a bishop to act as an impartial chairman. The two sides would then make all their documents available to the commission. De Valera had been so maligned by the press during the Civil War that the findings would undoubtedly have shown him in a better light. Even if he had been wrong about the Treaty in 1922, he was now following the course outlined by Collins while the latter's supporters were trying to frustrate his every move. Cosgrave's blunt refusal to have anything to do with the proposed historical commission may well have strengthened de Valera's conviction on the propriety of his own conduct in 1922.

Ever since the Civil War, relations between himself and Cosgrave had been embittered. Except on the floor of the Dáil, they did not speak to one another, and they would carry that feud almost to the end of their lives. In view of what had happened in 1922 their mutual distrust was understandable, but de Valera's feelings were certainly not helped by the whispering campaign being conducted against him by some of Cosgrave's supporters. There were snide insinuations, for example, about his foreign background, his religious heritage, and even his legitimacy. One "dirty innuendo" that particularly irritated him—for which he blamed the Opposition—was the suggestion that he was the bastard son of a Spanish Jew.

"There is not, so far as I know, a single drop of Jewish blood in my veins," de Valera told the Dáil in indignation. "On both sides I come from Catholic stock. My father and mother were married in a Catholic church on September 19th 1881. I was born in October 1882. I was baptised in a Catholic church. I was brought up here in a Catholic home." He added that he did not care who tried to pretend he was not Irish. "I say I have been known to the Irish and that I have given everything in me to the Irish nation." His comments were a further example of his insecurity about his foreign background.

CHAPTER 16

Throughout the period of his second government de Valera used the stepping-stone approach advocated by Collins to whittle away at the Treaty, dismantling the objectionable aspects one by one. Speaking at Arbour Hill on 23 April 1933 he outlined his policy. He explained he would not willingly assent "to any form of symbol" incongruous with the country's status as a sovereign nation. "Let us remove these forms one by one," he said, "so that this State that we control may be a Republic in fact and that, when the time comes, the proclaiming of the Republic may involve no more than a ceremony, the formal confirmation of a status already attained."

Although the previous Dáil had passed a bill doing away with the oath, it had been delayed by the Senate and therefore died when the Dáil was dissolved before the suspensory period had expired. De Valera promptly submitted the bill again in the new Dáil, where it passed without any difficulty. This time the Senate—which passed a resolution calling on the government to seek an amicable agreement on the issue with Britain—adopted a somewhat more facilitative approach, by not invoking its full suspensory powers. Instead of having to wait for eighteen months, the bill became law within sixty days. As a result the Treaty-oath, over which there had been so much fuss and bloodshed, was quietly confined to the scrapheap of history on 3 May 1933.

In August de Valera introduced three separate pieces of legislation limiting the country's connections with the British Crown. The first two curtailed the powers of the Governor-General and the other bill abolished the right of appeal to the judicial committee of the Privy Council. All three bills became law in November 1933.

While de Valera's efforts to dismantle the Treaty were essentially unilateral, the Americans suddenly found themselves in the midst of the affair in March 1934 when the newly appointed United States Minister to Ireland, William McDowell, formally presented his Credentials to de Valera instead of to the Governor-General, as had been customary. The State Department, which only learned of this from the press, was taken aback to read reports the same day of a triumphalist speech by the Irish Vice-President. "One by one we are cutting the ropes and chains England has wound around us here," Seán T. O'Kelly proudly declared. "Every day something is being done to oust the British from control in our country." Nothing was going to stop this process, because the Dublin government was determined and would resort to force, if necessary. "We will use every effort to reestablish the republic for the thirty-two counties," he emphasised.

The whole affair received extensive international publicity because the press thought he had used the arrival of the new American Minister as an occasion to insult the representative of the British King, but in fact the new procedure had been cleared with the British beforehand. McDowell was shown a letter initialled by King George V, approving of the new arrangement.

Under instructions from de Valera, the Irish Minister in Washington asked Secretary of State Cordell Hull to have the State Department publish a full explanation of the affair, but Hull was extremely reluctant to become embroiled in Anglo-Irish affairs. Some months earlier he had committed a *faux pas* by proposing a toast to the "Irish Republic" during a stopover in Cobh. Now, once he learned the King had approved of McDowell presenting his credentials to de Valera, the Secretary of State wanted nothing more to do with the affair.

Nevertheless the whole thing received a good deal more publicity less than a fortnight later when McDowell dropped dead at a state banquet in his honour at Dublin Castle. He actually suffered his fatal heart attack while he was responding to a toast to his health made by de Valera. In view of the ironic circumstances, his death received extensive international publicity, and the press naturally referred back to the events surrounding the presentation of his credentials twelve days earlier.

During 1934 de Valera simultaneously introduced three further bills giving effect to his concept of External Association. The first, the Citizens Bill, was to define Irish citizenship, while the Aliens Bill defined British subjects as aliens in the Irish Free State, and the third bill accorded British subjects the same privileges as Irish citizens while residing in the Free State. By the time the bills became law, confusion about the legality of the unilateral dismantling of the Treaty had been eliminated when the judicial committee of the British Privy Council ruled that "the Statute of Westminster gave to the Irish Free State a power under which it could abrogate the Treaty."

In some ways the British were coming off worst in the Economic War, despite their economic superiority. They had initially resorted to this coercion not only to get the annuities, but also to to bring de Valera down, or at least force him to observe the Treaty and abandon any idea of establishing an Irish republic. As soon as de Valera secured the overall majority in 1933, Ramsay MacDonald seemed to question the wisdom of continuing the Economic War because, he told the special cabinet committee on Irish affairs, Britain "was coming badly out of the situation."

Despite being Prime Minister, he was in a particularly weak position at the head of a national government in which his own faction of the Labour Party had only a handful of representatives. The government was dominated by the Conservative Party, and its strongman, Neville Chamberlain, the Chancellor of the Exchequer, was anxious to increase the economic pressure on the Dublin government by banning all Irish cattle imports into Britain. This was ruled out, however, by the cabinet committee which concluded that de Valera would retaliate and the end result would "damage our trade more than Free State exports." As they were basically collecting the annuities in the form of tariffs, the cabinet committee was content to let relations with the Free State drift.

A number of unofficial intermediaries had discussions with de Valera and reported to the British government, but little ever came of these talks. People like Lord Granard, the senator and Anglo-Irish businessman, simply had no rapport with the President.

"He is," Granard wrote to the Dominions Office after a conversation with him on 25 August 1934, "a most curious personality, very pleasant socially and possessed of good manners, but he is certainly not normal. He is on the borderline between genius and insanity. I have met men of many countries and have been Governor of a Lunatic Asylum, but I have never met anybody like the President of the Executive Council of the Irish Free State before. I hope that the Almighty does not create any more of the same pattern and that he will remain content with this one example." Such comments, coming from a member of the Free State parliament, merely encouraged the British to persist with their existing Irish policy.

Although they were recouping the lost annuities with their tariffs, it was costing them even more in the form of lost trade. In the autumn of 1934 *The Manchester Guardian* and *The Economist* had both come out with blistering condemnations of the government's Irish policy. They noted that Britain's trade was actually suffering. "If the British public allows the Economic War with the Free State to continue," *The Economist* concluded, "it does so in ignorance of the magnitude of the issues involved."

From Britain's economic perspective, the policy was obviously not a success, and from a political standpoint her policy was little short of disastrous, because, "de Valera used the 'Economic War' to brilliant political effect in domestic Irish terms." He entrenched his own political position by leading his party to an overall majority in the Dáil, and the British government's own political position was totally undermined in early 1935 by no less an authority than the judicial committee of the Privy Council, which ruled that—as a result of the Statute of Westminster—the Irish Free State had the right to abrogate the 1921 Treaty unilaterally. By this time the Irish had already begun to tighten some screws on the London government.

In the autumn of 1934 Dulanty informed the British that Irish officials were investigating the feasibility of replacing British coal with imports from Germany and Poland.

As the changeover to continental coal would entail costly alterations to Irish industrial plants, the British suddenly found themselves faced with the permanent loss of the Irish coal market, because those industries were unlikely to take British coal again. The London government therefore agreed to increase the British quota of Irish cattle by one-third in return for a similar Irish agreement to buy more British coal. This coal-cattle agreement, signed in January 1935, betrayed the first weakness in the British resolve to pursue the trade war.

Following the ruling by the judicial committee of the Privy Council, the British softened their approach to Irish affairs. They indicated Dublin had a right to eliminate the remaining connections with the Crown, but they warned this would mean giving up membership of the British Commonwealth, with the consequent denial of the privileges of British citizenship to the Irish people living in Britain and the dominions. The British hoped this would prompt de Valera to think very carefully before including any Republican symbols in the new constitution being drafted.

When a constitutional crisis erupted in Britain in late 1936 over the plans of King Edward VIII—who had succeeded his father in April—to marry a twice-divorced woman, de Valera seized the opportunity to take a far-reaching step towards formal External Association. As divorce was legal in Britain he had advised that the King should be allowed to marry the woman of his choice, but when the crisis was brought to a head in December and the dominions were asked to legitimise the King's abdication, de Valera took the opportunity to formalise the real position of the British King in Irish affairs. The new bill was designed "to eliminate the King from all those articles of the Constitution which seem to give him functions here in our internal affairs," the President explained. He wanted the position clearly understood from the very moment of the new King's accession to the throne.

As long as the Free State was associated with the dominions and as long as they recognised the British King "as the symbol of their cooperation" in matters like the appointment of diplomatic representatives, the External Relations Act authorised the Executive Council to ask the British King to act on behalf of the Irish Free State in such matters, but the King could only do so on the advice of the Executive Council. Some people thought de Valera should go all the way and declare a republic, but he ruled this out for the time being.

"I do not propose to use this situation to declare a republic for the twenty-six counties," he explained. "Our people at any time will have their opportunity of doing that. We are putting no barrier of any sort in the way. They can do it, if they want to do it, at any time."

Britain was suddenly confronted with a *fait accompli*. The cabinet's committee on Irish affairs held an urgent meeting to consider whether the External Relations Act provided the minimum "necessary to secure membership of the British Commonwealth." By all previous reckonings, the legislation clearly did not, but members of the committee were anxious not to complicate the abdication crisis. They decided that the Irish action did not alter the country's standing within the Commonwealth because there had been no change to Article I of the existing Free State constitution, which affirmed the country as "a co-equal member of the Community of Nations forming the British Commonwealth of Nations."

But, much to the dismay of the British, de Valera dropped that article from the draft constitution which he introduced a few months later. It was purely a Republican document that paved the way for the full implementation of External Association envisaged by de Valera in 1921. The new head of state was to be a popularly elected President, and the head of government would relinquish the title of President of the Executive Council to become Taoiseach (chief). There was no mention of any ties with the British Crown or Commonwealth; this was left to ordinary legislation. The External Relations Act remained on the statute books to be changed at will by the Irish parliament, unlike the provisions of the constitution, which were to be ratified by popular referendum and could therefore after a brief introductory period be amended only by the Irish electorate.

For all practical purposes, the new constitution would be in line with Document No. 2. Even on the Ulster issue de Valera would achieve what he had advocated should be done during the Treaty debate.

Article 2 of the new constitution would claim sovereignty over the whole thirty-two counties of Ireland, but Article 3 then stipulated that "pending the re-integration of the national territory," the laws enacted in Dublin would extend only to the "twenty-six counties." In other words, Northern Ireland's existence was accepted, but its right to exist was not formally recognised.

As it was hoped the constitution would ultimately apply to the whole island, de Valera said he aimed "to produce a constitution which would not require any fundamental change when the unity of Ireland was accomplished." Subject to "public order and morality," there were guarantees of "fundamental rights" such as freedom of speech, conscience, association, and assembly, habeas corpus, and the inviolability of one's home. In addition, all citizens were recognised as equal before the law and there was protection against religious discrimination, but the constitution nevertheless accorded closely with Catholic thinking. "The Most Holy Trinity" was attributed as the source of all authority in the Preamble.

The actual clause dealing with religion was to cause de Valera the greatest anxiety of all in drawing up the document. While the draft was being printed, he showed the proofs to some colleagues, who raised strong objections to one segment which basically recognised the Roman Catholic Church as the one true church. "The State acknowledges," the draft read, "that the true religion is that established by Our Divine Lord Jesus Christ Himself, which he committed to his Church to protect and propagate, as the guardian and interpreter of true morality. It acknowledges, moreover, that the Church of Christ is the Catholic Church." The Roman Catholic Church was further recognised "as a perfect society, having within itself full competence and sovereign authority, in respect of the spiritual good of man."

Gerry Boland, the Minister for Lands, was appalled. "If this clause gets through as now worded," he said, "it would be equivalent to the expulsion from our history of great Irishmen." Protestant patriots like Wolfe Tone, Robert Emmet, Henry Joy McCracken, Charles Stewart Parnell, Erskine Childers and many others would never have lived in Ireland "under such a sectarian constitution" he argued. "And I would not live under it either. I would take my wife and children and put myself out of it."

211

The religious clause was so contentious that de Valera had it removed from the draft constitution circulated to the whole cabinet on 16 March 1937. He explained the missing clause needed further work, and he proceeded to consult personally with leaders of the various churches. Eventually he came up with a cause merely recognising the existence in Ireland of the main Protestant churches, as well as the Jewish religion, and afforded recognition of "the special position" enjoyed by the Roman Catholic Church "as the guardian of the faith professed by the great majority of the citizens."

Cardinal MacRory opposed the new wording and both he and de Valera appealed to the Pope. "The Holy Father at first agreed with me," MacRory wrote. But de Valera sent Joseph Walshe to the Vatican to explain the difficulties which a triumphal recognition would cause, in view of the delicate sectarian situation in Northern Ireland. Although Walshe did not get a promise of outright support, he did return convinced that the Vatican would not actually oppose the new wording.

The constitution was clearly in line with Roman Catholic thinking. Divorce was prohibited in order to protect the family, which was described "as the natural primary and fundamental unit group of Society, and as a moral institution possessing inalienable and imprescriptible rights, antecedent and superior to all positive law." A whole series of social principles were outlined "for the general guidance of the legislature." These encouraged the State to ensure that mothers would "not be obliged by economic necessity to engage in labour to the neglect of their duties in the home," that all citizens would have an adequate means of livelihood, that they would be protected against exploitation by private industry, that the health of workers should "not be abused," that they should "not be forced by economic necessity to enter avocations unsuited to their sex, age or strength," that the country's material resources were distributed in such a way as to serve "the common good," and that "the economic interests of the weaker section of the community" be safeguarded. It was further advocated that as many families as practicable should "be established on the land in economic security."

Since the social principles were simply for the general guidance of the legislature and were specifically placed outside the jurisdiction of the courts, some people viewed them as mere platitudes, but it was not inappropriate to mention them boldly in the constitution, if only as a reminder to legislators to strive for those lofty ideals. De Valera skilfully used this aspect of the constitution as a kind of manifesto solemnly outlining his own ideals, or rather what he believed were the ideals of the Irish people.

The contemporary criticism of the document fell into four broad areas. There were charges of ambiguity over Articles 2 and 3, and the government was accused of hypocrisy over the stipulation that, in the event of any discrepancy between the Gaelic and English wordings, the Gaelic would take precedence, which was an essentially absurd situation because the constitution was drafted in English and only translated into Gaelic. Other criticisms were that it was insensitive about the rights of women, and there were ridiculous charges that the office of President was being created to pave the way for de Valera to take over as a national dictator. He, on the other hand, envisaged the office as largely ceremonial, and this would become obvious enough when he suggested a non-political figure—Douglas Hyde, the founder of the Gaelic League—as the first President.

There would later be much criticism of the Roman Catholic ethos permeating the new constitution, and the clause about the Church's "special position" would come in for particular criticism, but at the time even the document's most vociferous critic, Frank MacDermot, believed this "really means nothing," though he astutely warned it would be misunderstood in Ulster. It was basically intended as a mere positional statement to circumvent clerical demands for a more triumphalist recognition. At the time Fine Gael was not inclined to argue that the constitution was not secular enough, but rather that it should be more confessional.

The *Irish Times*, for long the voice of Irish Protestants, basically welcomed the constitution: "We are glad to admit that in many ways President de Valera's government has confounded its former critics including ourselves; that it has acted fairly and uprightly towards political and religious minorities, and that its Ministers, on the whole, have done their job conscientiously and well." This testament was all the more extraordinary in that it came on the eve of a general election called by de Valera to coincide with the popular referendum to ratify the constitution on 1 July 1937.

Calling a simultaneous general election was a shrewd political move on de Valera's part. He was able to justify it both on the grounds of convenience and saving money, seeing that the electorate would have to go to the polls in the near future anyway as the government's mandate had little over six months to run. More important from a tactical standpoint, it allowed Fianna Fáil to make the constitution the main election issue, rather than the economy, as would undoubtedly have been the case if he had delayed the general election. This was politically important because Ireland was still coming off worst in the continuing Economic War.

Although Britain's share of the Irish import market had declined from eighty-one per cent in 1931 to fifty per cent in 1937, Irish efforts to find new international markets were a dismal failure; only five per cent of the country's exports were redirected, which meant that a staggering ninety-one per cent still went to Britain. At the same time the value of Irish exports to Britain dropped by fifty per cent, which led to a record trade deficit of £20.7 millions in 1937. Those were figures on which no government could have relished fighting an election.

Hence de Valera emphasised the sovereignty issue as he concentrated on the constitution in his campaigning. "It is a renewed declaration of national Independence," he declared in an eve of election address. "It consolidates the ground that has been gained and forms a secure basis from which we can move forward the recovery of the national sovereignty over our ports and the reunion of the whole national territory into one state."

The result of the balloting obviously justified his decision in calling the general election. The constitution was ratified by 56.5 per cent of the voting electorate, whereas only 45.2 per cent voted for Fianna Fáil. With the relative popularity of the constitution inevitably reflecting on Fianna Fáil, the party undoubtedly fared better under the circumstances. It lost its overall majority, but only by the narrowest of margins. The eight seats it lost were largely due to the rationalisation of the new Dáil, which was fifteen seats smaller. As a result Fianna Fáil's 69 seats were exactly half of the 138 seats in the Dáil. The party could still depend on the support of the Labour Party, so de Valera retained power at the head of a minority government.

In less than five years since Fianna Fáil first achieved an overall majority, he had dismantled the most disagreeable aspects of the 1921 Treaty, implemented External Association, and essentially proved that Collins had been right in contending that the Treaty provided the freedom to achieve freedom. The British, faced with the choice of accepting what he was doing, or expelling Ireland from the British Commonwealth, announced they were "prepared to treat the constitution as not affecting a fundamental alteration" in Ireland's position, "as a member of the British Commonwealth of Nations." De Valera had, in effect, remodelled the Commonwealth concept.

Although he could have felt satisfied that the new constitution had gone a long way towards the realisation of Irish national aspirations, there were still major outstanding differences in Anglo-Irish relations over such things as partition, the defence clauses of the Treaty, and the continuing Economic War. The time had clearly come to resolve the economic conflict and tackle the remaining constitutional issues. He had gone just about as far as Ireland could go unilaterally, and he would set about tackling the other matters by diplomacy in the coming months.

CHAPTER 17

"WE OUGHT TO STAND FOR JUSTICE FOR OTHERS"

De Valera, with his vivid political discernment, was quick to appreciate the domestic advantages of a high international profile. He seized on the dramatic phase of international relations in the 1930s to earn an enviable reputation for himself as a statesman at the League of Nations.

He had distinguished himself with his forthright analysis of the League's shortcomings in the course of his opening address to the Assembly in September 1932. His words were not mere platitudes; he backed them up in the following months and years by energetically supporting moves to secure the withdrawal of Japanese forces from Manchuria, calling for the League's intervention to stop the war between Bolivia and Paraguay over the Chaco region, advocating League membership for the Soviet Union, and demanding firm action to stop the Italian invasion of Ethiopia. He took these stands even when his actions might have been expected to be unpopular at home with the Irish people.

In November 1932 he presided over the Council of the League when it considered the report of the Lytton Commission, which had been set up to investigate the Manchurian dispute. The report accused Japan of aggression and denounced the so-called independent Manchurian state of Manchukuo as an occupied Japanese puppet. In the face of obstructionist tactics by the Japanese, de Valera instilled an "energetic tone" into the proceedings and proved "an effective presiding officer," according to the *New York Times*. Over strong Japanese objections, he insisted on giving members of the commission the opportunity of replying to the comments made by the Japanese and Chinese representatives, and he also ensured the report was referred to the Assembly, with the warning that "it would be an intolerable defiance of public opinion," if the League's machinery was not used to end the dispute.

When the Assembly convened on 6 December 1932 the Irish government took a strong stand by co-sponsoring a resolution—along with Czechoslovakia, Spain, and Sweden—calling on the League to take action "with a view to ensuring a settlement of the dispute on the basis" of the Lytton Commission's recommendations. De Valera had chosen Joseph Connolly, his Minister for Posts and Telegraphs, to represent the Free State at the session, and Connolly spoke forcefully in favour of the resolution introduced by the "small four" as they were dubbed. "If the League falters or hesitates, fearing lest by its actions it may offend," he said, "then it will not survive and will not deserve to survive."

The great powers vacillated, however. It was the first major example of the disastrous policy of appeasement. The French representative adopted a timid approach, though he did at least imply France would carry out her obligations under the Covenant. John Simon, the British Foreign Secretary, implied the opposite, if anything. Stressing the difficulties of the situation and the need to be "practical," he delivered a devastating blow. Britain sided with Italy and Germany in arguing that the hardline approach advocated by the small four would probably prevent reconciliation by offending Japan.

The energetic approach taken by de Valera within the Council and the strong stand adopted by his government in the Assembly went for naught therefore, when the problem was merely turned over to a committee of the League for its suggestions. Although the Assembly did eventually adopt the Lytton report, its temporising had virtually killed any chance of decisive action, and Japan treated the League contemptuously by withdrawing from it in protest.

When other thorny questions arose later, de Valera took similarly strong stands, advocating the strict implementation of the League's Covenant. He supported the entry of the Soviet Union into the League, at the risk of exposing himself at home to renewed charges of being a Communist. Of course, he did score some political points with the Irish electorate by calling on the Moscow regime to institute religious freedom in the Soviet Union.

While his remarks about the need for religious liberty went down well at home, it would be wrong to suggest he did not sincerely believe in what he was advocating. A few days later he spoke out on another aspect of human rights, or to be more specific, the problem of minority rights which were soon to lead to—or at least become the pretext for—a series of European crises which eventually culminated in the outbreak of Second World War in August 1939, and which would still be threatening European peace more than half a century later. De Valera supported a Polish proposal calling for a uniform code for the protection of minority rights. The League had a particular responsibility in this issue, he said, because those who had framed the Covenant in Paris had contributed to the problem by raising the expectations of minorities everywhere.

"President Wilson used to protest against the cynical 'handing over of peoples from sovereignty to sovereignty as though they were chattels'," de Valera explained, "And when we were looking at the treaties that were being worked out at Versailles, some of us, at any rate, could not help thinking that that protest had been completely lost sight of when the war was over." The major powers had arbitrarily handed over minorities at Versailles, and the League now had a duty to defend the rights of those people. "I suggest," he said, "we could begin by a convention to universalise those sacred rights of the individual which should not be taken from him under any pretext by any majority whatever." To this end he proposed a committee be established to "obtain agreement on a universal measure of protection for minorities against unfair discrimination anywhere."

During the same session de Valera was elected chairman of the League's Sixth Committee, which dealt with political questions—the most thorny of which was the ongoing war between Bolivia and Paraguay over the region known as the Chaco. As President of the Council he had first suggested the League intervene in this dispute in 1932, but the United States—with its jealous attachment to the Monroe Doctrine—objected to outside interference in the American hemisphere. A number of American republics tried to settle the conflict, and when they failed the League eventually placed an embargo on the export of munitions to either Bolivia or Paraguay. The effects of the embargo were already being felt when Bolivia asked the League to intercede in the dispute in September 1934. De Valera angered the United States at this point by making what the *New York Times* described as the "sensational suggestion" that the League establish a peace-keeping force to keep the belligerent forces apart.

"It seems to me that this dispute can be brought to an end quickly if we are determined to act up fully to our responsibility," he said. Actually, it was not necessary to intervene because the war ground to a halt due largely to the effectiveness of the League's embargo, coupled with war weariness on both sides. As a result of the limited success in settling the Chaco dispute, de Valera had hopes the League would be able to prevent Italian aggression in Ethiopia the following year. From the outset he looked on the Ethiopian crisis as the crucial test for the League. As the Italians were preparing to invade Ethiopia, he announced his government's attitude was going to be "determined by its desire to see the League of Nations preserved as an effective guarantee of peace." Consequently, he said, he would "be in full sympathy with an effort that may be made to avert hostilities."

While in Geneva he delivered a broadcast to the United States over Radio Nations, the League's radio station. As things stood, people throughout the world had not been prepared to forego the opportunity of satisfying their own selfish ambitions at the expense of others. "Theoretically, and in the abstract, they assent and subscribe to the principle that the rule of law should be substituted for that of force," he said. "But, in practice, each nation wants to reserve to itself the right to interpret the law, to be the judge in its own case, and, if its interest should require it, to defy and disobey." The various alliances, treaties and non-aggression pacts entered into by members of the League showed how little confidence those countries had in the Covenant as a guarantee of security. "Each distrusts the professed good faith of its neighbour and rival, and those who depend upon the League and the Covenant for their security find themselves in danger of being taken unawares because of their confidence." As a result the League was "in imminent peril," and in drastic need of revision. In particular, he emphasised, the theory of absolute national sovereignty should be abandoned and the unanimity rule of the League changed. The organisation's rigid structures also needed to be changed so that some chronic wrongs could be righted.

"Only what is fundamentally just has a right to last," de Valera declared. "The rights of the haves and have-nots need to be adjusted from time to time in the case of States as of individuals within the State, and when a wrong cries out for redress or an evil for a cure, there must be some means of providing them in time without waiting for a threat of war to compel attention." He therefore suggested the establishment of "some tribunal by which the law shall be interpreted and applied, and, finally, there must be some means by which its judgments can be enforced against a State which might think it to its advantage to ignore them." Although the League had serious shortcomings, it was nevertheless a real attempt "to order international affairs by reason and justice instead of by force." Many people, including himself, had been suspicious of the motives of its founders, but this should not deter them from supporting it because the alternative as far as Europe was concerned was "a return to the law of the jungle," he said. "To destroy it now would be a crime against humanity. To maintain it we must live up to its obligations."

There was no doubt he was prepared to live up to those obligations. Prior to his election as chairman of the Sixth Committee, he had made overtures to secure the presidency of the Assembly, and it was ironic that the British Minister for League Affairs, Anthony Eden—who later came to international prominence as a critic of appeasement—actually opposed de Valera's prospective candidacy on the grounds that the Irish leader was a "firebrand" who would use the presidency to attack Italy.

"The final test of the League and all that it stands for has come," de Valera told the Assembly on 16 September 1935. "Our conduct in this crisis will determine whether it is better to let it lapse and disappear and be forgotten. Make no mistake, if on any pretext whatever we were to permit the sovereignty of even the weakest state amongst us to be unjustly taken away, the whole foundation of the League would crumble into dust. If the pledge of security is not universal, if it is not to apply to all impartially, if there be picking and choosing and jockeying and favouritism, if one aggressor is to be given a free hand while another is restrained, then it is far better that the old system of alliances should return and that each nation should do what it can to prepare for its own defence. Without universality, the League can only be a snare. If the Covenant is not observed as a whole for all and by all, then there is no Covenant."

He emphasised that the Irish people were determined to uphold their responsibilities in the impending crisis. "By our own choice and without compulsion we entered into the obligations of the Covenant," he said. "We shall fulfil these obligations in the letter and in the spirit. We have given our word and we shall keep it."

His logic was clear and simple. People should put the same effort into preserving peace as they would squander on war. "Yesterday," he said, "there were no finances to give the workless the opportunity of earning their bread; tomorrow, money unlimited will be found to provide for the manufacture of instruments of destruction." He may have been expecting the worst when he talked about "the final test," but he realised there was still a chance the Ethiopian crisis could be turned to the League's advantage by providing the impetus to weld members of the organisation together in "a common purpose of self-preservation."

He was particularly encouraged by the attitude adopted by Britain. Unlike John Simon's vacillation at the time of the Manchurian Crisis, the new British Foreign Secretary, Samuel Hoare took a strong stand against Italy's threatened aggression, and his speech won widespread international approval. People who had for years been highly sceptical of the League's ability to function as envisioned by its founders, suddenly discovered the organisation might after all be effective, if not in preventing aggression, at least in ensuring the aggressor would not profit by aggression. The support of world opinion which de Valera had said was so vital to the League in his first appearance before the Assembly three years earlier, was now undoubtedly aligned behind the organisation.

Even though Ethiopia offered important concessions to the Italians, Mussolini was bent on conquest. Ignoring the Ethiopian offer and his own country's obligations under the Covenant, he ordered Italian troops to Invade on 3 October 1935.

De Valera went on Radio Eireann next day to explain the situation to the Irish people. Japan's violation of the Covenant had shaken the League to its very foundations at the start of the decade, he said. "It is obvious that if a second similar successful violation takes place, the League of Nations must disappear as an effective safeguard for individual members." People are always prepared to exploit the advantages of an organisation like the League, but there was "no such alacrity in fulfilling the corresponding obligations to bear the burdens or make the sacrifices which the common interest may demand." He had "consistently held that the obligations of the Covenant should be enforced. That was our position in the case of the Sino-Japanese conflict. That is our position in the present case." The British were proposing economic sanctions against Italy, and he not only favoured these but also suggested military action should be taken if the economic pressure was not successful. Although his government did not have the authority to commit the country to such measures without the formal parliamentary approval, he intimated publicly that such consent should be given. He had already warned his cabinet that "it would be contrary to the spirit of the Covenant" to refuse to take part in any "collective military actions to be taken by the League."

"Whether or not one accepts Mr de Valera's views on these grave issues," one long-standing critic wrote, "one must realise that he has approached them sincerely and in no petty spirit, and that he is prepared to carry his opinions to their logical conclusions." Nevertheless his unequivocal support of the League met with a certain amount of criticism at home, even from within his own party. Kathleen Clarke, a widow of one of the 1916 leaders, contended that the government should have used its stand at the League "for bargaining purposes" in order to extract economic concessions from the British in return for supporting their call for sanction against Italy.

"If we want justice for ourselves, we ought to stand for justice for others," de Valera contended. "As long as I have the honour of representing any government here outside, I stand, on every occasion, for what I think is just and right, thinking thereby I will help the cause of Ireland, and I will not bargain that for anything."

On another occasion when opposition critics commented cynically about him pursuing the same policy as the British, he replied that a person on the road to Heaven would not turn around and go to Hell, simply because his worst enemy was taking the same route. Unfortunately some of his opponents at home were still so bitter towards him that they automatically tended to oppose anything he favoured.

Cosgrave initially came out against the sanction, much to the disgust of Frank MacDermot. "The line of argument adopted seems to me to offend everything we stand for," MacDermot declared publicly. "It is one that can be renewed every time that Mr de Valera behaves with ordinary decency in international affairs, and when it would be more becoming for us to commend than to attack him." MacDermot felt so strongly on the issue that he resigned from Fine Gael in protest. His actions apparently had a salutary influence because when it came to the actual Dáil vote on the sanctions against Italy, only three backbench members of Fine Gael—all from what might be called the lunatic fringe of the party—voted against the bill.

At first it looked like the sanctions might succeed under Britain's strong leadership. Hoare's speech at the League met with tremendous approval in Britain and the Prime Minister, Stanley Baldwin, capitalised on the popularity by calling a general election in which his party won a handsome majority. Baldwin and his colleague had campaigned on a promise to pursue the sanctions with full vigour and to do everything in their power to uphold the Covenant. "If ever there was an opportunity of striking a decisive blow in a generous cause with the minimum of risk," Churchill wrote, "it was here and now."

But Baldwin and his colleagues were just exploiting the crisis for their own political advantage. In December Hoare concluded the abortive pact with the French to appease Mussolini by giving him half of Ethiopia. De Valera rightly concluded that the British and the French were not in earnest about stopping the Italians. "If the powers were really serious and were prepared to take definite measures, the closing of the Suez Canal would have been resorted to as one measure," de Valera told the Dáil afterwards. "Consequently, it was obvious the League of Nations was taking half-measures which could not in the ultimate fail to be ineffective." As Churchill later wrote, the economic measures adopted "were not real sanctions to paralyse the aggressor, but merely such half-hearted sanctions as the aggressor would tolerate."

Although de Valera was often accused of exploiting anti-British feelings at every opportunity, he made no effort to do so in this instance. He behaved with impeccable diplomatic decorum throughout the whole crisis—right to the very end. He did not try to blame either Britain or France for the failure, but the League as a whole. "My view is," he told the Dáil, "that there was never a better chance for the League of Nations to be successful against a great power as there was in this case, and that if it failed in the case of Italy it was bound to fail in the case of other powers." Consequently, the League no longer had the "confidence of the ordinary people of the world," and, he emphasised, "it does not command our confidence."

Following the League's failure to stop Italy, de Valera believed another major war was virtually inevitable, and he reversed the whole trend of his policy on international affairs. From being an outspoken proponent of resisting aggression, he suddenly became a strong advocate of international appeasement.

Speaking in Geneva on 2 July 1936, for instance, he called for the lifting of the sanctions against Italy. "We have now to confess publicly that we must abandon the victim to his fate," he said. Common sense dictated something should be done to avert the drift towards catastrophe, but he realised the League would not stop it. "If the great powers of Europe would only meet now in that Peace Conference which will have to be held after Europe has once more been drenched in blood," he said, they would only have to make a fraction of the sacrifices they would have to make after the outbreak of another major war. "The problems that distract Europe should not be abandoned to the soldiers to decide," he said. "They should be tackled now by the statesmen. If these problems cannot be settled by conciliation, let them be submitted to arbitration." Of course, this was all talk but, as the leader of a small nation, he recognised there was little else he could do to avert the coming disaster.

"Despite our judicial equality here, in matters such as European peace the small states are powerless," he told the Assembly. "Peace is dependent upon the will of great states. All the small states can do, if the statesmen of the greater states fail in their duty, is resolutely to determine that they will not become the tools of any great power, and that they will resist with whatever strength they may possess every attempt to force them into a war against their will."

Meanwhile, there was a thaw in Anglo-Irish relations following the resignation of J.H. Thomas as Dominions Secretary and his replacement by Ramsay MacDonald's son, Malcolm. The latter took the initiative in asking for a secret meeting with de Valera in a room of the Grosvenor Hotel, London, on 24 March 1936. The President had stopped off on his way to Geneva, where he was to undergo surgery for his failing eyesight. The meeting, which lasted only about an hour, was mainly to break the ice. They met again, this time for more than four hours, when de Valera was returning from Geneva on 7 July. "It is perhaps an indication of his present practical mood," MacDonald reported, "that in the course of it he never mentioned Oliver Cromwell or any character or event which troubled Ireland prior to 1921."

In the following months de Valera was deeply involved in the drafting of the new constitution, but still found time to take stands on international matters. During the Spanish Civil War he supported the League's non-intervention policy, even though this was not popular with the overwhelming majority of Irish people. They tended to see the conflict in the over-simplistic terms of a struggle between Roman Catholicism and the most virulent form of atheistic communism. When Eoin O'Duffy announced he was forming a brigade to help the Nationalist forces of General Franco, some six thousand men volunteered within a fortnight. Even within the Labour Party, sentiment was so strong at the annual conference that Conor Cruise O'Brien, a young student from Trinity College, Dublin, had to be protected from physical abuse when he courageously denounced Franco.

To de Valera, the war was a struggle between fascism and communism, and while he publicly said he hoped Franco's forces would be victorious, he merely looked on them as the lesser of two evils. He introduced legislation supporting the non-intervention policy by making it a criminal offence, punishable by two years in jail and a £500 fine, to go to Spain without special permission.

The bill was vociferously opposed by Fine Gael. Desmond FitzGerald, a Minister for Foreign Affairs in Cosgrave's last government, castigated de Valera for taking a stand which, he said, was "applauded by all the Communistic, liberal, pinkish newspapers in Europe". "If I remember rightly," FitzGerald added, "he actually implied criticism of the Nazi Government in Germany and their treatment of Jews."

Sean Lester, who had been the permanent Irish representative in Geneva before joining the secretariat of the League, was particularly critical of the attitude adopted by members of Fine Gael towards de Valera's foreign policy. "They have tried to rally all our abysmal ignorance of foreign affairs against him," he noted. Surely it plumbed the depths of absurdity when the Fine Gael spokesman on Foreign Affairs attacked de Valera for having "implied criticism" of Nazi behaviour towards Jewish people.

Since de Valera thought there was little to choose between the Spanish sides, it was hardly surprising he refused to support the nonintervention states in September 1937 when they introduced a resolution at the League of Nations calling for the abandonment of the policy of non-intervention if all states did not comply with it. The resolution was really an attempt to end the foreign interference in Spain and isolate the conflict, but de Valera was convinced Germany and Italy would continue to support Franco, and if the non-intervention states then intervened on the other side it would lead "to a fatal competition which could only result in a general European disaster." Although he had just been elected Vice-President of the Assembly of the League, he abstained from voting on the resolution in order to demonstrate "beyond any possibility of misunderstanding" that he no longer considered the Covenant binding and would not be committed to any course of action resulting from the resolution.

He dramatised his repudiation of the Covenant before the end of the year by appointing a Minister to the Court of King Victor Emmanuel III in his capacity as both King of Italy and Emperor of Ethiopia. This meant the Irish government was formally recognising Italy's annexation of Ethiopia in contravention of a League resolution obligating member states "not to recognise any situation" resulting from a breach of the Covenant.

"There is a *de facto* position staring us in the face," de Valera told the Dáil, "and we must take account of that. If we wish to have a representative in Italy, as has been our wish, then we give to the sovereign of that country the title which he has taken or which his own people have taken." This had nothing to do with approving what Italy had done; it was merely recognising a reality.

CHAPTER 18

"We Whipped John Bull Every Time"

While in Geneva in September 1937 and again the following month while passing through London on his way home, de Valera had discussions with Malcolm MacDonald. Following those de Valera suggested the two governments should formally negotiate a settlement of their outstanding differences, and it was agreed to hold formal talks in London in the new year.

The British were, of course, well aware of de Valera's attitude on the various issues. He wanted them to renounce their rights to Irish bases and drop their claim to the land annuities, but he was primarily concerned with the partition question. "Throughout all my conversations with him during the last two years," MacDonald told his cabinet colleagues, "he has been at pains to emphasise in his view that no final settlement of the relations between the two countries is possible whilst partition remains."

Although the Irish people would probably wish to remain neutral in the coming war, de Valera told MacDonald they would likely come to Britain's aid, if all the outstanding difficulties were settled beforehand. There could be no formal assurance in the matter, however; Ireland would have to be free to decide on her own course when the time came, but he was prepared to assure that Irish territory would not be used as a base for an attack on Britain. MacDonald, who described de Valera as "a transparently honest and sincere man who never concealed, or even half-hid, his beliefs and aims," had no doubts. "I am convinced," he wrote, "that he is really genuine in desiring whole-hearted friendship and co-operation between the Irish Free State and Great Britain."

The British were not all that interested in Irish opinion; they were more concerned about the impact which Irish affairs had on American opinion towards Britain. De Valera had long ago recognised this and, as Britain would need all the American help she could get in the event of another war, he hoped to persuade the British that an Anglo-Irish settlement would greatly enhance their standing with the American public. "Real, unqualified friendship with the United States would be vastly more valuable to Britain than satisfaction of a claim for a sum of money, or than our occupation of the three Irish ports against the will of almost the whole Southern Irish population," de Valera told MacDonald.

The formal negotiations, which began in London on 17 January

1938, involved senior members of the two governments, backed up by senior civil servants, who did most of the background work in between three separate rounds of talks. De Valera, who did most of the talking for the Irish delegation, was accompanied by Lemass, MacEntee, and Ryan. On the other side Prime Minister Neville Chamberlain had the two former Foreign Secretaries most closely identified with Britain's appeasement during the Manchurian and Ethiopian crises, John Simon, now Chancellor of the Exchequer, and Samuel Hoare, now Home Secretary. Other members of the British delegation included Malcolm MacDonald and Thomas Inskip. The talks centred on four areas of contention—partition, defence, trade, and finance.

During the opening session, which extended over four days, the Irish hinted vaguely about being willing to make some kind of accommodation on defence in return for the ending of partition. If the British would bring the two parts of Ireland together, MacEntee said, co-operation on defence matters "might develop with remarkable rapidity," but de Valera tempered this by observing that "time would be required." Thereafter MacEntee said little.

Chamberlain was primarily anxious to secure Irish goodwill. He had decided what he was giving away beforehand. Very early in the talks he indicated that Britain would hand over the three ports and renounce her rights to the other Irish facilities. De Valera instinctively assumed the British were offering to hand these over on condition they would be made available to Britain later, if needed in an emergency. He argued they should be handed over unconditionally because it "was beyond the wit of a man to draw up a formula" handing them over and at the same time retaining rights to them. But there was no argument, as far as Chamberlain was concerned. He was making no conditions.

Members of the Irish delegation were stunned. This was certainly not the way farmers in east Limerick did business, nor the way Irish people had been conditioned to expect the British government to act. And that was not all; Chamberlain also indicated that Britain would drop her claim to the land annuities and abandon the duties on Irish imports, but he emphasised there could be no settlement of partition against the will of the majority in Northern Ireland. Privately he admitted partition was an anachronism about which he could do nothing, because the British public would not stand for putting pressure on Belfast in the matter. The only real concessions the British were demanding were some payment of the outstanding debts, exclusive of the land annuities, as well as the removal of import duties on goods imported from Northern Ireland.

Another man might have been tempted to reciprocate and offer the British something in return, but De Valera argued he could make no concessions unless partition were ended. And he stuck firmly to this line.

At the end of the first round of talks Chamberlain was very hopeful. He described de Valera as a "queer creature" in many ways but no enemy of Britain. "I shall be grievously disappointed if we don't get an all-round agreement on everything except partition," the Prime Minister wrote. "That is the difference that cannot be bridged without the assent of Ulster."

De Valera, on the other hand, provided John Cudahy, the American Minister, with a very gloomy account of the negotiations. He gave no indication that the British were prepared to make substantial concessions. Instead, he depicted the talks as doomed unless progress could be made on the partition question. He referred to an article in the *Irish Independent* the previous day in which Mary MacSwiney warned against any compromise. Although he had shown scant regard for her views over the years, he was prepared to use them when it suited his purposes. He gave Cudahy to believe her views "represented the sentiment of the Irish people."

"No leader would dare go counter to such sentiment," he explained. "Any leader who did would be repudiated."

In the following days de Valera launched a press campaign by giving interviews to correspondents of the *New York Times*, *Manchester Guardian* and *International News Service*. In each he emphasised the partition issue, and the interviews were given prominent coverage, especially in his own *Irish Press*. He also sent Frank Gallagher of the *Irish Press* to the United States on a mission to drum up American support. He gave him a letter for Roosevelt, outlining the importance of ending partition, which was the only obstacle preventing the ending of the centuries-long quarrel between Britain and Ireland.

"The British Government alone have the power to remove this obstacle," de Valera wrote. "If they really have the will they can bring about a united Ireland in a very short time. I have pressed my views upon them, but it is obvious that they recognise only the difficulties and are not fully alive to the great results that would follow a complete reconciliation between the two peoples. Reconciliation would affect every country where the two races dwell together, knitting their national strength and presenting to the world a great block of democratic peoples interested in the preservation of peace."

"Knowing your own interest in this matter," de Valera continued, "I am writing to ask you to consider whether you could not use your influence to get the British Government to realise what would be gained by reconciliation and to get them to move whilst there is time. In a short while, if the present negotiations fail, relations will be worsened."

Although Roosevelt refused to intervene formally, he did instruct Joseph P. Kennedy, the newly appointed ambassador to Britain, to tell Chamberlain privately he was anxious for an Irish settlement. "You will realise, I know, that I cannot officially or through diplomatic channels accomplish anything or even discuss the matter," Roosevelt wrote to de Valera, on 22 February 1938. "But I have taken the course of asking my friend, Mr Joseph P. Kennedy, who sails today for England to take up his post as Ambassador, to convey a personal message from me to the Prime Minister, and to tell the Prime Minister how happy I should be if reconciliation could be brought about."

The second round of talks, which was due to begin on 19 February, was delayed for some days due to a political crisis over the resignation of Anthony Eden as Foreign Secretary. Even if Chamberlain had wished to do something about partition, his room for manoeuvre was seriously restricted by this crisis. Within his own delegation, there was criticism of his willingness to give away too much. He was prepared to settle the dispute over all annuity payments for just £10 million of the more than £105 million claimed by Britain. It was ironic that Chamberlain, the most vociferous proponent of a hardline policy in the early years of the Economic War, was now more prepared to compromise than any of his colleagues. MacDonald, for instance, wanted to hold out for £26 million, but the British opened with a demand for £39 million for negotiating purposes, and the Irish side offered £2 million initially. De Valera actually asked for financial concessions for being prepared to take the ports. To the astonishment of the British, he indicated that the Irish people might not welcome the ports, because they would have to undertake the financial burden of defending them.

"I am lost in admiration of Mr de Valera's skill in dialectics," Chamberlain told colleagues. It might have been better "to spare Mr de Valera the embarrassment of having the treaty ports offered to him," he added sarcastically.

By launching his media offensive in January, de Valera may well have restricted his own field of manoeuvre. He had already lost his majority in the Dáil, and he was under strong pressure from some people not to conclude any agreement which did not resolve partition.

"I am afraid," explained Joseph Connolly—who had served in two different ministries in the Fianna Fáil governments from 1932 to 1937, "I argued rather vehemently that, if the partition of the country was not solved then when the other matters were being settled, the prospects of having it raised and decided in the near future were not very bright." People like him felt it was a mistake to conclude any agreement without settling the partition issue first.

De Valera told Cudahy he would be defeated if he agreed to such a settlement. "The important thing for statesmen in a democracy was to express the sentiment of the people, otherwise their action had no effect," he explained. He was at pains to stress that there was nothing anti-British in his attitude. The Germans had just invaded Austria, and he remarked that Ireland would undoubtedly suffer a similar fate if England did not act as a shield against the continent. "He was convinced," according to Cudahy, "that the international political outlook of Ireland would more and more fuse with that of England." In fact, he gave the American Minister to believe he was afraid the Irish race would be absorbed by the English, and hence he was anxious to promote the Irish language because it was vital as "a distinct racial influence of Irish permanency."

In the past de Valera had stirred up the partition issue for his own political purposes. He had deliberately created the impression it had been the cause of the Civil War, and having fooled the people to lead them, he was now forced to serve the folly he had created. Even if he had wished to do otherwise, which was by no means certain, he had no choice because he had only a minority government and—given the implacable hostility of Fine Gael at the time—the defection of a mere handful of Fianna Fáil deputies would have been enough to bring down the government.

While in London for the third round of talks in March, a Nationalist delegation from Northern Ireland had called on de Valera and urged him to take a firm stand against partition. "We would regard it as a betrayal of our interests if he ignored the problem of partition by getting trade and defence agreements only," Cahir Healy, the Nationalist leader, told the press afterwards.

Under existing circumstances Chamberlain reluctantly concluded that de Valera's government could not make economic concessions to Northern Ireland. "I am afraid," he wrote to Lord Craigavon, "we must face the fact that a Government without a majority in the Dáil could not get these particular provisions through."

At this point came Roosevelt's timely intervention. Kennedy delivered the President's message as the talks were deadlocked over de Valera's refusal to phase out duties on imports from Northern Ireland. The Taoiseach felt that the American intervention provided the necessary impetus for Chamberlain to drop his trade demands. The Prime Minister told his cabinet that Kennedy "had spoken strongly to him of the valuable effect on opinion in America of an agreement with Éire." The British dropped their insistence on trade concessions to Northern Ireland, and the two governments formally concluded three separate agreements renouncing Britain's rights to Irish bases and ending the Economic War by settling Britain's financial claims for a lump sum payment of £10 million. In addition, Britain agreed to remove her duties on Irish imports, while the Dublin government was only obliged to review its own import duties and to provide preferential treatment to some British imports.

There was no doubt de Valera got the better of the negotiations. Privately he credited Chamberlain, but he was unwilling to do so publicly because, he told Cudahy, he was already being criticised for being on "too friendly terms with the British." His only significant concession to them had been in agreeing to pay £10 million, which was less then one-tenth of the amount claimed by the British, and even then he pandered to anglophobic elements by characterising the payment as a kind of extortion. "I have repeatedly stated my belief," he told the Dáil, "that, if we were making agreements on the basis of justice—if sheer equity was to decide these matters—instead of paying money to Britain, whether a big or small sum, the payments should be made the other way." Deputies could, if they wished, he said, regard the payment "as ransom money" for the ports.

While de Valera professed to be disappointed with his failure to make progress on partition, he knew the agreements were popular and he capitalised on this by calling a general election in June 1938 after losing a minor vote in the Dáil. Although he adopted a statesmanlike posture during the campaign, his Tánaiste (Deputy Prime Minister) Seán T. O'Kelly, took a rather demagogic approach. "In the past six years look how we whipped John Bull every time," he said at an election rally in Dublin. "Look at the last agreement we made with her. We won all round us, we whipped her right, left and centre, and, with God's help, we shall do the same again."

Fianna Fáil had a resounding victory at the polls, winning fifty-two per cent of the first preference votes and securing an overall majority of fifteen seats. This was the largest vote the party enjoyed during its first fifty years. And de Valera was further honoured in September by being elected President of the Assembly of the League of Nations.

The League met that September under the dark cloud of the Sudetenland crisis. Germany was demanding the annexation of the Sudetenland of Czechoslovakia with its German majority. De Valera believed Hitler had a valid complaint because the Versailles Treaty had cut off the people in the Sudetenland from Germany with disregard for the principle of self-determination. In fact, the Irish leader saw a distinct parallel between the Sudeten problem and the situation in Northern Ireland. On his way to Geneva he told the British Attorney General that Dublin had its "own Sudetens in Northern Ireland" and he sometimes considered "the possibility of going over the boundary and pegging out the territory, just as Hitler was doing."

De Valera considered making a personal appeal to Hitler for peace, but this was obviated by Chamberlain's decision to go to Berchtesgaden for talks with the German leader. On hearing of the decision, which he described as "the greatest thing that has ever been done," de Valera sent the British Prime Minister a congratulatory message assuring him that "one person at least is completely satisfied that you are doing the right thing—no matter what the result."

Chamberlain wrote back that he "would be very grateful for any steps" de Valera might take to mobilise opinion within the Assembly for a settlement. Believing the best hope of avoiding war was for the American President to convoke an international conference to settle the issue and rectify the mistakes made at the Paris Peace Conference following the First World War, de Valera made his appeal to Roosevelt in the form of a broadcast to the American people over Radio Nations on 25 September 1938.

Even if the Sudeten crisis were settled amicably, he said, there would not always be a leader around prepared to swallow his pride as Neville Chamberlain had done by going to the potential enemy in an effort to secure peace. "The time for something like a general European Peace Conference, or at least a conference between the greater powers, is overdue," he declared. "If nations be called to make certain sacrifices at such a conference, these will be far less than the sacrifices they will have to make in the event of war."

There was a simplistic optimism in those sentiments, and de Valera realised this himself. He knew Hitler might not, indeed probably would not, be satisfied with everything Germany was justly entitled to, but if the Germans then went to war, their wanton aggression would be clearly exposed. And de Valera was convinced such a war should not be as feared as a conflict in which people believed the aggressor had legitimate grievances. "If by conceding the claims of justice or by reasonable compromise in a spirit of fair play we take steps to avoid the latter kind of war," he told his American audience, "we can face the possibility of the other kind with relative equanimity. Despite certain preaching mankind has advanced, and the public conscience, in a clear case of aggression, will count, and may well be in a European war a decisive factor." It was not that peace-loving people should always surrender to those who would not be deterred by the horrors of war. Rather, he said, they should "concede unhesitatingly the demands of justice" and then adopt a policy of wait and see. "To allow fears for the future to intervene and make us halt in rendering justice in the present, is not to be wise but to be foolish."

De Valera's address was not so much a personal appeal to Roosevelt as an attempt to mobilise public opinion. On 27 September he sent an open telegram to Chamberlain urging him to do his utmost to preserve peace.

"Let nothing daunt you or defeat you in your effort to secure peace," he urged as President of the Assembly. "The tens of millions of innocent people on both sides who have no cause against each other, but who are in danger of being hurled against each other, with no alternative to mutual slaughter are praying that your efforts may find a way of saving them from this terrible doom."

The ill-fated Munich agreement was signed in the early morning of 30 September 1938, so it was to a greatly relieved Assembly that de Valera delivered the closing address later the same day. Having deliberately avoided giving Chamberlain any public credit for the Anglo-Irish agreements earlier in the year, he was now effusive in his praise of the British leader, whom he described as a "knight of peace" who had "attained the highest peak of human greatness, and a glory greater than that of all the conquerors."

While on his way home from Geneva, de Valera met Chamberlain in London and tried to persuade him to move decisively on the partition question. Earlier in the year the Prime Minister had privately admitted he would like to see partition ended, but felt unable to do anything about it. Now, however, in the aftermath of the Munich agreement, he was riding the crest of a wave of popularity, and de Valera thought the time was ripe for a settlement. "Anybody who has studied Irish history must have learned this fact, that, if ever

233

there was to be a settlement between Ireland and Britain, that settlement would have to come in a time, not when you had a Liberal government, but when you had a Conservative government in office," de Valera believed. Once a Conservative government convinced its own supporters about the need for an agreement, it would have little difficulty with the Liberal Party, or the Labour Party for that matter, because both of those had always been more sympathetic to Ireland but had never had the ability to effect a settlement in the face of Conservative opposition.

Chamberlain still believed there would not be the public support necessary to take a stand on the issue, so de Valera set about trying to win over public support for a settlement. Upon his return to Dublin he gave a widely publicised interview to Hessel Tiltmann of the *London Evening Standard* in which he held out the possibility of concluding an alliance with Britain in return for the ending of partition. He had, of course, made a similar offer during the talks earlier in this year, but this time he talked about it publicly. It was possible, he said, "to visualise a critical situation arising in the future in which a united free Ireland would be willing to co-operate with Britain to resist a common attack." If the British would only convert their friends in Northern Ireland to the idea of Irish unity on fair terms, the Irish people would feel they had something worth fighting for, he said, but "no Irish leader will ever be able to get the Irish people to co-operate with Great Britain while partition remains. I wouldn't attempt it myself, for I know I should fail."

"Keep your local Parliament with its local powers if you wish," was the Taoiseach's message to the people of Northern Ireland. "The Government of Éire ask for only two things of you. There must be adequate safeguards that the ordinary rights of the Nationalist minority in your area shall not be denied them, as at present, and that the powers at present reserved to the English Parliament shall be transferred to the all-Ireland Parliament."

At the Fianna Fáil Árd Fheis a few weeks later de Valera announced he was asking AARIR—the American organisation he had helped to found in 1920—and the two ethnic Irish newspapers which had consistently supported him, the *New York Irish World* and *San Francisco Leader*, to inform the American public of "the nature of partition and the wrong done by it to the Irish nation." He was clearly embarking on another propaganda venture to marshal Irish-Americans to use their influence to get the American people to put pressure on Washington to get the British to do something about partition.

The British were told de Valera had no option politically but to campaign against partition in order to prevent the IRA getting control of the issue. "No man sitting in his chair could stand out of the partition campaign," Dulanty told MacDonald. Unless de Valera kept "some sort of control over it" by taking part, "it would get into unconstitutional channels." There was undoubtedly a good deal of truth in this, but de Valera was largely responsible himself for whipping up the issue, not only in the 1920s when he used it to obscure his real reasons for objecting to the Treaty, but also during the Anglo-Irish talks leading to the return of the ports.

In January 1939 the IRA declared war on Britain and launched a sporadic bombing campaign in English cities. The bombs—most made up in small packages and transported by bicycle to pillar boxes and the likes—were intended to force the British to abandon Northern Ireland, but this campaign was never likely to be successful, as became so evident the following year when the resolve of the British people stood up to German bombings which made the IRA's look like mere pinpricks.

Although de Valera had ruled out the use of force to settle partition, he appeared to pander to his more militant supporters when he said he would be willing to use it if he thought it would be successful. Addressing the Senate on 7 February 1939, for instance, he said he would use force to secure Irish unity, if he thought force would be successful.

"I am not a pacifist by any means," he said, "I would, if I could see a way of doing it effectively, rescue the people of Tyrone and Fermanagh, south Down, south Armagh, and Derry City from the coercion which they are suffering at the present time, because I believe that, if there is to be no coercion, that ought to apply all round." There was "not the slightest doubt," he said, "that if there were no British military forces in those areas, those people would move to come in with us, and we would certainly take them."

He certainly had a valid complaint when he talked about the contiguous Nationalist areas of the six counties. There was no moral justification for compelling them to remain within Northern Ireland. But in all his talks, had he never asked the British to transfer those Nationalist areas?

"I have not," he admitted, "because I think the time has come when we ought to do the thing properly. That would only be a half-measure." In other words he wanted all of the six counties or nothing, and he was only harping on the northern Nationalist grievances for propaganda purposes.

Having ruled out the use of force to end partition, de Valera said in 1934 that the only way to settle the problem was to convince a majority north of the border that they would be better off in a united Ireland, but he did very little to try to win over the predominantly Protestant Unionist community. In fact, his government had effectively promoted partition by failing to demonstrate a spirit of proper tolerance and broadmindedness.

Ever since the foundation of the state there had been discrimination against Protestant values in various matters. Although the Fianna Fáil government did not start the discrimination against Protestant values in matters like divorce, birth control, and censorship, it did intensify the discrimination. Divorce, hitherto illegal, was made unconstitutional in 1937, and a ban on the advertising of contraceptives was extended to their sale and importation, while censorship reached virtual draconian proportions with many Irish writers of international distinction being banned, sometimes on ludicrous grounds. On top of all this de Valera had effectively justified job discrimination during the Mayo library controversy in 1931. While in power de Valera and his colleagues often made the mistake of implying that "the only true Irishmen were Catholics," although he was not personally bigoted. In fact, he was instrumental in the selection of the founder of the Gaelic League, Douglas Hyde, who happened to be a Protestant, as the first President under the 1937 constitution.

De Valera openly advocated institutionalised discrimination within the civil service and the educational system in favour of those able to use the Gaelic language—for which northern Unionists had little or no affection. He publicly endorsed giving jobs to less qualified candidates with the "essential national qualification of the language." He even said he would prefer the restoration of Gaelic as the everyday language of the people to the ending of partition.

"If I were told tomorrow, 'You can have a united Ireland if you give up the idea of restoring the national language to be the spoken language of the majority of the people'," he said, "I would, for myself, say no." On another occasion he explained if he "had to make a choice between political freedom without the language, and the language without political freedom," he would choose the latter. Faced with such reasoning, northern Unionists could hardly be blamed for thinking their freedom would be denied in a united Ireland, if they refused to use the Gaelic language. They had no time for the Gaelic revival, or such features of southern life as the pervasive influence of the Catholic hierarchy and clergy, the rigid censorship, or the economic nationalism. The North's more industrialised economy—which was heavily dependent on export markets in Britain and further afield—would have been devastated by the kind of economic nationalism pursued by the Fianna Fáil governments.

While de Valera realised the northern people found such policies extremely objectionable, he made no real effort to change because he did not believe any changes his government might make would alter attitudes in the North. He challenged his critics to point out "any statements by any responsible representative of the people of the six counties that they are prepared to enter an all-Ireland Parliament on any conditions." As far as he was concerned, the 1937 constitution went as far as possible to reconcile the conflicting aspirations of the two parts of the island.

He was probably right, in the short term at any rate. No matter what changes or conciliatory gestures he made, the Protestant community in Northern Ireland were no more likely to accept local autonomy under an all-Ireland parliament than that the majority in the rest of the island would agree to re-entering the United Kingdom and according ultimate authority to the Westminster Parliament. The 1937 constitution was, in effect, as far as de Valera was prepared to compromise, so he was basically ruling out the possibility of winning over a majority in the North by conciliatory gestures and, as he had ruled out the use of force, this raises the question of how he proposed to solve partition.

When speaking in Geneva about the problem of European minorities in 1934, he had said the best solution was to transfer the minority to its ancestral homeland, if possible. He was thinking on the lines of the Treaty of Lausanne (1923) in accordance with which Greece and Turkey exchanged certain populations. When applied to the Irish situation, he was not thinking of transferring Catholic nationalists from the six counties to the south, but the Protestant Unionists of Scottish extraction to the mainland of Britain and replacing them with a similar number of Catholics of Irish extraction from Britain. He was planning on an international propaganda campaign, and he could hardly have chosen a more offensive setting in the eyes of Northern Protestants to launch his initiative.

In March 1939 he went to the Vatican for the coronation of Pope Pius XII and used the occasion to deliver a St Patrick's Day address over Vatican Radio. Describing partition as "an open wound," de Valera appealed "to all who may hear me, and especially the millions of our race scattered throughout the world—to all who glory

237

in the name of Ireland—to join us in a great united movement to bring it quickly to an end."

He had already made plans to visit the United States in early May, ostensibly to open the Irish pavilion at the World's Fair in New York, but his "chief aim" was to enlist American help to end partition. When he arranged a six week, coast-to-coast tour of American cities, there was a certain amount of uneasiness in American circles. John Cudahy, the United States Minister, was particularly worried.

Hitler had violated the Munich agreement in March 1939 by invading areas of Czechoslovakia to which Germany had no legitimate claim. It was obviously only a matter of time before another major war erupted. De Valera astutely predicted the conflict would begin following the next harvest in the autumn of 1939, and he was desperate for some kind of settlement of the partition issue before then because he feared the Nationalists in Northern Ireland would otherwise revolt during the war and the whole island would be dragged into a conflict with Britain. If the British tried to introduce conscription, he said his government would find itself in a similar position to the Redmondites in 1918.

Cudahy, who was certainly no anglophile, warned de Valera to be careful in his American speeches not to say anything which might be construed as anti-British. Even though the American people intended to stay out of the coming war, he explained they sympathised strongly with the democracies and would resent any anti-British remarks. "I told Mr de Valera that I was certain only an insignificant, die-hard, recalcitrant Irish element would support him if he dwelt upon the partition issue during his visit to the United States," he reported. "I said I was sure the great bulk of the American people would deplore the introduction of this note which they would regard as a most discordant one during this time of gravest tension in Europe."

The Taoiseach promised to speak "with tact and discrimination," but Cudahy was sceptical. "I wish," he wrote to President Roosevelt, "you would hammer home to him the necessity of treading very lightly on any controversial issue directed against England."

The warning was unnecessary on this occasion because de Valera cancelled the visit at the last moment when a political crisis erupted over British plans to introduce conscription. Under pressure from de Valera, Northern Ireland was excluded from the Conscription Act passed at Westminster. He therefore rescheduled his American visit for September 1939, but it, too, was cancelled with the outbreak of the war in September 1939.

"It will be a long war," de Valera told James A. Farley, the American Postmaster-General, that August, "but in the final analysis, the Allied powers should win. From our point of view it will be best to stay out of the war. By doing so we will be able to keep intact and at the same time be friendly to England. We are desirous of being helpful, in this or any other crisis in so far as we are able, short of actual participation in the war. That would be ruinous for us and injurious to England."

On the eve of the German invasion of Poland, the German Minister called on de Valera to find out his attitude in the event of war and to pass on an assurance from Berlin that Germany would respect Ireland's neutrality. In reply, de Valera explained that Ireland desired peace but, out of economic necessity, would have to show "a certain consideration" for Britain.

CHAPTER 19

"The Moral Postion Would Tell"

Nobody should have been surprised when de Valera announced that Ireland would remain neutral at the start of the Second World War. Ever since the League's failure to take effective action against Italy over the Ethiopian invasion, he had repeatedly emphasised his determination to avoid involvement in the coming war.

While he was influenced by a number of factors, the most important consideration in the last analysis was his belief that a small country like Ireland would only be hurt by involvement because it would be unable to influence the course of the conflict and would carry no real weight in drawing up the peace settlement afterwards. By staying out, on the other hand, she might escape, and he could at least demonstrate for once and for all that Ireland was a completely independent state, in spite of her remaining ties with the British Commonwealth.

He could have justified his policy on democratic grounds, seeing that the overwhelming majority of the Irish people wished to stay out of the war, but he told the Dáil on 2 September 1939 that it was "not as representing the sentiment or feelings of our people" that the government was taking its stand but "as the guardian of the interests of our people." In the 1930s he had stood boldly for what was right at the League of Nations while the major powers pursued their own self-serving policies. Now he was taking a leaf out of their book; it was his perception of Ireland's interest which was the determining factor of his policy. Everything else was secondary, though on occasions, especially when he was looking for international sympathy, he found it advantageous to stress secondary considerations, like the lack of proper defences, or the existence of partition.

Declaring Irish neutrality was one thing; keeping the country out of the conflict was something else. The government proclaimed an emergency and the Emergency Powers Bill was rushed through the Dáil and Senate authorising the government to use sweeping powers to deal with the wartime situation. De Valera also undertook the most extensive reshuffle of the government. Two new ministries were established to deal with the special problems caused by the war. Lemass was appointed Minister for Supplies and Aiken Minister for Coordination of Defensive Measures. O'Kelly moved to Finance and was replaced by Paddy Ruttledge at Local Government and Public Health, while MacEntee moved to Industry and Commerce, Gerald Boland to Justice, and Oscar Traynor to Defence. With the lone exception of James Ryan at Agriculture, de Valera moved all his ministerial colleagues to different portfolios. He retained External Affairs himself and even took over Education as well for a period. But despite the extensive nature of the changes, he only introduced one new face into the cabinet, P.J. Little as Minister for Posts and Telegraphs.

Britain was barely at war an hour when an RAF seaplane violated Irish neutrality by setting down in Dun Laoghaire harbour. Another set down to the north of the capital, off Skerries, shortly afterwards, and rumours of an impending British invasion spread about Dublin like wildfire. The rumours were ludicrous; one of the planes had merely got lost and the other was waiting for word to come to its assistance. The pilot of the second plane went ashore and made some telephone calls. The Gardaí were instructed to hold him pending a decision of the Minister for Defence, who, after consulting with de Valera, ordered that the two planes be allowed to leave.

The incident was a foretaste of what was to come. If de Valera was going to facilitate RAF planes, he would have to do likewise for the other side, and the country might then become a haven for the Germans, which would inevitably lead to problems with Britain. In the circumstances, therefore, all belligerent aircraft, surface vessels and submarines were forbidden to enter Irish territorial waters. The British were taken aback on being informed of this decision, and they sent an emissary to discuss the situation with the Taoiseach on 14 September 1939.

De Valera insisted the visit be kept strictly secret. Sir John Maffey, a veteran of the colonial service, arrived in Dublin incognito, using the name of "Mr Smith." He went, not to the Taoiseach's office, but to the Department of Agriculture, where de Valera was waiting for him.

From the outset de Valera emphasised his desire to pursue as benevolent a policy as possible towards Britain. "There was a time when I would have done anything in my power to help destroy the British Empire," he said. "But now my position has changed." There was no doubt the British had right on their side in this struggle. By doing "everything a man could do to prevent this tragedy," Chamberlain had allowed the moral issues at stake to be clearly defined. "England has a moral position today," the Taoiseach said. "Hitler might have his early success, but the moral position would tell."

Even though two-thirds of the Irish people "were pro-British, or at any rate anti-German," de Valera explained there was "a very active minority" bitterly opposed to any co-operation with Britain as a result of partition. He proceeded to give Maffey what was known in diplomatic circles as "the map treatment," outlining the anomalies of partition on a wall chart. The Nationalist population in Northern Ireland was living under "the petty tyrannies and oppressions" of the Unionists. "If I lived there," he said, "I should say 'I'll be damned if I'll be ruled by these people'."

De Valera was genuinely afraid northern Nationalists would provoke trouble by adopting the traditional Irish practice of exploiting Britain's difficulties. If the Nationalists rebelled as their southern brethren had done during the First World War, the rest of the island would inevitably become involved. He was already under a certain amount of pressure himself to do something about partition.

"My friends in America say to me 'why don't you take a leaf out of Hitler's book and work the Sudeten-Deutsch trick in Northern Ireland?" he explained.

Partition hurt the British in two rather different ways, according to de Valera. Firstly, if there was a united Ireland the Unionist elements "would be of real use to England" because they would be able to exert a tremendous political influence on the Dublin government. In fact, with southern politics still rent by Civil War bitterness, the Unionists would probably hold the balance of power. Secondly, he contended the ending of partition would remove the last remaining barrier to closer Anglo-Irish relations, which would, in turn, eliminate the hostility of the Irish-American community towards Britain. "Look at what a picture we might have!" he said. "A united, independent Ireland! Think of the effect in America where the Irish element had ruined and would ruin any possibility of Anglo-Irish understanding!"

While the decision to exclude all belligerents from Irish territory was designed to keep Ireland out of the war, de Valera explained that it was also a means of helping the British. He knew they would wish Dublin to have strict rules regarding submarines, but if he only acted against U-boats this would lead to complications with Germany. Although the government had censored all mention of the recent incidents involving the RAF seaplanes, the whole thing had still been the subject of widespread public comment, and this could not be permitted in future. Consequently it was necessary to ban all belligerent aircraft, submarines and surface vessels of war.

As he was explaining the situation the telephone rang.

De Valera picked it up and, after a brief conversation, turned to Maffey. "There you are!" he said. "One of your planes is down in Ventry Bay. What am I to do?" He felt he would have to intern the crew.

"It was quite obvious he found this course most unpalatable," Maffey reported. "I said that in view of the Skerry [sic] precedent he should warn the British Government before introducing any procedure of internment in such cases. The men concerned had probably had no warning of any such possibility."

The RAF flying boat, with twelve men on board, had set down in Ventry at nine o'clock that morning. It had been having engine trouble, due to a ruptured fuel pipe. The pilot and a mechanic brought the pipe ashore and got it repaired in a Dingle garage. They then returned to the plane and flew away around two o'clock in the afternoon.

"We were both much relieved when the telephone rang again an hour later to report that the plane had managed to get away—or rather had been allowed to get away," Maffey reported. He thought it was just "a strange coincidence" that the initial call came as de Valera was talking about the Skerries affair; he apparently never suspected that the Taoiseach knew about the incident beforehand and had skilfully exploited it.

The clandestine nature of the whole proceedings—with Maffey coming under an assumed name and meeting with the Taoiseach at the Department of Agriculture—was calculated to create an atmosphere of intrigue. It was a way of impressing on Maffey that de Valera was sympathetic to Britain but had to be very careful not to rouse anglophobic elements. It was a masterful piece of staging. Maffey left the meeting utterly convinced of the Taoiseach's desire "to maintain neutrality and to help us within the limits of that neutrality to the full extent possible."

Some British politicians were reluctant to recognise Ireland's neutrality. From their constitutional standpoint, the King was at war, and so were his dominions. If the Irish had wished to exercise their right to remain neutral, they should have withdrawn from the British Commonwealth beforehand.

De Valera, who had already shown himself to be a stickler on such constitutional matters, had carefully prepared the ground to counter any such arguments by challenging the theory of the indivisibility of the Crown, with both the new Irish Constitution and the appointment of an Irish Minister to Italy at a time when

Britain and the other dominions had no diplomatic relations with the Italians. By not taking a constitutional stand, the British accepted the precedent of Crown divisibility. Any British legal right to interfere in Irish affairs had been eliminated by the implementation of External Association, and de Valera took a further stand to highlight the issue when the British decided to open a diplomatic mission in Ireland following the outbreak of the war.

Normally the senior diplomat from one independent country to another was given the title of ambassador. The United States sent an ambassador to the Court of St James in London, but only ministers were exchanged between the United States and the dominions, because the dominions were in theory subject to the British King, to whom the ambassador was already accredited. The dominions, in turn, merely exchanged high commissioners among themselves. The British wished to appoint Maffey as High Commissioner in Dublin, but de Valera was determined to emphasise a constitutional difference between Ireland and the dominions by insisting on a different title in Maffey's case. The titles of ambassador or minister were unacceptable to the British, who, as a compromise, suggested calling him "British Representative in Ireland." De Valera—ever determined to have the last word—replaced "in" with "to", and so Maffey became the first "British Representative to Ireland."

Although Ireland's right to remain neutral was legally established, Churchill—who had become First Lord of the Admiralty following the outbreak of the war—had little time for such technicalities when they got in his way. "Legally," he wrote, "I believe they are 'at war but skulking'." Believing the Admiralty needed Irish bases, he advocated seizing them at a cabinet meeting on 24 October, but Chamberlain warned that the move "would have most unfortunate repercussions in the United States." At the time the Americans were in the process of amending their neutrality laws in order to allow Britain to purchase armaments. Unless it became a question of life or death for Britain, the cabinet decided against seizing Irish bases.

When the British secretly suggested a joint Anglo-Irish force to patrol the Irish coast, de Valera rejected the idea and countered with a scheme of his own. Information concerning the location and direction of any belligerent submarines, surface vessels, or aircraft spotted by Irish coastwatchers would be broadcast. "Not to you especially," the Taoiseach told Maffey. "Your Admiralty must pick it up. We shall wireless it to the world. I will tell the German Minister of our intention to do this."

In accordance with the arrangement, Irish coastwatchers reported all sightings to a regional command from where the messages were radioed to Dublin. They were ostensibly reporting to their headquarters and the belligerents were free to listen into the reports. This was of little help to the Germans, whose forces would be too far away to act against any Allied craft, but the British would be near enough to take advantage of any German sightings. Before long these messages were sent in a code secretly supplied by the British, with the result that Irish coastwatchers were effectively working for the British, though only de Valera and very few others knew this at the time.

The Irish government also co-operated in other ways. Britain was allowed to take over seven Irish-registered (though British-owned) oil tankers and—in an effort to keep chartering rates down by minimising competition—Dublin agreed not to charter any neutral ships except through the British who, in return, promised to make a certain amount of shipping space available to the Irish government.

Maffey appreciated Dublin's helpful approach and soon realised that the Taoiseach was in no position to give up the ports, even if he wished to do so. "There is no gainsaying Mr de Valera's view that any tampering with the neutrality of the ports would raise a storm here, the consequences of which are beyond computation, and which would certainly bring him down," Maffey reported. "It is remarkable how even the 'pro-British' group, men who have fought for the Crown and are anxious to be called up again, men whose sons are at the front today, loyalists in the old sense of the word, agree generally in supporting the neutrality of Éire. They see no possible practical alternative."

As the conflict settled into the "phoney war" on the continent, de Valera was primarily concerned with domestic political matters, especially the threat posed by IRA efforts to exploit Britain's difficulties. One of Gerald Boland's first acts as Minister for Justice was to issue warrants for the internment of some seventy people who were believed to be active in the IRA. One of those arrested in the initial swoop was Patrick McGrath, a veteran of the Easter Rebellion and the War of Independence. McGrath became the focus of particular attention when he and some colleagues went on hunger-strike to protest their internment. Tension mounted as de Valera emphasised his determination not to free the hunger-strikers.

"If we let these men out we are going immediately afterwards to have every single man we have tried to detain and restrain going on hunger-strike." But he was soon dealt an embarrassing blow when the High Court ruled in early December that the government had acted unconstitutionally by interning the men under the Offences Against the State Act, which had been passed during the summer to deal with the IRA's bombing campaign.

The internees were therefore released, and this was quickly followed by another setback for the authorities when the IRA raided the Irish Army's main armoury at the Magazine Fort in Phoenix Park. A considerable amount of arms and ammunition was seized in the raid, but it proved a pyrrhic victory for the IRA, because the government used the disquiet caused by the raid to rush through an amendment to the Emergency Powers Act, which was not subject to judicial review under the emergency provisions of the constitution. This amendment authorising internment closed the constitutional loophole recently exploited in the courts. In addition, most of the arms and ammunition seized in the raid were recovered in the following weeks.

De Valera was so busy with domestic matters in December 1939 that he declined to attend an emergency session of the Assembly of the League of Nations called to discuss the Soviet Union's invasion of Finland. Cudahy urged him to go to Geneva, but he rejected the idea. If he denounced what the Soviets were doing in Finland, he said he would also have to speak about the Nazi invasions of Slovakia and Poland, and this might complicate relations with Germany.

"There is no use in an oration at this time," the Taoiseach explained. Words were useless; what was needed was "tanks, bombs, and machine-guns." His voice "shook with agitation" as he said he felt "like a man behind a glass wall witnessing the destruction of everything he held dear, but absolutely paralysed and impotent to take any action to avert universal destruction."

When two members of the IRA were sentenced to death in Britain for their part in a Coventry bombing in which a number of civilians had been killed, de Valera pleaded with the London government to commute the sentences. "The reprieve of these men would be regarded as an act of generosity a thousand times more valuable to Britain than anything that can possibly be gained by their death," he pleaded with Chamberlain. "Almost superhuman patience is required on both sides to exorcise the feelings which the knowledge of centuries of wrongdoing have engendered." But Chamberlain decided against intervening and the two men were hanged.

Things were otherwise quiet on the diplomatic front. In fact, they were so quiet that Cudahy thought he was going to miss out on all the action. He pleaded with Roosevelt to move him to the continent, nearer the action, and he even suggested that the President replace him in Dublin with David Gray, a retired newspaper publisher who was married to an aunt of President Roosevelt's wife. The President took the bait, moved Cudahy to Brussels and replaced him with Gray. Since the latter had direct access to the White House, de Valera initially welcomed his appointment, but before very long he would come to regret it because the new Minister viewed his mission as primarily one of helping Roosevelt to give as much aid as possible to the British to defeat the Nazis. Even before taking up his post Gray visited the Vatican and London to investigate the possibilities of getting Ireland into the war, or at least promoting better Anglo-Irish relations in order to allieviate the hostility of Irish-Americans towards Britain and thereby mollify their likely opposition to Roosevelt's efforts to help Britain.

De Valera placed great emphasis on the partition issue during his first private meeting with Gray on 8 April 1940. As with Maffey, he gave him "the map treatment," using a wall chart to explain the anomalies of partition in which Counties Fermanagh and Tyrone, with their Nationalist majorities, were being compelled to remain as part of Northern Ireland, as were other contiguous Nationalist areas. 'That is his line," Gray wrote to Roosevelt. "The British refuse to coerce Belfast but connive at the coercion of these two counties and elements in the others."

When Gray asked if Ireland would break off diplomatic relations with Germany and allow the British to use Irish ports in return for an end to partition, the Taoiseach was adamant. "No," he replied without hesitation. "We could never bargain with our neutrality."

He was under increasing Republican pressure at the time because a number of IRA prisoners were reaching the critical stage of a hunger-strike protesting their imprisonment. Jack Plunkett, a brother of one of the 1916 leaders, and Sean MacCurtain—a son of the Lord Mayor of Cork murdered by British agents in front of his family in March 1920—were among those nearing death. As a result the hunger-strike was the focus of considerable public attention. Having backed down and released hunger-strikers before Christmas, in the wake of the adverse court decision, de Valera was now determined there would be no further surrender.

"Prisoners would not be allowed to dictate the conditions under which they would be kept in detention," he wrote. The IRA was de-

manding, in essence, that any of its members "sentenced for any offence whatsoever should 'serve their sentence in military custody,'
and thus be treated as though they were members of a military force
engaged in legitimate warfare and entitled to be treated as such," de
Valera complained to the widow of another of the 1916 leaders. The
whole thing was a test of wills, and this time the Taoiseach held his
nerve. After the first of the prisoners died on 19 April, the hunger-
strike was called off, but by then it was already too late for another
of the men. Both Plunkett and MacCurtain survived.

De Valera was certainly in an unenviable position. He had further alienated the Republicans and he was still despised by the opposition on the other side because of his role in the events leading to
the Civil War. On top of this the war on the continent had heated up
with the recent German invasions of Denmark and Norway in early
April, followed by the invasions of the Low Countries on 10 May
1940. The so-called "phoney war" was well and truly over.

Two more small neutrals had been attacked and Maffey seized
on the occasion to talk with de Valera, who, he hoped, would now
be more amenable to join with the Allies. But the Taoiseach immediately talked about his difficulties as a result of partition.

"If the partition question were solved today, would you automatically be our active ally?" Maffey asked.

"I feel convinced that that would probably be the consequence,"
de Valera replied.

"I said that the question was obviously only an academic one
as in wartime no attention could be given to the solution of such
questions," Maffey reported. These would disappear with time, but
for the moment there was the Nazi menace. He knew de Valera
recognised this menace and he now wanted to know if Ireland was
going to help resist it.

"But we always travelled back to the old prejudice, to Partition,
to the bitterness in the hearts of the active and extremist elements,"
Maffey continued. "I suggested that with clear leadership the ad-
venturous spirits would respond to a better call. But Mr de Valera
held to his narrow view. He seems incapable of courageous or original thought and now on this world issue and in every matter he
lives too much under the threat of the extremist."

De Valera did, however, publicly denounce the invasions of
Belgium and Holland. "Today," he said, "these two small nations
are fighting for their lives, and I think I would be unworthy of this
small nation if, on an occasion like this, I did not utter our protest
against the cruel wrong which has been done them." He did not

actually mention Germany by name, but nobody doubted he was denouncing the Germans, and the German Minister actually protested against the remarks to the Department of External Affairs.

From the Irish standpoint there were also some rather ominous political developments in Britain, with the election of Winston Churchill as Prime Minister. He had an erratic temperament and a dismal record on matters relating to Ireland. The notorious Auxillaries—the elite corps of Black and Tans responsible for the infamous attack on innocent spectators at Croke Park on Bloody Sunday in 1920—had been his brain-child, and de Valera held him largely responsible for stampeding Collins into attacking the Four Courts at the start of the Irish Civil War in 1922. In addition, Churchill had been the most vocal opponent of the Chamberlain government's decision to return the ports in 1938 and he tried to persuade the government to take them back the following year. As a result Churchill posed an even more immediate threat to Ireland than Hitler.

De Valera's response was to turn to the United States for help. He asked Gray to enquire confidentially if Roosevelt would be prepared to state publicly that the United States was interested in the preservation of the status quo in regard to Ireland. Even though the President was supposedly determined to keep America out of the war, he had little sympathy for Irish neutrality.

Just how serious the situation was at the time became apparent on the day the State Department transmitted Roosevelt's refusal. Irish authorities learned that the IRA had been harbouring a German Abwehr spy. Although the spy, Hermann Goertz, escaped and managed to remain at large for eighteen months, his papers were captured. These contained details of Irish defences as well as an IRA plan for a German invasion. In accordance with the plan, code-named "Kathleen," the Germans would invade at Donegal Bay, announce they had come to liberate Northern Ireland and invite all Irish Nationalists to assist them.

Since collusion between the IRA and the Nazis would provide the British with an excuse for seizing Irish bases in order to forestall a German Invasion, de Valera sent Joseph P. Walshe to London together with Colonel Liam Archer—the head of Military Intelligence—to assure the British that if Germany invaded, their government would fight and would also "call in the assistance of the United Kingdom the moment it became necessary." They even suggested secret talks between the British and Irish military to draw up contingency plans to deal with a German invasion.

Edouard Hempel, the German Minister to Ireland, was under no illusions about either de Valera's sympathy for the Allies or his aversion to the Nazi regime. Hempel predicted that the Taoiseach would maintain his "friendly understanding" with Britain "even in the face of the threatening danger of Ireland becoming involved in the war."

Measures to bolster Irish defences were intensified, and hundreds of suspected would-be German collaborators in the IRA were interned without trial for the duration of the war, much to the disgust of people like Mary MacSwiney. "Was there ever a period in which England's difficulty was more surely Ireland's opportunity than now?" she wrote to de Valera. "You could unite the country for the Republic. You still have the chance to do that. Failure to do so, here and now, will write you down in the time to come as the greatest failure Irish history has ever known. The pity of it! If you bring a new civil war on this country, and you are going the right way to do just that, you will deserve a fate worse than Castlereagh's."

Unmoved by her hysterical appeal, de Valera launched an intensive army recruiting drive, and invited the two major opposition parties to join with Fianna Fáil in a National Defence Conference to advise the government on security matters. On 1 June he went on national radio to warn of the dangers facing the country. "When great powers are locked in mortal combat," he said, "the rights of small nations are as naught to them; the only thing that counts is how one may secure an advantage over the other, and if the violation of our territory promises such an advantage, then our territory will be violated, our country will be made a cockpit, our homes will be levelled and our people slaughtered."

CHAPTER 20

"It Would Have Meant Civil War"

For the next twelve months there was a whole series of crises as Irish authorities feared either a British or German invasion. De Valera sought assurances from each government to respect Irish neutrality, but both initially refused. He then sought to play them off against each other, making it clear he would invite help from the enemy of any country that invaded Ireland. He told the Italian Minister his confidence in the Germans had been so shaken by the discovery of the Abwehr spy that he needed some guarantee in order to withstand mounting British pressure. He was basically using the Italian Minister to pass on a veiled threat that he would make concessions to the British unless the Germans gave an assurance to respect Irish neutrality.

Meanwhile Churchill launched quiet diplomatic moves asking friendly governments to use their influence to persuade Dublin to allow Britain to use Irish bases, but de Valera was unmoved. Smuts, the South African Premier, advised Britain to seize Irish bases forthwith, but Churchill rejected this because it would have undesirable repercussions in the United States. "Although as a last resort we should not hesitate to secure the ports by force," he told his cabinet on 16 June, "it would be unwise at this moment to take any action that might compromise our position with the United States of America, in view of the present delicate developments."

Chamberlain was assigned to try his hand with the Taoiseach, but the latter refused the invitation to go to London. As Chamberlain would be readily recognised in Dublin, Malcolm MacDonald went instead. He had a three-and-a-half-hour meeting with de Valera on the evening of 17 June.

The Taoiseach seemed a somewhat different man. "His mind is still set in the same hard, confined mould as of yore," MacDonald reported. "But in another way he appeared to have changed. He made no long speeches; the whole procedure was much more in the nature of a sustained conversation between two people than used sometimes to be the case. He seemed depressed and tired, and I felt that he had neither the mental nor the physical vigour that he possessed two years ago."

MacDonald's approach was in the form of a friendly warning that Ireland was too weak to defend herself against an inevitable German attack. She was going to need Britain's help and he suggested de Valera should abandon neutrality immediately and join with Britain "in resistance to Germany so that from this moment onwards co-operation could be complete and we could put whatever naval and military forces were required at his disposal," MacDonald explained. "We did not give this advice simply because it would help us; indeed, we gave it principally in the interests of Éire itself."

De Valera, who could hardly be blamed for being sceptical about MacDonald's concern for Ireland, rejected the suggestion. If partition had been ended before the war, as he had wanted, he said he might now be in a position to invite the British in. MacDonald suggested a united defence arrangement with Northern Ireland, but de Valera rejected this because it would be a violation of neutrality. As things stood, he felt he had no option but to remain neutral.

"The whole force of public opinion was against any abandonment of neutrality," he explained. The Irish people did not understand the real Nazi menace because they knew little of what the Germans were doing on the continent, and their ignorance was bolstered by a strong prejudice against Britain which, he said, would "take a long time to remove."

It was only twenty years since the British let the Black and Tans loose on Ireland and many Irish people felt it would do Britain some good to suffer some of her own medicine for a change. An Assistant Under Secretary from the Dominions Office who had visited Dublin the previous summer actually reported that he got the general impression that the Irish people felt "the United Kingdom should suffer, and should suffer to an extent which should teach her lessons." But this did not mean they wanted the Nazis to win the war. While many on the extremes of both sides of the Irish political spectrum—Republicans and Blueshirts—believed Germany would liberate the six counties, their views were representative of a mere minority. The vast majority wanted the British to win ultimately. According to Gray, the real Irish attitude was epitomised by the man who said he would like to see England "nearly bate."

Under the circumstances de Valera was in no position to invite British forces into Ireland, even if only to guard against an Axis attack. If Germany attacked, he said "his men would fight magnificently," according to MacDonald. "The Germans would not find things easy, for the Irish were very skilful at guerilla warfare; they were very good hedge fighters and would fight the invader from hedge to hedge." It was as if he had learned nothing over the years and was still thinking in terms of 1916 when he thought the people of Dublin should have come to the aid of the rebels whether with hayforks, or just knives and forks. Now he seemed to be talking in the absurd terms of the Irish people resisting by hiding behind hedges when they would have little more than rocks to throw at advancing Germans.

When the British cabinet discussed MacDonald's report, Chamberlain suggested offering to end partition in return for de Valera's co-operation. Cralgavon should "be told that the interests of Northern Ireland could not be allowed to stand against the vital interests of the British Empire," the former Prime Minister argued. MacDonald was sent back to Dublin to explore "to what extent any advance towards a United Ireland would help Mr de Valera in dealing with Irish opinion on this matter." In other words he was to find out if de Valera would bargain on neutrality in return for an end to partition. "If anything useful came out of these conversations," the cabinet concluded, "it would, of course, have to be put to Lord Craigavon."

If there was "a declaration of a United Ireland," MacDonald asked de Valera if he would agree to the setting up of a "joint Defence Council" in which the six counties would remain a belligerent while the rest of the island would stay neutral but allow the British to use Irish bases "in order to secure Éire's neutrality against violation by Germany."

The best way of ensuring that the Germans did not get hold of Ireland, the Taoiseach replied, was for Northern Ireland to withdraw from the war and agree to Irish unity, and then have Britain and the United States guarantee Irish neutrality. Since Britain was already a belligerent, its forces would not be able to take an active part in guaranteeing this neutrality but, he said, American ships could come into the Irish ports, and American troops could perhaps be stationed in Ireland "to effect this guarantee." MacDonald dismissed this as "entirely impracticable," which of course it was, seeing that the Americans had already refused to take any public stand in regard to Ireland for fear of complicating their country's avowed aim of staying out of the war.

This was getting away from the point. MacDonald wanted to know that if Britain declared a united Ireland in principle, with the practical details of this union to be worked out later, would de Valera be prepared to abandon neutrality and join the Allies?

"If there were not only a declaration of a United Ireland in principle, but also agreement upon its constitution, then the Government of Éire might agree to enter the war at once," de Valera replied. "But the constitution of a United Ireland would have to be fixed first."

The British government would need more than just a "might" to go on, MacDonald said. But this was as far as de Valera would go. In fact, he candidly added there was "a very big question mark after the 'might'." Even if he supported the proposition himself, he said he was not sure it would pass because some of his colleagues would undoubtedly be opposed to it.

The Irish people "were really almost completely unprepared for war," he explained. The army was not a properly equipped army to resist tanks or mechanised troops, and Dublin was practically undefended. "There were not even any air raid shelters in the city and the people had not got gas masks," de Valera continued. "They would be mercilessly exposed to the horrors of modern war, and he and his colleagues could not have it on their consciences that in this state of affairs they had taken the initiative in an action which so exposed them." If the British had offered to end partition a few months earlier, Maffey was convinced de Valera would have jumped into the war. Indeed, he still thought such an offer might yet sway the Irish cabinet.

"I suggest that we should test this," Chamberlain said when the British cabinet considered the latest report on 25 June. He advocated making a formal offer to end partition in return for Irish co-operation. The cabinet agreed, but at Churchill's insistence the offer was to be conditional on Northern Ireland's acceptance. He was too much of a politician to agree to an unqualified offer, especially when even Chamberlain thought there was little likelihood of success. The British offer was incorporated in a six-point memorandum, personally approved by Churchill and endorsed unanimously by the war cabinet.

MacDonald handed the document to de Valera next day, but the Taoiseach had great difficulty reading it as his eyesight was failing, so MacDonald read it to him:

(i) A declaration to be issued by the United Kingdom Government forthwith accepting the principle of a United Ireland.

(ii) A joint body including representatives of the Government of Éire and the Government of Northern Ireland to be set up at once to work out the constitutional and other practical details of the Union of Ireland. The United Kingdom Government to give such assistance towards the work of this body as might be desired.

(iii) A Joint Defence Council representative of Éire and Northern Ireland to be set up immediately.

(iv) Éire to enter the war on the side of the United Kingdom and her allies forthwith, and, for the purposes of the Defence of Éire, the Government of Éire to invite British naval vessels to have the use of ports in Éire and British troops and aeroplanes to cooperate with the Éire forces and to be stationed in such positions in Éire as may be agreed between the two Governments.

(v) The Government of Éire to intern all German and Italian aliens in the country and to take any further steps necessary to suppress Fifth Column activities.

(vi) The United Kingdom Government to provide military equipment at once to the Government of Éire.

There followed an elaborate list of armaments which the British were prepared to hand over immediately.

Mindful of the betrayal of the Redmondites on the Home Rule Act after they had supported Britain in the First World War, de Valera complained the offer was much too vague and really amounted to little more than "a pious hope." There was no assurance that northern Unionists would not undermine the proposed commission's efforts to draw up the new constitution. The British had reneged not only after leading Redmond to believe they would implement Home Rule for the whole island if he supported the war effort in 1914, but also after persuading the Irish signatories of the 1921 Treaty that the Boundary Commission would transfer the contiguous Nationalist areas of Northern Ireland to the Irish Free State. Now they were paying the price for their duplicity.

"Will you come into the war if we create a united Ireland straight away?" MacDonald asked.

"If we have a united Ireland," de Valera replied, "it will be neutral for at least twenty-four hours. We will then call a meeting of our assembly and it will decide if we—as an independent nation—will come into the war."

Next morning de Valera's cabinet rejected the proposals. With France having already fallen, Britain seemed on the verge of defeat and an alliance with her seemed a preposterous proposition, especially when it was inconceivable that Irish help would make the difference between victory and defeat for the British. Most of the Irish ministers sympathised with the British against the Nazis, but there were some like Frank Aiken and P.J. Little, who were utterly convinced that Germany was going to win the war, and they were therefore anxious to curry favour with the Germans. They were so nervous, according to Seán MacEntee, that they gave the impression at cabinet meetings that Hempel might be looking over their shoulders.

De Valera, Lemass and Aiken met with MacDonald that afternoon. "Aiken did most of the talking on their side and was even more persistent than de Valera himself had been in urging that the proper solution is a United Ireland which is neutral," MacDonald reported that night. "Lemass seemed to be prepared to discuss our plan in a more reasonable way, but his contributions to [the] discussion were usually cut short by fresh uncompromising interventions from one or other of his colleagues." MacDonald repeated his assurance that once the declaration of unity was proclaimed, Northern Ireland would not be able to go back on it.

"I think Lemass, and even Aiken was impressed," MacDonald continued. Lemass was particularly interested when MacDonald said it would not be necessary for Dublin to declare war on Germany. If Ireland handed over selected bases, she could try to remain neutral. Although MacDonald thought it was worth amending the formal proposals in this regard, he still held out no hope of success. "I am definitely of [the] opinion that the cabinet here will reject our plan," he wrote.

De Valera and his colleagues were understandably suspicious of the British offer. The British were really playing a double game. Chamberlain informed Craigavon the British were only sounding out de Valera and it had "been made clear" through the talks that it would be necessary to obtain Northern Ireland's assent, but this was not really true, as MacDonald's reports made patently clear.

What the British were offering was to end partition "lock, stock, and barrel," according to Maffey. It was only after they were sure that the Dublin government would not agree to their proposals that the British assured Craigavon that the whole thing was contingent on Northern Ireland's acceptance.

"The whole plan depends on our obtaining the assent of Northern Ireland," Chamberlain wrote to de Valera on 29 June. "I cannot, of course, give a guarantee that Northern Ireland will assent, but if the plan is accepted by Éire we should do our best to persuade Northern Ireland to accept it also in the interests of the security of the whole island."

On 2 July de Valera informed Richard Mulcahy, one of the Fine Gael members of the National Defence Conference, of the British proposals. Although Mulcahy offered his party's support, should the government decide to accept them, the Taoiseach explained they were too vague. Privately Mulcahy thought that, even with Cosgrave's support, de Valera would be unable to carry the Dáil on the British terms. He figured "perhaps more than half" of Fianna

Fáil, one third of Fine Gael and the whole Labour Party would be opposed. James Dillon, the deputy leader of Fine Gael and the only member of the Dáil to openly advocate abandoning neutrality during the war, agreed with Mulcahy's assessment. "If de Valera tried to carry the country for abandoning neutrality on the strength of the present British promises," he said, "he would be beaten."

Although the British were no longer asking for a formal declaration of war, this made little practical difference. "If we invite military assistance from one side," de Valera reasoned, "immediate attack by the other, with all its consequences, will be almost inevitable." He therefore formally rejected the proposals in a letter to Chamberlain on 5 July. "The plan would involve our entry into the war. That is a course for which we could not accept responsibility," he wrote. "Our people would be quite unprepared for it, and Dáil Eireann would certainly reject it." The whole thing was too vague because "it gives no guarantee that in the end we would have a united Ireland," unless the Unionists were given concessions which would be "opposed to the sentiments and aspirations of the great majority of the Irish people."

Over the years the Unionists of Northern Ireland had proudly adopted an uncompromising attitude. They were unwilling to give an inch, and de Valera now adopted his own variant of their attitude. "Our present Constitution," he wrote, "represents the limit to which we believe our people are prepared to go to meet the sentiments of the Northern Unionists, but, on the plan proposed, Lord Craigavon and his colleagues could at any stage render the whole project nugatory and prevent the desired unification by demanding concessions to which the majority of the people could not agree. By such methods unity was prevented in the past, and it is obvious that under the plan outlined they could be used again."

De Valera made no attempt to obtain any assurances which would have precluded the same thing happening again. Churchill, who had only weeks earlier put forward a plan for a political union between France and Britain in a vain attempt to keep the French in the war, was desperate and in his desperation he would probably have been prepared to compel the Unionists to accept some form of Irish unity if he had been given any encouragement from Dublin.

Staying out of the war, however, was now more important to de Valera than ending partition. Frank MacDermot visited Belfast to sound out Sir Basil Brooke (later Lord Brookeborough) one of the strongmen of Craigavon's government, only to be told upon his return to Dublin that the Fianna Fáil government was not interested.

257

"Get this into your head, MacDermot," Aiken said to him, "there are no terms on which we would abandon neutrality."

A couple of weeks later the Taoiseach told Maffey, "it had gone hard with him to turn down any scheme which would bring about a united Ireland, the dream of his life. But in the present circumstances acceptance had been impossible. It would have meant civil war."

"The real basic fact is that it is not partition, which stands in the way at this moment but the fear of Dev and his friends that we shall be beaten," Chamberlain wrote. "They don't want to be on the losing side and if that is unheroic one can only say that it is very much the attitude of the world from the USA to Rumania and from Japan to Ireland."

Events were closing in on de Valera in early July. Hitler ordered German propaganda to give the impression that Germany was about to invade Ireland. This, in turn, exacerbated fears of a preemptive British assault, and those fears were intensified on 4 July when Churchill referred to the German threat to Ireland in a speech justifying the British attack on the French fleet at Oran. Having only hours earlier authorised the attack on ships of his recent ally in order to ensure that they did not fall into German hands, there could be no doubt that he would endorse drastic action to prevent the Germans getting hold of Irish bases. Indeed he told his cabinet next day that he intended to warn Roosevelt that "it might be necessary" in the near future "to make a change in our policy towards Éire" in order to forestall the Germans.

De Valera had already read the ominous signs and his reaction was to turn to the United States for help. He tried to enlist the support of American public opinion by stressing his determination to stay out of the war in an interview with Harold Denny of the *New York Times*. "We do not have the slightest intention of abandoning our neutrality. We intend to resist any attack, from any quarter whatever," he said. "And whoever comes first will be our enemy."

When addressing an American audience on such a topic, there was a real danger his words would be interpreted as a veiled attack on Britain, the traditional enemy and nearest belligerent. Even though he did not pass up the opportunity of raising the partition issue, he was nevertheless quite positive in his remarks about Britain and there was an unmistakably negative twist to his references to Germany.

"We have got on very well with Britain," he said. "All questions between us have been amicably settled except the most important one of all—partition." There was still a great deal of Irish bitterness against Britain, he explained, but this did not translate into support for the Nazis. "Probably few are actually pro-German," he said, "for many Irishmen realise that the Irish with their passion for individualism are the last people in the world who could endure fascist rule." In the United States, where the rugged individualist had been elevated to the stature of a cult figure, few people were likely to miss the anti-fascist undertone of his remarks.

The interview was basically an attempt to build up a kind of common identity with the Americans and remind them that the Irish people shared their desire to avoid involvement in the war. Any British attack on Ireland would thus make Churchill look little better than Hitler and would certainly damage the popular support needed by the Roosevelt administration to provide Britain with effective aid. Before the week was out Secretary of State Cordell Hull cautioned the British ambassador against any attack on Ireland, and he was given an assurance that no such venture would be undertaken unless the Germans attacked first.

The British were never prepared to give Dublin the same assurance, but de Valera manage to extract a guarantee from the Germans by contending he needed it if he was to resist British pressure. On 11 July Berlin instructed Hempel to say that "as long as Ireland conducts herself in a neutral fashion it can be counted on with absolute certainty that Germany will respect her neutrality unconditionally." While the Taoiseach never placed any real faith in the German guarantee, it was something at least, especially as efforts to obtain a similar British guarantee were futile.

He was understandably nervous. Churchill had already attacked the French and there could be little doubt he would have even less compunction about attacking Ireland. "Who would have guessed three months ago that the British would attack the French fleet?" de Valera asked Maffey.

He was particularly disturbed by British propaganda, especially ludicrous stories about massive spy centres in the German and Italian legations in Dublin, or U-boat bases off the west coast. There was a report of a U-boat captain proposing a toast in a Dingle bar. There were many rumours of U-boat sightings, but these were usually unfounded. One investigator concluded that most of the U-boats were seen in pubs.

De Valera was confronted not only with the danger that Germany might try to get a foothold in Ireland, or that Britain would seize Irish bases, but also with the threat of a pre-emptive British strike in order to forestall the German invasion, as well as the risk that loose talk about secret Anglo-Irish co-operation might provoke the Germans to attack Ireland in retaliation.

"Of course, there were other more subtle causes all combining to give the impression that we were almost eager for the Germans to come in so that we could get in ourselves," Maffey reported. "Talk of a military 'pact' had been published and had done great harm." De Valera "begged" him to ensure that the Anglo-Irish military liaison "should be kept as secret as possible." If the Germans found out, they might retaliate, but if the Irish people learned, it would undermine the importance of the country's supposed neutrality as an expression of Irish independence.

Maffey assured de Valera that a British officer recently caught collecting military information in Ireland, had been sent without the authority of the government, and he promised "nothing of this kind would occur again."

"This had a tremendous effect," Maffey noted, "and I felt the whole atmosphere changed."

De Valera agreed to release the British spy and then pressed Maffey for arms. The British had offered weapons recently, so they were available. "Why will you not trust us?" he asked. "If you think we might attack the North I say with all the emphasis we will never do that. No solution can come there by force. There we must now wait and let the solution come with time and patience."

Following strong representations from Maffey, the London government decided to provide a limited quantity of arms for the Irish army in the following weeks, and this alleviated the tension. On 3 September 1940, at the height of the Battle of Britain, the *Irish Press* published a front page photograph of de Valera, together with Maffey and Gray, at the All-Ireland hurling final the previous afternoon. In this case the picture was worth the proverbial thousand words. Its prominent publication in his own newspaper was tantamount to a public endorsement. The Taoiseach never accorded this kind of recognition to the German Minister.

Any remaining doubts about de Valera's determination to curb the activities of the IRA were well and truly dispelled later the same week with the execution of two members of that movement. They had been involved in an incident in which three detectives were shot, two fatally, during a police raid on 16 August. The government reacted immediately by eliminating the right of appeal from the findings of the Military Tribunal set up to deal with political offences. Two men arrested at the scene of the latest shootings were summarily tried and sentenced to be shot. One of the men was Patrick McGrath, who had been freed while on hunger-strike the previous December. The leniency previously shown by the government had merely earned the contempt of the IRA, whose intransigence seemed to thrive on concessions. Henceforth de Valera was determined that there would be no more concessions and the two men were duly executed by firing squad on 6 September. This marked an irrevocable step in his break with the IRA.

CHAPTER 21

"You Have Seen What Happened to London"

Although the British refused to give an assurance that they would not violate Irish neutrality, the fear of an attack temporarily disappeared during the autumn of 1940. President Roosevelt was running for an unprecedented third term and any British action against Ireland would undoubtedly cause problems with his Irish-American supporters. It was largely to shore up his support among them that he went to Boston in the last days of the campaign and made his famous promise to stay out of the war. "I have said before," he declared, "but I shall say it again and again and again: *Your boys are not going to be sent into any foreign war!*"

The climate of complacency was shattered in Dublin on 5 November, the day the Americans went to the polls. Churchill complained publicly that the denial of Irish bases was "a most heavy and grievous burden and one which should never have been placed on our shoulders." His speech was followed up by a propaganda barrage on both sides of the Atlantic calling on Dublin to allow Britain to use the ports.

Maffey argued that nothing sinister should be read into the speech, seeing that Churchill had only "stated a bold and obvious fact, the tragic fact that the loss of Irish ports greatly handicapped our vital connections at sea," but de Valera contended—quite rightly as it turned out—that the importance of the ports was being exaggerated. He added he would not have been as worried about the Prime Minister's outburst, had it not been for the ensuing propaganda campaign.

Obviously the British press, operating under the strict wartime censorship, would not have been permitted to make such comments unless those reflected government policy. If the Irish side responded with its own propaganda, it would lead to heightened tension and a dangerous deterioration in relations between the two countries. "Mr de Valera said," according to Maffey, "that he could not contemplate how we could allow our press to play with fire in times such as this."

The Taoiseach was afraid the propaganda might have been designed to minimise the possible American reaction to a British attack on Ireland, and his fears could only have been confirmed by the brazen attitude of Gray, who told the Department of External Affairs that American opinion would support a British seizure of Irish ports. There was obviously little point in appealing to the American Minister, so de Valera turned directly to the Irish-Americans and asked them to drum up American support for Irish neutrality. His call was received enthusiastically by organised Irish-American elements, who combined to set up the American Friends of Irish Neutrality.

The British, Canadian and American representatives in Dublin all quickly concluded that the propaganda campaign was counter-productive. "As we see it here," Gray wrote, "any attempt by Churchill to negotiate for the ports will be hopeless. He has the choice between seizing them and paying the price in possible bloodshed and certain hostility and doing without." Believing that de Valera's power was based "on his genius for engendering and utilising anti-British sentiment," Gray thought there was little point in the British trying to pressurise the Taoiseach with arguments.

"He is probably the most adroit politician in Europe and he honestly believes that all he does is for the good of the country," Gray explained. "He has the qualities of martyr, fanatic and Machiavelli. No one can outwit him, frighten or blandish him. Remember that he is not pro-German nor personally anti-British but only pro-de Valera. My view is that he will do business on his own terms or must be overcome by force."

Churchill had little sympathy with the Taoiseach, and absolutely no intention of placating him. "I think it would be better to let de Valera stew in his own juice for a while," he wrote. "The less we say to de Valera at this juncture the better, and certainly nothing must be said to reassure him." He added that "Maffey should be made aware of the rising anger in England and Scotland and especially among the merchant seamen, and he should not be encouraged to think that his only task is to mollify de Valera and make everything, including our ruin, pass off pleasantly."

With the British unwilling to placate his fears, de Valera had little choice other than to make the best of the protection afforded by American opinion. He knew that the British were likely to appeal to the White House, and he astutely anticipated the move by giving an interview to Wallace Carroll of United Press, the American wire service.

"If we handed over the ports to Britain, we would thereby involve ourselves directly in the war, with all its consequences," de Valera explained. "You have seen what has happened to London, notwithstanding its defences. Ireland is not a nation which can spend ten million pounds a day on armaments and if London is suffering as it is what would happen to Dublin, Cork or other Irish cities relatively unprotected? If we are attacked, we should no doubt have to face those dangers, but no nation can be asked to court them."

Within hours of this interview the State Department instructed Gray to impress on de Valera that Irish freedom and democracy would vanish if Britain lost the war. He was to tell him that "virtually the entire American press and the vast preponderance of public opinion" believed Britain should be allowed to use Irish bases.

Gray adopted a rather threatening tone when he met the Taoiseach on 22 November 1940. "Americans could be cruel if their interests were affected," he warned, "and Ireland should expect little or no sympathy if the British took the ports."

There was no intention of handing over or leasing any Irish territory to anyone, de Valera replied, adding rather pointedly that it was strange that the United States, a neutral, should be denying the right of neutrality to a small country.

"I replied," Gray reported, "that we were not denying any rights but that as all right ultimately depended on power he might be relying on the power of American public opinion to support him and that he might fail to receive this support."

De Valera's authorised biographers contended that Gray had by then already "revealed a powerful dislike" of de Valera, but this was not really so. He certainly disliked aspects of Irish policy, but he still professed to like the Taoiseach personally and even admired his government's domestic policies. "I like him very much, though I despair of coping with him," Gray wrote to Eleanor Roosevelt on 10 February 1941. "The great thing the de Valera government has done and is doing, is to govern in the interest of the underprivileged as far as possible. They have a real new deal here." It was de Valera who first developed a strong aversion to the American Minister, and this was understandable under the circumstances.

Gray was an enthusiastic amateur with firm convictions which he rather naively expected all people of good faith to share. Hence he expressed his views with an almost reckless imprudence, especially in the circles in which he socialised. He liked to hunt and fish, and this brought him into contact with the old landed gentry of the ascendancy class, who were often pro-British to the point of still considering themselves British. Gray and his wife also liked to entertain extensively. De Valera and Sinéad attended one dinner party, but it was not their scene and they politely asked not to be invited again. This was a pity because if there had been a little more social contact between them perhaps they might not have eventually developed such an intense aversion towards one another. People like Seán T. O'Kelly, Seán MacEntee and Erskine Childers were frequent guests, and Gray expressed his views candidly in front of them, so they were able to report on what he was saying.

"Gray is very imprudent," de Valera wrote to Robert Brennan, the Irish Minister in Washington. "He repeats these views publicly in the diplomatic corps and amongst his ascendancy friends." The American Minister was saying that the Roosevelt administration wished the Taoiseach to allow the British to use Irish bases. Fearing this was giving the impression "that America wants the British to seize our ports," de Valera instructed Brennan to take the matter up at the State Department.

The following month the Taoiseach actually used the continuing British threat to frustrate Berlin's efforts to increase the size of the German Legation in Dublin. On 19 December Hempel informed Walshe that a Lufthansa airplane would fly in with additional diplomatic personnel around dawn two days later. On instructions from de Valera, the Irish Chargé d'Affaires in Berlin was cabled to tell the Germans that the whole thing was "politically impossible from our point of view." No doubt mindful of the so-called German Plot of 1918, de Valera was afraid that allowing the Germans to land a special aircraft would give Britain a pretext for alleging some kind of sinister collusion between Dublin and Berlin. While the Germans undoubtedly had a "technical right" to increase their staff, the Taoiseach insisted that the new people should come "by the ordinary ways of travel"—all of which involved a stop-over in Britain. Hence Berlin reluctantly dropped the idea.

While this crisis was coming to a head, there were signs of another impending crisis, when the British began to exert economic pressure, calculated by Churchill "to bring de Valera to his knees in a very short time." In December 1940 the British terminated their agreement to allocate Ireland shipping space in return for Dublin's agreement not to charter neutral shipping. By then Britain had most of the available neutral shipping under contract, and it was estimated that the Irish would only be able to secure enough ships to fulfil about a quarter of their needs. The British were acting within their rights in terminating the arrangement, but this was certainly contrary to the spirit in which the agreement had been made.

De Valera again turned for American help, this time by appealing directly to the American people. In a Christmas broadcast over the Columbia Broadcasting System (CBS), he asked for the United States to sell Ireland some ships to carry food because the country was facing serious shortages as a result of a blockade by the belligerents. In the text of the speech released by CBS and published in the *New York Times*, he was actually quoted as having said that "the overshadowing anxiety" of his government was the "possibility of incitement which would force our people once more to do battle against Britain and the British." In fact, he never mentioned either Britain or the British by name, but it was some days before a correction was published, and by then the damage had been done.

Roosevelt was furious. With Britain in dire straits and no longer able to pay for armaments, he had just sent up a trial balloon to gauge the possible reaction to lending or leasing war material to the British. Some opponents of his pro-British policy were basically contending the British were not worth helping because they were starving millions of innocent people with their blockade of the continent. The remarks attributed to de Valera fitted neatly into this "Starving Europe Campaign." Anglophobic elements, especially in the Irish-American community, instinctively concluded that de Valera was accusing Britain of trying to cause another famine in Ireland.

Roosevelt was so annoyed that he took time to ridicule Irish neutrality during a radio address on 29 December. What would happen, he asked, if Britain were defeated? "Could Ireland hold out? Would Irish freedom be permitted as an amazing exception in an unfree world?" There was no doubt he was insinuating that Ireland was acting as a parasite, while the British were fighting for her freedom as well as their own.

Gray denounced the Christmas broadcast as an attempt to appeal to the American people over the head of the President. If de Valera wished to explain his situation, he should send an emissary to the United States and not try to go over the head of the President. Early in the new year the Gallup Poll published the findings of a public opinion survey which found that 63 per cent of the American people felt the British should be allowed to use Irish bases, and even among the Irish-American community, 40 per cent of those whose fathers were born in Ireland believed Irish bases should be given to Britain. Gray gleefully passed on these figures to the Taoiseach, who was obviously worried by the drift of American opinion.

"Mr de Valera is more uneasy today than he has ever been at any stage of his non-stop political career," Maffey reported. "His congregation is melting away."

Although Churchill had instructed that the Irish should be told that "only dire necessity" had forced Britain to cancel the shipping agreement, de Valera realised what was happening, and Maffey sought to temper the approach of his own government, which was in danger of overplaying its hand. "Our best hope of achieving anything here lies and always will lie in the actions and thoughts of America and of Irishmen overseas," he advised. "For that reason we must be careful not to work the economic pressure in such a way as to revive that fatal sympathy for Ireland by lending colour to the cry that we are blockading her out of resentment."

The mass of the Irish people were ignorant and still liable to be stirred by politicians exploiting the old hatred of England, so the British Representative warned that de Valera needed to be handled carefully. "He is still the chosen tribal leader for their feuds," Maffey wrote. "Mr de Valera hitherto has used this Irish fanaticism on a bigger stage than his platform today. Through it he has achieved prestige in America, in England, and Geneva. He would stir world-wide interest in the soul of Ireland. But it is the soul of England which stirs the world today, and Éire is a bog with a petty leader raking over old muck heaps. He has in the past enjoyed world prestige, he is vain and ambitious, but the task he has followed without looking either to right or to left is now leading into insignificance."

Maffey's harsh comments should be considered against the backdrop of Churchill's virulent attitude towards de Valera and Irish neutrality. The Prime Minister, who was taking a personal interest in the Irish situation, asked to be informed regularly "as to how the screw is being applied to Ireland." He had already expressed misgivings about Maffey's friendly disposition towards de Valera, whereas Maffey thought that Churchill was being too severe and was in the process not acting in Britain's best interest. Maffey wanted further weapons supplied to the Irish as a means of showing that Britain intended to respect Irish neutrality and thereby minimising the possible danger of de Valera being able to exploit the economic pressure for his own political advantage.

The Dominions Office agreed with Maffey, but Churchill would have none of it. Having placed an approving tick in the margin and drawn a heavy black line beside the description of de Valera as "a petty leader raking over old muck heaps," Churchill wrote a resolute "No" beside the suggestion about supplying arms. He had no intention of giving the Irish any assurance about respecting their neutrality. For one thing, he still did not accept that Ireland had a right to remain neutral.

"I do not personally recognise Irish neutrality as a legal act," the

Prime Minister wrote on 17 January 1941. "Southern Ireland having repudiated the Treaty, and we not having recognised Southern Ireland as a Sovereign State, that country is now in an anomalous position. Should the danger to our war effort through the denial of Irish bases threaten to become mortal, which is not the case at present, we should have to act in accordance with our own self-preservation and that of our Cause."

"Hateful as their neutrality is," Maffey noted two days later, "it has been a neutrality friendly to our cause. I need not give in detail what we have got and are getting in the way of intelligence reports, coded weather reports, prompt reports of submarine movements, free use of Lough Foyle and of the air over the Donegal shore and territorial waters, etc., etc. He explained in another report three days later that Ireland's military "plans and details were revealed to us with the greatest frankness. The catastrophic fall of France stiffened the country's resolve to maintain neutrality, but the Éire Government continued to help in every way which did not expose them to German action."

Churchill wanted the ports, however, and he was not going to be satisfied with anything short of them. He instructed that the influence of the United States on Ireland should "be invoked by every means open to us." One such means was Wendell Willkie, the man whom Roosevelt had recently defeated. After visiting London, he hopped over to Dublin and had what he described as a "brutally frank" talk with de Valera.

Willkie told the Taoiseach that he was foolish thinking Ireland could stay out of the war by remaining neutral, because Hitler would attack Ireland when he was ready. De Valera complained that Ireland was unable to get arms and he said he was afraid Dublin would be bombed.

At this, Willkie said he could no longer conceal his contempt. He saw no reason why the British should supply arms when Dublin was unwilling to give them bases. He added that the Irish owed their freedom to American sentiment, and they would stand condemned in American eyes if Britain fell. "American opinion will not be with you," Willkie declared.

Jolted by Willkie's blunt approach on top of the latest public opinion polls and Roosevelt's contemptuous reference to Ireland, de Valera decided to take up Gray on his suggestion about sending an emissary to the United States. Seán T. O'Kelly was his first choice, but he declined, so Frank Aiken was selected instead. He proved a most unhappy choice, because Gray and the British informed the

White House he was pro-German, and they asked Roosevelt to ensure he returned empty-handed.

Aiken was kept waiting in Washington for several days before he finally got to meet the President, who proceeded to lecture him on Ireland's responsibilities. Aiken held his ground and the meeting ended in a blazing row when he persisted in maintaining that Ireland was in danger of a British attack. Afterwards Aiken travelled to various Irish-American centres throughout the country and associated publicly with some of Roosevelt's bitterest critics—people like Charles A. Lindbergh and John T. Flynn.

On instructions from the State Department, Gray complained forcefully to de Valera about Aiken's actions, and this lead to a heated exchange between them. Afterwards the Taoiseach let it be known that he would demand Gray's recall if it were not for the latter's close friendship with Roosevelt. Married to an aunt of the President's wife, Gray not only had direct access to the White House but also enjoyed the President's confidence. With Ireland needing all the friends she could get, it was no time to provoke a diplomatic incident with the United States by expelling Gray.

That same month, April 1941, the horrors of war came perilously close when more than a thousand people were killed in two German bombing raids on Belfast. De Valera ordered fire brigades from Dundalk, Drogheda and Dublin to help fight the fires. Although it was clearly an unneutral act, he was able to brush aside German complaints because the Irish constitution claimed legal sovereignty over the area.

"They are all our people," he explained in Castlebar. "Any help we can give them in the present time we will give to them wholeheartedly, believing that were the circumstances reversed they would also give us their help wholeheartedly."

The partition issue itself threatened to erupt the following month when Churchill announced that the government was thinking of extending compulsory military service to Northern Ireland. This was probably the move de Valera feared most, because it had the potential to drive the country into the arms of the IRA by undermining the constitutional parties in the Dáil in much the same way as the conscription crisis had undermined the Irish Parliamentary Party in 1918. The Nationalist population reacted predictably, voicing vociferous objections, and de Valera launched a diplomatic offensive to stave off the move.

This time he found Gray most helpful. The American Minister bombarded Washington with urgent messages for Roosevelt to intercede with Churchill. When Gray suggested an escape clause for Northern Catholics, de Valera initially agreed but telephoned some hours later to say that he had changed his mind after discussing it with cabinet colleagues.

"If Mr Churchill is determined, as he seems to be, to go ahead with the proposal, the prospect is indeed as dark as it can be," the Taoiseach warned Gray. "Almost inevitably this will lead to a new conflict between Ireland and Britain in which we shall all be involved. We are truly in a world gone mad."

De Valera also appealed directly to Churchill. Dulanty, who delivered the message, described his meeting with the Prime Minister as "exceedingly unsatisfactory." Churchill fulminated; he asked if de Valera wished a public answer. "If he does," he added, "I will give it and it will resound about the world."

Despite strong representations from Roosevelt and Prime Ministers Mackenzie King of Canada and Robert Menzies of Australia, together with most of the British cabinet, Churchill still wished to press ahead. To back down would, in his view, show irresolution.

"That is all very well," the cabinet secretary noted. "But what he does is to jump to decisions—ill-considered—and then say that it shows weakness to recede. It shows stupidity to jump to them." Fortunately saner heads prevailed and the idea was dropped.

The people of the twenty-six counties had their starkest reminder of the danger facing them later the same week when a German plane bombed Dublin, killing over thirty people and injuring scores more. The Luftwaffe bombed Bristol and Liverpool the same night and Dublin was apparently mistaken for one of the British cities by the lone bomber, whose crew was disorientated. It was, for the Irish, the most serious incident of the war.

Within three weeks, however, the real threat to Ireland would disappear as Hitler turned eastward and invaded the Soviet Union. It was not realised then, but in hindsight it would become apparent that Ireland was no longer in danger of a German invasion. Some of the war's greatest battles had yet to be fought, but as long as the Germans were occupied on the eastern front de Valera could breathe easier.

The only person who ever spoke out in the Dáil against neutrality was the deputy leader of Fine Gael, James Dillon. On 17 July 1941 he stunned even his own party colleagues by contending that "the government's present policy of indifferent neutrality" was wrong even though he acknowledged that it had the support of the majority not only of the Dáil and the Irish people, but also of his own party. Dillon did not challenge the right of the Irish people to remain neutral; he just contested the wisdom of the policy.

At the time American technicians were building a naval base on Lough Foyle and there was speculation that the United States would soon begin convoying lend-lease materials to Britain. If this happened, the Americans would probably want bases in the twenty-six counties.

When Roosevelt first hinted about lend-lease, he used the analogy of lending a garden hose to a neighbour whose house was on fire. Later the analogy was taken a step further to cover delivering the material, by suggesting that one would deliver the garden hose to the neighbour. Now, the analogy was being carried even further with de Valera, who was told one would allow firemen on one's roof to put out the fire next door.

"Of course, we would," de Valera told the Dáil, "but that is not the analogy to what we are being asked to do. What we are being asked to do is to set our own house on fire in company with the other house. We have been asked to throw ourselves into the flames-that is what it amounts to." Since providing bases to the United States, or any of the belligerents, would probably involve Ireland in the war, he resolutely rejected all overtures for such facilities, and it quickly became apparent that he had the broad support of the Dáil. Dillon's views were repudiated by Cosgrave. When Dillon spoke out in a similar vein some months later he was not only repudiated but also forced to resign from Fine Gael.

It was the American Minister who posed the greatest threat to de Valera's policy from mid 1941 onwards. "Although America was still neutral," Maffey later recalled, "Gray was outspoken in his condemnation of the Axis aggressors, in his support of Britain's determined stand for liberty and in his criticism of the unhelpful attitude of the de Valera Government towards our cause." There were things the British would like to say about de Valera's policy but could not speak out for fear of stirring up old passions, but Gray was in a different position. "He recognised the need of extreme patience on our side of the table and continued to say exactly what he thought in the ideal setting of the American Legation," Maffey continued. "An American Minister had the temerity to make it plain to Irish Nationalists that they were no longer the darling Playboys of the Western World, and to point out that the audience were bored."

On 21 April Gray invited Walshe and six different members of de Valera's cabinet to a dinner at the Legation in honour of Thomas

Campbell, an American wheat expert and friend of Roosevelt who was passing through Ireland. During the dinner Campbell made a blatant pitch to persuade the cabinet ministers—O'Kelly, Lemass, MacEntee, Ryan, Boland and Ruttledge—to abandon neutrality. "There was a general look of puzzlement on all the ministers' faces, arising, no doubt, mainly from the realisation that David Gray had brought them there to put them on the defensive and to influence them through this powerful friend of Roosevelt," Walshe reported. "I had personally never seen such an example of incorrectness and undiplomatic behaviour, and I think it should never be forgotten for Gray, who once more showed himself the worst enemy of the policy of neutrality."

Roosevelt thoroughly approved of the way Gray was handling Irish affairs. "Praise the Lord, you have got the number of certain persons in the Emerald Isle!" he wrote to Gray on 2 August 1941. "People are, frankly, getting pretty fed up with my old friend Dev."

Gray was so indiscreet, de Valera had little time for his judgement and the Department of External Affairs made quiet moves to have him recalled. If Gray were replaced, Joseph P. Walshe told John D. Kearney, the Canadian High Commissioner, the Irish government would probably be amenable to American approaches for Irish bases, but the Canadian representative soon learned that de Valera had no notion of giving bases to anyone. "I ascertained that even a promise of unity of Ireland would not alter his attitude," Kearney reported.

Not only did the Taoiseach show no inclination to allow the Americans to use bases in the twenty-six counties, he actually demanded that his government should be consulted if they wished to use a base being built by American technicians on Lough Foyle in Northern Ireland. In October he instructed the Irish Minister in Washington to find out what the Americans intended to do with the base.

When an informal enquiry was brushed aside, Brennan sent a formal note, which provoked a terse response. Roosevelt authorised the State Department to reply that the request related to territory recognised by United States as part of the United Kingdom and, therefore, "the Irish government should address its inquiry to the United Kingdom government." This contemptuous treatment of the Irish claim to sovereignty over Northern Ireland was indicative of the deterioration in relations between Dublin and Washington before the Americans entered the war in December 1941.

CHAPTER 22

"Why Should Éire Suffer?"

It was ironic that relations between the United States and Ireland should have deteriorated to such an extent when de Valera and Roosevelt were both professing a desire to stay out of the war. While de Valera openly proclaimed his determination to remain neutral, he quietly provided the British with essentially all the help his government could give them. He was, in fact, secretly pursuing Roosevelt's avowed policy of giving Britain all-out aid short of war, but there was a big difference in that the Irish leader believed in non-belligerency, whereas the American President apparently wished to get into the war.

Gray candidly admitted that it was only a matter of time before Roosevelt would lead the United States into the conflict, but de Valera did not believe the White House could do this because the approval of Congress was necessary for an American declaration of war. The Taoiseach did not foresee the Japanese attack on Pearl Harbour or Hitler's subsequent declaration of war on the United States. Gray, on the other hand, predicted the Japanese attack on American forces in the Pacific once Japan joined the Rome-Berlin Axis in September 1940, and in the weeks leading up to the attack on Pearl Harbour he was writing in terms of an imminent Japanese assault, which he apparently believed Roosevelt was deliberately provoking.

"Before you get this," he wrote to Roosevelt on 21 October 1941, "Japan may have touched things off. You have handled that situation as miraculously as every other as far as I can see."

Gray's astute assessment of Japan's intention probably bolstered his confidence in assessing Irish policy, but here his assessment was unquestionably distorted. He did not know of the extent of the secret Anglo-Irish co-operation, though in the long run it was unlikely this knowledge would have made much difference to his hostility towards Irish policy, any more than it influenced the hostility of Churchill, who was aware of it. Gray simply believed everyone had an obligation to fight fascism. Hence he welcomed the attack on Pearl Harbour, because it brought America into the war. "Our first reaction to the news that Japan had attacked us was, 'Thank God! the country is now behind the President'," he wrote.

Churchill likewise welcomed the Pearl Harbour attack and, intoxicated with his own elation, if not something stronger, he apparently hoped Dublin could now be persuaded to enter the war. "Now is your chance," he cabled de Valera. "Now or never. 'A Nation Once Again.' Am ready to meet you at any time." The reference to "A Nation Once Again," the anthem of the Irish Parliamentary Party in the days of Parnell and Redmond, raised the spectre of a deal to end partition, but Churchill had not intended to imply this.

"I certainly contemplated no deal over partition," Churchill wrote. "That would only come about by consent arising out of war comradeship between North and South."

Maffey caused considerable anxiety when he insisted that Walshe rouse the Taoiseach at "an unseemly hour" in the dead of night in order to deliver the message personally, as he had been instructed. Fearing some kind of ultimatum, Walshe alerted the cabinet secretary and Army chief of Staff to stand by, but the crisis quickly evaporated when de Valera read the message. "Our opinion was that Churchill had been imbibing heavily that night," Walshe later wrote, "and that his effusion flowed in the message."

"I considered it was Churchill's way of intimating 'Now is the chance for taking action which would ultimately lead to unification of the country'," de Valera recalled. As he did not see any opportunity of this himself, he felt a meeting with Churchill might lead to a disagreement which would only do harm. He therefore refused to go to London but suggested "the best way towards a fuller understanding" of the Irish position would be for Lord Cranborne, the Dominions Secretary, to come to Dublin instead. He was not offering to negotiate but merely proposing to explain his policy personally to the Dominion Secretary.

Speaking publicly in Cork on 14 December 1941 de Valera reaffirmed his determination to stay out of the war in the course of sympathising with the United States on being dragged into the conflict. "We can only be a friendly neutral," he repeated. From the moment the war began, neutrality was the only policy possible. Yet he recognised that there were dangers and difficulties on the road ahead. "In a world at war, each set of belligerents are ever ready to regard those who are not with them as against them, but the course we have followed is a just course," he added.

During the first two years of the war de Valera had used American opinion to keep the British in line, but henceforth the opportunities to do so were going to be severely limited because the vast majority of Irish-Americans would be supporting their country's war effort and would no longer have any time for Irish affairs. The American Friends of Irish Neutrality, set up at de Valera's behest in November 1940, had already disbanded itself within days of America's declaration of war.

Previously de Valera had been able to fend off Allied requests by contending he had to be careful not to give rise to speculation about secret Anglo-Irish deals which might inflame anglophobic elements at home. Now, the United States could "carry the ball" for the Allies.

On 22 December 1941 Roosevelt thanked de Valera for the expressions of sympathy in Cork but went on to indicate that mere sympathy was not enough. "If freedom and liberty are to be preserved, they must now be defended by the human and material resources of all free nations," he wrote. "Your freedom too is at stake. No longer can it be doubted that the policy of Hitler and his Axis associates is the conquest of the entire world and the enslavement of all mankind."

In June 1940 de Valera had told Malcolm MacDonald that the United States would be allowed to use Irish bases and station troops on Irish soil in order to guarantee Irish neutrality, but America's entry into the war changed all this. The Taoiseach displayed "considerable nervous excitement" on 23 December 1941 when Maffey brought up the possibility of providing bases for the Americans.

"Let it be clearly understood the answer to any such approach would be a plain 'No'!" de Valera said. "Éire has the right to choose her own way. She did not start the war, nor does she wish to get into it. The war was caused by the blunders of the great powers. I have seen opportunities missed, but the little powers could do nothing. Why should Éire suffer? If there is a conflagration why should she be thrown into the fire?"

"Today, we are a people united as perhaps never before in our history," he declared next day in a Christmas broadcast to the United States. "Unless we are attacked, any change from neutrality would destroy this unity. It is our duty to Ireland to try to keep out of this war, and with God's help we hope to succeed."

When Churchill and Roosevelt met in Washington in January 1942, they decided to station American troops in Northern Ireland. De Valera was informed of their arrival on 26 January by Maffey, who pleaded with him not to object, but the Taoiseach seized on the occasion to make another denunciation of partition. While the Irish people harboured no hostility towards the United States, he emphasised he had a "duty to make it clearly understood that, no matter what troops occupy the six counties, the Irish people's claim for the union of the whole of the national territory and for supreme jurisdiction over it will remain unabated."

His remarks alluding to American troops as an army of occupation were deeply resented by the American authorities, especially as he had made no protest to the Germans over the bombing of Northern Ireland. Although most Irish newspapers and the international press generally described de Valera's remarks as a protest, he explained privately that they should be considered a mere statement. "He felt obliged to make some statement in case silence might be interpreted as acquiescence in the status of partition," Kearney reported after a meeting with the Taoiseach. "He also told me that he feared a worsening of relationships between Ireland and the United States by reason of the presence of the American troops in the North, because the American soldier would not understand the Irish the way the British soldier did." He was afraid that the Nationalist minority would resent the arrival of United States troops, and that the Americans would take offence.

Even if the Taoiseach only intended his pronouncement as a simple statement, it was viewed as a protest in the United States, and there were reports of strong anti-Irish feelings. These reports, coupled with American newspaper editorials calling on de Valera to allow the Allies to use Irish bases, lent credibility to German propaganda about the Americans preparing industriously to invade the twenty-six counties from Northern Ireland. As Berlin had already used this kind of propaganda to justify what were supposedly pre-emptive invasions of neutrals, like Norway, Belgium and Holland, there was speculation that Hitler might make a desperate effort to gain control of Ireland in order to knock Britain out of the war before the United States could mobilise properly.

Roosevelt assured de Valera with a personal message that the United States never had "the slightest thought or intention of invading Irish territory or threatening Irish security." Instead of posing a danger to the Irish people, the President contended that the American troops in Northern Ireland "can only contribute to the security of Ireland and of the whole British Isles, as well as furthering our total war effort."

As far as de Valera was concerned, the comparatively small force of American soldiers were not needed to defend Ireland. In thanking Roosevelt for his message, the Taoiseach explained that there were already 250,000 Irishmen prepared to defend their country if they could only get the necessary arms.

"If he would only come out of the clouds and quit talking about the quarter of a million Irishmen ready to fight if they had the weapons, we would all have a higher regard for him," Roosevelt complained. "Personally I do not believe there are more than one thousand trained soldiers in the whole of the Free State. Even they are probably efficient only in the use of rifles and shotguns."

For the remainder of the war the United States took most of the initiatives in Allied relations with Ireland. In March 1942 Gray was let in on the secret Anglo-Irish co-operation and was genuinely surprised. "A mutual good feeling and confidence have been established between the Irish and British Military chiefs beyond what might reasonably have been believed possible," he informed the State Department on 23 March. The same facilities were extended to the Americans, but relations between the two countries continued to deteriorate. In fact, at times they were so strained that many Irish people feared an American invasion.

Although the Americans never did seriously consider invading Ireland, Gray outlined various contingency plans for invasions in his letters to Roosevelt. These sinister proposals certainly showed that there were valid grounds for Irish uneasiness. During the summer de Valera became decidedly worried over American propaganda about the bases in Northern Ireland. He complained that it was a deliberate attempt to provoke a German attack on the six counties. On 6 July Gray found him "in a sour, discouraged mood, evidently labouring under some acute apprehension of hostile conspiracy."

Their suspicions were clearly mutual. After assuring him that the United States was not trying to provoke a German attack, Gray turned the conversation to the subject of secret talks recently arranged between the Commander of the United States forces in Northern Ireland and the Chief of Staff of the Irish Army. He brought this up even though he knew de Valera did not want to discuss the topic, or even let on officially that he knew about the talks. "I did not wish," Gray wrote, "ever to give Mr de Valera the opportunity to disavow all knowledge of the liaison and to charge me, and possibly also Sir John Maffey, with tampering with his General Staff without his knowledge."

After personally authorising secret co-operation, de Valera normally left the technical details of the co-operation to Walshe in diplomatic matters, or in military affairs to people like General McKenna, or Colonel Dan Bryan, the head of Military Intelligence. He preferred not to discuss such matters at diplomatic level, an understandable precaution because the diplomats concerned would naturally report such conversations to their governments, and there was always the danger that their reports would be intercepted by the Germans.

While his door was always open to Maffey, Gray, and Kearney, he tried to keep his meetings with Hempel and Vicenzo Berardis, the Italian Minister, to a minimum. He left as much as possible of the dealings with them to Walshe and Frederick H. Boland.

When things looked bleak for the Allies in 1940 and early 1941, Walshe believed Germany was going to win the war, so he adopted what might be called a line of constructive ambiguity in order to ingratiate himself with Hempel. He congratulated him, for instance, on Germany's victories in western Europe. Walshe also pretended that he was afraid the British were so annoyed over the denial of Irish bases that they would retaliate against Ireland after the war; he actually expressed the hope that Germany would not abandon the Irish to Britain's ire. On another occasion he intimated to Hempel that the Irish-Americans could be used to Germany's advantage in keeping the United States out of the war as long as the Germans did not antagonise them by violating Irish neutrality.

Hempel duly reported all these conversations, much to the uneasiness of the Allied intelligence people who were reading his reports throughout the war. Their suspicions about Walshe were alleviated, however, by de Valera's use of him as a conduit for secret offers of cooperation. It was Walshe whom he sent to London to suggest staff talks with the British in May of 1940, and Walshe also conducted the discussions in November 1942 leading to the agreement not to intern Allied airmen who landed in Ireland while on "non-operational flights," such as training missions or delivering aircraft from the United States. The Allied argument was basically that any Germans who might land in Ireland would be on operational flights because they would be so far from base, but Allied pilots frequently got lost on non-operational flights and landed in the twenty-six counties by mistake.

According to Winston Churchill's son, Randolph, the whole "nonoperational" argument was merely a "convenient fiction." It was a way for Ireland to help the Allies, while still preserving the appearance of neutrality.

Irish authorities did not even bother to check the "non-operational" claims of Allied airmen who landed in Ireland. In fact, the pilots of five of the next six American planes which landed failed to claim they had been on non-operational flights, but they were released anyway. "Under the circumstances," the Canadian High Commissioner wrote, "the meaning of the words 'non-operational flight' has sometimes been stretched almost beyond recognition."

In all, 142 Allied planes came down in Ireland during the war. Forty-seven were allowed to fly away, most after being refuelled, and a further twenty-seven were salvaged and returned by road to Northern Ireland. Although forty-five of the survivors were officially interned for a time, these men were really little more than window dressing to preserve the appearance of neutrality. The vast majority—493 of the 538 Allied airmen who survived their landings—were promptly released, whereas all fifty-five German airmen were interned for the duration of the war, with the exception of one seriously injured man who was handed over to the British for repatriation to Germany in 1943. Any information about new equipment extracted from the wreckage of the sixteen German planes that came down on Irish territory was immediately passed on to the British.

The discriminatory aspects of internment were particularly apparent in the case of sailors. No Allied seamen were ever detained by the Irish, but 214 German sailors were held at the Curragh. The 166 survivors picked up in the Bay of Biscay by the Irish ship *Kerlogue*, and the forty-eight survivors from the U-boat sunk by the RAF in international waters off the south coast after its sighting had been reported by Irish coastwatchers, were all distressed mariners and should therefore have been freed under International law, but they were interned anyway.

Throughout the war all German spies caught in Ireland were jailed and anyone even suspected of collusion with the Germans was interned without trial, whereas the British soldier caught spying in July 1940 was quietly let go. In September 1942 Irish Military Intelligence uncovered an escape organisation which had been setup in conjunction with MI9 in Britain to help Allied internees to escape to Northern Ireland. It was made up largely of Irishmen who had served in the First World War. A Dublin doctor and a friend had been arrested as they were helping a New Zealand pilot who had escaped from the Curragh. Maffey pleaded with de Valera not to intern the doctor or his friends, but the Taoiseach was in a tricky position. He was anxious not to be seen to be interfering too much with the military.

In July a whole unit of the Local Defence Force had quit after learning of the release of the crew of a British aircraft which crashed near Strokestown, County Roscommon. It should be remembered that the security forces were controlled by people who had fought against de Valera during the Civil War. Many of them were still very bitter, and it was important for morale purposes that they should not be antagonised by political interference. Before agreeing to go easy on the doctor and his friends, de Valera discussed the situation privately with the head of Military Intelligence, Colonel Dan Bryan, who raised no objections.

Around the same time the newly formed Office of Strategic Services (OSS), the American forerunner of the Central Intelligence Agency, sent two undercover agents to Ireland. Both were quickly uncovered but, rather than expelling them, the Irish authorities actually welcomed them in the obvious hope that they would correct the distorted American perception of Irish neutrality, because the Americans seemed ready to believe the most ridiculous stories. In November 1942, for instance, the State Department asked the Irish Minister in Washington for an explanation about the rumoured presence of hundreds of Japanese tourists. It was a ridiculous request and de Valera sought to exploit its absurdity as a means of getting rid of Gray.

The Irish Minister expressed exasperation to the State Department that such an inquiry had ever been made. There were, he explained, only four Japanese people in the whole of the twenty-six counties, the Consul General, his wife, a vice-consul and a stranded seaman. The inquiry showed that the United States government was determined to believe that the Irish were "permitting every kind of Axis subversive activity to be going on in Ireland notwithstanding the frequent and official denials on the part of the Irish government." If Gray had been reporting properly, the Irish Minister added, the State Department would never have made such a ridiculous enquiry. He therefore asked the Americans to appoint someone who would be "an independent and unprejudiced witness to seek and make known the truth."

Gray, however, had the full confidence of Roosevelt, who thought he was doing a magnificent job in Ireland. As a result the State Department rejected the request as "offensive in the extreme." If de Valera wished to get rid of Gray, he would have to demand the Minister's formal recall, which would undoubtedly have led to a diplomatic incident, and it was no time to provoke such an incident.

Probably the most striking example of the real benevolence of Irish policy was in the area of intelligence. In January 1943 Walshe approached the Americans with an official offer to co-operate with the OSS. In the following months the Irish turned over voluminous Intelligence reports on such things as IRA strength, radio interceptions, reports on aeroplane and submarine sightings, the names and addresses of people in America with whom German nationals living in Ireland or pro-German Irish people had been corresponding, as well as detailed files on the interrogations of German spies and internees already captured.

Following Allied successes on the North African and Russian fronts in early 1943, de Valera's government gave "additional tangible evidence" of a willingness to help the Allies, according to the Canadian High Commissioner, who noted that news of the Allied successes had been received in Ireland with "a satisfaction approaching enthusiasm." The Irish people had begun to worry about the country's post-war standing and in such a climate, he thought the Taoiseach might even be willing to provide bases, if President Roosevelt asked for them. "De Valera had repeatedly stressed the importance of unity in regard to Ireland's attitude towards the war," Kearney wrote, "and I believe he would stretch a point to maintain such unity, and in case he is doubtful as to what course to pursue he might be influenced in favour of acceding to the request if such a course found favour in other quarters."

Maffey agreed and went to London in early March to discuss the situation with leaders there, but the British government could no longer envisage any use for the bases it had coveted in 1940. So long as the Germans controlled the coast of France, shipping routes off the south coast of Ireland were so susceptible to German attacks that practically all shipping to and from Britain went around Northern Ireland, where the Allies already had bases. It was ironic that the importance of Irish bases should have been dismissed at this time because the Allies were actually in the midst of their most serious crisis in the on-going Battle of the Atlantic. The British Admiralty later recorded, for instance, that "the Germans never came so near disrupting communications between the New World and the Old as in the first twenty days of March 1943."

When Gray brought up the question of Irish bases during a visit to the United States in the summer of 1943, the American Joint Chiefs of Staff concluded that the bases would not only be of no use, but would actually be a liability. The wartime fuss over the bases had therefore been pointless. It could be largely attributed to what the British cabinet secretary had earlier described as Churchill's tendency to jump to ill-considered decisions.

The extent of the Irish co-operation was such that the head of the Éire desk at OSS headquarters, R. Carter Nicholas, came to Dublin on 27 September 1943 to enquire if Irish diplomats in occupied Europe could be used as American spies. De Valera was consulted and arrangements were made for the OSS to furnish questions which the Department of External Affairs asked Irish diplomats in Berlin, Rome and Vichy, then transmitting the answers to the OSS. Such co-operation made a mockery of Ireland's supposed neutrality.

In mid-September de Valera had also agreed to release most of the Allied internees secretly on the pretext that they had been on nonoperational flights when they came down. Before releasing them, however, it was first necessary to move them to a new camp, away from the German internees. The new camp was ready on 18 October and in the course of the transfer all but eleven of the men were let go. Maffey tried to get the others released also, but Walshe explained that the government was afraid of German retaliation.

"Why not allow the eleven men to escape?" Maffey asked.

"I got the impression that we shall be able to work matters out this way if no better way presents itself," Maffey reported. He also assured London that henceforth Allied planes could operate off Ireland "on the assumption that no risk of internment exists."

Even though de Valera had refused to give bases to the British, he did allow them to station two armed tugs in Irish waters on the south and west coasts for air-sea rescue purposes. The Irish operated wireless direction equipment at Maim Head and Valentia for Allied planes to get their bearings, and Dublin permitted the British to establish a radar station on the south coast for use against submarine activity. In addition, thousands of Irish people volunteered for service in the Allied forces, some with great distinction. Eight men born in the twenty-six counties won the Victoria Cross, Britain's highest award for gallantry. Those eight, in relation to the country's population, actually constituted a higher ratio than for those born in Britain.

By the end of the war de Valera could honestly say he had helped the Allies. "For the first time in history the British Cabinet have been able to conduct a long war without any anxiety about Ireland," Maffey wrote the week after hostilities concluded. "When any German activity developed, I was the first to be informed."

In truth it was a myth to describe de Valera's wartime policy as neutrality because it should more accurately be called determined non-belligerency. The British and Canadian representatives in Dublin had repeatedly acknowledged that the Taoiseach was secretly prepared to give the Allies all the help he could short of involving Ireland in the war and, since the British and American service chiefs concluded that Ireland's involvement would actually be a liability to the Allied war effort, then one must conclude that de Valera really gave the Allies all the help he could. It was therefore ironic that after the war he was widely depicted as having been a Nazi sympathiser. It was just another of the many myths surrounding his career, but it was a myth the origins of which need closer examination.

CHAPTER 23

"They Would Mock Me"

In March 1943 as the Battle of the Atlantic was at its height, de Valera went on Radio Éireann to deliver a St Patrick's Day address in which he described the restoration of the Gaelic language as the most important issue facing the nation, and he proceeded to describe his kind of ideal Ireland. It would be a united Gaelic-speaking island, "whose countryside would be bright with cosy homesteads, whose fields and villages would be joyous with the sounds of industry, with the romping of sturdy children, the contests of athletic youths, the laughter of happy maidens, whose firesides would be forums for the wisdom of old age. It would, in a word, be the home of a people living the life that God desired that man should live."

De Valera's folksy picture could hardly have contrasted more starkly with what was happening in the war-torn countries of the continent. While critics howled with derision, his supporters were captivated. The Irish people were suffering materialistic deprivations as a result of the economic dislocation brought about by the war, and the comfort he was offering was of a romantic, spiritualistic kind. But it was still a comfort which contrasted with the horrific destruction elsewhere. In a subtle way the Irish people were reminded of their good fortune in avoiding the war.

To foreigners like Gray, reared in a more materialistic society, the speech was out of touch with reality. "Mr de Valera is living in his dream Ireland and still shutting out the rest of the world," he wrote to Roosevelt. The Irish people did not appear to know any better, they were cut off from the outside world and thus reality, and the American Minister held the country's censorship largely responsible.

Some aspects of Irish censorship plumbed really absurd depths while de Valera was in power. Not only were films banned on ridiculous moral grounds, but so were the books of some of the country's foremost writers, people like George Bernard Shaw, James Joyce, Seán O'Casey, Frank O'Connor, Liam O'Flaherty, and Seán O'Faoláin. The whole censorship mentality must have reached its most ridiculous extreme during the war years when the records of Bing Crosby were banned from the air by the controller of Radio Éireann for fear "crooning" would undermine the moral fibre of Irish youth.

"Ireland is a puritanical country with a clergy, many of whom have never been away from the island and whose reading and general culture is limited," Gray complained with justification. "It is honestly believed by these elements of the clergy that the Irish people must be protected from what in America seems innocent and amusing fun." Many of the actions of the censors did indeed seem mindless, but the censoring of war news was not without justification.

The routine wartime censorship, which came under the aegis of Aiken's department, was undertaken by three men, Joseph Connolly, who had been a member of the first Fianna Fáil government and a de Valera confidant until the late 1930s, T.J. Coyne, who had been seconded from the Justice Department, and Michael Knightly, a former newspaper-man. According to Robert Smyllie, the editor of the *Irish Times*, which tended to suffer most at the hands of the censor, Knightly was "reasonable, and even sympathetic, Coyne casuistically helpful, Joe Connolly a bitter anglophobe and Aiken unintelligently impossible." On a number of occasions Smyllie appealed directly to de Valera and found him eager to be fair. "Whenever I have appealed to Caesar—and I have done so more than once," he wrote, "I have found the long fellow more than anxious to be fair."

De Valera was anxious to prevent the press rousing passions. "We think that a great deal of the trouble in the world is caused by newspapers stirring up antipathies between people," he explained in Navan on 12 January 1942. His aim was to limit public debate about the war and generally discourage participation in the foreign policy process. This was done by implementing a strict censorship policy. News reports from the battle fronts had to be balanced—giving equal credence to Allied and Axis versions of various matters. In addition the press was forbidden to mention anything about Ireland's secret cooperation with the Allies, and when the secret release of Allied airmen was raised in the Dáil, de Valera refused to answer questions on the grounds of national interest.

His government contended that the stringent censorship actually favoured the British, and Maffey appreciated his reasoning. "Anti-British feeling was the dynamic of Irish opinion, always there though often latent," Maffey reported after one conversation with the Taoiseach. "Propaganda produces counter propaganda and the mind of the younger generation, brought up in an age and atmosphere of bitter hostility to England, would respond more rapidly to propaganda directed against us."

Of course, even impartial censorship was unfair to the Allies because it placed them on the same moral plane as the Nazis. Gray actually persuaded himself that the censorship policy, under the ministerial control of Aiken, was weighted towards the Axis powers. When the bishop of Achonry denounced the activities of the Nazi regime, for instance, his pastoral was censored, as was a report that the Vatican organ, Osservatore Romano, had refuted rumours that the Pope favoured Hitler and Mussolini. But when Cardinal MacRory denounced the presence of American troops in Northern Ireland, his remarks were published, much to the indignation of Gray, who was still seething with indignation over de Valera's critical comments about the stationing of American troops there.

De Valera may well have had the American Minister in mind in December 1941 when he warned of belligerents who would consider anyone hostile who did not give unquestioning support to their cause. "David Gray in that crisis of human affairs felt that 'those who are not with us are against us'," Maffey later explained. "That was his stern unshakeable principle. In his diplomacy there was no room for compromises." The Taoiseach was not prepared to give unquestioning support, and hence trouble between them was virtually inevitable.

Gray did come to the Dublin government's assistance in August 1942, however, when trouble threatened in Northern Ireland after six members of the IRA were sentenced to death for killing a policeman. It was just a quarter of a century since the executions of 1916, and de Valera feared a mass execution in the latest case would be a recipe for disaster. He was particularly critical of the sectarian undertones to the case; he noted that the Crown prosecutor had objected to thirty-nine Roman Catholics on the jury panel before coming up with twelve Protestants to try the six Roman Catholic defendants. Fearing that American soldiers would inevitably become involved if the executions led to likely trouble, Gray implored Washington to use its influence to get the British to commute the death sentences. Maffey and Kearney also exerted pressure on their own governments to use their influence, and the crisis was largely defused when the sentences of five of the six men were commuted.

De Valera sent an urgent personal message to Churchill on behalf of the sixth man, Thomas Williams. "The saving at this last moment through your personal intervention of the life of young Williams, who is to be executed on Wednesday morning in Belfast, would profoundly affect public feeling here," he explained. "I know the difficulties but results would justify—and I strongly urge that you do it."

The final decision was left to the Northern Ireland government, which refused to move. Williams was hanged on 1 September 1942.

Although Gray had helped the Dublin government in the affair, it was simply because he believed it was in America's interest. He was not trying to help the Taoiseach. The whole thing highlighted the vast potential for an unscrupulous politician to exploit the explosive situation in Northern Ireland, as far as Gray was concerned and, in a kind of perverse way, it probably contributed to his desire to discredit de Valera, because he considered him the most unscrupulous of politicians.

In the summer of 1943 Gray visited the United States and persuaded Roosevelt to ask for Irish bases. The whole thing was designed as part of a political ploy to discredit de Valera in order to undermine the American support the Taoiseach might get for an anti-partition campaign after the war. While there was no likelihood of settling partition in the near future, there were signs that de Valera intended to appeal to Irish-Americans to force Washington to put pressure on the British to abandon Northern Ireland as part of the post-war peace settlement.

Gray's judgement on Irish affairs was certainly suspect, but his uneasiness over the partition issue was understandable from an American political perspective, especially after Cardinal MacRory publicly contended in April 1943 that the Atlantic Charter's promise to restore the rights "to those who have been forcibly deprived of them" amounted to a commitment to end partition. De Valera got into the act himself in the following weeks by highlighting the partition issue for electoral purposes. With his government's mandate due to run out in June, he called a general election and proceeded to exploit the partition issue during the campaign.

The disruptive potential of Irish-Americans should not be underestimated, especially those who had been prominent in isolationist circles prior to the attack on Pearl Harbour. They were facing the political oblivion to which Hitler's appeasers were condemned, and there was a real danger that they might try to use the partition issue to stir up popular support in order to salvage their waning political fortunes.

Gray gradually became obsessed with a fear that the Ulster question would be used to undermine post war Anglo-American relations. He was terrified of a repetition of events following the

First World War when de Valera had helped to wreck Woodrow Wilson's peace plans simply because the Paris Peace Conference had not recognised Ireland's claim to independence. "Whatever the rights and wrongs of partition," Gray wrote, "it should be clearly understood that a solution on any basis of reason and compromise is not the primary object of the de Valera leadership at this time."

On 3 June de Valera told Gray a solution to partition was not beyond the bounds of good statesmanship, "especially since the precedent for the exchange of populations had been established." The implications were unmistakable. He was going to demand that the post-war peace settlement should end partition, if necessary by imposing a solution whereby Protestants In Northern Ireland would be moved to Britain and replaced by Roman Catholics of Irish extraction from Britain. Of course, Gray never seriously considered this scheme a workable solution, which was hardly surprising. After all the Protestants in Northern Ireland could trace their ancestry in the area back to the early seventeenth century, which was a great deal earlier than the vast majority of people in the United States could trace their ancestral roots in America.

As an astute politician de Valera would have realised that there was no real chance of getting the United States to insist on the ending of partition as part of the international post-war peace settlement, but this was not likely to stop him campaigning for the American government to take such a stand, any more than his realisation that there was no real hope of official recognition had stopped him campaigning for such recognition in the United States in 1920. In order to protect Roosevelt from the kind of destructive Irish influence exerted against Woodrow Wilson, Gray proposed taking on the Irish leader at his own game and beating him to the punch with propaganda to discredit him in the eyes of the American people.

"The important thing from the viewpoint of Anglo-American co-operation," Gray wrote, "is to bring to the notice of the American people the unfair and destructive policy of the de Valera politicians at the time when British and American interests are essentially the same and to obtain a verdict of American disapproval which will remove the pressure of the Irish question from Anglo-American relations." This could be done by getting de Valera to refuse a request from the American President for the use of Irish bases. He had no doubt that the Taoiseach would reject the request because he had told Maffey in April that Ireland could not jump on the Allied bandwagon.

"They would mock me," he said, "if I changed after it appeared certain that you were going to win."

It was the height of egotism to reduce such an important consideration as participating in a war against fascism to such a personal consideration, as far as Gray was concerned. He suggested it would be possible to exploit "this egotistical vanity" to get de Valera on record as refusing to give help to the Americans. The idea was for Roosevelt to offer the Taoiseach a chance to share in the inevitable Allied victory by inviting him to allow the United States to use Irish bases.

Roosevelt liked the idea. "I think Mr Gray is right in his desire to put de Valera on record," he wrote. "We shall undoubtedly be turned down."

Churchill, too, approved when Gray personally outlined the scheme for him at Roosevelt's home in Hyde Park, New York, in August, but the American service chiefs had reservations.

De Valera's political position had been weakened in June when Fianna Fáil lost its overall majority in the general election. The party easily remained the largest party in the Dáil and actually gained ground on Fine Gael, but it had to depend on the support of some independents to form a government. The Taoiseach was therefore politically vulnerable and the American Joint Chiefs of Staff feared he might agree to an Allied request, and they did not want to take any chances of this because they believed bases in the twenty-six counties would only be a liability. Instead, they argued, de Valera should just be asked to promise to make the bases available if they should be needed in future. The British vetoed this for fear he would comply and thus wipe out the stigma of his refusal to provide bases in 1940.

Having been frustrated in his efforts to get Roosevelt to ask for bases, Gray next suggested that the President demand the expulsion of the German and Japanese representatives from Ireland on the grounds that they posed an espionage threat to the forthcoming Allied invasion of Europe. They did indeed pose some danger, but this was not really a consideration in the whole affair.

The German legation had a radio transmitter and the use of a telegraph line to Berne, Switzerland, from where messages were forwarded to Berlin. Early in the war Hempel made frequent use of the radio transmitter. In August 1941 de Valera asked him not to use it again. Thereafter the transmitter was monitored by Irish authorities with radio detection equipment supplied by the British, and there were no further transmissions until December 1941, when there were three transmissions followed by three more in February.

Disturbed by British Sunday newspaper stories that the German legation had sent weather information to help two German battleships in a recent dash through the English Channel, de Valera instructed Walshe to tell Hempel that "he must cease absolutely using the transmitter." If he used it again, he was warned, he would be required to hand it over.

Although Hempel objected, de Valera was adamant; Ireland was not going to be used as a base to hurt Britain. Eventually Hempel agreed to deposit the transmitter in the vault of a Dublin bank from where it could be retrieved only with the approval of the Irish Department of External Affairs.

The Germans, of course, still had the use of a telegraph line to Berne, but it passed through London, and was therefore controlled by the British, who could cut it off at any time. They left it open as a quid pro quo for the Germans not blocking messages for Britain from Berne. Leaving the line open also allowed them to keep a better watch on Hempel because they had broken his code and were reading his messages. They were also using their own agents to feed him with bogus information. They must have known he warned Berlin in August 1942 of Canadian troops massing in southern England for an imminent assault on the French coast, only days before the disastrous landing at Dieppe. Hence there were valid grounds for uneasiness about the security situation in Ireland, but Gray's suggestion that Roosevelt should formally ask for the expulsion of the German and Japanese representatives was motivated strictly by political considerations.

The OSS was satisfied with the security situation and made it clear to the State Department that the proposed note was purely a political matter. A draft note was prepared for Roosevelt. It would remind de Valera of his promise to maintain a friendly neutrality towards the United States, but contended that Irish policy actually favoured the Axis countries by allowing them to retain diplomatic missions which posed an espionage threat to Allied plans for the invasion of occupied Europe. While the Americans wished that de Valera would sever all diplomatic relations with the Axis nations, the note just asked "as an absolute minimum" that the Irish government take steps to secure the recall of the Axis representatives.

If the Allies were serious about trying to get the Axis representatives expelled, Maffey suggested the Taoiseach be approached informally first. "Ought we not to give Mr de Valera the opportunity of making the break of his own motion?" Maffey asked the Dominions Office. "Up to date we have always felt our way with him. In matters of the release of our airmen and in getting secret service co-operation we have certainly done far better than we should have done by formal requests. We also avoid being told afterwards that things would have been quite different if they had been handled in a different way."

Gray told Maffey, however, that the purpose of the exercise was not to secure the removal of the Axis diplomats, but to have de Valera refuse to expel them. "The American line is to play for the answer 'No'," Maffey reported. "Mr Gray, who has just left my office, tells me that that is what his President wants."

After the British approved the note, Gray handed it in personally on the afternoon of Monday, 21 February 1944. De Valera looked "very sour and grim" as he read the note slowly, pausing frequently to re-read certain passages carefully. He rejected the request without hesitation. "Of course our answer will be no," he said before he had even finished the note. "As long as I am here it will be no." On coming to the phrase calling for the removal of the Axis diplomats "as an absolute minimum," he asked if the document was an ultimatum.

"I have no reason to believe that it is more than a request to a friendly state," Gray replied. "As far as I can see there is no 'or else' implication in this communication."

"As long as I am here Éire will not grant this request," the Taoiseach emphasised on finishing the note. "We have done everything to prevent Axis espionage, going beyond what we might reasonably be expected to do and I am satisfied that there are no leaks from this country; for a year and a half you have been advertising the invasion of Europe and what has got out about it has not been from Éire; the German Minister, I am satisfied, has behaved very correctly and decently and as a neutral we will not send him away."

When Maffey delivered a British note welcoming the American initiative next day, de Valera turned pale and became quite angry. "This is an ultimatum," he said. "This is an outrage!" He saw it as "an attempt to push him into the war and deprive Éire of the symbols of neutrality and independence," according to Maffey. "It was obvious that he attached tremendous importance to this symbolic factor."

The Americans gave an assurance that retaliatory measures were not contemplated. "The note was intended solely to warn you that if you refused request, the responsibility would be on you in case any leak should be traced to Ireland," Brennan cabled.

Nevertheless de Valera, who had already put the Army on alert, went ahead and talked publicly about it being "a time of extreme danger." In the process he generated a crisis which he exploited to his own political advantage.

Since the Canadians were interested in demonstrating dominion independence, de Valera turned to them for help. Contending that there was no evidence to justify ordering the removal of the Axis representatives, he asked the Canadian government to use its influence to have the notes withdrawn. Although he would not demand expulsion, he said he "would take any [other] measures" the Allies might suggest "to eliminate any possible espionage."

Prime Minister Mackenzie King initially sympathised with de Valera's request but then changed his mind under pressure from Churchill. Canada was fighting alongside both Britain and the United States and could hardly strain the alliance by supporting de Valera against the wishes of her own allies.

After Ottawa declined to intervene, de Valera's formal reply rejecting Roosevelt's request was delivered to the State Department on 7 March 1944. "The removal of representatives of a foreign state on the demand of the Government to which they are accredited is universally recognised as the first step towards war," he explained. "The Irish Government could not entertain the American proposal without a complete betrayal of their democratic trust. Irish neutrality represents the united will of the people and parliament. It is the logical consequence of Irish history and of the forced partition of national territory."

The press soon learned of the story, and the State Department decided to publish the notes on 10 March 1944. As there was little important news next day, the Irish refusal received banner headlines on the front pages of newspapers across the United States. For the next fortnight the American press depicted Ireland as being infested with Axis spies, and de Valera was portrayed as a Nazi sympathiser.

"The German and Jap embassies in Éire are nothing less than spy bases from which helpful information can be furnished to Hitler and Tojo," thundered the *Fort Worth Star-Telegram*. While the *Atlanta Constitution* accused the Irish of being "notoriously loose" in dealing with the Axis diplomats, the *New York Times* warned that they might possibly pass on information "to endanger the lives of many thousands of Allied soldiers." James Reston, the renowned political correspondent of the *New York Times*, noted that de Valera would never again "have quite the same political support from the United States that he has always counted on in his ancient battles with the British." That, of course, had been Gray's aim from the beginning.

Sumner Welles, who had recently resigned from the State Department under the cloud of a threatening sex-scandal, would have been aware of Gray's aim, and he sought to bolster it in an article which he wrote for the *New York Herald Tribune*. Observing that "de Valera had never been noted for possessing an elastic mind," he complained that the Irish "will not even lift a finger to help" the Allies. "Those who will not lend a hand in the supreme effort to make it possible for a real peace once more to exist," Welles added, "have no right to be heard by the victors when the war is won."

The whole thing was being exaggerated, Maffey warned London. "The German Legation, as I have often said, is the Symbol, and if I could say to Mr de Valera: 'Keep your Symbol but put it in the zoo,' he would say: 'Now you are talking'. We could be sure, in fact, that Germany would not be much more effectively represented in Dublin by Hempel than Greenland is by the Polar Bear."

"When it comes to practical measures for caging the Axis," he continued, "they will co-operate to any length." De Valera had already demonstrated his good faith towards the Allies by authorising the extraordinary secret assistance to the OSS. It was therefore ironic that he should have been pilloried in the American press for supposedly being indifferent and even hostile to Allied Interests. "He had always been anxious to help us to the utmost, though his course was not easy," Maffey noted.

The Irish government could have countered the unfavourable propaganda by disclosing some of its secret co-operation with the Allies. The Irish minister in the United States was under strong pressure and he was anxious to tell what he knew about the security co-operation, but Walshe instructed otherwise. De Valera "fully appreciates your great difficulties and has highest appreciation of way you handled situation," the Department of External Affairs cabled Brennan. "He knows you understand that we may have to suffer much abuse abroad for sake of home front which is the paramount consideration." The political damage to his standing abroad was being more than compensated for by what was happening at home.

De Valera's popularity with the Irish electorate was greatly enhanced by the way he stood up to the Americans. After losing a minor vote on a transportation bill in the Dáil on 12 May he called a snap general election. Fianna Fáil, which had lost its overall majority less than a year earlier, now romped home, gaining seventeen seats to give the party a comfortable majority in the Dáil.

Although his authorised biographers later contended that the American Note "benefited nobody except de Valera," this was an oversimplification, because Gray had achieved his aim of discrediting the Taoiseach in American eyes, which was the main purpose of the whole exercise. Henceforth de Valera would never again enjoy the international reputation for statesmanship which he had earned at the League of Nations during the 1930s. His standing as the personification of Ireland abroad would actually be enhanced, but not always in the way in which he would have wished. For those outsiders, deluded by the hostile propaganda, the Ireland which he personified was a small-minded, backward, selfish place from which people emigrated in droves.

CHAPTER 24

"I Do What I Think is Right"

The controversy surrounding the American note had clearly done enormous damage to de Valera's international reputation, as Gray had intended, but the Taoiseach was still able to secure international publicity. At the height of the public controversy over the American Note he had publicly appealed to the belligerents not to fight over Rome, "this great centre of the Christain Faith and civilisation."

If the Germans defended the city and the Allies attacked it, priceless and irreplacable artifacts would inevitably be lost, so de Valera expressed "the deep distress" of the Irish people, which he said was "shared by the three hundred million Catholics throughout the world." He was undoubtedly reflecting the wishes of the great majority of the Irish people, and this could only have enhanced his party's prospects in the May general election. Although his appeal to spare Rome probably had no impact on the belligerents, he inevitably got credit at home when the Germans suddenly withdrew from the city and allowed the Allies to liberate it without a fight on 4 June 1944.

The successful Allied landing in Normandy followed two days later and whatever German threat there had been to Ireland essentially vanished. But de Valera soon found Maffey taking a more hardline approach on the question of eight remaining British internees. In October 1943 when the bulk of the Allied internees were secretly let go, it had been possible to use the political instability at home as a justification for retaining eleven of the men to preserve the semblance of neutrality. Three of them were released in the following months on compassionate grounds, but eight still remained in June 1944. De Valera had been ready to release the Allied internees on a number of occasions, but he was dissuaded by opposition within his own cabinet. Following the Fianna Fáil victory in the general election of May 1944 and the success of the Normandy landing, the British were no longer interested in any excuses. Maffey was returning to London for consultations and he warned de Valera on 10 June that "quite unforeseeable complications would accrue" if the remaining Allied internees were not released. Now that Fianna Fáil had a safe majority in the Dáil, London would attach "a special significance" to the first actions of the new government.

"Mr de Valera paced about the room uneasily and said that as today was a Saturday he would not be able to get in touch with his cabinet before my departure," Maffey reported. "I said that we required to have his answer in London at the latest before early on Tuesday morning. I should expect a telephone message in London from Mr Walshe one way or the other on Monday evening."

"He was obviously shaken," Maffey continued. "It is impossible to forecast what his decision will be. He has the martyr complex and would hunger-strike for a principle. But there are one or two hard-headed men in the government and we can only wait and see. At any rate the long chapter of arguments and dialectics on this subject is now closed. It may be necessary to give a turn of the screw." He left the Taoiseach in no doubt that supplies were not "a kind of manna dropping as the gentle dew from Heaven," and if the Dublin government persisted in holding the eight internees, then Britain would cut back on her supplies to Ireland. "Fortune has spoiled Mr de Valera by paying him unfailing dividends for his untiring obstinacy," Maffey noted.

There were no political dividends for standing against the British this time, however. De Valera had his safe majority and the whole thing was not the kind of issue that was worth raising to a matter of principle. In the circumstances the government decided to release the eight men.

While Maffey was content to extract concessions from de Valera quietly, Gray was practically obsessed with the fear that the Taoiseach planned to cause an Anglo-Irish rift after the war. During the summer of 1944, for instance, Gray was alarmed when a number of Irish doctors proposed to send medical supplies to liberated areas of France. He thought de Valera would use the gesture to ingratiate himself with General Charles de Gaulle, the Free French leader. "Now he wants to get in solid with de Gaulle because he knows de Gaulle is out to make trouble for the British and Americans," Gray warned Roosevelt.

The American Minister, therefore, came up with a further scheme to discredit de Valera, this time by getting him to refuse to give a blanket assurance on the question of granting political asylum. On 22 September 1944, Gray formally asked the Taoiseach for an assurance that Ireland would not grant political asylum to any German war criminals. The request for a blanket assurance was tantamount to asking Ireland to surrender her right to grant asylum. It was clearly designed to provoke de Valera's rejection by challenging the country's rights as an independent nation.

"He was very sour about it," Gray reported. "It put him on the same spot as our note about Axis missions." As with the earlier note, Gray was not really looking for co-operation at all; he was again hoping that the Taoiseach would reject the request. "If he should say 'no' as he would like, that would be best," Gray wrote.

De Valera duly obliged by refusing to give a blanket commitment. "The Irish Government," he explained, "can give no assurance which would preclude them from exercising that right should justice, charity or honour or the interest of the nation so require." He added, nevertheless, that his government had no intention of altering the existing practice of denying "admission to all aliens whose presence would be at variance with the policy of neutrality, or detrimental to the Irish people, or inconsistent with the desire of the Irish people to avoid injury to the interests of friendly states." In short, war criminals were unlikely to be granted political asylum, but he was not prepared to sacrifice the country's freedom to do so by making a prior commitment. The State Department published the reply, and thereby opened de Valera to further ridicule in the American press.

In time it would become apparent that even if Gray had exaggerated the danger, he was justified in his suspicions about the likelihood of de Valera seeking to exploit the partition issue after the war. But Maffey tended to see the Taoiseach more in terms of a prisoner of circumstances on the issue. "De Valera has good cause for uneasiness," he reported, acknowledging that there was something rotten about partition.

"The fabric established by the Act of Partition is not a durable fabric," he warned. "It is certainly not a case of 'leaving well alone.' The active Catholic minority in the North are well aware that if they stage a blood sacrifice Mr de Valera and his patriots are bound in honour to stand by Irishmen who are only carrying on the fight of Easter 1916."

When de Valera argued that there were no grounds for compelling the Nationalist majority in Counties Fermanagh and Tyrone to remain within Northern Ireland, Maffey quietly agreed. Indeed, he actually suggested to the Dominions Office that the two counties should be given to the twenty-six counties and the remaining four counties in which there were Unionist majorities should be attached to Scotland. De Valera, of course, wanted all six. "If the difficulties of amalgamating the North with the South were insuperable then," he said, "there should be a transfer of population out of the North so that nothing insuperable remained." In other words, he explained, "such people should be physically transferred to the country to which they wished to adhere."

As the war in Europe entered its final weeks, Gray was still working on schemes to discredit de Valera. This time he wanted to ask for the Taoiseach's permission for the United States to seize the German Legation in Dublin before Hempel would have time to destroy documents. The British were consulted and Churchill warmly approved of the idea. He doubted that there was "anything of any value" in the German archives, but then he realised that the Irish were unlikely to accede to the request anyway. Indeed, if the Allies seriously wanted the German documents, they would have looked to someone other than Gray to approach the Taoiseach.

Before Gray could act, however, Roosevelt died suddenly on 12 April 1945. De Valera had lost his most powerful critic, but there was no rejoicing. "Personally," he told the Dáil, "I regard his death as a loss to the world, for I believe his whole career has shown that he could ultimately be depended upon, when this war has ended, to throw his great influence behind and devote his great energy to the establishment of a world organisation which would be just and which, being just, could hope to save humanity from recurring calamities like the present war."

"This is indeed a strange country," Gray wrote to the late President's widow next day. "All this forenoon members of the government, their wives and leaders of the opposition have been coming in a stream to pay their respects. Mr de Valera made a very moving tribute to the President in the Dáil this morning and moved adjournment till tomorrow. I thought I knew this country and its people but this was something new. There was a great deal of genuine feeling."

Yet this did not soften Gray's determination to embarrass de Valera at every opportunity. On 30 April 1945 he presented the Taoiseach with the formal request for permission to seize the German Legation.

Reading from a memorandum, Gray observed that Allied forces were almost in total control of Germany and that Ireland had, in effect, recognised the collapse of the Third Reich by withdrawing the Irish Chargé d'Affaires to safety in Switzerland. Once Germany had been defeated, title to all German property would be vested in the Allies, so he asked that the Americans be allowed to take control of the Legation early in the hope of getting their hands on German codes before the Legation staff could destroy them. He contended that the codes could then be used to save the lives and property of Irish nationals as well as others in the event that some

U-boats tried to carry on the struggle, or if there were armed pockets of German resistance.

"As I proceeded," Gray reported, "Mr de Valera grew red and looked very sour. He was evidently annoyed, but his manners were correct. When I finished, he slapped the copy of the memorandum, which I had presented him, on his desk."

"This is a matter for my legal advisers," de Valera said. "It is not a matter that I can discuss with you now."

Time was of the essence, Gray argued, but the Taoiseach refused to discuss it further. Next day Walshe informed the American Minister that Hempel would be instructed to hand over his keys, once Germany's surrender had been announced, and the Americans could then, and only then, take charge of the Legation.

It was obvious they were not going to have to wait very long, because the news broke that day of Hitler's death. De Valera responded by going to the German Legation to express condolence to the German Minister. Hempel realised there could be trouble over the visit, but the Taoiseach seemed unconcerned.

"I do what I think is right," he said.

Although de Valera made no favourable comments about Hitler and did not ask the Dáil to adjourn as a mark of respect, as he had done following the death of Roosevelt, his gesture of condolence set off a fire-storm of criticism in the Allied press. The widespread international criticism was not reflected in the heavily censored Irish newspapers, but there was a great deal of uneasiness about the affair in Ireland. "Nothing which Mr de Valera has done during the years which I have been in Dublin has evoked such widespread criticism and much of it comes from persons who are normally supporters of his own party," the Canadian High Commissioner reported.

De Valera made no attempt to account publicly for his actions, and he instructed the Department of External Affairs not to defend his gesture. "An explanation would be interpreted as an excuse, and an excuse as a consciousness of having acted wrongly," he wrote to Robert Brennan. "I acted correctly, and, I feel certain, wisely." If he was so sure of himself, however, why was he explaining his actions to Brennan?

The Buchenwald extermination camp had already been liberated, so he was in no doubt whatever about the nature of the Nazi regime. Only a few days earlier, for instance, Walshe told Maffey that Hempel "was horrified" by the Buchenwald revelations. In the light of all this de Valera's action in expressing official regret at the death of Hitler seemed inexplicable. He could have delayed on the pretext of waiting for official confirmation of Hitler's death.

"It was even far from certain at the time that Hitler was dead," Maffey contended, adding that "it was more than possible that Dr Hempel was delighted to think that Hitler was dead." It was not as if he had to make the gesture in order to maintain Ireland's neutrality. It had been largely notional throughout most of the war because de Valera had willingly co-operated on some matters and somewhat reluctantly abandoned even the semblance of neutrality on the issue of the British Internees.

Why did the Taoiseach go to such lengths to express sympathy for the death of a man he really despised? "Common gentlemanly feelings of sympathy with Dr Hempel in the hour of the country's collapse called for a gesture," de Valera explained privately. "I was damned if I was going to treat him any different from other representatives on whom I had called in similar circumstances, especially as Hitler was dead and there was no possibility of my reinforcing an already lost cause."

John Gunther, the famous American author and journalist, thought de Valera was probably just "tweaking" the tail of the British Lion, but a more correct analogy would probably have been that he was ruffling the feathers of the American Eagle. Maffey believed that the gesture had been in reaction to Gray's efforts to gain "possession of the German archives before VE day." It was de Valera's way of showing that he "was no 'bandwagoner'."

De Valera's annoyance at Gray had probably played an important part in the whole affair. Having recently paid what even Gray described as "a moving tribute" to Roosevelt, it would—in de Valera's view—have been an "unpardonable discourtesy to the German nation and to Dr Hempel himself," if official Irish condolences had not been proffered. And the Taoiseach was not about to insult Hempel, for whom he had a much higher regard than he had for Gray. "During the whole of the war," de Valera wrote, "Dr Hempel's conduct was irreproachable. He was always friendly and invariably correct—in marked contrast with Gray. I certainly was not going to add to his humiliation in the hour of defeat."

The public reaction in Ireland to de Valera's condolence gesture was slow to develop because, after years of strict press censorship, the Irish people knew very little about the holocaust in Europe. But censorship was lifted the following week and people were suddenly confronted with the full horrors of the Nazi reign of terror.

"In the public mind," Maffey wrote, "Mr de Valera's condolences gradually took on a smear of turpitude, and for the first time, and at a critical time, a sense of disgust slowly manifested itself and a growing feeling that Mr de Valera had blundered into a clash with the ideals of decency and right and was leading away from realities."

Although the Canadian High Commissioner in London thought it was in reaction to the condolence gesture that Churchill delivered a stinging attack during a broadcast victory address on 13 May 1945, it was more likely that the Prime Minister was taking a leaf out of Gray's book in a calculated attempt to highlight Northern Ireland's loyalty in contrast with de Valera's public attitude towards the Allies. By speaking out strongly in such an historic speech the Prime Minister would help to further weaken de Valera's ability to cause trouble over partition at the expected post-war peace conference.

Churchill pulled out all the stops in his speech as he referred contemptuously to de Valera, emphasising the different syllables of his name in such a way as to conjure up a subliminal suggestion of him as the personification of the devil and evil in Éire by pronouncing the name as if it were "D'evil Éire." The Prime Minister said:

OWING TO THE ACTION OF MR DE VALERA, SO MUCH AT VARIANCE WITH THE TEMPER AND INSTINCT OF THOUSANDS OF SOUTHERN IRISHMEN WHO HASTENED TO THE BATTLE-FRONT TO PROVE THEIR ANCIENT VALOUR, THE APPROACHES WHICH THE SOUTHERN IRISH PORTS AND AIRFIELD COULD SO EASILY HAVE GUARDED WERE CLOSED BY THE HOSTILE AIRCRAFT AND U-BOATS. THIS WAS INDEED A DEADLY MOMENT IN OUR LIFE, AND IF IT HAD NOT BEEN FOR THE LOYALTY AND FRIENDSHIP OF NORTHERN IRELAND WE SHOULD HAVE BEEN FORCED TO COME TO CLOSE QUARTERS WITH MR DE VALERA OR PERISH FOR EVER FROM THE EARTH. HOWEVER, WITH A RESTRAINT AND POISE TO WHICH, I SAY, HISTORY WILL FIND FEW PARALLELS, HIS MAJESTY'S GOVERNMENT NEVER LAID A VIOLENT HAND UPON THEM, THOUGH AT TIMES IT WOULD HAVE BEEN QUITE EASY AND QUITE NATURAL, AND WE LEFT THE DE VALERA GOVERNMENT TO FROLIC WITH THE GERMANS AND LATER WITH THE JAPANESE REPRESENTATIVES TO THEIR HEART'S CONTENT.

There was an air of anticipation in Ireland as people waited for de Valera to respond. It was assumed he would answer with a tirade and expectations were heightened as he delayed for three days. Then on 16 May he went on Radio Éireann. The occasions on which an individual is able to captivate the imagination of a whole nation are few and as a result memorable. This was one of those rare occasions that listeners would never forget. They would remember always where they were when they heard de Valera deliver what was probably the best and most effective speech of his long career.

He began by thanking God for sparing Ireland from the conflagration which had left much of Europe in ruins, and he expressed gratitude to the various people who had contributed to the successful efforts to keep the country out of the war. And then he turned to Churchill's speech. He knew what many people were expecting him to say and what he would have said twenty-five years earlier, but the occasion now demanded something else. With an exquisite touch of condescension, he explained that Churchill could be excused for being carried away in the excitement of victory, but there would be no such excuse for himself. Speaking calmly de Valera said:

> MR CHURCHILL MAKES IT CLEAR THAT, IN CERTAIN CIRCUMSTANCES, HE WOULD HAVE VIOLATED OUR NEUTRALITY AND THAT HE WOULD JUSTIFY HIS ACTION BY BRITAIN'S NECESSITY. IT SEEMS STRANGE TO ME THAT MR CHURCHILL DOES NOT SEE THAT THIS, IF ACCEPTED, WOULD MEAN THAT BRITAIN'S NECESSITY WOULD BECOME A MORAL CODE AND THAT, WHEN THIS NECESSITY WAS SUFFICIENTLY GREAT, OTHER PEOPLE'S RIGHTS WERE NOT TO COUNT. IT IS QUITE TRUE THAT OTHER GREAT POWERS BELIEVE IN THIS SAME CODE—IN THEIR OWN REGARD—AND HAVE BEHAVED IN ACCORDANCE WITH IT. THAT IS PRECISELY WHY WE HAVE THE DISASTROUS SUCCESSIONS OF WARS—WORLD WAR NO. I AND WORLD WAR NO. 2—AND SHALL IT BE WORLD WAR NO.3?

He then turned to praise Churchill for resisting the temptation to violate Irish neutrality. "It is, indeed, hard for the strong to be just to the weak," he continued. "But acting justly always has its rewards. By resisting his temptation in this instance, Mr Churchill, instead of adding another horrid chapter to the already bloodstained record of the relations between England and this country, has advanced the cause of international morality an important step."

The public reaction to the address in Ireland was overwhelming. Even before the Taoiseach had time to leave the Radio Éireann studio in the General Post Office, people had begun gathering to cheer him. With his use of modern technology, he had struck a chord in the whole nation, as no Irish leader had ever done before.

"With little exception," Kearney reported, "Mr de Valera's broadcast is regarded in Ireland as a masterpiece, and it is looked upon as probably his best effort. It has served to almost still the criticism which his visit to the German Minister provoked, and, in so far as I can judge, on balance, Mr de Valera now stands in higher favour in Ireland than he did before his visit to the German Minister."

"We had him on a plate," Maffey said the morning after the Taoiseach's speech. "We had him where we wanted him. But look at the papers this morning!"

Churchill's remarks had been a great mistake, according to the British Representative, because they gave de Valera the opportunity to escape from the consequences of his actions following Hitler's death.

"Mr de Valera assumed the pose of the elder statesman and skilfully worked on all the old passions in order to dramatise the stand taken by Éire in this war," Maffey explained. "So long as he can work his mystique over Irishmen in all parts of the world Mr de Valera does not worry about the rest of humanity. Orations and resolutions are the order of the day. His speech is acclaimed in all quarters, even in T.C.D. and by the *Irish Times*, and it is to be printed in the history books."

The British Representative was particularly critical of the suggestion that it would have been natural for Britain to seize Irish bases. "I felt that something was lost in the moral plane by suggesting that we might have seized them," Maffey explained. "However, where we lost most tricks in the rubber here was in the fact that after five and a half years of war the British Prime Minister, in a historic speech, gave prominence to Mr de Valera, attacked him personally and thereby introduced him to the spotlight and a world radio contest."

While the Dominions Office agreed with Maffey's assessment of the Irish reaction to de Valera's speech, it observed that the international perspective of this so-called "radio contest" was quite different. The latest events had had a comparatively similar impact as the American note of February 1944 in that de Valera's image at home was enhanced while his international standing was seriously damaged. The Dominions Secretary, who had just returned from the San Francisco Conference establishing the United Nations Organisation, noted that news of de Valera's condolence gesture, coming so soon after the gruesome revelations about the Buchenwald concentration camp, had "inflicted a profound and enduring shock on the American people," with the result that Churchill's "severe remarks were therefore accepted and even applauded as a salutary rap over the knuckles." Likewise in much of Europe, where Churchill was idolised as a liberator and hence, his speech was the one which made the impact. "On balance", the

Dominions Office concluded, "we have certainly gained in the eyes of the world, whatever may be the effect in Éire itself." "For the Irishman in the homeland and overseas," Maffey wrote, "it is once again a case of 'Up Dev!' "

There were still some loose ends to be cleared up at home, such as the thorny questions of what to do with the 266 interned German air and seamen, the handful of captured agents, and the staff of the closed German Legation. During the month of June the Americans asked for all German diplomatic personnel and captured agents to be interned or kept under house arrest, and the British asked for the internee airmen and sailors, as well as the spies, to be handed over to them. De Valera refused to surrender the spies, but was willing to hand over the internees on condition that Britain guaranteed that none of the men would be executed nor forced to return to the Soviet zone of Germany.

Gray, who was bitterly opposed to de Valera's conditions, accused Dublin of trying to split the victorious Allied alliance by getting the British to discriminate against the Soviet Union. He tried to persuade the State Department to put pressure on the British to reject the conditions but he no longer enjoyed the same influence in Washington now that Roosevelt was dead. The British agreed to the condition and arrangements were made for the British to pick up the internees at Rosslare on 11 July, but the week beforehand Maffey informed the Department of External Affairs that Britain could no longer guarantee that none of the men would be returned to the Soviet Zone. With this, de Valera cancelled the arrangements.

After further negotiations the British relented and again agreed to the conditions, so in the early hours of 13 August 1945, the day before the Japanese formally surrendered thereby ending the Second World War, the German internees boarded a British battleship at the North Wall, Dublin. Twelve men were missing. Eight of them had absconded and gone into hiding with Irish friends. All of them were recaptured in the following months and handed over, but the other four were personally granted political asylum by de Valera. Two were ill—one suffering from tuberculosis and the other had cardiac problems—while the remaining two were Austrians, who feared they would unjustly be charged with war crimes in Austria because they had apparently supported the German take-over in 1938. They were allowed to remain, on condition that they kept their presence in Ireland secret from the authorities in Austria.

Following the end of the war the myths about de Valera's policy persisted. In Ireland people continued to believe that the country had been neutral, while there was a widespread misconception abroad that, blinded by anglophobic bitterness, de Valera had been neutral against the Allies. What actually happened was, of course, very different.

During the war de Valera had to conceal the true nature of his policy in order to avoid the danger of Axis retaliation, but he allowed the myths to prevail in the post-war years. He never really tried to explain the gap which existed between the public perception and the reality of his foreign policy. National morale had been sustained by a feeling that neutrality was a significant achievement because it conclusively demonstrated the country's independence. This image could not as readily have been maintained if people had known the extent of his secret co-operation with the Allies, especially with Britain, the ancient enemy. "It was vital for the national psyche from the emotional viewpoint," Professor Joseph J. Lee wrote, "that the extent of Irish co-operation should not receive indecent exposure." It might have been more true to say that avoiding such exposure served de Valera's political purposes best.

None of this should be allowed to detract from his enormous accomplishment. He had steered Ireland through a prolonged, perilous crisis; he had conclusively demonstrated not only Irish independence but also that Britain really had nothing to fear from an independent Ireland, and he could also have honestly said that he gave the Allies just about all the help he could in the struggle against Nazi Germany. To borrow a Churchillian phrase, it was de Valera's "finest hour."

CHAPTER 25

"We Don't Pay Any Attention to Frank's Ideas"

During the war years de Valera presided over a united cabinet in which there were deep ideological divisions. Lemass, on the one side, was arguing for distinct social and economic changes in order to forestall Irish disillusionment which he believed would inevitably follow the implementation in Britain of the welfare policies outlined in the Beveridge Report of 1942. Others, like Seán MacEntee, resisted moves towards a welfare state, apparently believing that it was little more than a kind of creeping communism. He waged a protracted battle within the cabinet against the introduction of children's allowances, but de Valera eventually sided with Lemass.

The latter was a dynamic minister with a pragmatic outlook and little time for sentimentality. In the 1920s and 1930s he had been the most outspoken advocate of industrial protectionism, but he was not afraid to reverse his views when he saw tariffs being used merely to preserve and protect inefficient industries, nor was he afraid to call for the abandonment of de Valera's pet policy of settling more people on the land. Irked by the inefficiency of Irish agriculture in 1943, Lemass advocated the displacement of inefficient farmers. He felt the right of ownership should not include the right to allow land to be underproductive. "Only a limited number of families" could be settled on the land, he warned the cabinet in January 1945. Therefore the government's policy "must be directed to ensuring that ownership will be confined to persons willing and capable of working them adequately."

Having grown up on a small farm, de Valera realised that what Lemass was proposing was political dynamite, especially for Fianna Fáil, which was heavily dependent on the support of small farmers. Consequently he was unwilling to have anything to do with a policy of displacement, but he also resisted efforts from people within the party at the other extreme. Joseph Connolly, who had been a member of the first Fianna Fáil government, was annoyed at de Valera's unwillingness to contemplate the land reform promised in 1932.

"I formed the opinion that he no longer welcomed discussion much less criticism," Connolly wrote. "What he wanted beside him was a group of 'yes-men' who agreed with everything and anything the party (with himself as leader) approved." The party had grown stale and had little of the idealism it had brought into office in 1932.

De Valera's vision of the happy maidens dancing at the crossroads was an image from a romanticised past, not a projection of the future. After more than a dozen years in power, many of the same people were still to be found in the government. They were just the most available, and in some cases the least exceptional of a class of institutional survivors.

Following the end of the war, for example, there was no longer a need for both a Minister for Defence and a Minister for the Coordination of Defensive Measures, so Aiken's position was eliminated and he was appointed Minister for Finance following the election of Seán T. O'Kelly as President in June 1945. Aiken had little to recommend him for the position. Although his integrity was unquestionable, he was not renowned for his intelligence. In fact, some people referred to him as "the iron man with the wooden head."

Both Maffey and Gray had been particularly scathing in their assessments of him. The former described him as "rather stupid," while Gray wrote to Roosevelt that Aiken had "a mind half-way between that of a child and a baboon."

In February 1941 after Aiken had expounded on his financial views, which were based on the Social Credit experiment of the provincial government of Alberta, Canada, Gray questioned the Taoiseach, who just laughed. "We don't pay any attention to Frank's ideas about finance," he said. Yet this did not stop him slotting Aiken in as Minister for Finance when the position became vacant in June 1945.

O'Kelly's elevation to the Presidency also left a vacancy in the office of Tánaiste, and the Taoiseach appointed Lemass. It has been suggested that this appointment was de Valera's way of designating Lemass as his successor, but it was more likely just a sop to prevent his most dynamic minister becoming disillusioned with the government's conservatism. Usually the position of deputy leader in a parliamentary democracy is accorded to someone providing a political or ideological balance to the leader's views within the government or party, and this was the most likely explanation for the latest appointment, because even though de Valera was already in his sixties, he had no intention of retiring.

Unlike Lemass, a supreme pragmatist, de Valera was a prisoner of his own past, haunted by the need to justify his actions prior to the Civil War. He liked to think that he had acted in the interest of Irish freedom. Having won a name for himself as the champion of Irish independence, he was not about to allow anyone to knock him off that political pedestal.

The IRA's campaign launched in 1939 to drive the British out of Northern Ireland posed a distinct threat to de Valera's position. But he had little difficulty in justifying his resolute suppression of the IRA on the grounds of national security when it colluded with the Nazis during the Second World War. The external threat to the country posed by the collusion with the Nazis was obvious, but when the war was over and the foreign threat had been eliminated, he and his Minister for Justice, Gerald Boland, persisted in their refusal to accord political treatment to IRA prisoners.

Some IRA leaders, like Seán McCaughey, had been protesting by refusing to wear prison garb. Although they waged a determined prison campaign, news of their efforts was suppressed during the war years by the censor. In April 1946, after more than four years in solitary confinement, McCaughey went on hunger-strike to protest his imprisonment. It was a foolhardy gesture because de Valera had already demonstrated his determination to withstand such tactics six years earlier, and would do so again on this occasion. McCaughey, who may have been mentally disturbed as a result of his solitary confinement, was allowed to die, despite a strong public campaign, which soon led to the formation of a new political party, Clann na Poblachta, under the leadership of Seán MacBride, a former IRA chief of staff.

The new party began making serious inroads into Fianna Fáil's political support among Republican and radical elements. A number of the more radical Republicans who had voted for Fianna Fáil in the twenties and early thirties had long since become disenchanted.

In the past de Valera had been able to exploit the political advantages of a high international profile and he kept foreign policy firmly in his own hands. When he had to enlist the help of cabinet colleagues for missions abroad, he was careful to spread the load so thinly that nobody could ever be seen as having remotely near the expertise to challenge his pre-eminence. At different times he selected Connolly, O'Kelly, Lemass, Aiken, Ryan and MacEntee. For some time after the war, Ireland was virtually isolated diplomatically. It was still nominally a member of the British Commonwealth but de Valera had never taken part in any of the Imperial Conferences. There was, therefore, a certain amount of confusion over the country's actual status and its relationship with the Commonwealth, and he was deliberately evasive.

"In all political systems," he said, "there are relationships which it is wiser to leave undefined." By any definition, however, he contended that the state itself was "a republic." And he supported his argument by quoting the definitions of a "republic" from four of the most commonly used dictionaries of the English language.

De Valera wished to get back on the international stage by applying for membership of the United Nations Organisation, but before applying, he first sought the approval of the Dáil. He dismissed suggestions that membership could be used to end partition and thus complete the quest for full national independence. It was the most effective way of defending what had already been achieved, he contended, adding candidly that membership would actually involve a certain loss of independence because it carried with it responsibilities under the Charter of the United Nations which could lead to involvement in military conflicts.

"The difference between a war such as may arise under the obligations of the Charter and other wars is," he said, "that that type of war would be a war of enforcement, enforcement of obligations and also enforcement of rights. If there is ever to be a rule of law, nations must make up their minds that they will take part in such enforcement, because, if there is not enforcement, then, of course, the duties and rights that are guaranteed will be thrown aside." If the League of Nations had decided on military sanctions at the time of the Ethiopian crisis in the mid 1930s, he said he would have felt the country was obliged to take part. Now he wanted all the ramifications clearly understood, if the Dáil decided to apply for membership.

The Dáil agreed but the application was vetoed the following month by the Soviet Union whose Foreign Minister, Andre Gromyko, complained that Ireland had maintained friendly relations with fascist countries during the war yet had continuously refused to open relations with the Soviet Union. "Her behaviour," Gromyko said, "is hardly calculated to help her to admission to the United Nations."

Seán Lester, who had gone to Geneva as Irish Minister and later joined the Secretariat of the League and eventually became its Secretary General during the war, had infuriated Moscow by condemning the Soviet Union's invasion of Finland in 1940. As a result the Soviets blocked his transfer to the Secretariat of the United Nations. He then tried to rejoin the Irish Department of External Affairs, but he was the one Irishman who might have rivalled de Valera's international standing and his request was shamefully ignored.

If de Valera had blocked Lester's request just to ingratiate himself with the Soviets, it had no effect. It was ironic that the Soviet representatives should be so critical of the Irish government, seeing that de Valera had helped the hard-pressed Soviet representatives in the United States back in 1920 by loaning them some twenty thousand dollars for which he received some jewels as collateral. Nevertheless the Soviet Union—which repaid the money and got the jewels back in January 1948—persisted with its veto of Ireland's application to the United Nations. As a result de Valera was denied the international stage which he might have used to divert public attention from his government's growing difficulties at home.

He was hurt politically by a seven-month-long strike of national teachers in 1946. As a former teacher de Valera tended to have very definite views on education, as it was one of the areas in which he was most interested. In fact, in addition to being Taoiseach and Minister for Foreign Affairs, he was also Minister for Education between September 1939 and June 1940. During this time he laid the foundations for the controversial Primary Certificate Examination, despite strong opposition from the Irish National Teachers' Organisation (INTO).

"We will have to take the bull by the horns," he told the Dáil while acting as Minister for Education, "and, even though the teachers do not like it, we will have to insist on such an examination at the end of the primary school course." Many teaching authorities thought his approach retrogressive, but he believed that the educational system should be geared totally towards results. "I do not care what teachers are offended by it," he said. "I am less interested in the teacher's method of teaching than I am in the results he achieves."

His use of the masculine pronoun was not intended to be sexist, seeing that he thought women were just as good teachers. He professed to believe, for instance, in the right of women teachers to equal pay with men. "But," according to John Coolahan, "he was not prepared to support such a policy in practice because of its spill-over effects to other occupations, where the suitability of women was less obvious than teaching." This kind of thinking certainly did not reflect very favourably on his sense of justice. And the national teachers would eventually find themselves at loggerheads with him over the question of pay.

For one thing, de Valera insisted that national teachers should not be paid as much as their secondary colleagues, even though he had publicly acknowledged that their responsibilities were every bit as great, if not greater, both from the national and individual standpoint. "What the national schools are, the nation must be," he told the annual congress of the INTO while Minister for Education. The national teachers had the vital task of educating children while they were most impressionable. "The habits which the child acquires at this most plastic period are of as vital importance as any knowledge he or she will acquire later in the school, for habit is the foundation of character, and the training of character is your greatest task, more fundamental than any training in any particular branch of knowledge," he explained.

Having acknowledged their great responsibilities, however, he was not only unwilling to grant them parity with secondary teachers, but he even refused to meet their more modest pay demands. The Department of Education made an offer, which the INTO rejected as inadequate, and the Taoiseach then adopted the attitude that they could take it or leave it. "I told the Minister that he need not come back for more," de Valera explained to the Dáil. The teachers were told "that they had got their final offer," he added.

When the teachers went on strike, de Valera viewed their demands as a challenge to the authority of his government, and he resisted their demands with the same kind of determination which he had resisted hunger-strikers. He even went to the point of straining his long friendship with the Roman Catholic Archbishop of Dublin, John Charles McQuaid, who tried to intercede on behalf of the teachers. Eventually the archbishop persuaded the INTO to capitulate, but many teachers remained bitter and they would become enthusiastic supporters of Clann na Poblachta.

After years of shortages brought about by the Economic War with Britain and followed by the dislocation of the Second World War, people were impatient. Emigration was running at around 30,000 people a year and even with this exodus, unemployment was over nine per cent. It was going to be an extremely difficult time for any government. The country's wheat crop failed as a result of one of the wettest summers on record in 1946 and this was followed by an extremely severe winter. In January 1947 the government was forced to reintroduce bread rationing, and Lemass explained that the people were facing a situation "more difficult than at any stage of the war." Things were further complicated by a serious energy crisis brought about by a drastic cutback on coal supplies from Britain. As a result rail transportation was disrupted and an already chronic shortage of raw materials was exacerbated, forcing many industries to close and causing widespread redundancies.

Faced with growing disenchantment at home and near ostracism abroad, de Valera moved to improve his relations with the British in December by indicating a willingness to comply with their repeated request for his government to hand over two German spies, Hermann Goertz and Walter Unland, who had been arrested in Ireland during the war. Initially de Valera had refused to hand them over because there was no question of them having committed any war crimes. They had entered the country illegally and engaged in espionage, but that was a crime against Ireland, not the Allies. On hearing that they were to be handed over, Gerald Boland, the Minister for Justice, was so annoyed that he wrote out his resignation, but de Valera persuaded him to withdraw it on turning the whole matter over to him.

Boland was acting on purely compassionate grounds because Goertz was overwrought. The Irish authorities tried to assure him that he had nothing to fear, but he was terrified that he would be persecuted by the communists because he had taken part in the suppression of the Spartacist Revolt in Berlin following the First World War. Eventually Boland gave in to the British and Goertz was taken into custody, whereupon he killed himself. The deportation order against Unland, who was similarly threatening to kill himself, was promptly quashed and the British let the matter drop quietly.

When the United States proposed a conference to discuss a European Recovery Programme, de Valera sent Seán Lemass and Paddy Smith to Paris for the initial talks, before taking over himself at the latter stages. From a financial standpoint Ireland had come out of the war better than most. The country had a healthy balance of payments surplus, being owed over £400 millions by Britain, but the latter was essentially bankrupt, with the result that the Irish government was seriously strapped for hard currency. It applied for a grant under Marshall Aid, but the Americans—still annoyed over what was perceived as de Valera's indifferent neutrality during the war—were only willing to provide a £10 million loan.

The independence dream was turning sour on the Irish. Despite the achievement of political independence, the haemorrhage of emigration was increasing rather than diminishing. It had been customary to blame British rule for all of Ireland's difficulties in the past, and political independence was held out as a kind of panacea. Even though the country officially gained its independence in the early 1920s, de Valera had exploited the old wounds, by contending that the country could not be really free as long as partition existed.

Clann na Poblachta, which essentially adopted the approach initially advocated by Fianna Fáil in the 1920s, began making definite inroads into Fianna Fáil support, and de Valera therefore sought to protect his republican flank, especially on the partition issue. There were two ways of ending partition, he explained, by force or by persuasion. He again ruled out the use of force because, even in the unlikely event of it being successful, it would leave the island "in an unstable position." Hence persuasion was the only course open.

"It would make for a solution of this problem," he told the Dáil on 24 June 1947, "if at the present time the British Government would make a simple declaration to the effect that they were desirous of seeing partition brought to an end, that they would do anything that they could do to help bring it to an end, and that if agreement was reached here in Ireland, there would be no hesitation on their part in giving effect to the agreement." Everyone should realise, he said, that the three different parties involved would have to agree with one another before partition could be ended. In the meantime, he added, public opinion in Britain and the United States could play an important role.

David Gray, who was about to retire as United States Minister, warned de Valera against appealing over the head of the United States government and trying to involve the American people. The cold war was beginning in Europe, and he suggested that the Taoiseach could co-operate in making the British Isles a bridge-head for the defence of western freedom.

"We are free, but only in part," de Valera replied, interrupting with some vehemence. "We can take no part in the kind of thing you suggest while this wrong to our six northern counties continues."

"What do you wish us to do about it?" Gray asked impatiently. "Do you want us to send troops into the six counties to conquer them and hand them over to you?"

"Of course not."

"The only other course is in your hands," Gray said, "that is, to make conditions so desirable in Éire that the North will wish to join YOU."

"But," de Valera persisted, "if we cannot ask you to coerce the Six Counties why should the Protestant majority coerce the nation-alist minorities in two of them?"

"Suppose, for the sake of argument, we were able to arrange the handing over to you of the two counties of which you speak, would you not still have partition as to the remaining four?" Gray asked. "Would not the crime against your sovereignty of which you complain still subsist?"

313

De Valera did not answer. Although he had ruled out the use of force and talked about bringing about Irish unity by persuasion, he did nothing to alleviate even the legitimate fears of the northern majority on such matters as discrimination against Protestant values in the twenty-six counties. Over the years he made the mistake of implying that the only true Irishmen were Roman Catholics.

"Since the coming of St Patrick, fifteen hundred years ago, Ireland has been a Christian and a Catholic nation," he declared in a St Patrick's Day broadcast in 1935. "All the ruthless attempts made down through the centuries to force her from this allegiance have not shaken her faith. She remains a Catholic nation."

Whether through insensitivity, ignorance, or just blind indifference, he never seemed to realise that Northern Protestants had legitimate fears about a united Ireland. The religious persecutions which had blotted Irish history were not all one sided. The Protestants of Northern Ireland were only too well aware of the sectarian massacres perpetrated by Roman Catholics against their Protestant brethren, not only in the northeast, but also in the south, most notably in County Wexford during the 1798 Rebellion. Yet de Valera seemed conveniently oblivious to those.

"The pretext that partition was necessary to save a minority of Irishmen from religious persecution at the hands of the majority was an invention without any basis in the facts of our time or in the history of the past," he said. "No nation respects the rights of conscience more than Ireland."

He had adopted a somewhat bigoted attitude himself in relation to the Mayo library controversy in 1931 when he argued that a Roman Catholic community was entitled to insist on the appointment of Roman Catholics in the broad areas of health and education. While he did not carry those sectarian views to their logical conclusion after he came to power, his government did nevertheless intensify discrimination in the Twenty-six Counties against Protestant values in matters like divorce, contraception, and censorship. Censorship was carried to absurd lengths, especially during the war years when the censor banned the publication of notices regarding services at Kingstown Presbyterian Church because the Church insisted on retaining its name even though Kingstown had been renamed Dun Laoghaire some two decades earlier. As the head of the government, de Valera was responsible, but in fairness to him, he was not personally bigoted. After all it was he who was instrumental in having the founder of the Gaelic League, Douglas Hyde, a Protestant, selected as the first President of Ireland under the constitution of 1937.

For the Northern Unionists, however, the selection of Hyde was hardly reassuring, because in a way it highlighted the fact that there was positive discrimination in both the civil service and the educational sector in favour of those able to use the Gaelic language, for which most Northern Protestants had little time. Yet de Valera made no apologies for his discriminatory approach.

"I do not see why the people in this part of Ireland should sacrifice ideals which they hold dear—completely sacrifice these ideals in order to meet the views of people whose position fundamentally is not as just or as right as our position is," he declared.

It would be wrong to suggest that Northern Protestants were opposed to Irish unity simply because the Dublin government adopted discriminatory practices against their values. Had there been no discrimination, the overwhelming majority would still have opposed the ending of partition, if only on emotional grounds. They were no more willing to enter a united Ireland than the people of the twenty-six counties were prepared to go back into the United Kingdom.

The Unionists were also alienated by de Valera's attitude towards the British Crown, for which they had a strong emotional attachment. Before the war de Valera had deliberately skirted the issue, but he never ruled out even the nominal allegiance which dominions paid to the British King. "If being in the Commonwealth implied in any way allegiance or acceptance of the British King as King here," he declared "we are not in the Commonwealth."

"Twenty-six of our counties are a republic," de Valera told a Dublin gathering in October 1947, and if the Irish nation continued to give Fianna Fáil support, the party would have "a better chance of securing to the whole of Ireland as a republic than any other party." But Clann na Poblachta's impressive growth continued as it won two Dáil by-elections a few days later. Some people equated these successes with the Sinn Féin by-election victories of 1917, and MacBride predicted that the party would win an overall majority in the next general election.

In an obvious move to deny the new party further time to organise properly, de Valera called a surprise general election for 4 February 1948, even though the existing Dáil, with its safe Fianna Fáil majority still had some fifteen months to run.

When Clann na Poblachta candidates concentrated on the partition issue, de Valera sought to outflank them by campaigning on his own need to secure a renewed mandate to take up his anti-partition *efforts* where they had been interrupted by the Second World War. He said he was ready to go to the United States to drum up American support and that he would also appeal to other countries for help. "I promise that the pressure of public opinion of the Irish race, not in Ireland only, but throughout the world, will be concentrated on this question."

Offset against the radicalism of the new party, Fianna Fáil seem distinctly conservative, with little of the reforming zeal it had brought into office sixteen years earlier. Indeed, de Valera seemed satisfied with the social progress already made, but, of course, he had never even aspired to, much less promised the electorate more than frugal comfort. Since there was a certain candour about such an approach, it undoubtedly contributed to that intangible quality of passionate sincerity which so many people perceived in him. He was his party's greatest political asset, as evidenced by its most popular slogan, "Up Dev," which critics contended summed up the whole platform of Fianna Fáil.

The success of de Valera's election tactics in 1948 have long been a matter for conjecture. Clann na Poblachta won only ten seats, which was really a credible performance, but it appeared paltry in comparison with the inflated predictions made by MacBride and his party colleagues. As a result the party's momentum suffered an irreversible setback. The seats won were mainly from Fianna Fáil, which ended up six seats short of an overall majority, though it easily remained the largest party. The rest of the Dáil was so splintered that it took no less than six parties together with some independents to form a coalition government. Richard Mulcahy, the leader of Fine Gael, was unacceptable to Clann na Poblachta, so a compromise Taoiseach was found in John A. Costello, who had been Attorney-General in W.T. Cosgrave's last government. It was a coalition of misfits, who had little in common other than a burning desire to oust de Valera and his Fianna Fáil government.

CHAPTER 26

"We Have Heard Enoough"

In spite of the setback at the polls, de Valera went ahead with his planned visit to the United States. His trip, which lasted for four weeks, took in various American cities, including Washington, where he had what he characterised as "just a friendly chat" with President Harry Truman. Other stops included New York, San Francisco, Los Angeles, Chicago, Detroit, Philadelphia and Boston. He told gatherings in these cities that he had come to thank Americans for their past assistance in the struggle for Irish independence and to request further help. At every stop he harped on the partition grievance.

He was despondent about the international situation. "It seems to me," he said in New York, "that the action of Russia today is bringing war closer and making it inevitable." Yet he repeatedly indicated that the British were behaving worse in Northern Ireland than the communists had been in Eastern Europe. The communists were just acting blatantly, he contended, whereas the British were pretending to act democratically while behaving most undemocratically by maintaining the partition of Ireland against the wishes of the majority of the Irish people.

"If I were Stalin and wanted what Stalin wanted," he told the National Press Club in Washington, D.C., "I would imitate Britain and get away with it as Britain is getting away with it. It would be easy to pick an area somewhere in Europe with a Communist majority and, on pretence of safeguarding a minority, to cut off that area, and make it appear as if it was being governed by a majority."

"If what is happening in partitioned Ireland today were being done in eastern Europe by Russia," he told a Boston audience, "the people on whom it was being done would be entitled to ask assistance, and many who talk of democracy now would cry out against the injustice." He was not only anxious for the Americans to put pressure on Britain, but was also apparently hoping the United States would provide the necessary financial help. As things stood, he was still willing to back a settlement in which the six counties would retain Stormont, provided the powers vested in Westminster were transferred to Dublin. The Unionists of Northern Ireland would then be given the choice of staying or moving to Britian.

"We would say to them," he explained, "that we would prefer

that you stay, but if you prefer an outside power we cannot have our unity threatened by your loyalty. If you don't want to be Irish, we are prepared to let you go and compensate you. It would pay us because ill-will between the two countries would be a danger to both. We do not want to be kept in disunion because of a small minority."

Shortly after returning from America, de Valera set out on a tour of Australia and New Zealand, with a stopover in India, where he talked with Prime Minister Pandit Nehru and his daughter, Indira Gandhi. Upon his return home, de Valera told a Fianna Fáil Árd Fheis that plans had been made for a world-wide campaign to end partition. Things were ready in the United States, Australia and New Zealand, and he expressed high hopes that arrangements could be made in Canada, South Africa and India. "We have a splendid case," he said. "Partition is on a rotten foundation and it will totter and end. All we want to do is make up our minds to make the proper assault."

He seemed to be saying that the countries he had visited would support a campaign against partition, with the obvious implication being that he had arranged things. Yet in his travels he had generated little interest outside Irish ethnic circles. After the trauma of the war years those countries had enough problems of their own and their people were not even slightly interested in Ireland's. And if anything, an appeal from de Valera was only likely to be resented outside ethnic circles, because it was widely believed that he had been unsympathetic towards the Allies during the war. In his address to the Árd Fheis he adopted that constructive ambiguity which had served him so well during the war. He did not actually say that he had arranged the support of the United States, Australia and New Zealand, he just gave that impression. As an astute politician, he was never likely to have believed that himself. What he basically did in those countries was appeal directly to Irish emigrants, because they were likely to be most sympathetic. "If you want to bring the facts to the notice of the public," he explained afterwards, "you will go in the first instance to the people who are likely to be receptive and who do not start out with a feeling of hostility to you and who are not suspicious of you." When questioned after he had returned to power in 1951, he was unwilling to say whether he believed the emigrants could be effective. "I know they will do the best they can," he said, "but whether that will be effective or not I cannot say."

Of course he did not admit that until after he had regained power. While in Opposition, in the meantime, he hammered away at the partition issue with much the same emphasis as he had placed on it back in the 1920s. In July 1948, for instance, he criticised Seán MacBride, the Minister for External Affairs, for not challenging the British Nationality Act on the grounds that the legislation maintained "that our citizens in the Six Counties, who are natural born Irish citizens, owning allegiance to this nation and to no other, are now to be bound and dealt with exactly as if they were citizens of Britain."

"We cannot have in this country people whose first allegiance is not to our nation and we should make it clear that if there are such people, that we do not regard them as our citizens, and we should know where we stand in respect to them," he declared in the Dáil. Needless to say, the Nationality Act did not change anything; de Valera was just exploiting the issue to score political points.

When Costello made the surprise announcement some weeks later that his government intended to take Ireland out of the Commonwealth by repealing the External Relations Act, Maffey concluded the coalition was trying to "steal the 'Long Man's' clothes" by outmanoeuvring him on the Republican flank. Although the declaration of the Republic of Ireland was psychologically momentous, it was of little significance from the practical standpoint, because de Valera had long ago fulfilled his promise of dismantling the 1921 Treaty to the extent that the declaration of a Republic was a mere formality. Although the Opposition had sought to frustrate his efforts to use the stepping-stone approach first advocated by Michael Collins, he had no intention of making the same mistake. "You will get no opposition from us," he told the Dáil.

As the necessary legislation was being prepared, the government proposed an all-party conference at the Mansion House on 27 January 1949 to organise a campaign to end partition. On behalf of Fianna Fáil, de Valera supported the call and took an active part. The fanfare with which the anti-partition drive was launched was probably the strongest show of solidarity between the different nationalist parties since the Mansion House Conference of 1918 had met to oppose the extension of conscription to Ireland during the First World War.

De Valera contended the coalition government was acting "strictly in accordance with the plan and the programme announced by Fianna Fáil at its Inaugural meeting nearly twenty-three years ago. We then set before us the securing of full independence for this part of Ireland as the first step on which we would concentrate, so that this being achieved, the problem of partition might be isolated for the combined and converging attack of all who loved Ireland or were concerned with the broad right of the nation to be free."

De Valera attended anti-partition rallies in several English cities, including London, Birmingham, Newcastle and Sheffield. In his addresses he complained that those contiguous areas of the six counties which had Nationalist majorities should be handed over to the Dublin Government. "We demand that these counties where there is an overwhelming majority against partition should be given back to us in all fairness and justice," he told a rally in Newcastle in February 1949. He was exaggerating in a rather demagogic fashion. In a general election in Northern Ireland the previous week Nationalist candidates had won a majority of the votes in both Fermanagh and Tyrone, but neither could have been classed as having had an "overwhelming" majority, seeing that it was less than fifty-three per cent in each. He was now calling for those areas, something which he had never done while in power, but he made no pretence that he would be satisfied with such a settlement. "That would not solve the partition problem," he admitted, "because our ancient homeland would be severed and mutilated." In the past he had not asked for Nationalist territory because he thought that the whole partition problem should be solved at the same time. He was, no doubt, afraid that if the nationalist areas on the border were taken from the six counties, then the Nationalist minority in what would remain of Northern Ireland would be too small to pose a really significant force for Irish unity, with the result that the prospects for ending partition might be irreparably damaged. In short, he, and indeed his various successors, either really did not want the Nationalist people in Fermanagh, Tyrone, south Down, south Armagh, and Derry City, or else they were quite content to leave them as hostages in the hope that they might eventually help to secure Irish unity.

Like its Fianna Fáil predecessor, the Costello government used its foreign policy to exploit the unification issue. The popular irritation over partition was cited as the reason for refusing to join either the North Atlantic Treaty Organisation, or a suggested European federation. De Valera agreed with both decisions. He told the Assembly of the Council of Europe in Strasbourg in August 1949 that while he was not personally opposed to the idea of a united Europe, it would be very difficult to persuade the Irish people to enter a European federation at the time.

"I am sure," he said, "you can understand with what a cynical smile an Irish citizen would regard you if you spoke to him about uniting into a huge state the several states of Europe with their diverse national traditions so long as he contemplates his own country kept divided against his will." Those countries who believed in European unity should go ahead without Ireland, he continued. "It is from no desire to interfere with or delay them that some of us here have spoken against the attempt at immediate federation. It is simply because we know the task that would confront us in persuading our people to proceed by that road."

As international tension mounted with the outbreak of war in Korea, de Valera adopted essentially the same attitude as he had during the crises immediately prior to the Second World War. "As long as the evil of partition exists," he told a London gathering, "a divided Ireland would have no option but to remain neutral in a third world war." He had been saved from a most embarrassing position by the Soviet veto of Ireland's application for membership of the United Nations. In accordance with the scenario which he had outlined for the Dáil before applying for membership, Ireland would have been obliged to fight in Korea.

Although he seemed by implication to be holding out the possibility of co-operating with the western alliance if Irish unity were secured, he persisted with his refusal to make any commitment in advance. He would not bargain with Ireland's avowed neutrality even in return for Irish unity. "If you attempt to condition freedom," he said, "you have not got it."

A few weeks later the Costello government was rent by an internal squabble which developed after the Roman Catholic hierarchy demanded amendments to the Mother and Child Scheme, a health bill which some bishops felt smacked of creeping socialism. When Noel Browne, the minister in charge, refused to alter the bill to the satisfaction of the bishops, he was forced to resign. He then published his correspondence with the hierarchy, and this led to a political crisis. De Valera watched as leaders of the government parties vied with one another with fawning protestations of submissiveness to the church's authority.

"I as a Catholic, obey my Church authorities and will continue to do so," the Taoiseach told the Dáil. The whole affair should have been "adjusted behind closed doors" so that the public would not have become aware of it, he said. The Tánaiste and leader of the Labour Party, William Norton, proclaimed that "there will be no flouting of the authority of the bishops in the matter of Catholic social or Catholic moral teaching." Even MacBride, whose

Clann na Poblachta was posing as the real voice of constitutional Republicanism, got into the act. "All of us in the Government who are Catholics are, as such, bound to give obedience to the rulings of our Church and our hierarchy," he declared.

De Valera quietly agreed with Costello that the whole thing should have been settled behind closed doors. "You should not have published the correspondence between yourself and the hierarchy," he told Browne privately. "He appeared to resent the fact that I had deliberately set out, by use of the correspondence, to collect the evidence needed by me to prove conclusively that Rome did rule, which I had already learned from my experience in cabinet," Browne later explained. "De Valera appeared to know and condone it."

In public, however, the Fianna Fáil leader maintained an air of detached indifference, keeping a tight rein on his party colleagues and taking virtually no part in the Dáil controversy. "His sole comment at the end of a long heated debate was the dismissive and cryptic phrase, worthy of Pontius Pilate himself," Browne wrote.

"I think," de Valera said, "we have heard enough."

He had undoubtedly played a politically astute role in remaining aloof while his opponents attacked one another and brought down their own government. Of course, some people felt his was an ignoble part because he made no effort to dispel the distinct impression that the Irish government was quietly controlled by the Roman Catholic hierarchy. Yet in contrast with the fawning obsequiousness of his opponents, his behaviour had about it a certain dignified air of contempt.

In the ensuing general election Fianna Fáil gained only one seat, but this was enough for it to form a minority government with the help of a number of independent deputies, including Browne, who would soon join Fianna Fáil on a political excursion which would take him into two other parties before he finally retired from active politics. De Valera was already in his sixty-ninth year when he took over as Taoiseach again, re-appointing the same people from his last cabinet, with only one new face—Thomas Walsh as the new Minister for Agriculture. The most notable portfolio changes were the return of MacEntee as Minister for Finance in place of Aiken, who was moved to External Affairs. De Valera's eyes were giving him serious trouble, and he was forced to spend several months in the Netherlands while a Utrecht oculist tried to save his deteriorating eyesight. He underwent six operations before returning home in late 1952, virtually blind, except for some slight peripheral vision.

His decision not to take up the External Affairs portfolio was contrary to some solemn advice he had given to the Dáil ten years earlier. "In all small states," he had said, "it is almost absolutely vital that the head of the government should also be the Minister for External Affairs." In hindsight it would be suggested that he should have stepped down and handed over to Lemass, but at the time there were many people within the party who were deeply uneasy.

"Lemass had not the same statesmanship," MacEntee noted years later. "Lemass was essentially a merchant adventurer. He was prepared to take risks without some kind of deep thought."

In 1959 when Lemass did succeed de Valera, he performed magnificently, and this would give rise to profound regrets that he had not been given an opportunity to display his own leadership talents earlier, especially as de Valera's latest government seemed devoid of vision. Its only goal seemed to be to hold on to office.

Shortly after coming into power it looked like becoming embroiled in a controversy with the Roman Catholic hierarchy when James Ryan, the Minister for Health, moved to implement a somewhat revised version of the Mother and Child Scheme. The hierarchy wrote to the press condemning the legislation, but de Valera avoided an open confrontation by hurriedly going north to talk with John Cardinal D'Alton, his old classmate from Blackrock College. They met in Drogheda and agreed to certain modifications to the bill. The hierarchy then withdrew its letter before actual publication, but too many people had seen the document for the matter to remain secret for long. The whole affair was another example of the enormous influence which the Roman Catholic hierarchy had in the public life of the twenty-six counties.

Although the government buckled under the clerical pressure, de Valera had nevertheless—in marked contrast with his opponents—been able to give the impression over the years of being both closer to, and at the same time more independent of, the Roman Catholic hierarchy. He seemed closer because he was on good personal terms with prominent churchmen ever since his days as a teacher. He had used his clerical contacts adroitly during the 1917-1921 period when he did more than anyone to render Irish nationalism innocuous to the hierarchy. Yet he was no sycophant, as he clearly demonstrated during the Civil War. In the 1930s he "did much to make the Irish state more confessional" by strengthening legislation in line with Roman Catholic thinking on matters in which he firmly believed, like divorce, contraception and censorship, but at the same time he "also prevented it from becoming any more clerical" by withstanding pressure to include a triumphalist recognition of the Roman Catholic Church in the 1937 Constitution, and also by resisting pressure to support Franco's forces during the Spanish Civil War. What seemed like an unwillingness to submit blindly to the hierarchy was further enhanced by the tactics of his opponents, who criticised him for supporting the wartime censorship of comments made by the Bishop of Achonry, and also *Osservatore Romano*.

Whatever extremely remote prospects there might have been for a successful anti-partition campaign in these postwar years were well and truly demolished by the church-state controversies over the Mother and Child Scheme, but the new Fianna Fáil government showed no inclination of reviving the partition issue in any case. In fact, de Valera criticised the campaign conducted by his predecessors. Indeed, he had the galling audacity to say that partition should not have been made a political issue.

If the coalition government had been serious about ending partition, he told a meeting in Drogheda on 28 February 1954, the British ambassador would have been expelled and all trade with Britain severed. This, of course, raises the question whether he had ever been serious in his own campaigns, because he never advocated breaking off relations with the British. Now he contended a more moderate approach was needed. "There is one policy which we can pursue," he said, "a policy of trying to establish decent relations between the people of Britain and the six counties and ourselves."

"I don't want to make partition a political issue, because I do not believe there is any one of the parties who have got the solution for it."

During his years in power de Valera had invariably concentrated on questions of Irish sovereignty or international affairs, but now he would find little scope for those. He was still a kind of political outcast on the international scene. In 1953 he was reduced to going on official visits to two other outcasts, the neo-fascist dictators of Portugal and Spain—Salazar and Franco. It was only with some difficulty that F.H. Boland, who was serving as Irish ambassador to Britain, managed to persuade the Taoiseach to call on Churchill, then in his final term as Prime Minister. De Valera was afraid of being snubbed, but Churchill—with his keen sense of history—was anxious for them to get together, especially as they had never met before.

De Valera was accompanied to Downing Street by Aiken and

Boland. "Churchill met us at the door," Boland recalled. "He greeted de Valera warmly, took him by the arm and said: 'If you shout I shall be able to hear what you say. Now I will lead the way because I can see a little better.'" With their senses of humour, these two giants of British and Irish history immediately saw the comic side to their geriatric predicament. They laughed heartily and everyone else joined in.

"A pleasant atmosphere prevailed," Boland noted. De Valera and Churchill withdrew to a corner by a window and chatted privately for about twenty-five minutes. The Taoiseach brought up the partition question, but Churchill said no British government could drive the Unionists of Northern Ireland out of the United Kingdom. De Valera then raised the possibility of securing the return of the body of Roger Casement, who had been buried in a British jail following his execution in 1916. The Prime Minister agreed to consult his government, but nothing came of the initiative. It would be more than a decade before the body would be returned.

Meanwhile in Ireland the economy, having picked up under the coalition, took centre stage during the life of the Fianna Fáil government, which soon found itself dogged by inflation and an adverse balance of payments. MacEntee sought to restore financial probity through high taxation and reduced expenditure. Although honest and courageous, his policy was too severe, even in the opinion of conservative economists. The deflationary pressures eventually led to political difficulties which brought about the demise of the government and wrecked MacEntee's own chances of succeeding to the leadership of Fianna Fáil.

In 1954 de Valera called a general election, but it resulted in the poorest Fianna Fáil showing since 1927. Costello was able to put together another coalition Government.

In view of the earlier campaign against partition, it was not surprising that some members of the younger generation should become disillusioned with the apparent cynicism of politicians on the issue. The IRA was able to stage a revival from the near disastrous effects of its war-time collusion with the Nazis. Buoyed by fresh blood, the organisation began a bombing campaign on the border.

De Valera, who met privately and tried to discourage IRA leaders before the bombing began, publicly denounced the violence. Irish unity "could not be achieved by the exercise of force," he told the Fianna Fáil Árd Fheis in November 1955. "Even if it were militarily successful," he added, "we would not have the harmony essential" for real unity.

When the coalition government tried to move against the IRA, however, Clann na Poblachta withdrew its vital support in the Dáil and tabled a motion of no confidence. Faced with imminent defeat Costello asked for a dissolution and a general election was called for February 1957. This time de Valera campaigned on the need for a strong government to tackle the country's problems, especially its continuing economic ills. The result was a resounding victory for Fianna Fáil, which secured a majority of nine seats. Although the party had gained larger majorities in 1938 and 1944, the seventy-nine seats won in 1957 were the highest total ever held by the party during de Valera's lifetime.

Although a majority of the members of the new cabinet had been members of the 1932 government, there were a number of new faces this time, the most notable of whom were Jack Lynch as Minister for Education, Kevin Boland as Minister for Defence, and Neil Blaney as Minister for Local Government. Seán Moylan, who had lost his seat in the election, was appointed Minister for Agriculture as a Senator, but he died soon afterwards and was re-placed by another of the younger breed of politicians, Micheál O Móráin. The four new appointees would all figure prominently in the Arms Crisis of 1970, but this is getting ahead of the story.

In 1957 the new Fianna Fáil government lost little time in act-ing decisively against the IRA. It re-introduced internment without trial of IRA suspects and the level of violence in Northern Ireland soon showed a marked decline. The government also took what would eventually prove to be the most far-reaching step on the road towards economic growth by publishing the Whitaker Report, which called for drastic revision of the earlier economic policies pursued by Fianna Fáil and the coalition governments. In the fol-lowing years the implementation of the report would virtually revo-lutionise the Irish economy.

De Valera took a particularly admirable political stand in 1957 during a controversy which erupted in County Wexford near the village of Fethard-on-Sea. The whole thing had begun over the re-ligious education of a child of a Protestant woman and her Roman Catholic husband. In order that her husband could get his church's permission to marry her, she had agreed that their children would be reared as Roman Catholics, but when their oldest child came of school age she changed her mind and fled with her two chil-dren to her own family in Belfast. She said she would only return if her husband agreed to have the children reared as Protestants. His Protestant neighbours were blamed for helping her to flee, and there were calls for the community to boycott local Protestant business people. As the wife was a northern Protestant and northern Protestants had a long folk memory of the sectarian massacre committed in County Wexford during the 1798 Rebellion, the whole affair was ripe for sensational exploitation, especially when Michael Browne, the Roman Catholic Bishop of Galway, got into the act. Preaching to a congregation in Wexford which included Cardinal D'Alton and six other bishops, he essentially endorsed the sectarian boycott by describing it as "a peaceful and moderate protest" in the course of a sermon in which he went on to complain about what "seems to be a concerted campaign to entice or kidnap Catholic children and deprive them of their faith."

What had started out as little more than a marital spat suddenly became a national *cause célèbre*. De Valera was reluctantly dragged into the whole thing a few days later when Noel Browne tabled a question in the Dáil asking him to outline the government's position in the controversy. "I have made no public statement," de Valera explained, "because I have clung to the hope that good sense and decent neighbourly feeling would of themselves bring this business to an end." He denounced the boycott as ill-conceived, ill-considered, unjust and cruel. "I beg of all who have regard for the fair name, good repute and well-being of our nation to use their influence to bring this deplorable affair to a speedy end."

The Bishop of Galway, who had always been on particularly friendly terms with de Valera, responded the following Sunday. "It is not against charity or justice," he said, "to refuse special favours such as one's money or custom, to those whom one regards as responsible for, or approving of, a grave offence." The boycott continued for some months before the whole thing gradually fizzled out. The wife returned with her children to her husband, and the dispute was quietly resolved, as it should have been in the first place, within the family.

De Valera's independence of the hierarchy "was rooted in the fact that he knew he was right," according to Conor Cruise O'Brien. "His cold certitude on this point was at least the equal of that possessed by an Irish Archbishop. The bishops knew this characteristic and had a certain grudging respect for it. They were no more anxious than he was to provoke a confrontation." In fact, his personal certitude was more akin to that of papal infalliblity.

During the Civil War he had risked excommunication in defying the hierarchy. Indeed many people believed the Republicans had been excommunicated, and although de Valera never shared their conviction, he sought the reassurance of the Vatican. "I put the matter to the Pope," he explained, "and he agreed with me that I had not been excommunicated."

"But supposing he had said in fact that you were excommunicated, what would you have made of that?" Lord Longford asked him.

"I should have considered that His Holiness was misinformed."

De Valera was under mounting pressure to step down, but he made it clear to a Fianna Fáil Árd Fheis in November 1957 that he wished to hang on. "So long as this organisation wants me (if they do not want me, they can get rid of me easily) and as long as Dáil Éireann thinks I am doing my work and can do my work, then I stay," he declared. It was time for him to stand down, but Seán Lemass was too astute a politician to start a bruising leadership struggle. Instead, the chief was gently persuaded to move upstairs by standing for the Presidency, which was due to become vacant in June 1959 when Sean T. O'Kelly would complete his second term.

Noel Browne later suggested that questions asked by him about the running of the *Irish Press* group of newspapers may have led to de Valera's retirement, but there was no evidence to substantiate the unlikely story. De Valera had collected the money to set up the *Irish Press* as a means of promoting Fianna Fáil, but he ensured that he endowed the controlling director of the company "with absolute control over the public and political policy," as well as having the discretion to "remove or suspend all editors, sub-editors, reporters, writers, etc." Although he had these sweeping powers, he did not interfere in the running of the newspapers, because the various editors always knew what he wanted.

When he turned the company over to his son Vivion, a number of loyal Fianna Fáil supporters questioned the propriety of the move, but it never developed into any kind of scandal, probably because few people would give any credence to the idea that "the Chief" would be involved in any kind of financial scandal. He had always been willing to live in the frugal comfort he espoused. He never owned a palatial mansion, a large estate, race horses, yachts, or any of the other trappings of ostentatious wealth.

In January 1959 he told the Fianna Fáil parliamentary party of his decision to retire from active politics in the near future in order to give his successor enough time to prepare for the next general election. He said he had been approached about running for the Presidency, but would leave the "matter completely in the hands of the party." He was playing the role of the available yet reluctant politician to the very end, pretending he was not looking for office but merely making himself available out of a sense of duty. Of course, the party duly obliged by selecting him as its candidate.

Before retiring from active politics, he was anxious to tackle one last major issue. He wanted to reform the electoral system, which he believed had been responsible for the instability of the past decade. He therefore proposed the abolition of the single transferable vote of the Proportional Representation system. He got a bill through the Dáil to hold a constitutional referendum, which was scheduled for the same day as the Presidential election.

The results of the balloting were mixed from de Valera's viewpoint. In the Presidential race, he easily defeated his Fine Gael opponent, Sean MacEoin, but the attempt to abolish Proportional Representation was soundly defeated. In a way it was symbolic. The Irish electorate was accepting de Valera but rejecting his ideas. When De Valera resigned as Taoiseach to take up the Presidency, his ideal of frugal comfort in a self-contained, Gaelic, Roman Catholic republic was abandoned. Ireland was moving into the age of materialism and preparing to take her place in the European Community.

CHAPTER 27

"For Reasons Alike of Honour and Prudence"

On 25 June 1959 de Valera was inaugurated President. During the fourteen years he held the office, his duties were mainly ceremonial. He delivered the inaugural address at the opening of the national television service, Radio Telefís Éireann (RTE) on 31 December 1961. More than a quarter of a century earlier he had delivered the address at the opening of the radio broadcasting station in Athlone, and there was a curious contrast between the two addresses.

In 1934 de Valera had talked in terms of using the Irish radio station in "helping to save western civilisation." With the use of that modern technology he said that Ireland "might humbly serve the truth and help by truth to save the world." By the end of 1961, however, he was more apprehensive. "Never before was there in the hands of man an instrument so powerful to influence the thoughts and actions of the multitude," he warned. "A persistent policy pursued over radio and television, in addition to imparting knowledge, can build up the character of a whole people, including sturdiness and vigour and confidence. On the other hand, it can lead, through demoralisation, to decadence and dissolution."

Much of de Valera's official time was spent in receiving foreign visitors, especially diplomatic representatives, and welcoming numerous heads of state. The visit of President John F. Kennedy in 1963 was a particularly emotive occasion. When the American President was assassinated a few months later, de Valera undertook the arduous task of attending the funeral in Washington. It was one of many sad duties he was to fulfil during his tenure.

There were also happier moments such as when he represented the Irish people at the coronation of Pope Paul VI and made a state visit to the United States at the invitation of President Lyndon B. Johnson in 1964. It was forty-five years since he had gone to the United States seeking American recognition. Now he was returning as President of Ireland, an internationally recognised republic, and he was honoured with an invitation to address a joint session of Congress. It was a magnificent occasion as the blind eighty-one-year-old President delivered a moving twenty-five minute address without notes.

In April and May of 1966 he attended various ceremonies commemorating the fiftieth anniversary of the Easter Rebellion. Few questions were asked about the real consequences of the events of 1916, and no effort was made to put them in their proper perspective. It was just an orgy of unquestioning glorification, with de Valera—the sole surviving commandant of the Rising—at the centre of attention. Some former colleagues urged the press to investigate his real role in the events of Easter Week but, fifty years after the events, newspapers like the *Irish Times* were not interested in pursuing the charge that he had deserted his men. Even though he had clearly mellowed over the years, de Valera was still a controversial figure.

His predecessor, Seán T. O'Kelly, had not been challenged for a second term in 1952, but the opposition were not about to accord de Valera such an honour. Fine Gael nominated T.F. O'Higgins, a nephew of the assassinated Kevin O'Higgins. The President—already in his eighty-fourth year and almost totally blind—was not going to be able to match the much younger man on the campaign trail, so his campaign was put in the hands of one of the young rising stars of Fianna Fáil, Charles J. Haughey, who was already being talked about as a potential successor to Lemass, his father-in-law. Haughey, then Minister for Agriculture, was being afforded the opportunity of making a name for himself on the national stage as de Valera's national director of elections. He pulled off a political stroke in minimising the Fine Gael candidate's physical advantages by having de Valera virtually sit out the campaign and persuading RTE not to cover his opponent in the supposed interest of fair play.

The RTE Authority was, of course, controlled by Fianna Fáil appointees and the RTE news department accepted the spurious fair play argument, which was unfair to O'Higgins. He campaigned actively but got little radio or television coverage, whereas the President had received enormous exposure on both radio and television in connection with the fiftieth anniversary of the Easter Rebellion during the past couple of months. He was also able to get publicity for his official engagements which, of course, were supposedly unconnected with the campaign. In addition, various government ministers were dispatched by Haughey to rallies around the country, where they in turn were able to secure publicity for de Valera's campaign by using their official positions to make newsworthy pronouncements. In the circumstances nobody was surprised when de Valera won another seven-year term, but there was amazement that his margin of victory had shrunk by more than ninety per cent. He actually trailed badly in the large urban areas, but the rural constituencies had come to his rescue.

In a close election it is always possible to attribute the margin of victory to numerous factors. In this case Haughey's deft political footwork may have made a vital contribution, but it may well have been at the cost of his own ambition to succeed his father-in-law. When Lemass decided to step down as Taoiseach the following autumn, Haughey was in the midst of a bitter row with RTE newsmen, who clearly resented his political interference. While the ultimate significance of the row is a matter for conjecture, it certainly did not help Haughey, who withdrew from the race and threw his support behind Jack Lynch, one of the new breed appointed to the cabinet by de Valera in 1957.

The more noteworthy events of the President's second term included the publication of his own "quasi-official biography," the country's entry into the European Economic Community, the election of a coalition government headed by Liam Cosgrave, the son of his longtime rival W.T. Cosgrave, and finally the surprise election of the son of his own good friend Erskine Childers to succeed him as President. But it was affairs relating to the troubles in Northern Ireland which took centre stage in Irish politics during the latter years of his presidency.

De Valera actually played a role behind the scenes of some of those events. In August 1969, for instance, he helped to resolve a political crisis that threatened when Kevin Boland resigned from the cabinet in protest at the government's unwillingness to adopt a more active policy in relation to Northern Ireland. Boland, whom de Valera had first appointed to the cabinet along with Lynch back in 1957, was invited to Áras an Uachtaráin, where de Valera pleaded with him.

"The President talked of the constitutional crisis that would be caused by my resignation—particularly on this issue," Boland later wrote. "He foresaw a change to Fine Gael controlled Government and pointed out the seriousness of this in the circumstance that existed." Thereupon Boland resorted to a course worthy of the dialectics of de Valera himself.

"I agreed that I did not want to change the government, and, while I did not agree to withdraw my resignation," Boland wrote, "I said I would attend the next government meeting of which I was notified." Of course, he effectively withdrew his resignation, only to resign again, this time publicly, nine months later in the midst of the Arms Crisis of May 1970.

That political crisis centred around the activities of Haughey and Neil Blaney, who had allegedly tried to import guns earmarked for Northern Ireland. When asked to resign by the Taoiseach, they refused to stand down. Lynch therefore asked the President to remove them formally. With their removal the Arms Crisis erupted and there were widespread rumours of a *coup d'état*. It was unquestionably the most serious political crisis since the Civil War. Both Haughey and Blaney were arrested. Blaney was subsequently discharged and Haughey was acquitted. Following the trial Haughey made a brief bid for power himself, but the party rallied to Lynch, who was able to enforce a strict party discipline. Blaney was expelled from Fianna Fáil and Boland walked out to form a new party, but very few people followed him. Throughout the period Lynch was able to depend on de Valera's help in maintaining party unity, much to the disappointment of people like Boland.

Following the trauma of the famous Arms Trial of 1970 came the publication of de Valera's "quasi-official biography" by Lord Longford and Thomas P. O'Neill, who were given full access to his personal papers. It was the first book to deal with Britain's secret offer to end partition in 1940 and, as the troubles had already erupted in Northern Ireland, the book received extensive international publicity.

It depicted de Valera as a sincere, considerate, compassionate, and fearless patriot—a committed democrat, a brilliant thinker, an excellent strategist, a great statesman, and a dedicated family man. At one point the authors observed that "the Irish were wont to canonise their saints without waiting for Rome," and their hagiographical account was like a case for de Valera's canonisation to crown off his presidency. They sought to sanctify him both by glorifying his accomplishments and obscuring his failings with unsubstantiated and unsubstantiable repudiation, by omission, and by nuance.

The authors set the tone in the preface. "No famous statesman of our time can have centred his life more completely, or perhaps so completely, on religion," they wrote. "He represented a whole world of Irish Catholicism at its simplest and purest." Yet in over four hundred and seventy pages of text, this aspect of his life is essentially ignored. "Concerning his religion and its significance to him," the authors explained, "he concealed nothing, but revealed very little directly."

The book was actually quite good at times, especially on de Valera's successes and triumphs in the twenty years between 1925 and 1945. As these have already been discussed at length in the preceding chapters, it is intended to consider here only those aspects of the book in which de Valera's actions were depicted in a different perspective. For instance, the authors glossed over his part in events leading to the Irish-American split in 1920 with their assertion that "he never could be accused of interference with American internal politics," as if trying to influence domestic elections, or to inject himself into the American controversy over the League of Nations did not amount to such interference. At the time he admitted that the controversy was "purely an American affair attacked from a purely American angle."

The absurd conclusion was really only one of a number of generalised statements, made with little regard for historical accuracy. During the Treaty controversy, they asserted that "the foundation of his whole position, then as always, was democratic." They glossed over his contemptuous treatment of the Dáil in walking out in protest over Griffith's forthcoming election as President, and they ignored his admission about being so foolish as to defend Rory O'Connor's patently undemocratic stand in repudiating the Dáil. Instead they contended he did not renounce O'Connor's actions "for reasons alike of honour and prudence." Just how honour came into it, they did not explain.

Immediately after quoting the 1923 letter in which de Valera assumed the insight of an omniscient being to accuse Mary MacSwiney of vanity, they went on to observe that one of his "most remarkable characteristics, then as later, was a quality of detached judgment." It was as if they were endorsing his right to assume omniscient insight. "He was," they added, "fearless in the expression of his opinions, and on occasions did not hesitate to take a stand which would be seriously questioned in Ireland."

While this was undoubtedly true on occasions, especially at the League of Nations, there were other times when—for various reasons—he was obviously afraid to express his true feelings. The authors referred, for instance, to his "brave statement" denouncing the invasion of the Low Countries in May 1940, but his words were couched in vague diplomatic terms. At no point in his speech, or indeed at any time during the war, did he ever publicly denounce the Germans, the Nazis, or even Hitler. He only protested against "the cruel wrong" done to Belgium and Holland without blaming any country specifically. This did not necessarily conflict with the German claim that the British and French were responsible for provoking the attack.

Of course, there were prudent reasons for not speaking out, seeing that Ireland was virtually defenceless and the Irish people would undoubtedly have suffered greatly if the Germans had decided to attack in response to something or other which de Valera might have said. In the early months of the war he privately explained that words were useless against the Nazis. What was needed, he said, was tanks, bombs and machine guns. He did quietly give essentially all the help he could, but he never spoke out. In the latter stages of the war when the danger of a German attack had evaporated, he could easily have done so, but by then he was afraid the Allies would mock him and this fear may even have played a part in his fatuous condolence gesture at the time of Hitler's death. He had, in short, remained silent as some of the most despicable crimes that ever stained the pages of human history were being committed, and he capped the whole thing off with his inane gesture to the German Minister.

All this is not to suggest that de Valera was a coward, or even that he was not brave, but that he was not as fearlessly outspoken as his authorised biographers contended. If they had bothered they could have found similar examples in his failure to condemn openly either O'Connor's repudiation of the Dáil, or the Republican excesses during the Civil War, and there was also his admission that he feared the consequences of publicly acknowledging Chamberlain's role in the negotiations leading to the Anglo-Irish agreements of 1938.

On the partition question Longford and O'Neill also made assertions that simply did not stand up. In de Valera's eyes, they wrote, partition had "always been an Irish issue to be settled between Irishmen," and they added that "he never wavered in his insistence that unity must come about by consent and not by force."

Their use of words like "never" and "always" was historically reckless. Just one exception was enough to refute such statements and in those instances there were numerous exceptions. In early 1918 de Valera referred to the northern Unionists as "a rock" on the road to Irish independence, and he threatened to "blast" it out of the path, if necessary. In fairness to him, it should be noted that he did subsequently rule out the use of force on a number of occasions, but it was hardly accurate to contend that he "never wavered in his insistence," because he did indicate several times that he would favour its use if he thought it would be successful. Likewise on numerous occasions he stated it was Britain's responsibility to end partition. "The British Government alone have the power to remove this obstacle," he wrote to President Roosevelt in January 1938. If he "always" thought partition was an "issue to be settled between Irishmen," then one must ask how they could have thought that he ever tried to settle the problem, because they never cited any occasion on which he sought to talk with any member of the Northern Ireland government!

A whole chapter, albeit a short one, is devoted to de Valera's role as a family man. "The worldly success of an unworldly family has been astonishing, and possibly unequalled," they wrote. "Out of six surviving children, three are professors." They did not bother to mention that all three were professors at the university in which their father was Chancellor. As was mentioned earlier, the authors quoted liberally from reminiscences provided by his sons and daughters, but those memories were permeated with evidence that they hardly knew their father while growing up. In 1936 when the fifth child, Brian, died following a riding accident, there was only one photograph of the whole family together. The facts cited in the book were not really a depiction of a dedicated family man, but of a kind of stranger, an individual who was so committed to the national cause and to politics that his family life suffered.

Several of de Valera's former cabinet colleagues died during his second term, among them his successor as Taoiseach, Seán Lemass and Gerald Boland. Although his relations with the older Boland had cooled because of his support of the Lynch government during the Arms Crisis and afterwards, de Valera still called to the Boland home to pay his last respects following Gerald's death. Although other members of Fianna Fáil were told to stay away, de Valera was welcomed. He knelt down beside the bed where the body lay and, to the amazement of the family, suddenly leaned forwards across the corpse and began crying. "Gerald," he sobbed, "you were always the boss."

Having outlived most of his contemporaries, de Valera was a lonely man. He liked to chat about old times to visitors, or to talk off the record to reporters assigned to cover him. Despite his austere reputation, he usually kept a bottle of whiskey in his desk and was quite fond of the drop himself.

On public occasions he was always the essence of composure. Reviewing a guard of honour or performing ceremonial duties before football games, he would do a magnificent job of overcoming his blindness by walking in step with his aide-de-camps.

In view of his age RTE drew up contingency plans to cover his funeral in the event he died in office. On one occasion some technicians were taking measurements in Áras an Uachtaráin when, to their surprise, de Valera came groping along the hallway. They slipped into an alcove, hoping he would not detect their presence but as he passed them, he remarked with a laugh that he planned to outlive the lot of them.

Officially he was supposed to be above politics, so he did not take part in the referendum campaign on Ireland's admission to the European Economic Community. He had spoken publicly against membership in the 1950s, but now he kept his silence, and presided over the country's entry.

Even in his nineties he was still quietly able to be of political help to the Taoiseach. In 1973 a political crisis threatened within Fianna Fáil after Lynch called a general election. The Tánaiste, Frank Aiken, wished to block Haughey's nomination as a party candidate, but Lynch refused to go along with this. In disgust Aiken decided to retire from politics and tell the press his reason for quitting. This would, of course, have split the party going into an election. Lynch therefore sought the help of de Valera, who tried to persuade Aiken to keep his silence. It was then disingenuously announced that he had decided to step down "on doctor's orders." It was a sad end to the long political career of a particularly courageous man, and it was all the sadder that he should leave politics quietly while the truth about his reason for going was deliberately distorted. But this was not enough to save the government. Fine Gael and Labour won enough seats to form a coalition government, and Liam Cosgrave, the son of the President's old adversary, was elected Taoiseach.

De Valera hosted a state dinner for the new government and delivered a short address. "I have had reservations about the system of voting called Proportional Representation," he began, "because I foresaw that if persisted in this system would lead eventually to coalition government." Cosgrave, too, was known to have deep reservations about the system and something about what the President said struck him as "irresistibly funny" because he exploded into laughter and everybody else laughed with him.

The President then continued to make his point, which was that since the Irish people wished to retain Proportional Representation, coalition governments were inevitable and the politicians should make the best of the situation. The only way they could be made to work, he contended, was for the members of the coalition government to put loyalty to the Taoiseach before party considerations. That was all he had to say. "It was oddly impressive," according to Conor Cruise O'Brien, one of the new Ministers. "I felt a little ashamed of having laughed."

With de Valera due to retire in June of that year, it was confidently predicted that he would be succeeded by T.F. O'Higgins, the Fine Gael candidate he had so narrowly defeated seven years earlier. Fianna Fáil nominated Erskine Childers for the post. He was not given much chance of winning in view of the good showing made by O'Higgins against de Valera during the last presidential election. In addition, Childers had what was seen as another handicap—he was a Protestant running for national office in a country that was predominantly Roman Catholic, and sectarianism had come very much to the fore in recent years with the renewed outbreak of violence in Northern Ireland. In some ways the presidential election was like a rerun of Civil War politics.

Back in 1923 Kevin O'Higgins, as Minister for Justice, had been responsible for de Valera's arrest. The following week Erskine Childers, then a seventeen-year-old student, acted as a surrogate speaker for de Valera on the campaign platform. Thus de Valera took a keen delight in the surprise victory of Childers, who succeeded him to the office on 25 June 1973.

De Valera attended the inauguration and then retired to Linden Convalescent Home in Blackrock. He had already sold his old home in Blackrock and he had essentially given away most of his possessions. He had handed over the *Irish Press* to his son, Vivion, and had donated his personal papers and various memorabilia to the Franciscan Fathers. Those would have been worth a fortune on the open market, which prompted some cynics to describe his gesture as his insurance policy for the next life. At the end he left only £2,800 in his will, which could be compared with over £380,000 left by Vivion, when he died little over five years later.

While living in the nursing home de Valera appeared in public from time to time. He attended the funeral of Erskine Childers, who died suddenly in November 1974, and he also attended the inauguration of the new President, Cearbhall O Dálaigh, whom de Valera had appointed Attorney-General in his last government of the 1940s and again in his first government of the 1950s. In January 1975, on the eve of their sixty-fifth wedding anniversary, Sinéad de Valera died. Éamon was back in the public eye in March 1975, when, in a joint ceremony, Dublin conferred the freedom of the city on him and on the man who had twice succeeded him as Taoiseach, John A. Costello. It was really a measure of Civil War bitterness that after more than half a century, his opponents would accord de Valera this honour only in a joint ceremony with one of their own.

Despite his extreme age, de Valera never retired completely. He remained on as Chancellor of the National University and dutifully performed his functions until his death, after a brief illness, shortly before noon on 29 August 1975.

CHAPTER 28

"Our Eyes Have Seen The Glory' "

In the days following de Valera's death, his career was widely assessed. For many he had become the personification of Irish freedom and independence, while others took a different view. "One can only look on Eamon de Valera's life as a failure," the columnist Con Houlihan wrote. "By his own stated ambitions he was a failure—it is as cruelly simple as that."

"Speaking for myself," de Valera said to the Dáil on 29 April 1932, "if we were not able to achieve unity of this country, we had not much to boast of beyond what the Irish [Parliamentary] Party might ultimately have achieved." In other words, the Easter Rebellion, the War of Independence, and the Civil War would all have been for nought. Throughout his career he repeatedly stated that his two main ambitions were to secure the revival of the Gaelic language and the ending of partition, neither of which seemed even remotely near realisation at the time of his death. Yet while the language and Ulster questions led him into politics, one must look deeper, to his deprived childhood, for the reason he stayed active so long.

Children who lose their parents usually adapt by denying the loss with daydreams about their return. In de Valera's case, it was he who was sent away, and he must have thought that, if he had greater status, his mother would reclaim him and afford him that recognition which most people take for granted. Instead he was left in Bruree to be reared in loveless surroundings, amid lurid speculation about his legitimacy. There was no truth to the rumour that he was the illegitimate offspring of the randy son of the house where his mother had worked before emigrating, but the rumour persisted and de Valera was quite touchy about it.

Under the circumstances, he must have had doubts about his own value growing up and it was natural that he should crave recognition. Spurred on subconsciously by his early rejection, he had more than a mere yearning for distinction; he had a compulsion to become somebody. He first sought recognition in the academic field. He distinguished himself in secondary school but only achieved moderate academic success at the university level—a pass Bachelor of Arts degree. Despite some years of further study he never earned a Master's degree, nor did he obtain a professorship at the National University for which he initially decided to learn Gaelic, but he still got to the very top of the academic ladder. Through his political involvement he became Chancellor of the National University and held the position for more than half a century—a record which will probably never be equalled.

It was through his educational activities that he became interested in Irish nationalism, which he took to with the zeal of a belated convert. He was not Irish by birth or paternity, and this was highly important because it inflamed his sense of nationalism with an implacable patriotism. Only an outsider could take Irishness so seriously.

He first came to public prominence following the Easter Rebellion when he was one of only three participating commandants to survive the Rising and the subsequent executions. While in jail he was elected leader of the Irish prisoners, and following his release he became the first of the commandants to be elected to parliament. When the various separatist elements united under the Sinn Féin banner in October 1917, he was elected leader because he was able to appeal to moderate and militant elements alike by convincing each that he really shared their views.

The newly united Sinn Féin Party lost the first three by-elections it contested under de Valera's leadership. The Irish Parliamentary Party had begun to re-assert itself, until it was undermined by the conscription crisis in the spring of 1918.

De Valera's decision to allow himself to be arrested during the crisis, and his dramatic escape from Lincoln jail the following February, enveloped him in a cloak of heroism. Collins and the militants had expected him to lead a renewed military campaign against the British following his escape, but de Valera had other ideas. He believed that the independence movement's best hope of success lay, not in a military campaign, but in political agitation with the support of the United States.

America obviously had a deep-rooted attraction for him, seeing that he would turn to the United States again and again throughout his political career. Following his release from jail in June 1917, his first act had been to draw up an appeal to the United States, and he was in the process of drawing up another formal appeal to the United States when he was arrested again during the conscription crisis. Following his escape from Lincoln Jail, he announced his intention of going to America. During the latter half of the 1920s while he was out in the political cold he visited the United States on a number of occasions to collect money both for Fianna Fáil and for the establishment of the *Irish Press*. In 1932, during the critical interim between the general election and his election as President of the Executive Council, he again turned to the United States, as he would do during the Ethiopian crisis, the vital Anglo-Irish negotiations of 1938, and the Munich crisis.

"Without the moral support of American opinion," de Valera told John Cudahy, "the Irish Free State could never have become a reality." Before the start of the Second World War he made arrangements to tour the United States to drum up support for an anti-partition campaign, but it had to be cancelled with the outbreak of hostilities on the continent. Then, in the early years of the war he made repeated appeals for American help and basically used American opinion to ensure that Churchill did not violate Irish sovereignty. On losing power in 1948 de Valera's first act was to visit America.

"The United States, since the Declaration of Independence, has been looked upon by all freedom-loving peoples as the champion of human liberty, the liberty of nations and the liberty of individuals," de Valera told Congress during his visit in 1964. "We in Ireland have constantly looked to you as such a champion." This was during the Vietnam War when there were many people who would challenge his assessment, but there could be no doubt that the United States did have an extraordinary attraction for him. It was a deep-seated allurement which probably went back to his early childhood when he looked to America, longing for the security of his mother. When he went there in 1919 he was not only submitting to that attraction, but was also probably gratifying a subconscious need to demonstrate to his mother that he was indeed *somebody*, or as Owen Dudley Edwards put it, "to exhibit himself in glory in front of his mother." He was returning to America as *Príomh Aire* of *Dáil Éireann*. What Americans thought of his title was so important to him that he changed it to President of the Irish Republic, without any authority from the Dáil, or even informing—much less consulting—members of the cabinet at home.

Of course, it was not just a question of title alone. Without power, the title would have been meaningless. He was therefore determined to show that he had more power than anybody else in the movement; he had to be clearly seen as the Irish chief and resented it when Cohalan and Devoy interfered in Irish affairs. They, on the other hand, resented him depicting Irish-Americans as being prepared to support President Woodrow Wilson's plans for the League of Nations, if the White House would only recognise the Irish Republic. De Valera tried to set himself up as a power broker in American politics—the man who could deliver Irish-American support for the League of Nations, and also the one with the final say on whom the millions of Irish-American voters would support to succeed Wilson in the presidency.

De Valera contended that the feud was over a matter of principle, that Cohalan and Devoy were not asking for formal recognition of the Irish Republic but were merely calling for self-determination for the Irish people. This was the principle for which the United States had supposedly fought in the First World War. He had initially endorsed this approach upon his arrival in the United States and he would do so again repeatedly following his return to Ireland. He even took strong exception in April 1921 when Seán T. O'Kelly argued on the lines he had taken against Cohalan and Devoy, so there could be no doubt that his feud with them had nothing to do with principle; it was purely a power struggle. And upon his return to Ireland he became involved in a further power struggle, this time with Michael Collins, who was the real architect of the Black and Tan War, which had begun during de Valera's absence in the United States.

Prior to going to America de Valera had deliberately frustrated Collins's efforts to provoke a military confrontation with the British. He had pushed through measures within Sinn Féin that were designed to restrain the militants, and he entrusted the control of the movement to the hands of more moderate political elements. But the latter were undermined when the British administration proscribed both the Dáil and Sinn Féin. In the process Dublin Castle drove the Nationalist movement into the arms of militants like Collins.

On hearing that Collins had been appointed acting President following the arrest of Arthur Griffith in November 1920, de Valera abandoned plans to stay longer in the United States and returned to Dublin. Collins posed a real threat to his leadership, and de Valera hastily tried to despatch him to America. When this failed, he replaced him as deputy President. He refused to bring Collins with him to London in July, but later insisted on including him among the plenipotentiaries, to negotiate a treaty with the British.

The President played a dangerous game in selecting people like Griffith and Collins and then saddling them with the responsibility of concluding a treaty. He said he trusted them implicitly, but this was not so. He knew about their inclination to compromise, and he had Erskine Childers appointed as chief secretary to the delegation in order to keep an eye on them. When it came to this kind of conspiratorial thing, however, Collins was no slouch. He resented

Childers acting as a kind of spy and arranged to have him excluded from all discussions with the British. Yet de Valera still thought he could control the delegation, as its members had agreed to confer with the cabinet in Dublin before signing any agreement.

It was a bad miscalculation. Once the plenipotentiaries conferred with the cabinet, they were free to make their own decision. They had been sent with the aim of securing External Association, which was de Valera's plan to ensure that Ireland would have the *de facto* freedom of dominions like Canada. When the British countered with an offer to stipulate in the agreement that Ireland's status would be no less than the *de facto* status of Canada, Griffith and Collins were prepared to accept membership of the British Commonwealth, and they initially thought this was also acceptable to de Valera. They noted, for example, that in the course of the three meetings on the Saturday before the signing he never objected to this aspect of the draft treaty and never said anything about External Association. The only mention he made of holding out for External Association was towards the end of the final meeting in answer to a question from Childers, but neither Griffith nor Collins heard the exchange.

Later it was widely suggested that when the plenipotentiaries signed the Treaty, they expected de Valera to support it, but this was not so. Griffith and Collins realised that he would be opposed, but they were convinced that there was no practical difference between the Treaty and what de Valera wanted. Indeed, he later admitted to a private session of the Dáil that the actual difference was only "a small" one over a "little sentimental thing." The difference was so small that the British would not fight over it. Griffith and Collins, on the other hand, believed that Britain—with her strong attachment to her imperial symbols—would fight even though it was not worth fighting over. They were satisfied that they had secured not only the best terms possible but also the freedom to achieve everything else desired and, having been saddled with the responsibility of concluding a satisfactory settlement, they signed the Treaty.

De Valera publicly exaggerated the defects of the Treaty and pretended that his objections were a matter of fundamental principle, but there was no more principle involved than there had been in his dispute with Cohalan and Devoy. It was another aspect of the ongoing power struggle.

Some people felt that he was just annoyed because the delegation had signed the Treaty without calling him over and allowing him a chance to sign. "I felt the team should have played with me to the last and that I should have got the last chance which I felt would have put us over," he told the Dáil. On several occasions during the Dáil debate he mentioned that he would not have signed the Treaty as it stood. It was a curious thing to say, unless he had actually expected to be asked to sign. His remarks provided grounds for speculating that he had intended to go over to London at the last minute.

All of this must, of course, remain in the realms of speculation. It is not possible to state with any assurance what he had been planning to do. But there can be little doubt that he miscalculated, and he compounded the mistake by playing a highly irresponsible role in rousing public passions in the following weeks and months leading up to the Civil War. In his own words, he was "foolish enough" to defend people like Rory O'Connor "even to straining my own views in order to avoid the appearance of a split."

At the time the anti-Treaty activists were made up largely of people who tended to fit into two different categories. There were, on the one hand, the militants like O'Connor and later Liam Lynch—fanatics who wished to continue the fight in the belief they could eventually succeed militarily. On the other hand, there were the political types, like Mary MacSwiney and Count Plunkett, part of what Lemass would later call that "galaxy of cranks." To them words like "compromise" and "betrayal" meant exactly the same. They were preoccupied with the purity of their tactics and could never reconcile themselves with practical people who believed in achievement. De Valera did not really fit into either category, though in 1922 people could hardly be blamed for assuming he belonged among the purists who wallowed in the traditional Irish tendency to glorify heroic failure.

While in the United States, for instance, he had insisted on calling for formal recognition of the Irish Republic, even though he privately admitted there was no chance of success except in the extremely unlikely circumstances that the United States went to war with Britain over something or other. Likewise when he called on the Dáil to reject the Treaty and substitute his Document No. 2 instead, he admitted that no British politician would have anything to do with his alternative. Where he differed from the purists, however, was that he was not bound by principles but was merely following a course of political expediency, which would become quite evident in the following years.

De Valera's actual role in the Civil War was the subject of ill-founded rumour, misrepresentation, and sheer distortion. His heart was not in the fight; he quickly turned against it and tried hard to stop it. But he had very little control over events; it was the events which tended to control him. Although he was elected leader of the so-called Emergency Government set up by the Republican side during the Civil War, he had no real power and very little influence, because the Republicans were in the grips of militants who tended to distrust all politicians. He was actually regarded as little more than a nuisance by the real leaders of the Republican side until they were replaced by men who realised they had no chance of winning. Then he managed to convince them to dump their arms and quit the fight.

Afterwards when he tried to get the Republicans back on a political course, however, he was arrested by the Free State authorities. Although the government decided to have him charged as soon as possible, the state was unable to make a real case. According to the Attorney-General's office the only hard evidence of any misconduct by de Valera during the Civil War was a letter he had written, supposedly inciting the secretary of Cumann na mBan. Having accused him of starting the war and being the real Republican leader, it would have been ludicrous if he was only tried for inciting the secretary of Cumann na mBan—of all organisations! As a result he was never charged, but he was still held in prison for eleven months. In the process the government made a martyr of him in the eyes of Republicans.

During the Civil War de Valera had decided to boycott the Dáil on tactical grounds. It was just a temporary expediency, but when he got out of jail he found that the decision had been elevated to the level of fundamental principle. Even though he had serious reservations, he went along with this. He was basically fooling people in order to lead them and he would soon find himself serving the folly he begot.

In 1926 when he attempted to modify the abstentionist policy, his proposal was defeated, and he quit Sinn Féin to found Fianna Fáil. The supposed principles on which his abstentionism was based were then conveniently cast aside in 1927 as he led Fianna Fáil into the Dáil. "What we did was contrary to all our former actions, and to everything we stood for—contrary to our declared policy, and to the explicit pledges we gave at the time of our election," he admitted.

As leader of the opposition, he exploited every opportunity to oppose the government—going so far as criticising the Kellogg-Briand Pact, which sought to outlaw war. Describing England as "the never-failing source of all Ireland's political evils," he played the green card to good effect, especially when the government was coming off worst in its dealings with the British in matters like the Boundary Commission and the Ultimate Financial Settlement.

The Fianna Fáil programme also had an economic side with an ideological attraction. While de Valera was personally very conservative, critics depicted him as a radical. Even though his radicalism seldom extended beyond resisting reaction, he professed to sharing the outlook of James Connolly, who had been an avowed Marxist.

"During my whole time in struggling for the freedom of this country," de Valera told the Dáil in 1932, "I had only one object and that was to get free so as to be able to order our life for the benefit of our people. I never regarded freedom as an end in itself, but if I were asked what statement of Irish policy was most in accord with my view as to what human beings should struggle for, I would stand side by side with James Connolly."

Yet, as Professor John A. Murphy noted, the evidence from de Valera's "career as a whole is that he never gave any real thought to the ideas of James Connolly." Murphy saw the remarks as little more than platitudes to please the Labour Party, which was propping up the Fianna Fáil government at a time. Whatever the case, de Valera was able to excuse his failure to implement Connolly's ideals by explaining that Connolly had personally told him that "to secure national freedom was the first step in order to get the workers of Ireland the living they were entitled to in their own country."

By invoking the name of Connolly, de Valera enhanced his image as a radical, which allowed him to appeal to the idealism of radical elements and exploit the emotional resentment of the underprivileged sections of Irish society. The radicals and underprivileged had been alienated by the apparent insensitivity of the Cumann na nGaedheal government in pursuing stringent financial policies—like cutting the old age pension—with an almost sadistic zeal as the world slumped into the Great Depression.

The ten months from when de Valera took office in March 1932 and the general election of January 1933—when Fianna Fáil became the first party to win an overall majority of Dáil seats since the establishment of the Irish Free State—formed a watershed in Irish politics. It was during this period that the Economic War with Britain began. De Valera was accused of starting it, but it was really brought about by Britain's determination to bring him down by using economic pressure. Cumann na nGaedheal played a despicable role in the whole affair by secretly pleading with the British not to make concessions to him or his government.

Blinded by their own bitterness, de Valera's opponents never forgave him for his actions prior to the Civil War. They portrayed him as an austere, cold, vain, arrogant and ruthless individual. He certainly betrayed an arrogant streak with his behaviour at different times between 1919 and 1923 and also in his correspondence with erstwhile supporters like Mary MacSwiney and Joseph McGarrity. Under the circumstances it was understandable that his accession to power was viewed with a good deal of apprehension by the civil service.

People who crave power frequently take pleasure in humiliating those who work for them, often with profanity, bad manners and a savage sense of humour. In 1932 Irish civil servants could hardly be blamed for fearing that they—having loyally served the Cumann na nGaedheal governments—would be victimised by someone with an arrogant streak like de Valera, but, to their surprise, they found him a gracious and considerate, indeed, a modest individual with a disarming sense of humour. It was not that he was a barrel of laughs. People frequently had to explain jokes to him, and he would then laugh heartily, but there was no savagery in his humour. When he poked fun at people, it was usually at himself, which, of course, seemed to belie that insufferable arrogance of which his opponents accused him. The arrogant streak was there all right, but he normally kept it under tight control. It only surfaced when his leadership seemed under threat, which would suggest that it was born of a personal insecurity rather than a contempt for others.

He sought to retain power by trying to give the Irish people what the majority wished, not necessarily what he desired himself. "It is not what I want," he said. "It is what the people of Ireland want." Personally, for instance, he was most interested in the revival of the Gaelic language. Even though he acknowledged in 1933 "that half-measures are useless," he never attempted to implement more because he did not feel he would have the necessary popular support, and staying in power was his primary aim.

De Valera was not firmly committed to any form of government. As a young man he had been very critical of democracy, and he betrayed a certain contempt for democratic principles during the period leading up to the civil war. He openly stated he was not a doctrinaire republican in 1921, and twenty years later he admitted "that he had never held any strong views about any particular form of government." Yet from what he saw in Italy and Germany he did come to the conclusion that dictatorship inevitably led to disaster. "With all its faults," he added, "democracy seemed to him to be the best form of government. It might go through dark or disappointing chapters as in America, where rapid growth of wealth enabled forms of democracy to be abused, but it had in it inherent qualities which kept the ship of state on or near its course." In essence, de Valera was a political opportunist who seized the chances of gaining that sense of distinction which had been so sadly lacking in his formative years.

The leadership he sought was not one of humiliation, rather a blend of admiration and command. Those who liked him so admired his amiability and control that they served him without question. Except on those rare occasions when he felt threatened, he used his power adroitly, with an unostentatious but nonetheless exuberant self-confidence. Within his cabinet he ruled with extreme patience and used the force of exhaustion to get his way by seeking unanimity and rarely allowing any decision to be taken on a vote. He fostered a ministerial rivalry by assigning overlapping tasks to individuals with differing outlooks, thereby promoting a sense of dependency on himself because ministers—like the conservative MacEntee in Finance and the radical Lemass in Industry and Commerce—inevitably had to appeal to him, which cultivated his own image as the omniscient leader to whom everyone within the government had to turn.

De Valera did not engage in victimisation, notwithstanding the hysterical charges to the contrary by the opposition following the removal of Eoin O'Duffy as head of the police force. O'Duffy, who had sought to arrange a *coup d'état* to prevent Fianna Fáil coming to power, turned down the offer of another post. Even Cumann na nGaedheal had planned to remove him, so there were no real grounds for the charge of victimisation in his case, but the opposition still gave him reckless support in an attempt to embarrass the Fianna Fáil Government.

By reacting blindly in trying to block virtually everything de Valera tried to do in the 1930s, often for no other reason than the fact that he was trying to do it, the opposition did themselves irreparable harm. When he did the right or popular thing, they duly made the political blunder of opposing him, and in the process alienated open-minded elements of the electorate.

While members of Cumann na nGaedheal claimed that national freedom had been achieved in accordance with the terms of the 1921 Treaty (which were regularised by the Statute of Westminster a decade later), they undermined their arguments after de Valera came to power when they contended that his attempts at demonstrating Irish sovereignty could not be implemented without provoking the wrath of Britain. This was the last thing anybody should have said to a people who had just attained their freedom. It made it all the easier for de Valera to enlist popular support for his efforts to demonstrate that Britain had no business in Irish politics.

In 1926 he decided it was necessary to break with Sinn Féin because he was afraid Irish politics would otherwise develop in such a way that sectional interests would take precedence over the national considerations which he thought should be paramount. When he came to power in 1932 he stressed issues of national sovereignty and allowed them to dominate his political approach.

Changes like the abolition of the Treaty-oath, the replacement of the Governor General, the abolition of the right of appeal to the British Privy Council, and the introduction of an autochthonous constitution, may not have been immediately understandable to people from countries with long histories of political independence, but demonstrating national sovereignty was important to the people of an infant state unsure of itself. Hence he became "a master panderer to Irish national longings," in the words of one American diplomat.

Appreciating the advantages of a high international profile, de Valera used his foreign policy to domestic political advantage by taking bold, independent stands on international issues. At the League of Nations he adopted a firm yet temperate approach to international affairs, taking a courageous stance against Japanese aggression in Manchuria, and Italian aggression in Ethiopia. He irritated the United States by calling for League intervention in the Chaco War, and he risked the hostility of the Roman Catholic hierarchy at home both by advocating the Soviet Union's admission to the League, and by refusing to support Franco during the Spanish Civil War.

A staunch advocate of collective security, de Valera was ready to propose the use of Irish troops to help the League stop international aggression, until it became clear that the major powers were unwilling to live up to their international responsibilities in ensuring the effectiveness of the League's collective security system. Although he then became a strong supporter of appeasement, his services to the League were recognised by his election as President of the Assembly at the height of the Sudetenland crisis in 1938. In that position he played a significant role in preparing international opinion for the infamous Munich Agreement.

By taking strong moral stands on various international issues in which he was able to represent the nation as a whole, he not only bolstered the country's national identity but in the process diverted attention from divisions at home, and thus promoted a measure of unity. He won the admiration and support of Irish people who had never shared his outlook on domestic political matters, while he became the virtual personification of Ireland for people abroad, winning the respect of even British politicians.

It was during his trips to Geneva that he did the early ground-work for the negotiations leading to the Anglo-Irish agreements of 1938, which terminated the Economic War, settled the outstanding financial disputes, and paved the way for Ireland to stay out of the coming world war by getting the British to give up their bases in the twenty-six counties and renounce their other rights under the defence clauses of the 1921 Treaty. Capitalising on the popularity of the 1938 agreements, de Valera called a general election and Fianna Fáil candidates proceeded to win not only a handsome majority of Dáil seats but also an overall majority of the first preference votes cast. In fact, the party's percentage of first preference votes was greater than any party would gain either under himself or any of the five men who would succeeded him as Taoiseach in the next half-century.

Any lingering doubts about the independence of the twenty-six counties were irrefutably squashed when Ireland managed to stay out of the Second World War. Displaying an acute shrewdness and a tough, realistic decisiveness, he played the great powers off against each other. While Ireland's interest was the deciding factor, he managed to cloak his policy in a kind of constructive ambiguity in order to convince each set of belligerents that they had more to lose than gain by violating Irish sovereignty.

While Ireland was supposedly neutral, he secretly authorised essentially all the help he could to the Allies, by releasing their airmen who landed in Ireland, by operating radio directional find-ing equipment so that Allied airplanes could get their bearings, by permitting the Royal Navy to station armed tugs in Irish waters for air-sea rescue purposes, by providing the British with facili-ties for a radar station on the south coast, and arranging it so that the Irish coastwatching service effectively reported to the British. There was also extensive co-operation on intelligence matters, and de Valera authorised the use of Irish diplomats in occupied Europe as American spies. It was therefore ironic that he should have been depicted by the British and American media as being anti-British to the point of being pro-Nazi.

It was nonsense, but he was not too concerned about the gap between the public perception and the reality of his foreign policy, because he managed to use it to his own domestic political advantage. By standing up to the United States at the time of the American Note and responding so effectively to Churchill's verbal onslaught at the end of the war, de Valera won the unqualified approval of practically the whole nation, which was more united than at any time in more than two decades. He had put the Civil War behind him and acquired that most elusive and much sought-after quality of real charisma.

In the proper sense, a charismatic leader is not necessarily someone who possesses charm and popularity, but someone who is credited with having achieved seemingly impossible tasks and who, in the eyes of his followers, possesses qualities which mark him out not just as rare or exceptional but essentially superhuman. The vital dimensions of real charisma are not therefore necessarily attributes of the leader but, rather, qualities which he is believed to possess by his followers who place a blind trust in him.

In the concluding words of their biography of de Valera, for instance, Longford and O'Neill credited him with having had an influence of divine proportions. "He was," they wrote, "a creator of Ireland's destiny."

The various leaders who achieved charismatic acclaim in the twentieth century—people like Franklin Roosevelt, Hitler, Mussolini, and Gandhi—all performed what were seen as heroic feats, possessed outstanding rhetorical ability, and were identified with one or more of the dominant myths of their culture or society. De Valera was not generally considered a great orator, his words were not well phrased, and the dull manner of his delivery was not particularly impressive. There were none of Churchill's rhetorical flourishes, or Hitler's emotional histrionics, but the Irish leader was nevertheless an extremely effective speaker, as he demonstrated with his majestic reply to Churchill's broadcast in May 1945. The real secret of de Valera's success as a speaker was his facility to convey a sense of passionate sincerity. His open-minded listeners might not always have shared his pronounced convictions, but they were nevertheless convinced that he believed them himself, which, of course, was not always the case, seeing that he was not above cloaking more mundane considerations in the hypocritical garb of fundamental principle.

Having played what was seen as a heroic part in the Easter Rebellion, in which he was credited with having supposedly been the most effective commandant, he was acclaimed as a military genius by his admirers. They compared him to Napoleon, just as other admirers lauded his intellectual prowess by comparing him with Einstein. It was a measure of his charisma that he was compared to so many of the great, and indeed infamous, leaders of history. He assiduously promoted comparisons with Abraham Lincoln by keeping a bust of the American President in his office. Lincoln, the poor boy who made good, had engaged in the American Civil War to prevent a break-up of the United States, and, of course, de Valera liked to promote the myth that his own involvement in the Irish Civil War had been in connection with partition. Others compared him to Gandhi, Ataturk, Kerensky, Lenin, Stalin, Hitler, and Mussolini. Lloyd George had met those people but dismissed comparisons with the Irish leader.

"Quite frankly," he told the British parliament, "I have never found anyone like him; he is perfectly unique." The former Prime Minister added rather pointedly that "the poor distracted world has a good right to be profoundly thankful that he is unique."

The explanation for de Valera's charisma was to be found in the way in which he promoted a series of myths and assimilated himself with the dominant Irish myth about supposedly having struggled for independence for more than seven centuries. In his speeches he referred regularly to the Irish struggle as if it had been a seven-hundred-year-war, which he virtually sanctified by linking it with the struggle for religious freedom. There had been an over-lapping prior to Catholic Emancipation in the early nineteenth century, but de Valera managed to give the current cause a religious facet by using religious occasions like St Patrick's Day, Easter and Christmas for major addresses, by referring to the executed leaders of 1916 in hallowed terms, as "martyrs," and by referring to the area severed by partition as "sacred sod." Borrowing from "The Battle Hymn of the Republic," he even gave a religious twist to his speech commemorating the centenary of Parnell's birth.

"Our 'eyes have seen the glory' which Parnell and his comrades longed for and strove for but did not see," de Valera said. "Let us strive to be worthy of the great privilege which is ours." By invoking the names and singing the praises of the past heroes of Irish history, people like Tone, Emmet, O'Connell, Davis, Parnell, and especially the "martyred" leaders of 1916, he associated himself with them and used their historical precedents to sustain his own policy. It was a subtle way of telling people that great as those heroes were, they had all failed to achieve that elusive goal of independence, whereas he had attained it, for the twenty-six counties at any rate. By reminding people of the historical reverses, he also made his own accomplishments seem all the greater. It was all so subtle, especially as he frequently played down his own achievements himself, letting his lieutenants brag about whipping John Bull, while he stressed the unfinished nature of the work—whether it was the need to improve the economy, revive the language, or reintegrate the six counties.

He frequently referred to the six counties in highly emotional terms. "It is hard to be calm when one remembers that it is the fairest province that is being cut off," he declared during a public address following the agreement setting aside the findings of the Boundary Commission. "The Ulster that the Irishmen of every province loves best next to his own. The Ulster of Cúchulain, the Ulster of the Red Branch Knights. The Ulster of the O'Neills and the O'Donnells. The Ulster of Benburb and the Yellow Ford. The Ulster in whose sacred sod rests the bones of Patrick, Columcille and Brian of the Tributes."

In his speeches de Valera not only promoted but managed to secure widespread nationalist acceptance of a whole series of myths in regard to partition—that the thirty-two counties were one, united "nation from the dawn of history," that Britain was totally responsible for partition, that it had nothing to do with religion, that even the Unionists had opposed it, that a united, politically stable Ireland would result if the British would only withdraw from the six counties, and that the Civil War had revolved around the partition issue.

He adopted a somewhat ambivalent attitude towards violence, especially Republican violence. "There was," he said, "something in the Irish nature which revelled in heroic sufferings and sacrifice and this sentiment, which had prevailed throughout the generations could not disappear overnight." At times he resorted to sheer demagoguery, altering the emphasis of his position on the partition question for selfish political ends.

He was the first person to suggest in the Dáil that the people in each of the Ulster counties should be allowed to vote themselves out of the Irish Republic, but some weeks later he advocated using the Ulster question as a pretext for breaking off the Treaty negotiations, even though the real stumbling block was elsewhere. He incorporated the partition provisions of the Treaty in his own alternative document, yet later exploited the issue as a pretext not only for having opposed the Treaty, but also for Sinn Féin's abstentionism from the Dáil, and for his decision to stay out of the Second World War. When he lost power in 1948 he sought to upstage the government by embarking on an extensive international anti-partition tour.

Over the years de Valera complained about the discrimination against Roman Catholics in the six counties and denounced the incorporation within Northern Ireland of Counties Fermanagh and Tyrone, with their Nationalist majorities, but while in power he never asked for the transfer of those two counties or the other contiguous areas in which Nationalists were in the majority. He was content to leave the people in those areas as hostages, to perpetuate a legitimate Nationalist grievance, and thus keep the partition issue alive. He neglected to make any serious attempt at reconciliation with the northern Unionists. He was not even willing to take steps to eliminate from the twenty-six counties the discrimination against Protestant values which provoked legitimate fears among Unionists that they would be discriminated against in a united Ireland.

"For every step we moved towards them," he once told the Dáil, "you know perfectly well they would regard it as a sign that we would move another, and they would not be satisfied, in my opinion, unless we went back and accepted the old United Kingdom, a common parliament for the two countries." He was probably right, but in adopting his own variant of their policy of "not an inch," he prompted the suspicion that he was partitionist himself.

The suspicion was undoubtedly exaggerated; he wanted a united Ireland all right but on his own terms. As far as he was concerned, those Unionists who were not willing to accept the 1937 constitution should be transferred to Britain and replaced by Roman Catholics of Irish extraction from Britain. It was unfitting that he—the son of emigrants and the leader of a people who had for so long depended on emigration—should have even suggested a settlement which would compel the expulsion of the descendants of a people who had migrated to Ireland more than three centuries earlier.

During his final years in politics, de Valera abandoned his more demagogic approach to the Ulster question to emphasise what he had recognised as early as 1921, that partition could not—and indeed should not—be ended by force. When the IRA resorted to violence in the 1950s, his government reintroduced internment and quickly undermined the campaign, though it would erupt again during the latter years of his Presidency.

His ultimate political legacy to the Irish people was a mixed bag, with positive and negative aspects. No subsequent political action can condone his mistakes or erase his share of the guilt for the events leading to the Civil War, but history is replete with examples of leaders who surmounted disastrous mistakes to enrich the lives of their people. Since nothing succeeds quite like success, his past errors and miscalculations took on a different aspect as a result of his achievements in the 1930s and early 1940s when he made an invaluable contribution towards the preservation of democracy.

During the inter-war years Ireland was one of the few countries in Europe with a Roman Catholic majority which did not turn to a dictatorship. There was apparently something in the Roman Catholic psyche—possibly related to the Church's own authoritarian structure—which left such countries vulnerable. Italy, Hungary, Austria, Poland, Spain and Portugal all succumbed to dictatorships, and the most notorious dictatorship of all, that of Hitler, had its power base in the Roman Catholic state of Bavaria. Some Irish people genuinely feared that de Valera would try to set up a dictatorship when he came to power in 1932, but it was his most outspoken opponents (some of the same people who had kept the country on the democratic path when challenged by Rory O'Connor and the Republican extremists in 1922) who flirted with fascism under the hysterical leadership of Eoin O'Duffy. De Valera had promised to adhere to democratic principles, and he upheld his promise. In the process he managed to take the gun out of twenty-six county politics, an achievement which was probably his greatest contribution to the modern Irish state and his most important legacy.